THE RIGHTS OF STUDENTS AND TEACHERS

The RIGHTS of STUDENTS and TEACHERS

Resolving Conflicts in the School Community

LOUIS FISCHER
DAVID SCHIMMEL

University of Massachusetts, Amherst

1817

HARPER & ROW, PUBLISHERS, New York

Cambridge, Philadelphia, San Francisco
London, Mexico City, São Paulo, Sydney

Sponsoring Editor: George A. Middendorf
Project Editor: Pamela Landau
Designer: T. R. Funderburk
Production Manager: Willie Lane
Compositor: Lexigraphics, Inc.

This volume is a combination and revision of two earlier books, *The Civil Rights of Teachers* and *The Civil Rights of Students*.

THE RIGHTS OF STUDENTS AND TEACHERS
  Resolving Conflicts in the School Community

Fischer, Louis, 1924–
  The rights of students and teachers.

  Combination and revision of: The civil rights of teachers / Louis Fischer, David Schimmel, and The civil rights of students / David Schimmel, Louis Fischer.
  Includes bibliographical references and index.
  1. Teachers—Legal status, laws, etc.—United States.
2. College students—Legal status, laws, etc.—United States. 3. Civil rights—United States. I. Schimmel, David, II. Title.
KF4175.F59   344.73'078   81-6717
ISBN 0-06-042075-8   347.30478   AACR2

To all who are working to keep the
Constitution alive in the schools.

Introduction

The rights of teachers and students are often ignored and sometimes openly violated in the schools and communities of our nation. It is paradoxical that in the schools, which have as one of their major purposes "the preparation of citizens for effective participation in a democracy," the Bill of Rights has never been consistently applied.

There are many reasons for this. One reason is that a majority of parents, teachers, and administrators honestly do not think the Bill of Rights applies to most school situations. This is because these rights did not apply to them when they were students and because they learned almost nothing functional about this subject during their education. Even in those courses that taught about the history and principles of the Constitution, there were few texts or instructional materials that applied those principles to school conflicts. Today most materials continue to deal with great historical cases or other issues that seem remote from the personal experience of the average student. Thus for several related reasons, teachers, administrators, and parents are poorly prepared to apply the Bill of Rights to the public schools. They have had little education and almost no personal experience in the application of these rights to school controversies, and there is a lack of relevant educational material to assist them in the effort.[1] This book is intended to help meet these needs.[2]

Specifically, this book is designed to help readers become more aware of student and teacher rights and how these rights can be legally asserted. But its purpose is not to encourage litigation. On the contrary, its goal is to help resolve educational conflicts without going to court. How? By helping all participants of the school community become legally literate—by introducing them to the way the legal system works and to how it can work for them in their schools. With this kind of information, teachers, students, administrators, and parents will be able to practice "preventive law." This does not mean they will be able to be their own lawyer; it does mean that they will have a better understanding of how the Bill of Rights applies to the schools and thus will be less likely to violate these rights within the educational system.

This book is also intended to help readers become sensitive to the concerns and arguments on both sides of current civil rights controversies.[3] (Although we have chosen cases primarily concerning public schools, the constitutional principles considered here are also relevant to civil rights conflicts in the community.) In addition, the book suggests a model for teaching about the Bill of Rights in schools: Begin with cases concerning the rights of the students being taught *and* practice the Bill of Rights in formulating and applying school policy in all academic and extracurricular activities—thus simultaneously reinforcing and providing a laboratory for the lessons of the classroom

There are many misunderstandings concerning how our educational and legal systems work. First, many who know that their rights are being abridged feel that they are unable to do anything about it. Students think

---

[1]We recognize that some educators consciously resist applying the Bill of Rights in their schools because they feel that "kids are immature," that "schools are for education, not protest," that "students today already have too much freedom," and so on. However, we believe that such educators are in the minority and that most do not intentionally violate the law.

[2]Although there are a small but increasing number of books about the rights of public school teachers and students, we know of none that is designed for use by students and teachers in college courses and in-service training programs.

[3]We recognize that writers sometimes distinguish civil rights from civil liberties. But for most people, these distinctions have become blurred. In this book we include civil liberties within the term civil rights. As Professor Abraham wrote in his text on this subject: "Although some would object, the terms 'rights' and 'liberties' are used interchangeably in this book. They are to be distinguished from all the other rights and freedoms individuals may enjoy under law because they are especially protected . . . against violations by *governments.*" Henry J. Abraham, *Freedom and the Court: Civil Rights and Liberties in the United States,* New York, Oxford University Press, 1972, p. 3.

they must choose between obedience and rebellion; teachers think their choice is between conforming and resigning. This book suggests other alternatives.

Second, students and teachers frequently equate the Bill of Rights with their own interests. It is then easy to use the rhetoric of constitutional rights as a cover for asserting personal interests or as an excuse for simplistic thinking. A study of constitutional cases forces the reader to go beyond this easy rhetoric and to realize that these conflicts are rarely between right and wrong, but usually involve a tough choice between competing values.

Third, teachers and students frequently feel that their rights are inherently in conflict. They believe in a "fixed-pie" theory of legal rights, that is, that there is only "a limited amount of rights," and if students get more, teachers have less. We suggest that the rights of students and teachers can be complementary rather than competitive.

This book is designed not only for teachers and students, but also for administrators, parents, and others interested in the subject, and it can be used for several purposes.

• To learn the law. Chapters can be read selectively to learn what courts have said about specific issues such as freedom of speech, press, religion, or association as well as personal appearance, due process, and racial or sexual discrimination.

• To learn about current controversies. Through the use of court cases, the book examines a wide range of recent constitutional conflicts between teachers or students and school officials. The cases confront such student issues as distributing "obscene" publications, criticizing teachers and administrators in school-sponsored newspapers, wearing provocative symbols in the classroom, organizing radical groups on campus, and refusing to salute the flag or to conform to official dress codes. Similarly, we examine teacher rights issues such as criticizing school policies or officials, using controversial texts and teaching methods, joining subversive organizations, and engaging in allegedly immoral conduct. Conflicts involving racist and sexist practices by schools are also included.

• To learn the reasons courts give for their decisions. By borrowing generously from court opinions, we have attempted to show how judges think through their decisions from the facts of the case to their legal conclusions.

This book is intended to communicate with laymen about the law. But lawyers, like teachers and other professionals, often use a technical vocabulary of their own. This jargon or "legalese" serves as a shorthand to facilitate communication between attorneys but becomes a barrier to communication between lawyers and laymen. We have tried to minimize this problem by omitting legalese or "translating" it into English wherever possible.

• **The case approach.** Typically the law is explained to educators and laymen through a "text" approach. Usually a text first states the statutory or case law on a subject and then gives examples of how the rules have been applied and of any exceptions that might exist. This method has the advantages of brevity and simplicity; it states the conclusions of the courts and provides answers to legal questions. The problem with the method is that it seems abstract, "legalistic," and somewhat divorced from human conflict.

Instead we generally use the "case" method. Rather than starting with the answers, this approach begins by presenting a legal controversy in an educational setting. Most of the cases are recent. All describe real and complex situations that students, teachers, and school officials have been unable to resolve. After outlining the facts of the case, we often pose several questions to be considered in order to confront the implications of resolving the case for or against the plaintiff. Then we summarize the opinion of the court, accompanying the judges on their journey from the facts of the case to their legal conclusions, thereby enabling the reader to better understand the reasons behind court decisions. In addition, there are summaries of the law at the end of each chapter that integrate the rulings of the diverse cases that are presented. Thus instead of totally rejecting the text method, we have attempted to incorporate some of its features into our approach.

Generally, we have not chosen easy cases with obvious answers. Most illustrate a clash between alternative values and competing educational goals. Many are on the cutting edge of the law, in areas where the law is constantly changing. They raise questions about which reasonable parents, students, educators, and judges differ; and the answers are neither simple nor precise.[4]

A case approach to a legal question takes more time than a text approach, which can neatly "lay out the law." But the world of educational conflict is not a neat one, and court cases can provide readers with situations of human conflict that they can recognize and identify with. When feasible, we have selected cases that teachers and students could imagine happening in schools or to people they know.

[4]Because this book focuses on areas of conflict and change, a reader might conclude that most of the law is controversial and confusing. In fact the reverse is true. In over 90 percent of the cases that arise, almost all lawyers and judges agree on the law to be applied. Typically the facts are in dispute, but the law usually has been established through prior decisions of the legislature or the courts. This book generally deals with the other 10 percent, the atypical cases—the unresolved "hassles" that "end up in court."

Legal texts often begin with a description of the judicial system and the court structure. For some readers this information provides a helpful introduction. Many, however, become lost or bored with such initial descriptions because they do not yet care about jurisdictional issues or the various appellate systems; they have not yet asked the questions these descriptions answer. But as readers become involved with different types of cases, many begin to wonder about such questions as: What kind of case can I take to a federal court? Could I appeal to the Supreme Court? How can I look up a case in the library? Because different students ask these questions at different times (and some never ask them), we have put our explanations in Appendix B, How the System Works. In addition, Appendix A contains the constitutional amendments most frequently referred to in this book.

By the time this book is published, some of its cases may be outdated by more recent decisions.[5] Therefore, we note that our aims are (1) to help students and teachers understand the legal issues in a constitutional controversy—to ask the right questions, not to teach the final answers; (2) to indicate the trend of judicial decisions, not the latest case on each issue; (3) to present representative cases in the field, not a comprehensive statement of the law; and (4) to emphasize the legal aspects of cases rather than their educational, economic, political, or sociological dimensions.

This volume is a combination, revision and updating of our two earlier books, *The Civil Rights of Teachers* and *The Civil Rights of Students*. Although our book focuses on the many constitutional rights of students and teachers as well as on selected federal laws, most common law and state statutes are outside its scope. These include areas such as torts, collective bargaining procedures, and state tenure laws—which are typically included in basic school law texts.

On February 25, 1975, the U.S. Supreme Court ruled that school officials could be held personally liable if they violated a student's clearly established constitutional rights. In the case of *Wood* v. *Strickland*, the Court wrote that such an official "is not immune from liability . . . if he knew or reasonably should have known . . . that the action he took would violate the constitutional rights of the student affected."[6] Because of the Wood decision, many educators have been stimulated to learn more about the rights of students and teachers in order to protect themselves from liability.[7] We hope our book can assist such educators in practicing "preventive law" and in avoiding unnecessary litigation . More important,

[5]The legal conclusions in this book reflect most of the major cases on the subject as of June 1981.
[6]*Wood* v. *Strickland*, 420 U.S. 308 (1975).
[7]See Chapter 15 for an explanation of this issue.

we hope it will encourage teachers and administrators to practice what they teach about American law, to establish a system of rules and procedures in the schools that reflects the letter and spirit of our Constitution.

In response to teacher or student demands that their rights be respected, some educators have pointed out the administrative problems and risks in trying to run a public school in accordance with the Bill of Rights. We do not minimize these problems nor do we deny that some will abuse their rights. However, the Supreme Court has repeatedly said that the Bill of Rights applies to the public schools. Moreover those concerned that students and teachers "obey the law" cannot be unconcerned when school officials disobey the Constitution. And as one judge pointed out, the risk taken if a few abuse their rights "is outweighed by the greater risk run by suppressing" these freedoms in our nation's schools.[8]

Louis Fischer
David Schimmel

[8]*Eisner* v. *Stamford Board of Education,* 314 F.Supp. 832, 836 (D. Conn, 1970).

Chapter 1
Second-Class Citizens?

Only recently have efforts begun to apply the Constitution to schools, to the lives of teachers, and to students. Historically, teaching was considered to be a public trust, a privilege bestowed by local communities who could attach various conditions to this privilege. Similarly, being a child or a student carried with it all kinds of disabilities. Authoritarian practices were so widespread and so generally accepted that teachers were functionally "second-class citizens," whereas the status of students was aptly and angrily characterized even in recent years as *The Student as Nigger*.[1]

Although we shall not attempt a systematic presentation of the historical role of schooling nor the status of teachers or students during the first two centuries of our national life, some brief comments are in order to help provide perspective.* We shall first look at some of the traditional restrictions in the lives of teachers and then in the lives of students.

*For more detailed study, see Howard K. Beale, *Are American Teachers Free?*[2] and Willard S. Elsbree, *The American Teacher*.[3]

ARE TEACHERS SECOND-CLASS CITIZENS?

Pedagogue was the Greek word for a kind of slave, but to us it means *teacher*. Although no rational person contends that the conditions of teachers in the United States of America today are like those of slaves, until very recently teachers were certainly second-class citizens. The following excerpts from a teacher's contract illustrate conditions that were not uncommon in the 1920s.

> I promise to take a vital interest in all phases of Sunday-school work, donating of my time, service, and money without stint for the uplift and benefit of the community.
> I promise to abstain from all dancing, immodest dressing, and any other conduct unbecoming a teacher and a lady.
> I promise not to go out with any young men except in so far as it may be necessary to stimulate Sunday-school work.
> I promise not to fall in love, to become engaged or secretly married.
> I promise not to encourage or tolerate the least familiarity on the part of any of my boy pupils.
> I promise to sleep at least eight hours a night, to eat carefully, and to take every precaution to keep in the best of health and spirits, in order that I may be better able to render efficient service to my pupils.
> I promise to remember that I owe a duty to the townspeople who are paying me my wages, that I owe respect to the school board and the superintendent that hired me, and that I shall consider myself at all times the willing servant of the school board and the townspeople.[4]

In many localities teachers are still second-class citizens. Let us look briefly at some historical antecedents of these social and legal deprivations, keeping in mind that the values of a culture change slowly— certainly much more slowly than its material and technological aspects. Many of the values, beliefs, and attitudes of 100 years ago are still with us, although we have replaced stagecoaches with jets, frontier lawmen with a computer-assisted FBI, and lap-held slates with overhead projectors, videotapes, and "talking typewriters."

The Burdens of the Past Century

Teaching as an occupation is struggling to shake off a burdensome legacy of nineteenth-century restrictions. In frontier America, as well as in rural towns and villages across the nation, a powerful tradition developed that prevented separation of a teacher's private life from one's occupational life. This tradition remains strong in rural America and influences the urban scene as well. Significant changes have occurred and continue to occur; however, many of our leaders grew up in rural settings and accepted the dominant values of their childhood environment. In fact, millions of people who today live in urban centers spent their formative years on farms or in small towns. Consequently, although the majority of our population currently resides in metropolitan areas, values and attitudes formed in rural agricultural settings still influence the behavior of urban and suburban dwellers.

"BOARDING 'ROUND"

In the middle of the nineteenth century, it was common practice for teachers to live with the families of children who attended their schools. They would spend about a week at a time in the home of each family in lieu of higher cash wages. "The extent of boarding around was large. In 1862 the number of teachers in Vermont who were subjected to this mode of life was 3354, or 68 percent of all those employed. Connecticut reported a similar situation earlier. The proportion of winter teachers boarding in 1846 constituting 84 percent of those reporting . . . reliable statistics are not available for other states, but the policy appears to have been a common one before the Civil War."[5] Although many claims have been made for the benefits as well as the shortcomings of "boarding 'round," the arrangement undoubtedly encouraged the general attitude that teachers have no private lives at all.

With or without boarding around, a teacher's life has always been similar to that of a goldfish in a bowl. Like ministers—but unlike lawyers, physicians, businesspersons, or plumbers—teachers were closely regulated by public rules and expectations.

"The explanation for this lies in the nature of the business in which they are engaged. Entrusted with the responsibility of instructing the young, they stand *in loco parentis* before the law and the public and are expected to keep themselves above reproach and to be subservient to the wishes of the most pious patrons in the community."[6] Thus the teacher was seen as an adult model, a role he or she is expected to fulfill to some extent even today. Another reason for regulating the lives of teachers has to do with the constant face-to-face relationships that were integral to the folk culture of rural America. Urban centers provide anonymity, which tends to separate one's work from one's home and make it more possible for teachers to conduct their private life according to the dictates of their conscience.

SPECIFIC AREAS OF RESTRICTION

Since the Civil War period a wide variety of restrictions have surrounded the lives of teachers. These restrictions often paralleled the folkways and mores of the times but were more strictly applied to teachers. In fact, teachers risked dismissal for engaging in some activities (even away from school) that were perfectly acceptable for others. A brief catalog of common restrictions follows.

• Drinking. Although in colonial times teachers drank alcoholic beverages quite openly, the later temperance movement brought severe and lasting restrictions. Drunkenness almost certainly cost a teacher his or her job, and applicants for positions usually faced the questions, "Do you drink?" and "Do you smoke?" Contracts forbade drinking and smoking, and even an occasional drink in a private home could lead to chastisement or *punishment* dismissal. As in most other restrictions small towns were more severe than cities, and the Northeast was less restrictive than other parts of the country.

• Smoking. The use of tobacco, particularly by women, was frowned upon. In many places this was a specifically forbidden practice whose violation led to dismissal. There are schools today that will not hire women who smoke, and many states still require teachers to teach the "evil effects of smoking and alcohol."

• Theater. It comes as a surprise to many that theater attendance was a forbidden form of amusement in many communities. In fact, such restrictions lasted until about 1920.

• Dancing. Dancing and card playing were frowned upon even more than attending the theater. In connection with any socially marginal or questionable behavior, a much higher degree of abstinence was required of teachers than of their pupils' parents.

• Divorce. Divorce would generally lead to dismissal and a change of profession. "After all, divorce is immoral, and you don't want an immoral teacher influencing your children." Gambling and swearing were similarly treated.

• Marriage. Oddly enough, marriage could also lead to dismissal, particularly in the case of women teachers. Until the 1920s and 1930s, contracts tended to prohibit marriage, but later these were eliminated as unreasonable and against public policy.

• Sexual immorality. Sexual immorality was almost always disastrous. Whether it consisted of adultery or fornication, or even rumors of such conduct, dismissal would follow.

• Late hours. Going out on a school night or staying out until late at night was forbidden. In fact, "keeping company" was against the rules in many communities, whereas others specified in their contracts that a woman teacher might "keep company" with only one man and that he might not be another teacher.

• **Gossip.** Rumor or gossip, however unfounded, tended to be sufficient for dismissal, particularly if it were related to sexual immorality. Since a teacher was expected to be a model adult, she could be dismissed if her *reputation* for good character were tainted.

• **Publicity.** If the behavior of a teacher brought any unfavorable publicity to the school, his or her career was in jeopardy. Any unconventional behavior or nonconformity was treated as sufficient evidence of immaturity, instability, or immorality.

• **Grooming.** The personal appearance of teachers was closely controlled. Cosmetics, gay colors, bobbed hair, sheer stockings, short skirts, low-cut dresses, and the like, were forbidden.

• **Racism.** White teachers, particularly in small communities, were dismissed if they were seen in public with blacks or visited their homes. In the South white school boards would ignore sexual behavior on the part of black teachers that would lead to the dismissal of white teachers.

• **Organizations.** Membership in organizations was a very sensitive matter with many local variations. For example, in some communities teachers had to join the Ku Klux Klan to keep their job. In others, membership in the KKK led to immediate dismissal. There were many controversial and therefore "unsafe" organizations, including the American Civil Liberties Union. Teachers were not to take part in open, public criticism of issues, leaders, or organizations. The widely accepted exercise of free speech, press, or assembly was denied them. Any type of activity related to labor organizations was discouraged, and membership in teachers' unions would typically lead to dismissal.

• **Duties.** At the same time, a variety of formal and informal obligations were imposed on a teacher's private life. For example, if teachers were invited to a social function, they could not decline. Their contracts often obligated them to Sunday School teaching, Scout work, or 4-H club leadership. Amazingly enough, teachers tended to submit to these restrictions, meekly accepting them and helping to enforce them against their fellow teachers.

Toward Greater Freedom

Without a doubt giant strides have been made away from these restrictive practices. The reasons for increased freedom in the lives of teachers and in the occupation of teaching are many, and they are inseparable from general cultural developments in the United States. The major factors in this development are the demographic shift to urban centers, the development of teacher organizations, the influence of the mass media, and the increased militancy of teachers in pursuit of their constitutional rights.

Today's teachers, employed mostly in urban and suburban centers, tend to be fairly well protected by their organizations as well as by the anonymity of mass living. They find ludicrous the conditions of employment readily accepted by their forefathers two generations ago. However, the preceding material must not be dismissed as being merely historical information. History is not just "one damn fact after another." We are still influenced by earlier cultural patterns, and in many informal ways we are controlled by their consequences. One of the authors, for example, had the following conversation with the associate superintendent of public instruction for the state of California in 1969:

> SUPERINTENDENT: Teaching is a privilege, not a right. If one wants this privilege, he has to give up some of his rights.
>
> AUTHOR: Just what constitutional right does one have to give up in order to enter teaching?
>
> SUPERINTENDENT: Any right his community wants him to give up.

In other words, this educational leader (though no longer an associate superintendent) believes the Constitution does not apply to teachers the way it does to businesspersons, physicians, lawyers, taxi drivers, or plumbers. Is he correct in his beliefs? Do others share his convictions? What rights must one surrender in order to teach children and youth?

Current Practices

The educational leader just mentioned is not alone in his conviction that local communities can and should control the behavior of teachers. These controls, though well meant, often lead to at least partial revocation of the Bill of Rights for teachers. Specific cases and controversies are described in later chapters, whereas some rather widespread practices are noted here. These practices are particularly invidious when they are applied in a covert, unstated, and even dishonest fashion.

Extreme examples of control over teachers' private lives are found in many small communities where one religion is dominant and the selection of teachers and particularly administrators is systematically influenced by religious affiliation. Practices that occur at the point of *selection* are peculiarly difficult to eliminate or even attack, since selection committees are necessarily called upon to exercise discretion and make qualitative judgments when hiring people. For example, in a recent interview for an elementary school teaching position in the state of North Carolina, a well-qualified graduate of an excellent school was asked whether or not she smoked. This turned out to be the most dangerous question in the interview. The wisdom of smoking aside, no school board in the country would propose to dismiss a teacher who smoked away from school. Yet despite the common acknowledgment of the right to smoke, the overall qualitative judgment at the initial screening or selection stage often obscures violation of this right.

A more common example is the concern about beards, mustaches, and long hair. Although many courts protect a teacher's right to wear a beard, candidates for teaching positions are often passed over because of this factor. Many a young candidate faces a serious personal conflict when his friends or advisors tell him, "Shave your face and you'll get the job. Once the principal and the community come to appreciate your talents, you can grow your beard again."

Membership in certain organizations or political parties has similar consequences. Although we generally proclaim freedom of conscience and political commitment, open membership in the Socialist Party or the John Birch Society is an insurmountable barrier to initial employment in thousands of school districts throughout our "free" country. Moreover, many nontenured teachers are dismissed for membership in such organizations, although the stated reason for nonrenewal of a contract may be insufficient knowledge of the "new math" or the "new English," or some other apparently legitimate ground.

A known history of social dissent, though peaceful and lawful, is also commonly viewed with suspicion by hiring authorities. Screening committees and administrators are concerned with the efficient functioning of their schools. They tend to view social activists as potential troublemakers who will interfere with the smooth running of a "tight ship." Viewed with suspicion is a history of activism in "peace movements," "Black Power," "Women's Liberation," "World Federalism," and perhaps most suspect of all, "Gay Liberation."

Open support of similar causes by teachers often leads to harassment, disciplinary actions, and, at times, dismissal. Most teachers do not fight unwarranted disciplinary action, choosing rather to negotiate a quiet resignation with a positive letter of recommendation that makes possible a new job and, therefore, economic survival in some other community. Most administrators would rather "settle" the matter in the same way in order to avoid public controversy, which might endanger the next bond issue. Thus in a way both teachers and administrators contribute to the erosion of constitutional rights.

Vigorous participation in controversial political elections and local community issues, and outspoken criticism of school policies and practices are other legally protected activities that in practice are often abridged. The extent of such curtailment is not known. Inferences can be drawn from the cases that reach the courts, from the many incidents reported by the press, and from the files of the two major educational organizations, the National Education Association (NEA) and the American Federation of Teachers (AFT).

ARE STUDENTS SECOND-CLASS CITIZENS?

All human groups treat children and youth differently from adults, and in our American society we are no exception. Furthermore, in our complex, diverse nation there have always been significant disagreements over the proper upbringing of the young, including disputes over the application of the law to those "below the legal age of maturity." In our analysis we do not accept either of two extreme views: neither the one that equates the differential treatment of youth with oppression and slavery nor the one that accepts the traditional view that "children are to be seen and not heard." Powerful traditions support this latter view, whereas the counter-culture tends to assert the former. We believe, however, that there exist a large number of parents, schools, and legal principles that reject both of these extremes and choose a third, albeit more difficult, road.

This third road is more difficult because it calls for an endless series of situational decisions. It is based on the twin principles that there are significant differences between adults and youth and that basic constitutional principles are applicable to all. These two principles when taken together, however, are enormously difficult to apply in daily school activities. Before we explore the various current problems in the application of these principles, a brief historical discussion will help to provide some perspective.

The Legacy of History

The history of mistreatment of children throughout the world is gruesome and depressing. We will not recount this history; instead, we will limit our comments to the history of American education and to court cases that record the formal, legal efforts to exercise adult control over students, as well as efforts to extend constitutional rights to them.

A key legal doctrine established early in our history and still with us in modified form is encapsulated in the Latin phrase *in loco parentis,* which means "in place of the parents." Legally this doctrine empowered school officials to exercise the same control over students at school (or even to and from school) that parents could exercise at home. Technically this principle still left open the question of just what powers parents have over children; however, this generally has been interpreted as extensive, almost unlimited power, short of obvious, gross abuse. Thus, when *in loco parentis* was applied to the schools, it gave teachers, principals, and other administrators enormous control over students. This control extended not only to formal studies but also to clothing, hair style, speech, manners and morals, organizational membership, and even behavior away from school. For example, courts in the past have upheld the authority of public school officials to expel students for the following prohibited behavior: joining a social fraternity,[7] going home for lunch,[8] contracting a venereal disease,[9] smoking off campus,[10] and violating a school rule against going to the movies on week nights.[11] Similarly courts have held that students can be expelled for speaking against school policy at a student body meeting,[12] wearing a fraternity insignia to school,[13] expressing offensive sexual views,[14] arranging for a communist speaker off campus,[15] and even for refusing to tell who wrote dirty words on the school wall.[16] Most of these cases were decided decades ago.

Changing times have brought new opportunities and problems to both students and school officials. Henry Ford and our rising standard of living, for example, brought the student-owned automobile with its attendant problems. Inexpensive methods for reproducing written material facilitated the development of the student "underground press." Added to the technological developments of recent decades were the dramatic social and political events of the 1960s. The emergence of a massive student antiwar movement was symbolized by local and national demonstrations, by peaceful protest and civil disobedience, and by strikes, marches, and teach-ins. As a result of this movement, thousands of students were willing to go to court and even to jail over issues of principle.

This confrontation with legal and political authority had widespread side effects. One of these was to challenge the way things were done in families, in churches, and in schools. Many of the cases in this book are a product of these confrontations and the new thinking they provided. Another product of these events was the passage of the Twenty-sixth Amendment, which lowered the voting age to 18.*

These events also led educators and judges to change their views on *in loco parentis*.[17] As a result, the doctrine has been substantially altered and restricted by state departments of education and judicial decisions.

Some states are likely to follow the example of the New York State Department of Education, which restricted the powers of school officials to those expressly granted by the legislature: "the school and all its officers and employees stand *in loco parentis* only for the purpose of

*The Twenty-sixth Amendment was ratified in 1971 and provides: "The right of citizens of the United States, who are eighteen years of age or older, to vote shall not be denied or abridged by the United States or by any State on account of age."

educating the child. The Education Law does not give the school authority beyond that."[18]

One of the strongest statements against the principle came from a judge in a Louisiana case involving corporal punishment:

> It might have been said, in days when schooling was a voluntary matter, that there was an implied delegation of such authority from the parent. Such a voluntary educational system, like a system of apprenticeship . . . has long since disappeared. Parents no longer have the power to choose either the public school or the teacher in the public school. Without such power to choose, it can hardly be said that parents intend to delegate that authority to administer corporal punishment by the mere act of sending their child to school.[19]

Although the Supreme Court has not ruled directly on the continued viability of *in loco parentis*, it has indirectly modified its application by declaring that the Constitution does not stop at the door of the public school. Thus, to the extent that civil rights have entered the schools, the principle of *in loco parentis* has been modified. Even though some courts still use the Latin phrase in explaining the reasons for their decisions, the doctrine is in decline. In the future, courts are more likely to rely on the general principle that students in the public schools have constitutional rights and then proceed to apply that principle to the unique factors of each controversy.

The following chapters present cases highlighting current legal trends and contrast these with earlier decisions. Thus the reader will come to understand the pattern of expanding rights related to schooling. Although our presentation focuses primarily on legal sources, we are cognizant of the significant gaps between court decisions and the behavior of teachers, students, and administrators as well as parents. Furthermore, we acknowledge, although we do not address, the powerful influences exerted on these issues by economic, political, and ideological considerations. It is our conviction, nevertheless, that the more clearly everyone understands the constitutional rights of teachers and students, the more likely they will be practiced both in and out of schools.

Current Controversies

The hypothetical cases that follow illustrate current controversies related to teachers and students. They are presented for three reasons: (1) they suggest the types of issues that will be examined in the following chapters; (2) they alert and sensitize the reader to current controversies in this area; and (3) they illustrate rights in conflict, that is, the ways in which the rights of teachers and students may clash with each other as well as with those of school officials and members of the community.

FREEDOM OF EXPRESSION

• **Controversy 1.** A high school teacher in a city with a population of over a quarter million wrote a play. She wrote it on her own time, away from school, to be performed by a nonprofessional group in the city completely independent of the schools. The play turned out to be a controversial one and was considered by some people to be offensive in its references and implications concerning sex, religion, and interracial relationships. The state superintendent of public instruction entered the controversy to investigate whether or not the teacher's certificate should be revoked or suspended, or whether she should be disciplined in some other way.

It is clear that a lawyer, a physician, a plumber, or a business executive has a well-protected right to write such a play. Its performance, though controversial, would not jeopardize their jobs or state licenses. However, a teacher is regarded as a model who stands in a special relationship of example and trust to the children and the community. In her special position, is it not proper that higher standards of conduct be expected of her?

• **Controversy 2.** Three students at Raineer School began publishing an underground newspaper that they distributed to fellow students. The second issue contained an article entitled "High School Is Fucked," which criticized the quality of education that Raineer students were receiving. The school administration confiscated all the papers, suspended the three students, and threatened them with expulsion if they published any further issues. The students claimed that their constitutional rights were violated. Were they?

FREEDOM OF ASSOCIATION

• **Controversy 1.** Mr. B, an elementary school teacher, became an active member of the Black Panthers. His activities, though well known throughout the community, took place on his own time and away from school. His school is racially integrated, but his chapter of the Black Panthers advocates racial separation. The principal, also black, requested Mr. B to leave the organization or resign from his teaching position.

Should Mr. B have to choose between a teaching career and membership in the Black Panther Party? Does he have a right to do both? Can a community require that its teachers not join controversial organizations?

Would it make any difference if Mr. B were a member of the KKK? Of the American Communist Party? Of the American Fascist Party? Of the American Civil Liberties Union?

• **Controversy 2.** Students at Old Faithful High School organized a chapter of the Students for a Democratic Society (SDS). They requested recognition by the school, along with other clubs, in order to use school facilities and recruit students. The principal refused to grant recognition and prohibited any SDS activities at school. He claimed that SDS was part of an extremist national organization and was inconsistent with the educational purpose of the high school. The students argued that his action violated their right to freedom of association under the First Amendment. Were their rights violated, or do schools have the power to exclude certain organizations?

RIGHT TO PRIVACY

• **Controversy 1.** Two middle-aged male teachers shared a house and taught in the junior high schools of a large city for over ten years. Both were tenured and known to be competent teachers and willing workers. On the basis of secret surveillance, the local police accused them of homosexuality. In a closed hearing in the superintendent's office, the teachers admitted to being homosexuals, but stated that their private lives had no connection to their teaching and thus were irrelevant to the superintendent. The superintendent wanted to dismiss them "in order to protect the moral development of the students and to protect the schools from an angered and outraged community." Are teachers protected in their private sexual lives? Are there overriding public interests to be protected that outweigh whatever private rights exist in the situation?

• **Controversy 2.** During a search of school lockers authorized by the vice-principal of Emerson Junior High, various illegal drugs were found. The school administration immediately suspended all students in whose lockers the drugs were discovered. The students were notified that in five days hearings would be held at which they and their parents could be present and a school official would decide on the appropriate punishment. The students object to the search of their lockers as an "unauthorized invasion of their privacy"; they object to the "lack of due process"; and they demand representation by lawyers.

Do school officials have a right to search student lockers? What constitutes "due process" in school disciplinary situations? If lawyers enter such situations, isn't there a danger that our schools will become arenas of legal controversy rather than educational institutions?

EQUAL PROTECTION

• **Controversy 1.** School District Delta desegregated its schools and combined the racially separate schools into a single system. During this process it became clear that there were too many teachers for the unitary system, and the school board proceeded to dismiss some of them. Among them was Mr. Smith, a black teacher. Smith claimed that since the school board used no objective standards to determine competence, his dismissal represented racial discrimination and violated his civil rights. The board claimed that since there were no objective standards by which to judge teaching competence, the school administration must decide according to its best judgment. The board claimed that if it did not have such discretion it could not run the schools.

• **Controversy 2.** Elmwood High School has tennis, baseball, and swimming teams for boys but not for girls. Valerie X wants to try out for the tennis team, Cathy Y is eager to play competitive baseball, and Judy Z claims that her diving is as good as that of any of the boys on the swimming team. Each young woman wants a fair chance to try out for the school team.

Is it legitimate to segregate girls and boys in high school athletics? Do girls have a right to try out for boys' teams? Where would such a right come from? Is there a legitimate difference between sexual segregation in extracurricular activities and in academic courses (shop, typing, home economics, and others)?

Similar hypothetical cases could be presented illustrating current controversies involving other constitutional rights. The chapters that follow examine such controversies. Any sensitive reader will find similar conflicts reported in current newspapers and magazines. Although we cannot address them all, we believe that if educators understand and apply the principles we analyze, some progress will have been made toward fulfilling the ideals of our Constitution.

NOTES

1. Jerry Farber, *The Student as Nigger*, Contact Books, North Hollywood, Cal. 1969.
2. Howard K. Beale, *Are American Teachers Free?*, New York, Scribner's, 1936.
3. Willard S. Elsbree, *The American Teacher*, New York, American Book, 1939.
4. Quoted by T. Minehan, "The Teacher Goes Job-Hunting," *The Nation, 124* (1927), 606.
5. Id. at 288.
6. Id. at 296.
7. *Smith* v. *Board of Education*, 182 Ill. App. 342 (1913).
8. *Bishop* v. *Houston School District*, 35 S.W.2d 465 (Tex. 1931).
9. *Kenney* v. *Gurley*, 95 So. 34 (Ala. 1923).
10. This was a state college case; *Tanton* v. *McKenney*, 197 N.W. 510 (Mich. 1924).
11. *Mangum* v. *Keith*, 95 S.E. 1 (Ga., 1918). Courts have also upheld the suspension of students for eating at an off-limits lunchroom, *Board of*

Education v. *Luster,* 282 S.W.2d 333 (1955), and for getting drunk off campus, *Douglas* v. *Campbell,* 116 S.W. 211 (Ark. 1909).

12. *Wooster* v. *Sunderland,* 148 Pac. 959 (Cal. 1915).
13. *Antell* v. *Stokes,* 191 N.E. 407 (Mass. 1934).
14. *Morris* v. *Nowotny,* 323 S.W.2d 301 (1959). In this university case, the court held that administrators had discretion to expel a student whose sexual beliefs "were advocated in a manner calculated to be offensive" to the "dignified atmosphere of University life." Id. at 312.
15. This occurred at a state college, *Zarichney* v. *State Board of Agriculture,* 338 U.S. 118 (1949).
16. *Board of Education* v. *Helston,* 32 Ill. App. 300 (1889).
17. Although in *loco parentis* had not been widely challenged until recent years, a Vermont court as early as 1859 noted a major flaw in the doctrine. A parent's power, wrote the court, "is little liable to abuse, for it is continually restrained by natural affection. . . . The school master has no such natural restraint. Hence, he may not safely be trusted with all of a parent's authority, for he does not act from the instinct of parental affection." *Student Rights and Responsibilities: Courts Force Schools to Change,* Washington, D.C., National School Public Relations Association, 1972, p. 3.
18. Formal Opinion of Counsel, No. 91, I Ed. Dept. Rep. 800 (1959).
19. *Johnson* v. *Horace Mann Mutual Insurance Company,* 241 S9. 2d 588 (Ct.App.La. 1970).

Chapter 2
Student Freedom of
Speech

It can hardly be argued that either students or teachers shed their constitutional rights to freedom of speech or expression at the schoolhouse gate.[1]

—Justice Abe Fortas
in *Tinker* v. *Des Moines*

It is a myth to say that any person has a constitutional right to say what he pleases, where he pleases, and when he pleases.[2]

—Justice Hugo Black
Dissenting in *Tinker* v. *Des Moines*

During the first half of this century, the Bill of Rights rarely assisted students who challenged the constitutionality of school policies. Courts generally used the "reasonableness test" to judge whether disputed school rules were constitutional. If there was any reasonable relationship between the rule and the goals of the school, the rule usually would be upheld. It did not matter whether most educators (or even most judges) believed that the rule was unwise or unnecessary. Judges felt that school boards should have "wide discretion" and that courts should not substitute their judgment for that of school officials who were presumed to be experts in educational matters. In upholding a state educational policy that restricted student rights, the Supreme Court in 1915 held that it was up to the state to determine whether its regulations promoted discipline among its students.[3] For decades thereafter it was easy for school officials to make a "reasonable" defense of almost any challenged policy with the argument that its enforcement "promotes school discipline."[4]

In 1969 the Supreme Court handed down an historic decision that challenged many of the educational policies of the past. In *Tinker* v. *Des Moines* the Court bypassed the "reasonableness test" and ruled that students do not shed their constitutional rights to freedom of expression "at the schoolhouse gate." No other recent case has been so influential in advancing the rights of public school students.

Beginning with a brief historic perspective, this chapter focuses on the *Tinker* decision—its principles, its challenge, and the way it has been applied and interpreted in subsequent cases. A final section examines the question of academic freedom for students. It considers whether students have a "right to know" or a "right to read" controversial books, especially in school libraries.*

HISTORICAL PERSPECTIVE

The Wooster Case: Expulsion for Subversive Speech[5]

Earl Wooster was a high school student in Fresno, California, who, during a school assembly, made a speech to the student body that alleged that the auditorium and certain science rooms were unsafe because of the possibility of fire. Wooster denounced the Fresno School Board for compelling students to use these inadequate facilities. He also made some caustic comments concerning the board's management of the school and objected to its prohibition of an annual student event known as the "donkey fight," which often resulted in "cracked heads and injured bodies." During his talk Wooster argued that it was "not fair of the board of education to forbid a donkey fight, in which the boys took their own chances of being injured, and forced them to take chances of being injured in a fire trap."

This "incendiary" talk resulted in a student resolution criticizing the school board, which led the board to invite Wooster to appear and explain his actions. While attempting to justify his conduct, Wooster also acknowledged that his speech to the students "was intended as a slam" at the board. At the conclusion of the hearing the board decided that Wooster's conduct was a "breach of school discipline" and that it was "intended and calculated" to discredit the board in the eyes of the students. The board therefore demanded an apology and "a public retraction" of the "offensive remarks." Wooster refused. As a result he was expelled from high school. Since Wooster did not believe his conduct justified expulsion, he took his case to court.

Questions to Consider

1. Should students be free to publicly criticize, discredit, or humiliate school officials?
2. Can a student be punished for making an incendiary speech at a school

---

*For related cases concerning teachers' academic freedom, see Chapter 5.

assembly that may subvert school discipline? Or can a student say anything he wishes as long as there is no school rule that specifically prohibits his behavior?
3. If a student refuses to apologize for remarks that are intentionally offensive and insubordinate, can he be punished?

THE OPINION OF THE COURT
The trial court upheld Wooster's expulsion. It found that his address to the student body was delivered for the purpose of creating "a spirit of insubordination" among the students and was "subversive of the good order and discipline of the school."

Wooster appealed the decision. He argued that no school rules made his controversial speech a ground for expulsion. But the appeals court was not persuaded and quoted with approval an earlier judge who wrote that there are "certain obligations on the part of the pupil, which are inherent in any proper school system, and which constitute the common law of the school, and which may be enforced without the adoption in advance of any rules upon the subject." The court noted that the purpose of Wooster's speech was to belittle the school board, and "the tenor of the address was well calculated" to produce that result.

Thus the appeals court ruled that Wooster's conduct "cannot be classified as anything but a species of insubordination" that "required correction" in order that "the discipline of the school might be maintained." It acknowledged that the harsh penalty of expulsion is not appropriate until milder measures have failed. However, Wooster's refusal to make the apology demanded by the board not only "accentuated his misconduct" but also "made it necessary" to resort to expulsion as the "only effective means" of punishing Wooster and maintaining school discipline.

The Wooster case was decided in 1915. And none of the parties to the case even raised the possibility that Wooster's speech might be protected by the Constitution.

THE TINKER CASE: A LANDMARK DECISION

In 1965 the war in Vietnam was becoming more intense. United States involvement in the war was escalating rapidly, and the debate over American participation was becoming vehement. There were protest marches against the war in Washington, D.C., and a wave of draft card burning incidents swept the country.

In Des Moines, Iowa, a group of Quakers who were active in the antiwar movement planned to publicize their views by wearing black armbands during the Christmas season. Their purpose was to mourn those who died in the war and to urge a truce in the fighting.

The principals of the Des Moines schools became aware of the plan and adopted a policy that any student wearing an armband to school would be asked to remove it. If she refused, she would be suspended until she returned without the armband.* This policy was later ratified by the school board.

Although they knew about the policy, a group of seven students insisted on wearing the armbands to school. The students were sent home and suspended until they would return without their armbands. Two high school students (John Tinker and Chris Eckhardt) and a junior high school student (Mary Beth Tinker) did not return to school until after New Year's Day, when the planned period for wearing armbands had expired.

The students, through their fathers, brought suit in a U.S. District Court against the school officials to restrain them from taking disciplinary action. The students argued that the policy of prohibiting armbands in school deprived them of their constitutional rights.

Questions to Consider

1. Should the students have been suspended for deliberately disobeying the school policy prohibiting armbands?
2. The First Amendment provides that "Congress shall make no law abridging the freedom of speech."[6] Is wearing an armband protected by this amendment?
3. If a student is entitled to freedom of speech, should this freedom be limited by school officials under certain circumstances? If so, when and under what circumstances?
4. Should students have the same freedom of speech as adults? Should students have the same freedom of speech in school as out of school? In class as well as in the halls or in the cafeteria?

THE OPINION OF THE DISTRICT COURT[7]

In his opinion District Court Judge Roy Stephenson outlined the legal principles applicable in this case. First, the "free speech" clause of the First Amendment protects symbolic as well as "pure" speech, and the wearing of an armband to express certain views is the type of symbolic act protected by that amendment.† Second, freedom of speech is not an

---

*In our culture it is conventional to use the pronoun *he* to refer to the third-person singular. Since students usually include an equal number of women and men, we purposefully alternate *she* and *he* throughout the book, except where students are specifically identified. For a full discussion of this and related issues, see Nancy Frazier and Myra Sadker, *Sexism in School and Society*. New York: Harper & Row, 1973.

†Although the First Amendment restrains only Congress, courts have held that the freedoms of speech and press are among the "liberties" protected by the Fourteenth Amendment (which provides that no *state* "shall deprive any person of life, *liberty,* or property, without due process of law" [italics added]). By incorporating the First Amendment freedoms into the Fourteenth Amendment, courts have protected an individual's right of free expression against infringement by a state or state agency such as the school board.

absolute right and may be abridged by the state under some circumstances. Third, school officials have a responsibility to maintain a disciplined atmosphere in the classroom. Thus the question posed by this case is how to resolve a conflict between the rights of students and the need for discipline.

The court held that "school officials must be given wide discretion and if, under the circumstances, a disturbance in school discipline is reasonably to be anticipated, actions which are reasonably calculated to prevent such a disruption must be upheld by the Court." Judge Stephenson therefore ruled that under the circumstances of this case, the action of the school district was reasonable and did not deprive the students of their constitutional rights. Because of this ruling, Chris Eckhardt and the Tinkers appealed to the U.S. Supreme Court.*

Questions to Consider

1. Does the ruling of the district court seem fair and reasonable?
2. If you were a judge, under what circumstances would you allow school officials to restrict student speech?
3. Should freedom of speech be different for students of different ages? Should high school students, for example, have more freedom than primary school students and less freedom than college students?
4. Should evidence that the armbands caused some disruption make any difference in deciding the case?

THE OPINION OF THE U.S. SUPREME COURT[8]
On behalf of the majority of the Supreme Court, Justice Abe Fortas reviewed the history and legal principles of the case. "It can hardly be argued," he wrote, "that either students or teachers shed their constitutional rights to freedom of speech or expression at the schoolhouse gate." To support this assertion he cited a previous Supreme Court opinion that indicated that because school boards "are educating the young for citizenship is reason for scrupulous protection of constitutional freedoms of the individual, if we are not to strangle the free mind at its source and teach youth to discount important principles of our government as mere platitudes."[9]

On the other hand, the Court has also emphasized the need for school officials to be able to control student conduct. Thus this case

*Federal cases are generally tried in a U.S. District Court. A losing party has the right to appeal to one of 11 U.S. Circuit Courts of Appeals. (In the *Tinker* case the appeals court judges were evenly divided; this had the effect of affirming the district court opinion.) The party who loses the appeal may then submit a petition to the U.S. Supreme Court, asking the Court to hear his case. Because the Supreme Court receives more petitions than it can possibly consider, it generally reviews only those cases it considers especially significant. For more information on the American judicial process, see Appendix B, How the System Works.

presents a conflict between the rights of students and the rules of the school. To resolve this question Justice Fortas reviewed the facts of the case. He noted that there is "no evidence whatever" that the wearing of the armbands interfered "with the school's work or with the rights of other students to be secure or to be let alone." Nevertheless the district court had concluded that the action of the school authorities was reasonable because it was based upon their fear of a disturbance from the wearing of the armbands. This conclusion was rejected by the Supreme Court. "In our system," wrote Justice Fortas, "undifferentiated fear or apprehension of disturbance is not enough to overcome the right to freedom of expression."

Justice Fortas also noted that school authorities did not prohibit the wearing of all political or controversial symbols. Students in some schools wore political campaign buttons and some even wore the Iron Cross, "traditionally a symbol of Nazism." The school order prohibiting armbands did not extend to these. Singling out one particular symbol for prohibition is not constitutionally permissible, at least without evidence that the symbol caused substantial interference with school activities.

In an eloquent argument on behalf of free speech in the schools, the Court pointed out that:

> Any departure from absolute regimentation may cause trouble. Any variation from the majority's opinion may inspire fear. Any word spoken in class, in the lunchroom, or on the campus, that deviates from the views of another person may start an argument or cause a disturbance. But our Constitution says we must take this risk; and our history says that it is this sort of hazardous freedom—this kind of openness—that is the basis of our national strength and of the independence and vigor of Americans who grow up and live in this relatively permissive, often disputatious society.[10]

The school officials cannot prohibit a particular expression of opinion merely "to avoid the discomfort and unpleasantness that always accompany an unpopular viewpoint." Where there is no evidence that the forbidden conduct would "materially and substantially interfere" with school work, the prohibition is unconstitutional.

In a provocative and far-reaching defense of the freedom of public school students, Justice Fortas wrote:

> In our system, state operated schools may not be enclaves of totalitarianism. School officials do not possess absolute authority over their students. Students in schools as well as out of school are possessed of fundamental rights which the State must respect, just as they themselves must respect their obligations to the State. In our system, students may not be regarded as closed-circuit recipients of only that which the State chooses to communicate. They may not be confined to the expression of those sentiments that are officially approved. In the absence of a specific showing of constitutionally valid reasons to regulate their speech, students are entitled to freedom of

expressions of their views . . . [and] school officials cannot suppress "expression of feelings with which they do not wish to contend."[11]

The Court did not limit its decision to the protection of free expression in the classroom. Instead it specifically noted that the principles of this case are "not confined to the supervised and ordained" classroom discussion. First Amendment rights extend to the cafeteria, the playing field, and the campus. There, too, students may express their opinions on controversial topics. But conduct by students, in or out of class, which "for any reason . . . materially disrupts classwork or involves substantial disorder or invasion of the rights of others is, of course, not immunized by the Constitutional guarantee of freedom of speech."

In sum, there was no evidence in this case that led school authorities to forecast substantial disruption or material interference with school activities, and none in fact occurred. The students wore their armbands to express their disapproval of the Vietnam War and their advocacy of a truce. They wanted others to adopt their views, and they provoked discussions outside of classes. But they caused no substantial disorder or interference with school work. "Under these circumstances," concluded the Court, "our Constitution does not permit officials of the State to deny their form of expression." The opinion of the district court was therefore reversed.

A STRONG DISSENT

What are the implications of the *Tinker* case? Justice Hugo Black saw them as serious and unfortunate. He feared the decision would encourage a revolutionary era of permissiveness. Therefore, although he had been one of the Supreme Court's strongest defenders of free speech, he wrote a vigorous dissenting opinion.*

The crucial questions in the *Tinker* case, wrote Justice Black, "are whether students and teachers may use the schools at their whim as a platform for the exercise of free speech . . . and whether the courts will allocate to themselves the function of deciding how the pupils' day will be spent." Although frequently opposing government regulation of the "content" of speech, "I have never believed that any person has a right to give speeches or engage in demonstrations where he pleases and when he pleases."

As Justice Black read the record of the case, it showed that comments by some students made John Tinker self-conscious while attending school and that the armbands "took students' minds off their classwork and

---

*In most cases decided by the Supreme Court and other appeals courts, the judges reach unanimous agreement, but sometimes this is not possible. In such cases, a judge who does not agree with the majority may submit a dissenting opinion, which is published immediately after the opinion of the court. This is what happened in the *Tinker* case.

diverted them to thoughts about the highly emotional subject of the Vietnam war." Students, Black argued, cannot concentrate on school work when black armbands are being "ostentatiously displayed" to call attention to the wounded and dead of the war. And it was precisely "to distract the attention of other students that some students . . . determined to sit in school with their symbolic armbands." Thus Justice Black feared that "if the time has come when pupils of state-supported schools, kindergartens, grammar schools or high schools, can defy and flout orders of school officials to keep their minds on their own school work, it is the beginning of a new revolutionary era of permissiveness in this country fostered by the judiciary."

Justice Black denied that either students or teachers take with them "into the schoolhouse gate" full constitutional rights to freedom of expression. He wrote:

> The truth is that a teacher of kindergarten, grammar school or high school pupils no more carries into a school with him a complete right to freedom of speech and expression than an anti-Catholic or anti-Semite carries with him a complete freedom of speech and religion into a Catholic church or a Jewish Synagogue. . . . It is a myth to say that any person has a constitutional right to say what he pleases, where he pleases and when he pleases.

In two revealing sentences Justice Black shares his views and concerns about public education:

> The original idea of schools, which I do not believe is yet abandoned as worthless or out-of-date was that children had not yet reached the point of experience and wisdom which enabled them to teach all of their elders. It may be that the Nation has outworn the old fashioned slogan that "children are to be seen and not heard," but one may, I hope, be permitted to harbor the thought that taxpayers send children to school on the premise that at their age they need to learn, not teach.[12]

In a final eloquent paragraph Justice Black described his perception of the current breakdown of law and discipline in American schools and his fear that decisions such as this one would encourage a dangerous trend. Since his statement articulates a concern of many parents, teachers, and administrators, we quote from it at length:

> Change has been said to be truly the law of life, but sometimes the old and the tried and the true are worth holding. . . . Uncontrolled and uncontrollable liberty is an enemy to domestic peace. . . . School discipline, like parental discipline is an integral and important part of training our children to be good citizens—to be better citizens. Here a very small number of students have crisply and summarily refused to obey a school order designed to give pupils who want to learn the opportunity to do so. One does not need to be a prophet or the son of a prophet to know that after the Court's holding today some students in Iowa schools and indeed in all schools will be ready, able, and willing to defy their teachers on practically all orders. . . . Turned

loose with lawsuits for damages and injunctions against their teachers as they are here, it is nothing but wishful thinking to imagine that young, immature students will not soon believe it is their right to control the schools rather than the right of the States that collect the taxes to hire the teachers for the benefit of the pupils. This case, therefore, wholly without constitutional reasons in my judgment, subjects all the public schools in the country to the whims and caprices of their loudest-mouthed, but maybe not their brightest, students. I, for one, am not fully persuaded that school pupils are wise enough, even with this Court's expert help from Washington, to run the 23,390 public school systems in our fifty states. I wish, therefore, wholly to disclaim any purpose on my part to hold that the Federal Constitution compels the teachers, parents, and elected school officials to surrender control of the American public school system to public school students. I dissent.[13]

The Aftermath of Tinker

In the years following the *Tinker* decision, no case involving the issue of freedom of student expression was argued or decided without reference to the principles and holding of this crucial opinion. The following section illustrates the way in which *Tinker* has been applied by different courts in a variety of related situations.

This section also illustrates two legal concepts. First, courts generally follow "precedent." This means that when a court has ruled a certain way, the same court or a lower one is obliged to rule the same way in a similar case. However, a court is not bound by precedent if it can "distinguish" the case—that is, if it can show that the case before it is significantly different, despite its apparent similarity. The first three cases, *Guzick, Melton,* and *Banks,* illustrate the way courts distinguished the situations before them from the facts of the *Tinker* case. Second, we will examine *Butts* v. *Dallas* and *Aquirre* v. *Tahoka* to see how, in contrast, judges used the precedent of *Tinker* to decide two cases upholding student rights.

TINKER DISTINGUISHED: LIMITING STUDENT EXPRESSION

The Guzick Case: Forbidding All Symbols[14]

Shaw High School in Cleveland, Ohio, had a long-standing rule forbidding the wearing of all buttons, badges, or other symbols "whereby the wearers identify themselves as supporters of a cause or bearing messages unrelated to their education."[15] The rule had its origin in the days when strong competition between fraternities disrupted the educational process at Shaw. More recently a similar problem existed when the student population became 70 percent black and 30 percent white. Shaw officials had uniformly enforced the antibutton rule because they believed the wearing of such symbols fostered undesirable competition, magnified the differences between students, and polarized them into separate and unfriendly groups. In recent years students attempted to wear buttons expressing "inflammatory messages," such as "White Is Right," "Say It Loud, Black and Proud," and "Black Power." A fight had resulted when a white student wore a button that other students considered an insult to the memory of Dr. Martin Luther King. Whenever such controversial buttons appeared, school authorities required that they be removed.

Despite the school policy, Thomas Guzick, a junior at Shaw High School, wore a button in class that solicited participation at a Chicago demonstration against the Vietnam War.[16] The principal told Guzick to remove his button. Guzick replied that his lawyer told him that "a United States Supreme Court decision entitled him to wear the button in school" and that he would not remove it. The principal then suspended Guzick until he obeyed. Guzick, however, believed that the *Tinker* ruling applied to his case and went to court to require the principal to allow him to wear the button in school.

Questions to Consider

1. Under the circumstances of this case, was it unconstitutional for Guzick's principal to tell him to remove his button?
2. What arguments would you use in support of Guzick? What arguments could you use to defend the no-button policy of Shaw High School?
3. In what ways are the facts of *Tinker* similar to the *Guzick* case? In what ways are they different?

THE OPINION OF THE COURT

The trial court dismissed Guzick's complaint and concluded that revoking the no-button rule "would inevitably result in collisions and disruptions, which would seriously subvert Shaw High School as a place of education for its students, black and white."

Guzick appealed the court's ruling. He argued that the wearing of the button did not and would not disrupt the work and discipline of Shaw High School. The U.S. Court of Appeals acknowledged that if the facts of this case were similar to *Tinker*, the judgment of the district judge would have to be reversed. But the majority of the judges of the appeals court believed that *Guzick* could be distinguished from *Tinker* and that the facts of this case "clearly provide such distinction."*

First, the appeals court contrasted the rule of *Tinker* with the long-standing and uniform enforcement of Shaw's no-symbol rule. School

---

*Where the evidence is in dispute, the trial court first determines the facts of the case and then applies the appropriate law. An appeals court usually accepts the facts as determined by the trial court and focuses its attention on disputes concerning the proper legal principles to be applied to the case. For more information on this and related issues, see Appendix B, How the System Works.

authorities in the *Tinker* case did not prohibit the wearing of all controversial symbols. The evidence showed that some students wore political campaign buttons and a few even wore a Nazi symbol. The order prohibiting armbands did not apply to these symbols but only to black armbands worn in opposition to American participation in the Vietnam War.

A second distinction concerned probable disruption. In *Tinker* the trial court found no evidence to indicate that the wearing of the armbands would cause substantial disruption. In contrast the trial court in the *Guzick* case found that "if all buttons are permitted or if any buttons are permitted, a serious discipline problem will result, racial tensions will be exacerbated, and the educational process will be significantly and substantially disrupted."

On behalf of the appeals court Judge O'Sullivan pointed out that any rule that attempts to permit the wearing of some buttons but not others would be virtually impossible to administer. "It would occasion *ad hoc* and inconsistent application. It would make the determination of permissible versus impermissible buttons difficult, if not impossible." And it would deprive school officials of their position of neutrality.

The court emphasized the need for proper balancing in the exercise of the guarantees of the Constitution—in this case, the need is to balance First Amendment rights with the duty of the state to protect the public school system. In arriving at this balance, Judge O'Sullivan observed:

> Denying Shaw High School the right to enforce this small disciplinary rule could and most likely would, impair the rights of its students to an education and rights of its teachers to fulfill their responsibilities. . . . We must be aware in these contentious times that America's classrooms and their environs will lose their usefulness as places in which to educate our young people if pupils come to school wearing the badges of their respective disagreements and provoke confrontations with their fellows and their teachers. The buttons are claimed to be a form of free speech. Unless they have some relevance to what is being considered or taught, a school classroom is no place for the untrammeled exercise of such [a] right.[17]

Thus the court ruled that "the potentiality" of imminent rebellion among Shaw students supported the wisdom of the no-symbol rule. "Surely," concluded Judge O'Sullivan, "those charged with providing a place and atmosphere for educating young Americans should not have to fashion their disciplinary rules only after good order has been at least once demolished."[18]

The Melton Case: Symbolic Expression at a Tense School[19]

Rod Melton, a student at Brainerd High School in Chattanooga, Tennessee, was suspended because he refused to stop wearing a small Confederate flag patch on one sleeve of his jacket. The principal felt that Melton had violated the school code, which prohibited the wearing of provocative symbols on clothing; he construed "provocative symbols" to mean those that "would cause a substantial disruption of the student body." The principal was concerned about the tense racial situation and disturbances that had erupted the year before. The disruptions, which closed the school twice, resulted from controversy over the use of the Confederate flag as the school flag and the song "Dixie" as its pep song.

Melton believed that the principal overreacted to the sleeve patch and that his suspension violated his right to freedom of expression. Although he knew of the disturbances the prior year, Melton argued that the circumstances were substantially different. In the fall during the time he was suspended, the situation had become less tense, and there had been no threats of disruption or acts of violence. The protests the previous year had been against official school symbols, whereas the wearing of a small insignia was by a single student and did not indicate administrative approval. Moreover the symbol in this case was small and was worn by Melton in a quiet, peaceful manner. Thus Melton argued that the holding of the *Tinker* case should apply and that the wearing of this emblem "which was merely symbolic of one of the historic facts of American life" should be protected.

On behalf of the U.S. Court of Appeals, Judge Keith wrote: "This is a troubling case; on the one hand, we are faced with the exercise of the fundamental constitutional right to freedom of speech, and on the other, with the oft conflicting, but equally important, need to maintain decorum in our public schools." Unlike *Tinker,* the record of this case indicated that there had been substantial disorder at Brainerd High School during the 1969—1970 school year; that this disorder "most materially disrupted the functioning of the school, so much so that the school was in fact closed on two occasions"; that much of the controversy the previous year had centered around the use of the Confederate flag as a school symbol; and that the school officials had every right to anticipate that a tense racial situation continued to exist at the time that Melton was suspended. The court concluded that under the circumstances of this case, Melton's suspension did not violate his First Amendment rights, and the school authorities were permitted "to stave off any potential danger" resulting from his conduct.[20]

The Banks Case: Can Symbolic Expression Violate Minority Rights?[21]

Although somewhat different from other controversies in this section, a federal case from the midwest raises a related free speech issue and illustrates the difference between legal and educational questions. The controversy began in 1962 when students in Southside High School in

Muncie, Indiana, voted to adopt symbols associated with the Old South. Accordingly the school flag resembled the flag of the Confederacy, the name of the athletic team was the "Rebels," the glee club was named the "Southern Aires," and the homecoming queen was called the "Southern Belle." Black students, who constituted 13 percent of the enrollment of Southside, felt that these symbols were offensive and inflammatory and that they discouraged black participation in extracurricular activities. These students also felt that the symbols violated their right of free speech and were discriminatory and that they therefore should be prohibited.*

To support their case the black students cited an Indiana Civil Rights Commission report that urged the school administration to eliminate these symbols and that noted: "It is impossible for Negro students to feel loyal to a school whose official symbols represent a system that enslaved their ancestors."

The school administration refused to intervene on the grounds that they were pursuing a valid educational policy of allowing students of all schools to choose their symbols democratically. Moreover school administrators indicated that they would not prohibit students of a predominantly black school from adopting the "Black Panther" as their symbol, although it might offend white students.

Both the trail court and appeals court upheld the position of the administration. The court of appeals found no evidence that the policy on school symbols was motivated by racial discrimination. Furthermore there was nothing to indicate that black students were denied access to any school activities or facilities because of these symbols. Finally the court failed to find "any evidence in the record that the black students' rights of free speech and expression was being abridged by use of the Confederate symbols."†

This case illustrates the difference between legal and educational issues. Both the trial court and appellate court judges felt that the student body's choice of symbols was offensive and unwise, but they did not believe the choice was unconstitutional.[22] Although the courts ruled in favor of the schools, they approved neither the symbols nor the "educational policy" that maintained them. On the contrary, the trial judge specifically recommended that school authorities "exercise their discre-

---

*The *Banks* case involved several other issues such as affirmative action, school site selection, and busing. Here, as in a number of other cases discussed in this book, we do not mention all the issues involved in a case unless they are relevant to the subject of the chapter in which they are included.

†The students had also argued that the *Tinker* decision "precludes a school from compelling minority students 'to endure offensive official symbols at a tax supported institution which they are compelled to attend.' " But the appeals court held that the *Tinker* ruling protecting student symbolic speech did not apply to this case since the symbols here did not appear to restrict the black students' right to freedom of speech.

tion to bring about the elimination of school symbols which are offensive to a racial minority." Thus the court saw this as a matter that called for educational leadership rather than judicial intervention.

The Karp Case: Forecasting Disruption[23]

Prior cases indicated that administrators may restrict student expression in tense situations in which substantial disorder had occurred. Can officials also restrict student speech before serious disruption takes place? This is the question posed in the case of *Karp* v. *Becker*.

Steve Karp and several high school classmates wanted to protest the nonrenewal of an English teacher's contract. First, they planned a demonstration during an athletic awards ceremony. When this was canceled, Karp notified the news media and brought signs into school supporting the instructor. After news reporters, demonstrators, and increasing numbers of students gathered, the vice-principal feared violence and ordered the demonstrators to surrender their signs. Then some students began chanting, and shoving developed between the demonstrators and the lettermen, which was broken up by school officials. As a result, Karp was suspended for five days. Officials offered to reduce the suspension if he would agree not to bring similar signs on campus. Instead Karp refused and sued.

In this case there was more disruption than in *Tinker*, but no substantial disorder had occurred. May school officials impose restrictions in cases that fall between these extremes? Judge Wallace said "yes." The issue, wrote the judge, is whether the evidence is sufficient to support the school official's "forecast of a reasonable likelihood of substantial disorder." In cases such as this, Judge Wallace explained that courts should avoid the temptation to be a "Monday morning quarterback" and should focus upon "whether the apprehension of the school officials was unreasonable under the circumstances." After reviewing in detail the evidence of the case, the judge ruled that the vice-principal's forecast of substantial disruption was not unreasonable. Therefore the court concluded that the school's restriction of Karp's speech was not unconstitutional.

TINKER REAFFIRMED: SUPPORTING STUDENT EXPRESSION

The Butts Case: The Inadequacy of Administrative Intuition[24]

School authorities in Dallas, Texas, concluded that the Vietnam Moratorium of October 15, 1969, would be a day of disruption in their schools. Their conclusion was based on several events: Someone published a "manifesto" calling on high school students to "boycott" their classes or to attend them "wearing black armbands of protest"; a former pupil, not connected with the Vietnam Moratorium, threatened to bomb one of the schools; and, as the day approached, disruptive sit-ins occurred in schools in a nearby community. On the morning of the moratorium a group of students massed across the street from one of the schools displaying a large banner reading "Try Peace." One student who opposed the protest snatched the banner and ran away with it, and other moratorium opponents wore white armbands.

On learning of the plan to wear black armbands, school officials decided that it would be disruptive. Although officials did not expect the wearers of the black armbands to initiate disruption, they believed that these students would anger others not participating in the moratorium. They feared, for example, that wearers of white armbands would tear the black armbands from those who wore them. Hence officials prohibited the wearing of all armbands, which they anticipated "would substantially interfere with school work."

Questions to Consider

1. What argument could be made on behalf of the Dallas school officials in support of their action?
2. How would you argue this case on behalf of the students who were sent home?
3. If officials had evidence that the wearing of black armbands would anger and disturb other students, would this be sufficient to justify their banning these armbands? Or their banning all armbands?

JUDICIAL OPINIONS

The trial court upheld the action of the school officials,[25] but a U.S. Court of Appeals ruled in favor of the students. "Whatever the black armbands may have communicated," wrote the appeals court, "the record is devoid of any evidence that it did in fact communicate to any witness an intention on plaintiff's part to engage personally in the feared disruptive action."

The appeals court acknowledged that school officials were not prohibited by the First Amendment from action until disruption actually occurs. Similarly officials had a right and duty under the circumstances of this case to expect that disruption might occur on October 15. The court, however, disagreed that this "expectation" was sufficient to justify the suspension of the students' constitutional right of symbolic speech. What more was required? To justify the school's action, officials would have to determine, "based on fact, not intuition," that disruption would probably result from the exercise of the constitutional right and that not wearing the armbands "would make the expected disruption substantially less probable or less severe."

The court acknowledged that the school can restrict student symbols (e.g., in the case of a "provocative flaunting" of Nazi "swastikas"). But in most cases, something more than the *ex cathedra* pronouncement of the superintendent"* is required to establish that there would be disruption.

There is nothing in this record to show that school officials had developed solid information on the attitudes and intentions of the student protestors. They made no effort to bring leaders of the black- and white-armband factions together to agree on mutual respect for each other's constitutional rights. If actions such as this had been tried and failed, the court wrote, "the failure would have tended to establish that armbands of all colors should be banned." But in the *Butts* case, officials made no attempt to respond to the moratorium crisis through such democratic processes.

In conclusion, the court rejected the notion that the holding of *Tinker* is nullified whenever a school system is confronted with disruptive activities. "Rather we believe that the Supreme Court has declared a constitutional right which school authorities must nurture and protect, not extinguish, unless they find the circumstances allow them no practical alternative." Where there are no practical alternatives, the reasonable decisions of officials will be supported. "But there must be some inquiry, and establishment of substantial fact, to buttress the determination." Since no such facts were established in this case, the judgment of the trial court was reversed.

The Aguirre Case: Supporting Educational Change[26]

In Tahoka, Texas, a group known as "Concerned Mexican American Parents" had become dissatisfied with certain educational policies and practices in their school system. To support "corrective action," a number of students began to wear brown armbands to school. On the next day the board of education passed a regulation prohibiting any unusual wearing apparel that is "disruptive, distracting, or provocative so as to incite students of other ethnic groups."

After a number of students were suspended for refusal to remove their armbands, they sued to stop school officials from enforcing this regulation. School officials defended their action on two grounds: first, wearing of the armbands in violation of school policy "was a disruption in and of itself"; second, several incidents of "unrest and apprehension" were attributable to the wearing of the brown armbands. These included the testimony of one girl that several other girls attempted to force her to wear an armband in the gym. (But the evidence also indicated that they did not persist when she refused and that she was not harmed or

---

Ex cathedra means "authoritative"; it was originally applied to decisions of the pope from his *cathedra,* or chair.

frightened by the incident.) Two parents indicated that their children were afraid of "some unspecified trouble at school." (But in neither case was there evidence of force, threats, or violence.)

Based on this testimony, the trial court found school officials had not presented adequate evidence to show "that the wearing of the armbands by plaintiffs . . . would materially and substantially interfere with the requirements of appropriate discipline or be disruptive of normal educational functions."

The court concluded that the decision in this case should be based on the *Tinker* ruling that the wearing of an armband to express certain views is the type of symbolic act that is protected by the First Amendment. "The logic of such a conclusion," wrote Judge Woodward, "is obvious when the symbol, the armband, is translated back into the expression which it symbolizes—'I support those in the community who advocate certain changes in the educational system'—and of that expression it is asked, 'Is it within the protection of the First Amendment?' " In answer, Judge Woodward replied, "No room for doubt exists."

RELATED CASES

Lipp v. *Morris:* **Standing as Symbolic Speech**[27]

Deborah Lipp, a 16-year-old student at Mountain Lakes High School in New Jersey, refused to stand during the Pledge of Allegiance to the flag because she believed "the words of the pledge were not true." She claimed that the state statute that required her to stand "to show full respect to the flag while the pledge is being given" violated her First Amendment rights.

In defense of the statute, the attorney general of New Jersey argued that "mere standing does not rise to the level of symbolic speech, " and that it cannot be considered a protected political activity. But a federal appeals court disagreed. The court ruled that a state cannot require a student to "engage in what amounts to implicit expression" by standing at respectful attention while the flag salute is being administered. This interference with "the student's right not to participate in the flag ceremony is an unconstitutional requirement that the student engage in a form of speech and may not be enforced."

Fenton v. *Stear:* **Fighting Words Not Protected**[28]

On a Sunday night in May, Jeffrey Fenton, a high school senior from Pennsylvania, was sitting in a car with some friends at a shopping center. When someone told him that the teacher Donald Stear was passing by, Fenton loudly commented, "He's a prick." As a result, the high school principal punished Fenton by imposing an in-school suspension for 3 days and other restrictions for 11 days. Fenton claimed that being punished for his comment violated his First Amendment rights. A federal district court did not agree.

Instead of viewing this as a case of protected speech, the court said that Fenton's conduct involved "an invasion of the right of teacher Stear to be free from being loudly insulted in a public place." Judge Marsh acknowledged that many people might have ignored the insulting remark. Nevertheless, the court emphasized that Fenton's use of "insulting or fighting words—those which by their very utterance inflict injury"—directed at Mr. Stear in a public place is not safeguarded by the constitutional guarantee of freedom of speech.

Does this mean that school authorities can punish students for off-campus comments? Not usually. But in this case the judge wrote that when a student refers to a teacher in a public place by an "obscene name in such a loud voice that the teacher and others hear the insult, it may be deemed a matter for discipline in the discretion of the school authorities."

Commonwealth v. *Bohmer:* Convicting Student Disrupters[29]

In 1978 the Massachusetts Supreme Court upheld the constitutionality of a statute that provides up to one month in prison or a $50 fine for anyone who "willfully interrupts or disturbs school." Two students at the Massachusetts Institute of Technology were convicted under the statute when they tried to make announcements and distribute leaflets in classes and refused to leave after being asked to do so. The students wanted the court to declare the statute unconstitutional since it could prohibit protected speech. The court refused. It upheld the law because it only prohibited deliberate actions which create an "interruption or disturbance of the normal functioning of the school."

Although the First Amendment protects speech from government regulation, the court noted that this protection was not absolute since the restriction of disruptive expression may be necessary in the classroom. In this case the statute does not prohibit speech "that is compatible with the free flow of ideas essential to the learning process." It merely insulates the schools from activity that significantly disrupts their functioning. The court concluded that "no constitutional protection extends to [such] conduct."*

Fricke v. *Lynch:* Homosexual Views Protected

In an unusual 1980 free speech case, a homosexual high school student, Aaron Fricke, planned to take a male date to his high school senior prom.

*For other cases concerning the right of students to protest and demonstrate, see Chapter 8.

The plan was vetoed by the principal who said he could not guarantee the safety of Fricke or his date. But a federal judge in Rhode Island overruled the principal's objections saying that the right of Fricke to make a statement about his sexuality supersedes fears of disruption. "To rule otherwise," wrote the court, "would completely subvert free speech in the schools by granting other students a heckler's veto, allowing them to decide through prohibited and violent methods what speech will be heard."[30]

ACADEMIC FREEDOM FOR STUDENTS: SELECTING AND REMOVING BOOKS

This section examines the different ways courts have ruled on controversies concerning the selection of texts and library books and their "deselection" or removal in response to objections by parents or administrators.

Questions to Consider

1. Do teachers, students, administrators, or parents have the right to select books for the curriculum? For the library?
2. Which, if any, of these groups has the right to remove books they find objectionable?
3. What reasons would justify removing a book from the school library or from the curriculum?
4. Do students have a "right to know" or a "right to read" controversial material?

The President's Council Case: A Constant Process of Winnowing[31]

In New York City, some parents objected to the junior high school libraries stocking copies of Piri Thomas's *Down These Mean Streets*. The book is an autobiography of a Puerto Rican youth growing up in Spanish Harlem and contains vulgar words and graphic descriptions of violence, sex, and drug use. The objecting parents claimed that the book would have "an adverse moral and psychological effect on 11 to 15-year-old children." As a result, the Community School Board voted to remove the book from all junior high school libraries. (The board later voted to make it available to parents of children attending the schools.)

In response, a group of students, parents, teachers, and librarians went to court to prevent the removal of the book. They believed that it was advantageous to acquaint middle-class students with the bitter realities of Spanish Harlem, that the book had no adverse psychological effects, and that its removal violated the First Amendment.

The Second Circuit Court of Appeals acknowledged that city officials would not be able to remove Thomas's book from a public book store. However, it said that a public school was different. Some authorized body or person, such as the school board, has to decide what will be in the library. "It is predictable," wrote Judge Mulligan, "that no matter what choice of books may be made" by the board, some person or group may dissent. The judge observed that the "ensuing shouts of book burning, witch hunting, and violation of academic freedom hardly elevate this intramural strife to First Amendment constitutional proportions. If it did, there would be a constant intrusion of the judiciary into the internal affairs of the school."

The court noted that the action of the board does not preclude teachers from discussing the book in class or assigning it for outside reading. Judge Mulligan rejected the concept of a book "acquiring tenure by shelving" and wrote that the administration of any school library "involves a constant process of selection and winnowing based not only on educational needs but financial and architectural realities. To suggest that the shelving or unshelving of books presents a constitutional issue, particularly where there is no showing of a curtailment of freedom of speech or thought, is a proposition we cannot accept." The court concluded that "books which become obsolete or irrelevant or were improperly selected initially, for whatever reason, can be removed by the same authority which was empowered to make the selection in the first place. . . ."*

The Minarcini Case: Protecting the Right to Know[32]

In the Cleveland suburb of Strongsville, Ohio, a controversy erupted over the use of three contemporary novels as texts and library books. Disregarding faculty recommendations, the school board refused to approve Joseph Heller's *Catch 22* and Kurt Vonnegut's *God Bless You, Mr.*

*Because of the *President's Council* decision, two 1979 district court opinions in the second circuit upheld the authority of school boards to remove objectionable books from public school libraries. *Pico* v. *Board of Education Island Trees Union Free School District,* 474 F.Supp. 387 (E.D. N.Y. 1979); *Bicknell* v. *Vergennes Union High School Board of Directors,* 475 F.Supp. 615 (D. Vt. 1979). In a related Ohio case, a group of parents objected to the use of Brown's *Manchild in the Promised Land* and Kesey's *One Flew Over the Cuckoo's Nest* as part of the high school curriculum. The court ruled that these books had "no literary, artistic, political or scientific value whatever," and they were "offensive to prevailing standards in the adult community with respect to what is suitable for juveniles." For these reasons the state court prohibited assigning the books as part of the curriculum except when a parent "has knowledge of the character of the books and consents to their use." *Grosser* v. *Woolett,* 341 N.E.2d 356 (Ohio 1974). In 1980, the Seventh Circuit Court of Appeals agreed with the decision in the *President's Council* case. *Zykan* v. *Warsaw Community School Corporation,* 631 F.2d 1300 (1980).

Rosewater and *Cat's Cradle* as texts or library books. In addition, it ordered Vonnegut's *Cat's Cradle* and Heller's *Catch 22* to be removed from the library. A group of high school students and their parents believed that these two actions violated the First Amendment, and they took their case to court.

The court first considered whether the school board could disregard the recommendations of the faculty concerning the approval of the purchase of textbooks. "Clearly," wrote Judge Edwards, "discretion as to the selection of textbooks must be lodged somewhere, and we can find no federal constitutional prohibition which prevents its being lodged in school board officials who are elected representatives of the people." Therefore the court ruled that the school faculty could not make its professional choices prevail over the considered decision of the Board of Education.

The second issue involved the removal of *Cat's Cradle* and *Catch 22* from the school library. The board apparently removed the books because it felt that it had the power "to censor the school library for subject matter which the board members found distasteful." The court rejected this notion. Judge Edwards agreed with the *President's Council* case that a school could select and winnow books on the basis of financial or space considerations. But he ruled that school officials could not remove books simply because they objected to their content.

Access to school libraries is an important privilege created for the benefit of students. According to the court, that privilege cannot be withdrawn by succeeding school boards whose members might desire to "winnow" the library for books "the content of which occasioned their displeasure." Although the board was not required to provide a library or to choose any particular books, the court noted that once it provided one, it could not "place conditions on the use of the library which were related solely to the social or political tastes of school board members."*

The court recognized that this case deals with a First Amendment "right to know," with "the right of students to receive information" and ideas from their teachers. Judge Edwards observed that the First Amendment's protection of academic freedom would certainly protect a teacher's right to state in class that he regarded *Catch 22* to be an important American novel. According to the court, it would also protect "his students' right to hear him and to find and read the book." Removing the book from the school library would clearly hinder this option. Thus the court concluded that "the removal of books from a school library is a

---

*In a related Mississippi case, a federal judge ruled that a state Textbook Rating Committee violated student and teacher rights by refusing to choose a text simply because it referred to racial incidents that the board felt did not represent the "Southern and true American way of life." *Loewen* v. *Turnipseed*, 486 F.Supp. 1138 (N.D. Miss. 1980).

much more serious burden upon freedom of classroom discussion than the action found unconstitutional in *Tinker*."

The Chelsea Case: No Unlimited Right to Remove[33]

In 1978 a case related to *Minarcini* was decided by a federal district court in Boston. It involved a decision by a Chelsea school committee to bar from the high school library an anthology by adolescent writers entitled *Male and Female Under 18*. The committee objected especially to one poem, "The City to a Young Girl," written by a 15-year-old New York high school student. The chairman of the school committee characterized "City" as "obviously obscene," "filthy," and "vile and offensive garbage."* The committee said that because it was not required to purchase *Male and Female* for the library, it could therefore remove it at will.

In a liberal opinion strongly supporting students' "right to read," the court ruled against the committee. Judge Tauro acknowledged that books can be removed from school libraries when they are obsolete, irrelevant, or obscene. But there was no evidence that *Male and Female* was obsolete or irrelevant; and despite the controversy over its language, it was clearly not legally obscene. Instead, the evidence indicated that the book was banned because the school committee considered the theme and the language of "City" to be offensive and because they felt that it might have a "damaging impact" on the high school students. "But the great weight of expert testimony," wrote the court, "left a clear picture that 'City' is a work of at least some value that would have no harmful effect on the

---

*The text of the poem is as follows:

The City to a Young Girl
    "The city is
    One million horney lip-smacking men
    Screaming for my body.
    The streets are long conveyor belts
    Loaded with suckling pigs.
    All begging for
    a lay
    a little pussy
    a bit of tit
    a leg to rub against
    a handful of ass
    the connoisseurs of cunt
    Every day, every night
    Pressing in on me closer and closer,
    I swat them off like flies
    but they keep coming back.
    I'm a good piece of meat."

Jody Caravaglia, 15

students." Committee members assumed that language offensive to them and some parents had no place in their educational system. However, as another judge wrote, "with the greatest of respect to such parents, their sensibilities are not the full measure of what is proper education."

The court acknowledged that "City" is "not a polite poem." Its language is "tough but not obscene," it is "challenging and thought provoking," and it uses "vivid street language, legitimately offensive to some, but not to everyone." The committee claimed an absolute right to remove "City" from the school library. The court ruled that "it has no such right" and that no public authority should have "such an unreviewable power of censorship."

Judge Tauro emphasized that there is more at stake here than one particular poem.

> If this work may be removed by a committee hostile to its language and theme, then the precedent is set for removal of any other work. The prospect of successive school committees "sanitizing" the school library of views divergent from their own is alarming. . . . What is at stake here is the right to read and be exposed to controversial thoughts and language—a valuable right subject to First Amendment protection.

Finally, the judge observed that the exposure to controversial ideas, language, and philosophy in a high school library poses no danger to students. "The danger," he concluded, "is in mind control."

Summary and Conclusions

Although all courts recognize that the Bill of Rights applies to students, individual rights are not absolute. When a student's exercise of his rights comes in conflict with the rights of other students or the obligation of the school to keep reasonable order, then judges weigh and balance these competing interests in light of the circumstances of the particular case before arriving at their decision.

The *Tinker* case outlined the constitutional principles that are now applied to all public schools: (1) A student's First Amendment right of free speech is protected against infringement by a state agency (such as the public schools) by the due process clause of the Fourteenth Amendment. (2) The wearing of an armband, button, or other type of symbolic expression by students is protected by the free speech clause of the First Amendment. (3) Freedom of speech is not an absolute right and may be abridged by school officials under some circumstances. The question posed by the cases in this chapter is: Under what circumstances can school authorities restrict student freedom of expression?

The *Tinker* case held that restricting a student's right to freedom of expression is unconstitutional unless there is evidence to show that the forbidden conduct would "materially and substantially interfere" with school activities. "Apprehension of disturbance" on the part of school officials or their desire to avoid "the discomfort and unpleasantness that always accompany an unpopular viewpoint" is not sufficient to overcome a student's right to freedom of expression. This right extends beyond the classroom to halls, the cafeteria, and the entire school campus.

In the years following the *Tinker* decision other courts have sought to determine what rules regulating student expression were consistent with the principles of *Tinker* and under what circumstances the "substantial and material disruption" test would justify the restriction of free speech in public schools. In the process some judges tended to distinguish *Tinker* from the cases before them and limit the application of this landmark decision. In the *Guzick* case, for example, a court upheld a school rule prohibiting the wearing of all controversial buttons and badges when the wearing of such symbols had caused substantial disruption in the past and would have aggravated an already tense situation. Because of the "potentiality and imminence" of disruption, school officials were permitted to enforce disciplinary rules restricting freedom of expression before "good order" had been "demolished."

Just as *Guzick* limited the application of *Tinker*, other cases have reaffirmed and perhaps expanded its application. The *Butts* case, for example, indicated that an expectation of disruption by school officials is not enough to justify the suspension of students rights, unless (1) such an expectation is "based on fact, not intuition" and (2) the officials first made an honest effort to restrain those who might cause the disruption. The *Lipp* case suggested that a corollary of free speech is the right not to speak or engage in symbolic expression such as saluting or standing during the Pledge of Allegiance. On the other hand, freedom of speech does not protect "fighting words" because these expressions are designed to injure individuals and not to communicate ideas.

Does the First Amendment give students the right to influence decisions about school texts and library books? Courts usually distinguish between the right to select books and the right to remove books from a library or reading list. Judges generally agree that school boards have the authority to select textbooks, a power usually delegated to them by state law. If there is a conflict between students and teachers who recommend certain books and administrators and school boards who want to select other books, courts will usually uphold the board's selection as a matter of reasonable administrative discretion.

The removal of books from the library is a more complex matter. Nevertheless, certain principles are clear. First, administrators have no obligation either to provide a school library or to select any particular library books. Second, books can be removed if they are obsolete, irrelevant, or legally obscene, or because of space or financial limitations.

Can books be removed because they offend certain board members, parents, or community groups? Judges are in conflict, and the Supreme Court has not yet ruled on this issue. The *President's Council* case gives school boards broad discretion in "unshelving" as well as selecting books. On the other hand, the *Minarcini* and *Chelsea* cases clearly ruled that school officials cannot censor the library or reading lists simply because they object to a book's content or philosophy. Rather, they suggest that students have a "right to know," a right to receive information, and a right to "be exposed to controversial thoughts." This right appears to prohibit officials from "deselecting" a book just because it is offensive to some parents or administrators who are hostile to its language or theme. However, the scope of a student's right to know has not yet been fully clarified by the courts.

In reviewing the cases that followed *Tinker*, it seems clear that some of Justice Black's fears have been fulfilled and others have not. The *Tinker* decision did not begin a "new revolutionary era" of judicially fostered permissiveness. On the contrary, judges have repeatedly allowed authorities to protect schools from student expression that would lead to disorder. On the other hand, Justice Black was right in predicting that *Tinker* would lead students to demand their rights more frequently and to initiate "lawsuits for damages and injunctions" when they believed their rights had been violated. But this has not subjected "all the public schools in the country to the whims and caprices of their loudest-mouthed" students. Rather, it has led to a growing and active interest in the law on the part of students, faculty, parents, and administrators. Unlike Justice Black, we view this as a healthy development, educationally as well as legally.

NOTES

1. *Tinker* v. *Des Moines Independent School District*, 393 U.S. 503, 506 (1969).
2. Id. at 522.
3. *Waugh* v. *Board of Trustees*, 237 U.S. 589 (1915). In *Waugh* the Court indicated it would not annul state restrictions of student freedom "upon disputable considerations of their wisdom or necessity."
4. In 1966 federal courts were still using the "reasonableness test." For example, the trial court judge in the *Tinker* case wrote that unless the actions of the school officials in restricting student expression "are unreasonable, the courts should not interfere." *Tinker* v. *Des Moines*, 258 F.Supp. 971 (D. Iowa 1966).
5. *Wooster* v. *Sunderland*, 148 P. 959 (1915).
6. For the full text of this and other constitutional amendments especially relevant to students, see Appendix A.
7. *Tinker* v. *Des Moines*, 258 F.Supp. 971 (D. Iowa 1966).
8. *Tinker* v. *Des Moines*, 393 U.S. 503 (1969).
9. *West Virginia Board of Education* v. *Barnett*, 319 U.S. 624, 637 (1943).

10. Tinker at 508–509.
11. Id. at 511.
12. Id. at 522.
13. Id at 524–526.
14. *Guzick* v. *Drebus*, 431 F.2d 594 (6th Cir. 1970), cert. denied, 401 U.S. 948 (1971).
15. Symbols that supported high school athletic teams or advertised school plays were not forbidden. Id. at 596.
16. The button read: "April 5 Chicago, GI-Civilian, Anti-War Demonstration, Student Mobilization Committee."
17. *Guzick* at 600–601.
18. This is the text of Judge McAllister's brief dissenting opinion in the *Guzick* case:

> *When a few students noticed the button which appellant [Guzick] was wearing, and asked him "what it said," appellant's explanation resulted only in a casual reaction; and there was no indication that the wearing of the button would disrupt the work and discipline of the school.*
>
> *I am of the opinion that the judgment of the district court should be reversed and the case dismissed upon the authority of* Tinker v. Des Moines. [Id. *at 601.*]

19. *Melton* v. *Young*, 465 F.2d 1332 (6th Cir. 1972).
20. In a related case a federal court upheld the right of a North Carolina high school principal to prohibit all armbands worn by groups of pro- and anti-war demonstrators in an "explosive" situation that included belligerent student behavior and threats of violence. *Hill* v. *Lewis*, 323 F.Supp. 55 (E.D. N.C. 1971).
21. *Banks* v. *Muncie Community Schools*, 433 F.2d 292 (7th Cir. 1970).
22. Although he did not rule in favor of the black students, the trial court judge commented:

> *Tyranny by the majority is as onerous as tyranny by a select minority. The student body's choice of symbols has been shown to be personally offensive to a significant number of the students, no matter how innocuous the symbols may originally have seemed to the young, white students. An exercise in democracy which results in offense to a sizeable number of the participants should be seriously reconsidered by the student body. [Id. at 297–298.]*

> Similarly, the appeals court worte that "the symbols complained of are offensive and that good policy would dictate their removal." Id. at 299.

23. *Karp* v. *Becken*, 477 F.2d 171 (9th Cir. 1973).
24. *Butts* v. *Dallas Independent School District*, 306 F.Supp. 488 (N.D. Tex. 1969); 436 F.2d 728 (5th Cir. 1971).
25. 306 F.Supp. 488, 490 (N.D. Tex. 1969). In a paragraph that reflected his educational concerns, Judge Taylor wrote:

> *The simple fact of the matter is that in order to educate a large group of children, there must be some type of orderly process. This process may infringe on a child's freedom of expression in varying degrees. Hopefully, the process will teach him how to reason, assimilate ideas, and generally*

think for himself. To date, the Dallas Independent School District has been one of the most up-to-date and qualified districts in the Nation. It has maintained an admirable degree of order in these times when other large school systems are experiencing chaos and violence. . . . It occurs to this Court that one obligation students have to the State is to obey school regulations designed to promote the orderly educational process. [Id. at 491].

26. *Aguirre* v. *Tahoka Independent School District,* 311 F.Supp. 664 (N.D. Tex. 1970).
27. *Lipp* v. *Morris,* 579 F.2d 834 (3rd Cir. 1978). For related "freedom of conscience" cases, see Chapter 7.
28. *Fenton* v. *Stear,* 423 F.Supp. 767 (W.D. Penn, 1976).
29. *Commonwealth* v. *Bohmer,* 372 N.E.2d 1381 (Mass. 1978).
30. *Fricke* v. *Lynch,* 491 F.Supp. 381 (D. R.I. 1980).
31. *President's Council, District 25* v. *Community School Board No. 25,* 457 F.2d 289 (2nd Cir. 1972).
32. *Minarcini* v. *Strongsville City School District,* 541 F.2d 577 (6th Cir. 1976).
33. *Right to Read Defense Committee of Chelsea* v. *School Committee of the City of Chelsea,* 454 F.Supp. 703 (D. Mass. 1978).

Chapter 3
Freedom of the Press: The Publication and Distribution of Student Views

> *Tinker's* dam to school board absolutism does not leave dry the fields of school discipline. . . . It sets canals and channels through which school discipline might flow with the least possible damage to the nation's priceless topsoil of the First Amendment.
>
> *Shanley v. Northeast Independent School District*[1]

In a 1973 Supreme Court opinion, Chief Justice Burger wrote:

> The First Amendment protects works which, taken as a whole, have serious literary, artistic, political or scientific value, regardless of whether the government or a majority of the people approve of the ideas these works represent. "The protection given speech and press was fashioned to assure unfettered interchange of ideas for the bringing about of political and social changes desired by the people."[2]

Thus the First Amendment protects the freedom of citizens to suggest revolutionary change and to write critically about government policies and officials. Is a student equally free to propose radical change and to criticize publicly school officials and administrative policy? Can he publish such proposals or criticism in a school-sponsored paper? Or can faculty advisers eliminate material that attacks school policy?

What is the status of "underground" student newspapers? Can the distribution of such papers be prohibited in school? Or does a student have a constitutional right to distribute any material she wishes if she is not disruptive? These are some of the issues raised in this chapter.

The chapter is divided into three sections. After a brief examination of a 1908 case, we first consider the question of "prior restraint"— whether and under what circumstances school officials can require students to submit all publications for approval prior to distribution. Second, we examine a series of cases that probe the limits of student freedom concerning underground newspapers. Finally, we consider the extent to which officials can control the content, advertisements, and editorial policy in school-sponsored publications.

HISTORICAL PERSPECTIVE

The Dresser Case: A Traditional Approach to Student Publications[3]

Two high school students from St. Croix Falls, Wisconsin, printed a poem in the town newspaper that satirized the rules of the school. The principal believed that the poem tended to hold the "school, its discipline and its teachers to public contempt and ridicule." Therefore he told the students that they would be suspended unless they submitted a written apology "admitting that they did a wrong thing" and that they were sorry. The students refused and were suspended.

The father of the two students went to court and argued that the principal had no right to punish his daughters for publishing a "harmless" poem that they had written after school hours. The principal responded that it would be detrimental to the school and "subversive of proper discipline" to reinstate the students without a suitable apology.

The court held that school authorities have the power to suspend a pupil for an offense committed outside school hours that has "a direct and immediate tendency to influence the conduct of other pupils while in the schoolroom" and to impair the authority of the teachers. "Such power is essential" for the preservation of "decency, decorum and good government in the public schools." Since the judge believed that school officials are familiar with the effect such a poem would probably have, he ruled that they should be given "broad discretion" in disciplining students. The court concluded that the principal's action was not an abuse of discretion but rather "an earnest desire" to discipline the students "for their own good as well as for the good of the school."

This case was decided by the Supreme Court of Wisconsin on May 8, 1908. The court did not consider the possibility that the First Amendment's provision concerning freedom of press might have protected the action of these students.

ADMINISTRATIVE APPROVAL: CONSTITUTIONALITY, CRITERIA, AND PROCEDURES

The Shanley Case: The Limits of Administrative Review[4]

In 1972 Mark Shanley and four high school classmates in San Antonio, Texas, were suspended for publishing and distributing an underground student newspaper entitled "Awakening." The publication discussed current controversial subjects (such as the "injustice" of drug laws) and it offered information on birth control, venereal disease, and draft and drug counseling. In addition it expressed critical views of the school administration.

The administration believed the contents of Awakening" to be "potentially disruptive." Moreover, distribution of the paper was contrary to a school board policy that was developed to maintain "at all times a proper learning situation" in the San Antonio schools. The policy provided that any student attempt "to avoid the school's established procedure for administrative approval" concerning the production and distribution of petitions or printed documents of any kind "without the specific approval of the principal" shall be cause for suspension.

The suspended students had used their own resources and facilities to produce the underground paper. They distributed the paper peacefully before and after classes on a public street near the school. The distribution caused no disruption of class activities. The paper, however, was published and distributed "without the specific approval of the principal."

At a hearing before the school board, the students argued that they did not think the board policy applied to conduct outside school hours and off school grounds. The school board nevertheless affirmed the suspension. Objecting to the school board's "bootstrap transmogrification into Super-parent," the biological parents of the five students took the case to court. A federal district court upheld the school board and the parents appealed.

Questions to Consider

1. Are the First Amendment rights of students the same as those of adults? Is there a difference between freedom of press in a public school and on a public street? Should school officials be able to limit the former more strictly than city officials can limit the latter? If so, what factors might justify such differences?
2. Should school officials be able to review the content of student publications before they are distributed?
3. Under what circumstances, if any, can the distribution of a student publication be prohibited?

4. Does the Tenth Amendment, which reserves education to the states, protect school board policy from review by federal courts?*

THE LEGAL PRINCIPLES

On behalf of the U.S. Circuit Court of Appeals, Judge Irving Goldberg began his opinion on the *Shanley* case by reviewing the applicable law. First he took note of the principle that courts should interfere with day-to-day operations of schools as a "platitudinous but eminently sound maxim." On the other hand, he emphasized that "this court laid to rest more than a decade ago the notion that state authorities could subject students at public-supported educational institutions to whatever conditions the state wished." Of paramount importance, wrote the judge, is "the constitutional imperative that school boards abide by constitutional precepts."

The school board argued that the Tenth Amendment reserved education solely to the states and protects its policy from interference by the federal courts. In caustic and colorful language, Judge Goldberg characterized the school board's legal position as a "judicial believe-it-or-not" and a "constitutional fossil, exhumed and respired to stalk the First Amendment once again long after its substance had been laid to rest."

• **Students and adults.** Despite this dismissal of the board's argument, the court noted that there was a significant difference between the freedom of speech of students in a public school and adults on a public street. Thus, whereas the Supreme Court protected an "inflammatory and vitriolic exhortation" before a paying adult audience,[5] it would not protect the same speech before a high school assembly. Although a school is certainly a marketplace for ideas, "it is just as certainly not a market place."

The educational process, observed Judge Goldberg, "is thwarted by the milling, mooing, and haranguing, along with the aggressiveness that often accompanies a constitutionally-protected exchange of ideas on a street. Thus courts recognize the differences "between what are reasonable restraints in the classroom and what are reasonable restraints on a street corner." This is because students and teachers cannot easily disassociate themselves from expressions directed toward them during school hours, because disciplinary problems in a crowded school setting "seriously sap the educational process," and because schools have the

---

*The Tenth Amendment provides: "The powers not delegated to the United States by the Constitution, nor prohibited by it to the States, are reserved to the States respectively, or to the people."

"vital responsibility of compressing a variety of subjects and activities into a relatively confined period of time and space."

• **Reviewing Student Materials.** Given the necessity for discipline and orderly processes in high schools, the court ruled that it is not unconstitutional to require that materials destined for distribution to students be submitted to the school administration prior to distribution, as long as the requirement does not restrict student publications in an unconstitutional manner.

When the constitutionality of a school regulation is questioned, the burden of justifying the regulation falls on the school board. The test for curtailing student expression is whether it materially and substantially interferes with the activities of the school. The justification for allowing administrators to screen materials before they are distributed "is to prevent disruption and not to stifle expression."

In sum, the court outlined four principles applicable to student freedom of expression under the First Amendment: (1) expression by high school students can be prohibited if it materially and substantially interferes with school activities or with the rights of students or teachers; (2) expression by high school students cannot be prohibited solely because other students, teachers, administrators, or parents may disagree with its content; (3) expression by students may be "subjected to prior screening under clear and reasonable regulation"; and (4) student expression may be limited in "manner, place, or time" by reasonable and equally applied regulations.

Questions to Consider

1. Could school officials prohibit the distribution of "Awakening" if they believed it would cause disruption? What evidence would be necessary to support such a belief? Is the professional judgment of a school administrator adequate evidence?
2. Would the fact that a student newspaper dealt with topics that most students or parents considered highly controversial or disturbing justify restricting distribution?
3. Could student publications be restricted if they were critical, negative, and in basic disagreement with school policy?
4. Do you believe the San Antonio school board policy was constitutional? If not, how would you redraft it so that it would not violate the Constitution?

CAN "CONTROVERSY" STIFLE DISTRIBUTION?

The court next applied the legal principles to the facts of the case. There was no evidence that the distribution of "Awakening" caused any disturbances on or off campus. Hence there was no "disruption in fact."

The "reasonable forecast of disruption" that might result from student expression is a more difficult test to apply. However, for several reasons Judge Goldberg did not feel the test was difficult to apply in this case.[6] First, the "Awakening" contained no remarks that could be considered obscene, libelous, or inflammatory.* Second, even if the administration were genuinely concerned about the controversial topics mentioned in "Awakening," the discussion of controversial issues is no reason to restrict freedom of expression. "It should be axiomatic at this point in our nation's history," observed the court, "that in a democracy 'controversy' is, as a matter of constitutional law, never sufficient in and of itself to stifle the views of any citizen."

The "controversial" subjects in "Awakening" included a statement advocating a review of the laws regarding marijuana and a statement offering information about birth control, venereal disease, and draft and drug counseling. To the court it appeared odd that an educational institution "would boggle at controversy" to such an extent that "mere representation that students should become informed" about these widely discussed and significant issues should prompt a school to stifle the content of a student publication. Judge Goldberg observed:

> Perhaps newer educational theories have become in vogue since our day, but our recollection of the learning process is that the purpose of education is to spread, not to stifle, ideas and views. Ideas must be freed from despotic dispensation by all men, be they robed as academicians or judges or citizen members of a board of education.

The school administration also expressed concern over the negative attitude of the newspaper and its criticism of the administration. In response, the court noted that "negativism" is "entirely in the eye of the beholder, and presumably the school administration's eye became fixed upon the criticism by the students." As a person to whom public criticism has been directed, the judge asserted (with "some pained assurance") that "criticism" like "controversy" is not a "bogey," at least not in a democracy. Although constructive criticism is more helpful than other sorts of critiques, the court noted that almost any effort to explain an alternative way of doing things serves to illuminate the issue being questioned. If the criticism is irrational or ill-intentioned, "then surely the American citizenry, even that of high school age, will have enough good sense to attach that much more credibility" to the actions of those unfairly criticized. In any event, aversion to criticism is not a constitutionally reasonable justification for forbidding student expression. The First

---

*Libel is a false written expression that injures a person's reputation. A person who is libeled can sue for damages. What constitutes obscenity is considered in the Kitchen and Miller cases in the following section.

Amendment's protection of speech and press is part of the Bill of Rights precisely because those regulated "should have the right and even the responsibility" of commenting upon the actions of their appointed or elected regulators.

"One of the great concerns of our time," observed the court, "is that our young people, disillusioned by our political processes, are disengaging from political participation. It is most important that our young people became convinced that our Constitution is a living reality, not parchment preserved under glass."

NO LIMITS OR STANDARDS

The court was highly critical of the wording of the school board policy. Its questionable provisions stated that:

> Any attempt to avoid the school's established procedure for administrative approval of activities such as the production for distribution and/or distribution of petitions or printed documents of any kind, sort, or type without the specific approval of the principal shall be cause for suspension.

The court found this policy unconstitutional because it (1) was too broad and vague, (2) contained no standards to guide its application, and (3) contained no fair procedures for resolving disputes concerning its application.

The policy was "overbroad" because it established a "prior restraint" on all written expression by high school students at any time or place and for any reason.* There was no requirement that the prohibited activity (publishing or distributing any printed document without the principal's approval) have any relationship to maintaining orderly school activities. When questioned at the school board hearing regarding the scope of the policy, the assistant principal responded: "I think it is left up to the principal's good judgment." Although not derogating the good judgment of school administrators, Judge Goldberg noted that the Constitution cannot be interpreted loosely "because the motivations behind its infringement may be benign."

The policy was also unconstitutional because there were no standards to guide a principal in accepting or rejecting a student publication. The court emphasized that "our constitutional system does not permit any school or administrator, however well intentioned, to be the unaccountable imperators of the lives of our children." In order to remedy this lack of standards, the policy in question must include guidelines stating "clear and demonstrable criteria" that administrators should use to evaluate materials submitted to them for prior clearance.

The policy was further defective because it did not state what high

---

*Authorities exercise prior restraint when they prohibit, censor, or restrict the publication of materials prior to their distribution.

school activities were included in the rule. In fact the assistant principal conceded under questioning that one student handing *Time* magazine to another without the permission of the principal might be in violation of the policy.[7] In order to remedy such vagueness, the policy must include guidelines stating the relationship between the curtailment of distribution and the prevention of substantial disruption of school activities.

Finally, the policy was unconstitutional because it lacked the safeguards required for "due process."* There was no provision for appeal from a decision by a principal prohibiting distribution nor was there an indication of how long a principal could take to make her decision. Delays in reviewing newspapers "carry the inherent danger that the exercise of speech might be chilled altogether during the period of its importance." This illustrates the many frustrating and petty ways "the constitutional ideal can be thwarted" by a school administration. Therefore any requirement for screening publications distributable to high school students under a policy purporting to prevent disruption must: (1) state clearly the means by which students are to submit proposed materials to the school administration; (2) state a brief period of time during which the administration must make its decision; (3) state a clear and reasonable method of appeal; and (4) state a brief time during which the appeal must be decided.

In conclusion, Justice Goldberg wrote:

> *Tinker's* dam to school board absolutism does not leave dry the fields of school discipline. . . . It sets canals and channels through which school discipline might flow with the least possible damage to the nation's priceless topsoil of the First Amendment. Perhaps it would be well if those entrusted to administer the teaching of American history and government to our students began their efforts by practicing the document on which that history and government are based. Our eighteen-year-olds can now vote, serve on juries, and be drafted; yet the board fears the awakening of their intellects without reasoned concern for its effect upon school discipline. The First Amendment cannot tolerate such intolerance. This case is therefore reversed.

RELATED ISSUES
In addition to discussing criteria and procedures for administrative review of student publications, Judge Goldberg also commented on several related questions.

1. Does a "forecast of disruption" always justify prior restraint of student expression?

---

*The Fourteenth Amendment to the Constitution provides that no state shall deprive any person "of life, liberty or property without due process of law." The meaning and requirements of due process are discussed more fully in Chapter 12.

No, not always. The school administration could use its discretion to regulate the time, place, and manner of distribution more strictly if the content of a student publication could lead to a disturbance by those who hold opposing views. However, students who wish "to reasonably exercise their freedom of expression should not be restrained or punishable at the threshold of their attempts at expression merely because a small, perhaps vocal or violent, group of students with differing views might or does create a disturbance."*

    2. What evidence is needed to constitute a reasonable forecast of disruption? Is the professional judgment or intuition of a principal or superintendent adequate?

Although the court "has great respect for the intuitive abilities of administrators," freedom of expression cannot be stifled solely on this ground. On the contrary, Judge Goldberg emphasized that the judgment of school administrators must be "substantiated by some objective evidence" to support a reasonable forecast of disruption. Thus the court cautioned administrators against restricting student expression simply on the grounds that their professional intuition leads them to predict substantial disruption.

    3. Does the *Shanley* decision mean that *any* attempt by a school to regulate the off-campus distribution of student publications would be unconstitutional?

The decision does not go that far. Although Judge Goldberg pointed out that an offense is "usually punishable only by the authority in whose jurisdiction the offense took place," he noted that the distance from the school might be a significant factor in determining the breadth of the school board's authority. The San Antonio school policy was clearly unconstitutional as it applied to the peaceful distribution of "Awakening," but the judge declined to say that a school could never regulate off-campus distribution of student publications.

---

*In this regard Judge Goldberg quoted with approval a strong statement by the Supreme Court explaining the importance of protecting controversial speech:

> A function of free speech under our system of government is to invite dispute. It may indeed best serve its high purpose when it induces a condition of unrest, creates dissatisfaction with conditions as they are, or even stirs the people to anger. Speech is often provocative and challenging. It may strike at prejudices and preconceptions and have profound unsettling effects as it presses for acceptance of an idea. That is why freedom of speech, though not absolute . . . is nevertheless protected against censorship or punishment, unless shown likely to produce a clear and present danger of a serious substantive evil that rises far above public inconvenience, annoyance or unrest. There is no room under our Constitution for a more restrictive view [*Shanley* at 973 quoting *Terminiello* v. *Chicago*, 337 U.S. 1 (1948)].

SUMMARY

The *Shanley* case indicated that the distribution of student publications cannot be prohibited simply because school officials disagree with their contents. However, the time, place, and manner of distribution can be regulated, and distribution can be prohibited if it substantially interferes with school activities. *Shanley* also held that schools can require prior review of student publications under clear and reasonable regulations. In this case the rules requiring such review were unconstitutional because they vaguely applied to all written expression ("of any kind, sort, or type"), they lacked reasonable standard for evaluating student expression, and they lacked due process safeguards. Such safeguards include prompt, clear, and fair procedures for review and appeal.

Fujishima v. *Board of Education:* Prior Approval Prohibited (or the Case of The Cosmic Frog)[8]

In 1972 another federal court went even further than the *Shanley* decision in protecting the First Amendment rights of students to publish and distribute underground newspapers. The case arose when two Illinois high school seniors, Burt Fujishima and Richard Peluso, were suspended for distributing before and between classes about 350 copies of "The Cosmic Frog," an underground student paper. They were disciplined pursuant to the following Chicago Board of Education rule: "No person shall be permitted . . . to distribute on the school premises any books, tracts, or other publications . . . unless the same shall have been approved by the General Superintendent of Schools." Fujishima and Peluso challenged the constitutionality of this regulation.

The school board argued that its rule was constitutional because it does not require approval of the "contents" of a publication before it may be distributed. "Unfortunately," replied the court, "that is neither what the rule says" nor how the school board has "previously interpreted it." Because the rule requires prior approval of publications, the court held that it was "unconstitutional as a prior restraint in violation of the First Amendment." The court arrived at this conclusion by combining the Supreme Court's holdings in *Near* v. *Minnesota** and *Tinker* v. *Des Moines.* According to appeals court Judge Robert Sprecher:

*Near v. *Minnesota ex rel. Olson*, 283 U.S. 697 (1931). *Near* involved a Minnesota statute that allowed state authorities to bring the owner of a newspaper to court on charges of publishing "scandalous and defamatory matter" about public officials. According to the statute, unless the owner were able to prove that his charges were true, further publication of the paper would be prohibited. The Supreme Court ruled that the statute violated the freedom of press guaranteed by the First Amendment. The Court's opinion reviewed the rationale of the guarantee and noted that "liberty of the press, historically considered and taken up by the Constitution, has meant principally, although not exclusively, immunity from previous restraints of censorship."

What about writers and publishers that abuse this freedom and slander government

Tinker held that, absent a showing of material and substantial interference with the requirements of school discipline, schools may not restrain the full First Amendment rights of their students. Near established one of those rights, freedom to distribute a publication without prior censorship.

Cannot administrators restrict the distribution of a publication if they can "forecast" that it will cause substantial disruption? Not according to Judge Sprecher.[9] On the contrary, "the *Tinker* forecast rule," wrote the judge, "is properly a formula for determining when the requirements of school discipline justify *punishment* of students for exercise of their First-Amendment rights. It is not a basis for establishing a system of censorship and licensing to *prevent* the exercise of First-Amendment rights."

This does not mean that a school board may not regulate the distribution of student publications. It may issue rules concerning the time, place, and manner of distribution and may punish students who violate those rules. It may also establish rules punishing students who publish and distribute obscene or libelous literature on school grounds. But, according to Judge Sprecher, schools may not require that publications be submitted to the administration for their approval before students may distribute them.

NOTE: As *Shanley* and *Fujishima* illustrate, federal appeals courts are not in agreement about whether schools may require students to submit publications to them for review before distribution. And the U.S. Supreme Court has not ruled directly on this issue. With the exception of *Fujishima*, however, most federal courts that have considered the problem have indicated that prior review is not necessarily unconstitutional in public schools. But, in practice, courts that have examined prior review procedures have generally found flaws in them. Some cases such as *Shanley* have focused on the need for procedural safeguards. Others have focused on the need for clear, precise standards and have strictly limited administrative review. The following section examines some of these standards as well as the scope and limits of prior review.

Precise Standards Required: The Baughman and Williams Cases

In the *Baughman* case, two Maryland high school students asked a federal appeals court to prohibit any prior review of the content of their underground newspaper. The court declined this request. It did, however, provide clear guidelines and explanations on this issue.[10]

---

officials? In answer the Court wrote: "Public officers, whose character and conduct remain open to debate and free discussion in the press, find their remedies for false accusations in actions under libel laws providing for redress and punishment, and not in proceedings to restrain the publication of newspapers and periodicals."

Judge Craven explained that school rules imposing prior review "must be much more precise than a regulation imposing post-publication sanctions" because censorship may prevent the public from finding out what an administrator has refused permission to distribute. Therefore regulations requiring students to submit material for approval before distribution "must contain narrow, objective, and reasonable standards" by which the material will be judged. Such standards are required so that those who enforce the regulations are not given "impermissible power to judge the material on an *ad hoc* and subjective basis."

The court emphasized that the use of legal terms such as "libelous" or "obscene" without explanation "are not sufficiently precise and understandable by high school students and administrators untutored in the law" to be acceptable criteria to indicate what is forbidden. Although school authorities may ban obscene or libelous material, "there is an intolerable danger . . . that under the guise of such vague labels they may unconstitutionally choke off criticism, either of themselves or school policies, which they find disrespectful, tasteless, or offensive." And that, wrote Judge Craven, "they may not do." Therefore, prior review policies must contain "precise criteria sufficiently spelling out what is forbidden" so that a reasonably intelligent student may clearly know what he may and may not write.

In a subsequent Maryland case, *Williams* v. *Spencer*, the same federal appeals court upheld a school rule halting the distribution of any student publication that "encourages actions which endanger the health and safety of students." School officials had stopped students from distributing an underground newspaper that advertised waterpipes used to smoke marijuana and hashish. The students claimed the school rule was vague and violated their constitutional rights.

In contrast to the holding in *Baughman*, the court felt that the rule in *Williams* was clear and that high school students would have no difficulty understanding that advertisements encouraging "the sale of drug paraphernalia" were prohibited. In this 1980 decision, the court concluded that "the First Amendment rights of students must yield to the superior interest of the school in seeing that materials that encourage actions which endanger the health or safety of students are not distributed on school property."[11]

TESTING THE LIMITS OF FREEDOM

OBSCENITY

The Kitchen Case: What Is an Obscene Publication for Students?[12]

Prior to morning classes, Paul Kitchen was standing outside an entrance to Houston's Waltrip High School selling "Space City," a controversial local newspaper that was not approved by the principal. Kitchen was a junior at Waltrip, and most of his customers were students on the way to school. After he had made a number of sales, he was confronted by Gordon Cotton, the high school principal, who bought a copy of the newspaper, read a portion of the second page, and informed the student that he was violating several school board policies. But Kitchen refused to stop selling the paper. He was later suspended and responded with profanity as he left the principal's office. What provoked Cotton's action was the following letter to the editor, which was captioned "High Skool is Fucked":*

> Dear Brothers and Sisters,
> What ever happened to the skools where you learned? Now you compete for grades, memorize and spit it back out on test day. It is as boring as hell, you don't talk to your friends in class or you get your ass bit. You grow your hair long because you love it and its beautiful, then you get thrown out for being a radical and not wanting to conform to the fucked rules and regulations of the so-called "great-society." Big shit! Think about your brothers and chicanos and blacks getting fucked all the time, only because they weren't born white. You write up a leaflet, pamphlet or newspaper to get your friends to get it together, and see how they are getting fucked, and you get thrown out.
> The courses skools have are the same ones they had for fifty years. They don't try to teach, they just want you to pass and get the fuck out of there. It's their jobs—they are getting paid not us. You try to get the attention of the administration and skool board by boycotts or demonstrations and you get thrown out or busted.
> . . . . If you could be in a relaxed atmosphere you might could learn something. But not at skool, they're too busy telling you to "sit up straight," "don't chew gum," "you can't smoke in skool," "don't come back til you cut your hair and wear decent clothes," "don't talk or we'll bust your ass." Man it is a big fucking burn you just can't learn under those conditions.
> You have read and heard the same thing before, but we have to quit fucking around and do something. Right now! I don't mean petitions and talks with the administration because they have been tried and failed. Now is the time to go to actions and not talking. Do it! Venceremos!
> Gerald (Bushman) Smith
> MacArthur High
> Houston

Mr. Cotton suspended Kitchen because the issue of "Space City" Kitchen had sold was obscene, because it urged disobedience of school regulations, because its distribution would cause disturbance in the

---

*The substitution of "K" for "C" and "Ch" (e.g. "Amerika") was widely used by publications of the New Left.

school, and because it had not been submitted to the principal for approval.

Kitchen believed that the principal's action was unconstitutional and he took his case to court.

Questions to Consider

1. Should Paul Kitchen have been suspended for selling "Space City"? What are the legal and educational issues raised by this case?
2. Was the letter to the editor in "Space City" obscene? What makes material obscene? Who should decide this question and how? Should there be a different standard of obscenity for adults and for minors?
3. If students read and commented on "Space City" during class, would this disruption justify prohibiting the distribution of the paper near school?

THE OPINION OF THE COURT

In the opinion of the district court, Judge Seals considered the question of what constitutes an obscene publication and several other important free speech issues for students.

• **Obscenity.** In this case the principal testified that the distribution of "Space City" violated school board policy "because it had obscene words in it and these words are obscene in our area, and on the school campus at Waltrip High School." Although Cotton may have believed that a written statement that "High School is Fucked" violated school policy prohibiting obscene language, the trial court noted that the principal failed to consider several important limitations on the obscenity test.

First, he did not consider the issue of "Space City" as a whole. Cotton testified that he had not read the paper beyond the letter to the editor, which appeared on the second page. However, courts have ruled that "a publication must be considered as a whole in order to determine whether it is obscene." And as a federal judge noted: "A publication is not obscene merely because it contains a blunt, anglo-Saxon word."[13]

Second, Cotton failed to apply correctly another part of the obscenity test, the definition of the "common community standard" by which a word must be judged. The principal evaluated the newspaper in terms of its probable reception in the Waltrip High School area and concluded that its distribution was "unacceptable" there. However, the community whose "common standards" are at issue must be "the whole community of the Houston Independent School District" and not just the standards of the Waltrip High School community.

Third, Judge Seals ruled that the controversial letter (which was the basis for suspending Kitchen) was not in itself obscene and that "intermittent employment of 'fuck' and its ilk cannot, without more, render a publication obscene." As one expert witness on linguistics testified: "The use of 'fuck' in the declaration, 'High School Is Fucked,' has no reference to sex and, in fact, denotes that high school is 'in bad shape . . . in a pretty lousy state of affairs.' " Thus the court held that a key requirement of the obscenity test, that it appeal to a prurient interest in sex, had not been satisfied.[14]

Furthermore, the judge ruled that Houston school administrators forfeited their right to object to the appearance of *fuck* in "Space City" by sanctioning the presence of various books and articles in school libraries that contained similar "vulgarisms." Judge Seals observed that Cotton seemed to approve the use of vulgar language when it is used "to depict the speech of a bygone era, but not when employed by a contemporary young person to describe his current dissatisfaction with the educational system." The judge indicated that he was "unable to comprehend such a distinction." Consequently, he ruled that the school board failed to demonstrate a basis for discrimination between the use of vulgarity in "Space City" and its use in school-approved publications. Thus the court found that neither the letter "High School Is Fucked" nor the entire issue of "Space City" in which it appeared was obscene.

In concluding this section of his opinion, Judge Seals noted a recent trend toward a "greater toleration of words that were once scrupulously avoided," and he observed:

> In a society in which the old and the traditional is daily being challenged by the new and the unprecedented, those who seek to guard against the encroachment of taboo words appear to be waging defensive warfare. The court believes that, far from signaling the moral crisis of our civilization, such a development is a healthy indicator of moral progress. In a witchhunt to expunge the momentarily embarrassing, we frequently tolerate language and name-calling that degrades the human spirit, and leaves its heritage of bitterness long after we have forgotten the reddened face and temporary loss of composure that flash our instantaneous reaction to a string of four-letter words.[15]

• **Disruption.** Judge Seals considered as reasonable those school rules that regulated the distribution of materials "near campus" when this resulted "in possession by students on campus." This was because of the court's view that disruption was the proper criterion for restricting distribution. To clarify this question Judge Seals wrote that if a student complies with reasonable rules as to time and place for distribution and "does so in an orderly, nondisruptive manner, then he should not suffer if other students who are lacking in self-control tend to over-react, thereby becoming a disruptive influence." The court therefore concluded that in order to sustain suspension of a student distributor, school officials must demonstrate: "(1) substantial and material interference, and (2) a good faith, but unsuccessful, attempt to discipline the disrupting student or students."

• **Other Abuses.** According to Judge Seals, the possibilities of abuse in the application of the Houston School Board rules were numerous and were reflected in this case. Cotton, for example, deemed "Space City" to be "obscene" before seeking the opinion of any attorney, and the regulations did not provide any right to appeal a principal's decision that a publication was unacceptable. The court therefore found that the regulations "fail to obviate the risk" that untrained laymen will misconstrue "obscenity" and "libel" in violation of a student's First Amendment rights.

The court concluded that "the risk taken if a few abuse their First Amendment rights of free speech and press is out-weighed by the far greater risk run by suppressing free speech and press among the young."

Miller v. *California:* New Obscenity Standards[16]

In 1973 the U.S. Supreme Court reformulated the test for obscenity used by Judge Seals. In the *Miller* case Chief Justice Burger wrote that the first criterion for determining whether material is obscene is "whether the average person, applying contemporary community standards would find that the work, taken as a whole, appeals to the prurient interests." The second test is whether the work describes sexual conduct "in a patently offensive way," as defined by state law. The effect of these new tests is to indicate that "contemporary community standards" need not be national standards but could be those of a state or perhaps a smaller unit of government. The third test is whether the work, taken as a whole, "lacks serious literary, artistic, political or scientific value." (Here the Court rejected the old criterion that the work must be "utterly without redeeming social value" to be obscene.[17])

Might the new test allow some local governments to suppress unpopular or controversial ideas that could be potentially useful? Not according to Justice Burger, who reaffirmed an earlier opinion that stated:

> All ideas having even the slightest redeeming social importance—
> unorthodox ideas, controversial ideas, even ideas hateful to the prevailing
> climate of opinion—have full protection of the [First Amendment] guaran-
> tees. . . . But implicit in the history of the First Amendment is the rejection
> of obscenity as utterly without redeeming social importance.[18]

If a judge had applied the new Supreme Court test to the facts of the case involving Kitchen, would he have found that "Space City" was obscene? Probably not. Vulgar or "dirty" words still do not make a publication legally obscene. The work still must be judged "as a whole." And the community standards to be used in judging a work are those of the state (or perhaps a county or city), but not the standards of an individual school community.

The Kitchen Case on Appeal[19]

After Judge Seals ruled in favor of Paul Kitchen, the Houston School District appealed. Because of Kitchen's defiant conduct and flagrant disregard of school regulations, the Fifth Circuit Court of Appeals dismissed his suit. The appeals court did not disagree with the position taken by Judge Seals on most of the legal issues: that the distribution of "Space City" was protected by the First Amendment, that it did not substantially disrupt school activities, and that the language of the newspaper was not constitutionally obscene. The court did not deal with these issues. It merely considered whether Kitchen's conduct in this case "outweighs his claim of First Amendment protection" and gave school officials sufficient grounds for disciplining him.

On behalf of the court Judge Thornberry pointed out that "Paul's conduct can hardly be characterized as the pristine, passive acts of protest 'akin to pure speech' involved in *Tinker*." Rather Kitchen defied Cotton's request that he stop selling the newspapers; he shouted profanity at the principal; he persisted in returning to school during his suspension period; and he "never once attempted to comply with the prior submission rule."

The judge indicated that the results of the case might have been different if Kitchen had challenged the administrative approval rule by "lawful" means. Had he submitted the newspaper to the principal prior to distribution and had it been disapproved, then he could have promptly sought relief in the courts "without having been first suspended from school."

"Considering Paul's flagrant disregard of established school regulations, his open and repeated defiance of the principal's request, and his resort to profane epithet," the court held that school authorities could discipline him even though his actions were not substantially disruptive. Thus the appeals court did not consider whether the application of the school policy in this case was constitutional or not. Instead it simply asked whether there was "substantial evidence" to support Kitchen's suspension, and it ruled that there was.

The court hastened to point out that "by thus limiting our review in this case, we do not invite school boards to promulgate patently unconstitutional regulations" governing the distribution of student publications. "Today," concluded Judge Thornberry, "we merely recognize the right of school authorities to punish students for flagrant disregard of established school regulations; we ask only that the student seeking equitable relief from allegedly unconstitutional action by school officials come into court with clean hands."*

This does not mean that Judge Seals' ruling concerning the obscenity issue was wrong. Rather we believe the lower court's ruling that "Space City" was not legally obscene was correct and would have been upheld by the appeals court had it ruled on this question, even under the new Supreme Court criteria. This case, however, dramatically illustrates the dangers of ignoring and violating school rules and then objecting to them in court. Here the safer and more effective approach for Paul Kitchen might have been to try to follow the prior approval rules and then challenge them legally if their application by the principal appeared to be unconstitutional.

In the following case we see how a court in a situation that was similar to *Kitchen* reached a different result by focusing on the unconstitutionality of the school rules rather than on the manners of the student plaintiff.

The Quarterman Case[20]

In 1971 Charles Quarterman was a tenth grade student in North Carolina's Pine Forest High School. Without permission he distributed an underground paper that included this statement in capital letters:

> . . . WE HAVE TO BE PREPARED TO FIGHT IN THE HALLS AND IN THE CLASS-
> ROOMS, OUT IN THE STREETS BECAUSE THE SCHOOLS BELONG TO THE PEOPLE.
> IF WE HAVE TO—WE'LL BURN THE BUILDINGS OF OUR SCHOOLS DOWN TO SHOW
> THESE PIGS THAT WE WANT AN EDUCATION THAT WON'T BRAINWASH US INTO
> BEING RACISTS. AND THAT WE WANT AN EDUCATION THAT WILL TEACH US TO
> KNOW THE REAL TRUTH ABOUT THINGS WE CAN NEED TO KNOW, SO WE CAN
> BETTER SERVE THE PEOPLE! ! ! !

As a result of distributing the paper, Quarterman was suspended pursuant to a school rule that prohibited pupils from distributing any written material while under school jurisdiction without the permission of the school principal. Since Quarterman believed his suspension violated the First Amendment, he went to court to block the enforcement of the rule.

The appeals court acknowledged that federal courts should not intervene in the resolution of school conflicts "which do not directly and sharply implicate basic constitutional values." But the issue concerning the validity of the rule in this case, "is not a simple matter of school

*The "clean hands" doctrine allows a court to deny relief to a litigant if he did not act fairly, justly, or equitably in the case.

discipline; . . . it deals 'directly' and 'sharply' with a fundamental constitutional right under the First Amendment."

It might be argued that the newspaper distributed by Quarterman included inflammatory language. However, he was not disciplined because of the content of the publication, but because he had violated the school rule prohibiting distribution of printed material without permission. Therefore the appeals court did not consider the disruptive potential of the challenged publication but only the constitutional validity of the regulation under which Quarterman was suspended. Because the regulation included neither procedural safeguards nor guidelines for determining the right to publish or distribute, it was constitutionally defective.[21] Therefore the court ruled that Quarterman was entitled to "declaratory judgment that, as presently framed, the regulation is invalid," and its subsequent enforcement should have been prohibited.

STUDENT CRITICISM OF SCHOOL POLICY AND PERSONNEL

The Scoville Case[22]

In the fall of 1967 the administration of Illinois' Joliet Central High School published a pamphlet entitled "Bits of Steel." The purpose of the pamphlet was to improve communications between parents and the administration. It included information concerning attendance, discipline, school committees, and student problems. Beginning with a message by the principal, it also included pieces by the freshman and senior deans.

Arthur Breen, a student at Central High, was also senior editor of an underground newspaper entitled "Grass High," published by a fellow student, Raymond Scoville. Breen wrote a lengthy critique of the pamphlet, which was published as an editorial in "Grass High." The following excerpts reflect the content, style and intent of Breen's critique:

> . . . The pamphlet started with a message from the principal, David Ross. In this article, Ross states why the pamphlet was put out and the purpose it is supposed to accomplish, namely, the improvement of communications between parents and administration. He has to be kidding. Surely, he realizes that a great majority of these pamphlets are thrown away by the students, and in this case that is how it should have been. I urge all students in the future to either refuse to accept or destroy upon acceptance all propaganda that Central's administration publishes. . . .
>
> Next came an article on attendance. There's not much I can say about this one. It simply told the haggard parents the utterly idiotic and asinine procedure that they must go through to assure that their children will be excused for their absences. . . .
>
> The next gem we came across was from our beloved senior dean. Our senior dean seems to feel that the only duty of a dean or parent is to be the

administrator of some type of punishment. . . . An interesting statement that he makes is "Therefore let us not cheat our children, our precious gifts from God, by neglecting to discipline them!" It is my opinion that a statement such as this is the product of a sick mind. Our senior dean because of his position of authority over a large group of young adults poses a threat to our community. Should a mind whose only thought revolves around an act of discipline be allowed to exert influence over the young minds of our community? I think not. I would urge the Board of Education to request that this dean amend his thinking or resign. The man in the dean's position must be qualified to the extent that his concern is to help the students rather than discipline or punish them. . . .

The last thing of any interest in the pamphlet was about the despicable and disgusting detention policy at Central. I think most students feel the same way as I about this policy. Therefore I will not even go into it.

In the whole pamphlet I could see only one really bright side. We were not subjected to an article written by Mr. Diekelman.

Senior Editor, Grass High

The 14-page edition of "Grass High" that included this editorial also included poetry, essays, and movie reviews. It was distributed to 60 students and faculty at Central High for a price of 15 cents. A week later Scoville and Breen were suspended. They were later expelled from day classes for a semester by the Board of Education because the newspaper "constitutes a disregard of and contempt for the authorities charged with the administration" of Central Campus. Although the students were permitted to attend night school, they believed their rights had been violated, and they sued.

Questions to Consider

1. Should a student newspaper be permitted to "urge all students in the future to either refuse to accept or destroy upon acceptance" information a school gives them for their parents?
2. Should a student editor be allowed to characterize a school official as having "a sick mind" and posing "a threat to our community"?
3. Could either statement justify punishment by school authorities?
4. What arguments would you use before the court of appeals on behalf of the students?
5. To what degree and under what circumstances should students be permitted to criticize school officials and school policy or urge that school policy be disregarded?

THE OPINION OF THE APPEALS COURT

The district court found that the distribution of "Grass High" constituted a "direct and substantial threat to the effective operation of the high school." However, the court of appeals questioned whether the lower court had adequate facts to support its finding. No evidence was taken, for example, to indicate the ages of the students to whom "Grass High" was sold, what impact the newspaper had on those who bought it, or whether some teachers had approved its sale, as alleged by the students.

On behalf of the appeals court Judge Kiley acknowledged that the editorial imputing a "sick mind" to the dean reflected a "disrespectful and tasteless attitude toward authority." But that alone did not justify a "forecast" of substantial disruption or interference with school policies or the rights of others. "The reference undoubtedly offended and displeased the dean," wrote the judge. But as *Tinker* pointed out, mere expression of student feelings with which school officials do not want to contend is not enough to justify expulsion.

Nor did the published criticism of the school's disciplinary policies to 60 students and faculty justify the board's action. In fact, the court noted that "prudent criticism" by high school students may be socially valuable since students possess a unique perspective on matters of school policy.

The court concluded by recognizing the need for effective school discipline but emphasized that school rules must be related "to the state interest in the production of well-trained intellects with constructive critical stances, lest students' imaginations, intellects and wills be unduly stifled or chilled."[23]

RELATED ISSUES

The Jacobs Case: A Broad and Liberal Decision[24]

During the 1971–1972 school year, high school students from Indianapolis published an underground newspaper entitled the "Corn Cob Curtain." It contained cartoons and articles about politics, education, religion, movies, and music. School officials prohibited distribution of the paper because it violated school rules against obscenity, anonymous articles, and selling underground newspapers. This led to a liberal decision by a federal appeals court on several significant questions.

1. *May schools ban the sale of underground newspapers on campus?*
   School rules prohibited the sale of all literature except publications for the benefit of the school. Judge Fairchild acknowledged the legitimate interest of school officials in limiting commercial activities on campus by people not connected with the school. In this case, however, the paper was sold by students, and their purpose was to raise "the $120 to $150 necessary to publish each edition" of their paper. School officials also argued that newspaper sales and other "commercial activities are time-consuming, unnecessary distractions" that are "inherently disruptive" of school activities. The judge rejected this argument. He pointed out that school officials clearly have the authority to regulate the time,

place, and manner of distribution of newspapers "so as to avoid interference with others and littering." The court indicated that this power was adequate to maintain "good order and an educational atmosphere" without forbidding sales and restricting the First Amendment rights of the students.*

2. *Can school rules prohibit the distribution of any material that is not written by a student, teacher or other school employee?* Not according to Judge Fairchild. Such a rule, wrote the court, would prohibit use of materials by individuals of all walks of life "whose views might be thought by the students to be worthy of circulation." The judge indicated that he had "no doubt" that such a rule violated the students' First Amendment rights.

3. *May the school prohibit the distribution of all anonymous publications?* The school contended that such a prohibition is necessary so that those responsible for the publication of libelous or obscene articles can be held accountable. In considering this question, the court noted that historically anonymous publications have been an important vehicle for criticizing oppressive practices and laws and that anonymous student publications can perform a similar function in schools. "Without anonymity," wrote Judge Fairchild, "fear of reprisal may deter peaceful discussion of controversial but important school rules and policies." According to the court, the problem with this prohibition is that it is not limited to potentially libelous or obscene literature but that it applies equally to literature "the content of which is acceptable" and that would cause no substantial interference with school activities.

4. *May rules prohibit distribution of literature by students "while classes are being conducted in school"?* According to the court, the only way this rule could be upheld is if school officials "could reasonably forecast that the distribution of student newspapers anywhere within a school at anytime while any class was being conducted" would be substantially disruptive. Since the evidence did not support the necessity of such a broad prohibition, it was held to be unconstitutional. In short, schools generally cannot prohibit all student distribution "in-school" or "during classes," but it can restrict such distribution where and when it would cause material disruption of school activities.[25]

---

*In a related California case, the state supreme court wrote that "the right to publish a newspaper would be meaningless indeed if it did not include the right to sell it." It concluded: "We fail to see how the *sale* of newspapers on the school premises will necessarily disrupt the work and discipline of the school, whereas their distribution free of charge will not." *Bright* v. *Los Angeles United School District*, 134 Cal. Rptr. 639 (1977).

5. *Can schools prevent or punish the use of "offensive" language?* As previous cases indicated, schools can certainly punish students for distributing material that is legally obscene. But the court observed that the "earthy words" used in the "Corn Cob Curtain" were usually used as "expletives" and were not erotic or sexually explicit. Therefore the papers could not be considered obscene in a legal sense.

What about prohibiting "improper" or "offensive" language? The U.S. Supreme Court has ruled that universities cannot regulate language in an underground paper that it considers "coarse or indecent."[26] Although Judge Fairchild recognized the difference in maturity and sophistication between high school and college students, he concluded that the "occasional presence of earthy words in the Corn Cob Curtain" could not be prevented or punished because it was not likely to disrupt the school's educational activities. Thus this federal appeals court used the *Tinker* test to broadly defend the sale, publication, and distribution of student views in public schools.[27]

The Thomas Case: Restricting "Indecent" Off-Campus Publications[28]

High school students from a small rural New York community produced a vulgar and satirical off-campus publication entitled *Hard Times*. As a result of negative community reaction, the school punished the student publishers. They then took their case to court.

In a comprehensive and challenging 1979 opinion, Judge Irving Kaufman examined the principles governing the student press and the dangers of administrative control. The judge noted that school officials could certainly punish disruptive student expression in school. Here, however, they punished students because board members and other citizens found an off-campus publication objectionable. According to the judge, courts should not endorse such punishment "because the populace would approve." Judge Kaufman explained that school officials must be restrained in moving against student expression since they act "as both a prosecutor and a judge" and since their desire to preserve decorum gives them "a vested interest in suppressing controversy." The court concluded that the First Amendment "forbids public school administrators and teachers from regulating the material to which a child is exposed after he leaves school."

Could officials ban *Hard Times* if students distributed it on campus? In a concurring opinion, Judge Newman said "yes." In contrast to the *Jacobs* decision, Judge Newman felt that schools should be able to prohibit indecent and vulgar writing because schools have a responsibility to try to promote "standards of decency" among students. Since the Supreme Court has not ruled directly on this issue, it is possible that other judges also may feel that public school officials can legally restrict "indecent" writing that is not obscene.

CONTROVERSIAL VIEWS IN SCHOOL-SPONSORED PAPERS

This section includes cases from New York, Alabama, Virginia, and North Carolina. Two concern freedom of press in college-sponsored newspapers. Although the extent of freedom of high school and college students may not be identical, we have included the college cases because they confront important current issues of students' rights and because the principles outlined by the courts will generally apply to the publications of most public high schools.

The Zucker Case: Can a Principal Prohibit Political Ads?[29]

In 1967 a group of New York's New Rochelle High School students wanted to publish the following advertisement in the student newspaper: "The United States government is pursuing a policy in Viet Nam which is both repugnant to moral and international law and dangerous to the future of humanity. We can stop it. We must stop it." The group offered to pay the standard student rate for their advertisement. But the principal prohibited its publication. The students charged that this violated their First Amendment rights.

The principal based his action on an administrative policy that prohibits all advertising "which expresses a point of view on any subject not related to New Rochelle High School." School officials argued that the publication was not a commercial paper but an "educational device." The policy prohibiting paid political advertising was designed to prevent the paper from becoming "an organ for the dissemination of news and views unrelated to the high school." Since the war was not a school-related activity, school officials maintained that it was "not qualified . . . for advertising treatment."

The district court, however, disagreed. Judge Metzner pointed out that the paper carried a number of articles and letters on controversial political issues, including student opinions about the draft and the war, which shows that the war was considered to be a school-related subject. "This being the case," wrote the judge, "there is no logical reason to permit news stories on the subject and preclude student advertising."

The school newspaper was generally open to the free expression of student opinions in its news, editorials, and letters. Therefore the court held that it was "patently unfair" in light of the free speech doctrine to close to students the forum they wanted to use to present their ideas on the Vietnam War.

In conclusion, Judge Metzner observed:

> This lawsuit arises at a time when many in the educational community oppose the tactics of the young in securing a political voice. It would be both incongruous and dangerous for this court to hold that students who wish to express their views on matters intimately related to them, through traditionally accepted nondisruptive modes of communication, may be precluded from doing so by that same adult community.

The Trachtman Case: Preventing Emotional Harm[30]

In 1976 Jeff Trachtman was editor-in-chief of "The Voice," the student newspaper of New York City's Stuyvesant High School. He wanted to distribute a 25-question anonymous survey asking for personal and frank information about students' sexual attitudes, preferences, knowledge and experience, and to publish the results in "The Voice." After the principal, superintendent, and school board rejected his proposal, Trachtman sued.

The school officials argued that they were not trying to prohibit all student writing about sexual matters. Rather they wanted to prevent students from using school facilities "to solicit a response that will invade the rights of other students by subjecting them to psychological pressures" that could cause emotional harm.

To support their position, the school presented evidence from four experts in the field of psychology and psychiatry. One expert indicated that many adolescents are anxious about the whole area of sex and that their attempts to answer the survey could create anxiety and feelings of self-doubt that could result "in serious injury to at least some of the students." Five experts on behalf of Trachtman seriously questioned the possibility that any harm could be caused by high school students answering the questionnaire.[31]

Given this conflict of testimony, a federal appeals court ruled that the school officials did not act unreasonably in prohibiting the distribution of the proposed survey because of the probability that it would result in psychological harm to some students. According to Judge Lumbard, the school's inability "to predict with certainty" that a specific number of students would be injured does not mean they should be powerless to protect students from peer pressures that might result in their emotional disturbance. The court concluded that freedom of expression does not include the right to request anyone to answer questions when there is reason to believe that such requests may cause harm.

In a strong dissenting opinion, Judge Mansfield wrote that the right of a newspaper to conduct a survey on a controversial topic and to publish the results represents the "quintessence of activity protected by the First

Amendment." The judge argued that in this day and age, when New York City students "are literally bombarded with explicit sex materials on public newsstands" on their way to and from school, when they are encouraged to discuss sex topics in school-sponsored "rap sessions," and when large numbers of students are pregnant, school officials "failed completely" to demonstrate that the questionnaire poses any substantial harm to Stuyvesant High School students. Judge Mansfield concluded that by banning the distribution of the "non-disruptive, non-defamatory, and non-obscene material," the majority is supporting a "drastic type of censorship and prior restraint."

The Gambino Case: Controversial Information Protected[32]

Students in Virginia's Hayfield Secondary School wanted to publish an article entitled "Sexually Active Students Fail to Use Contraception." It included results of a survey of student attitudes on birth control and some information on contraceptives. The principal objected to the article being published in the student newspaper because (1) it was funded by the school, (2) students were a "captive audience," and (3) it would conflict with school policy against teaching about birth control in the curriculum.

After reading the controversial article, Judge Bryan indicated his surprise that such an "innocuous" piece could have led to a federal case. He also observed that, given the normal curiosity of youth, the controversy has assured that "copies of the offending article now have been secured" by most of the students the school "sought to protect."

The court ruled that financial support of a student newspaper by the school does not mean that "any manner of state regulation is permissible." On the contrary, he noted that "the state is not necessarily the unrestrained master of what it creates and fosters."

School officials asserted that they were able to regulate the contents of the paper because it was given out in homerooms to a "captive audience" of students compelled to be there. Judge Bryan disagreed. He noted that the Hayfield students were less captive than those in the *Tinker* case because here students had to pick up the paper and read it, whereas in *Tinker* students could not avoid seeing the armbands of the protesting students.

Finally, the judge ruled that the newspaper was not part of the curriculum. Schools could decide not to teach courses in contraception. The newspaper, however, was less like the curriculum and more like the school library that contained extensive and explicit information on birth control. The court concluded that the material "is not suppressible" merely because the school board or its constituents find it objectionable.

A similar New York case dealt with a principal's seizure of a sex information supplement to a high school newspaper. The court ruled that the supplement, which contained serious articles on contraception and abortion, deserved First Amendment protection. Although school officials feared that the supplement could cause various "dangers," the court concluded that "responsible presentation of information about birth control to high school students is not to be dreaded."[33]

The Dickey Case: Can Criticism of Public Officials Be Prohibited?[34]

In 1967 Dr. Frank Rose, the president of the University of Alabama, came under attack by certain legislators for his refusal to censor a controversial student publication. The publication provided background reading for a campus program entitled "A World in Revolution." It included speeches by advocates of violent revolution and black power as well as articles by antirevolutionaries such as the chairman of the Joint Chiefs of Staff.

Gary Dickey, editor of Alabama's Troy State College newspaper, prepared a thoughtful editorial criticizing the legislators for their "harassment" of Dr. Rose. But the faculty adviser and college president ordered Dickey not to publish the editorial. Their objection was based on a college rule prohibiting editorials in the school paper that were critical of the governor or the legislature. The reason for the rule was that a state institution should not criticize those who fund it.

The faculty adviser furnished substitute material concerning "Raising Dogs in North Carolina" to be published in lieu of Dickey's proposed editorial. Dickey, however, arranged to have the space that was to be occupied by the editorial left blank (except for the title, "A Lament for Dr. Rose") and the word *censored* printed diagonally across the blank space. Dickey was expelled for his action, which was termed "willful and deliberate insubordination."

In reviewing this case a federal judge observed that the rule against criticizing the governor and legislature apparently would have been invoked no matter how reasonable the criticism had been. Under these circumstances "the conclusion is compelled that the invocation of such a rule against Gary Dickey that resulted in his expulsion . . . was unreasonable."

"A state," wrote Judge Johnson, "cannot force a college student to forfeit his constitutionally protected right of freedom of expression as a condition to his attending a state-supported school." And the school cannot punish Dickey for exercising his right "by cloaking his expulsion . . . in the robe of 'insubordination.' " This attempt to characterize his conduct as insubordination "does not disguise the basic fact that Dickey was expelled from Troy State College for exercising his constitutionally guaranteed right of academic and/or political expression."

There may have been no legal obligation on the part of the college to operate a school newspaper or to permit Dickey to continue as editor, but since Troy State did authorize Dickey to be editor, its officials could not expel him for his conduct in this case without violating the First Amendment of the Constitution. Hence, the court ordered that "defendant [Alabama State Board of Education] immediately reinstate Gary Clinton Dickey as a student in Troy State College."

The Joyner Case: Is Restricting a Segregationist Paper Unconstitutional?[35]

In a 1973 case the president of predominantly black North Carolina Central University withdrew financial support from the official student newspaper because of its announced segregationist editorial policy. The first issue of the newspaper under this new policy opposed the admission of more white students. It stated:

> There is a rapidly growing white population on our campus. . . . We want to know why they are here? How many are here? Why more and more come every year (by the hundreds)? . . .
> Black students on this campus have never made it clear to those people that we are indeed separate from them, in so many ways, and wish to remain so.

The article concluded with the words of H. Rap Brown:

> "I do what I must out of the love for my people. My will is to fight. Resistance is not enough. Aggression is the order of the day." And moreover, we will take nothing from the oppressor, but only in turn get that which is ours.
> Now will you tell me, whose institution is NCCU? Theirs? Or ours?

The president wrote the student editor to inform him that the paper "does not meet standard journalistic criteria nor does it represent fairly the full spectrum of views on this campus." Therefore the president indicated he would withhold funds for future issues until agreement could be reached regarding publication standards. When no agreement was reached, the president "irrevocably terminated the paper's financial support." The editor believed this action abridged freedom of the press and sued to regain school support.

A federal appeals court acknowledged that a college need not establish a newspaper or may permanently discontinue publication for reasons unrelated to the First Amendment. But Judge Butzner noted that if a college has a student newspaper, "its publication cannot be suppressed because college officials dislike its editorial comment." According to the judge this principle has been extensively applied to strike down every form of censorship of student publications at state-supported institutions. In an extensively documented sentence (which summarized the holdings of more than 15 related cases), the court wrote:

> Censorship of constitutionally protected expression cannot be imposed by suspending the editors, suppressing circulation, requiring imprimatur of controversial articles, excising repugnant material, withdrawing financial support, or asserting any other form of censorial oversight based on the institution's power of the purse.*

Since the student publication caused no disruption, did not reject opposing viewpoints, and did not incite anyone to harass or interfere with white students or faculty, the administration was not justified in its restriction of free expression. Although the president found the paper's editorial comment to be abhorrent, contrary to university policy, and inconsistent with constitutional guarantees of equality, the court held that the president "failed to carry the heavy burden of showing justification for the imposition of a prior restraint on expression."[36]

Summary and Conclusions

Before *Tinker*, administrators generally had "broad discretion" to censor school newspapers and punish students for distributing publications that "damaged school discipline." This is no longer the law. Today expression by public school students cannot be prohibited unless it substantially and materially interferes with school activities or with the rights of others. In addition, expression by students cannot be restricted solely because teachers, administrators, parents, or other students disagree with what is being said or because the subjects discussed are unpopular or controversial. When students question the constitutionality of a restriction concerning the distribution of materials, school officials have the burden of justifying the restriction.

This does not mean that the First Amendment rights of students are always the same as adults. Because there must be order as well as free expression in the schools, authorities can impose reasonable restraints on the distribution of student material. In addition some courts hold that administrators can regulate distribution near school when this might result in substantial disruption on campus.

Distribution also can be restricted if school officials can demonstrate

---

*In a recent, related case concerning a high school sponsored newspaper, a federal court ruled that neither the principal nor the advisor could cut off funds or otherwise terminate or censor the paper because it criticized school policy and practice and published controversial political articles. *Reineke* v. *Cobb County School District*, 484 F.Supp. 1252 (N.D. Ga. 1980).

"reasonable cause to believe" that the expression would cause substantial disruption. But neither the discussion of controversial topics nor aversion to criticism is a constitutional justification for prohibiting student expression. And even a "reasonable forecast of disruption" would not always justify such a prohibition unless administrators first tried to control the potential disrupters.

PRIOR REVIEW

Courts differ on the question of whether school officials can constitutionally require students to submit publications to them for review prior to distribution. Most courts hold that school rules can require prior review of student expression. But such rules would be unconstitutional if they were overbroad and vague, had no clear, objective, and precise standard to guide their application, or lacked due process safeguards. Due process requires that any regulations for administrative screening of publications before distribution must state (1) a brief period of time for administrative review, (2) a reasonable method for appeal, and (3) the time within which the appeal must be decided.

In contrast, a few judges have held that prior restraint of student publications is unconstitutional, that schools cannot require administrative approval before distribution. Even these courts, however, usually recognize that schools can *regulate* the distribution of publications and can *punish* students who distribute materials that are libelous, obscene, or cause substantial disruption.

THE LIMITS OF FREEDOM

• Obscenity. Although the distribution of obscene materials is not protected, a publication is not legally obscene merely because it contains blunt, vulgar, or "dirty" words. Applying the new Supreme Court test, material for students would be considered obscene if the work (1) "appeals to the prurient interest" of minors, (2) describes sexual conduct "in a patently offensive way," *and* (3) "lacks serious literary, artistic, political, or scientific value." In applying these tests, the material must be judged "as a whole" and the "community standards" are not simply the standards of an individual school community. In addition school officials may not be able to object to certain vulgar language in student publications if the same vulgarisms are found in books and articles in the school library.

• Defying School Rules. When a student is disciplined for distributing materials in a manner that is "defiant" or "grossly disrespectful," then some courts may uphold his punishment without considering his claim that the rules restricting distribution were unconstitutional. Thus in the

Kitchen case an appeals court concluded that a student's "flagrant disregard" of school regulations precluded his seeking relief. On the other hand, when a student "lawfully" challenged an unconstitutional restriction concerning distribution of underground newspapers in *Quarterman,* the regulation was declared void even though the content of the publication was potentially disruptive.

School officials have a right to devise rules governing the time and place of distribution. They could, for example, prohibit distribution in classrooms and in narrow school corridors. But officials could not prohibit all distribution on school property, in school or during school hours. In addition, a federal appeals court ruled that school policy cannot totally prohibit (1) "sales" of student publications, (2) the distribution of anonymous material, or (3) students from publishing nonstudent materials.

• School-sponsored Publications. School officials naturally have some control over a publication they sponsor. They can, for example, probably determine its goals and focus, the criteria for selecting editorial staff, the level of financial support, or whether it should accept advertising. Although the limits of administrative control over public school publications are not precise, officials clearly do not have total control over their contents. Thus *Zucker* held that students could not be prohibited from placing an antiwar advertisement in a school-sponsored newspaper that had been used as a forum for the expression of diverse student views. *Dickey* ruled that a student editor could not be prohibited from publishing responsible criticism about public officials. And *Joyner* indicated that a state college could not terminate funding for a student newspaper merely because of its editorial policy. Although *Dickey* and *Joyner* concerned state-supported colleges, the holdings in these cases would probably apply to public secondary schools and prohibit principals from suppressing or censoring a student paper simply because they disliked its editorial content.

On the other hand, a federal court held that the First Amendment does not include the right of student editors to seek information from other students where there is some evidence that the survey could cause emotional harm. Generally, however, courts have ruled that responsible presentation of controversial information in a school-sponsored paper (e.g., about birth control) cannot be prohibited because the topic is excluded from the curriculum or because administrators or parents find it objectionable.

NOTES

1. 462 F.2d 960, 978 (5th Cir. 1972).
2. *Miller* v. *California,* 413 U.S. 15 (1973).

3. *State ex rel Dresser* v. *District Board of School District No. 1*, 116 N.W. 232 (Wisc. 1908).
4. *Shanley* v. *Northeast Independent School District*, 462 F.2d 960 (5th Cir. 1972).
5. *Terminiello* v. *Chicago*, 337 U.S. 1 (1948).
6. Justice Goldberg noted that the content of the underground publication in this case "could easily surface, flower-like, from its underground abode. As so-called 'underground' newspapers go, this is probably one of the most vanilla-flavored ever to reach a federal court." *Shanley* at 964.
7. To illustrate further the problems with the wording of the policy in question, Judge Goldberg wrote:

> If the school board here can punish students on the strength of this blunderbuss regulation for passing out any printed matter, off school grounds, outside school hours and without any disruption whatsoever, then why cannot the school board also punish any student who hands a Bible to another student on a Saturday or Sunday morning, as long as it does so in good faith? We resist the temptation to answer [Id. at 977].

8. *Fujishima* v. *Board of Education*, 460 F.2d 1355 (7th Cir. 1972).
9. Judge Sprecher listed several cases that seemed to support his position. He also acknowledged that some cases, like *Shanley*, allowed schools to require prior submission of publications if accompanied by reasonable procedural safeguards. The court, however, believed that cases such as *Shanley* erred in interpreting *Tinker* to allow prior review "as a tool of school officials in 'forecasting' substantial disruption" of school activities. The judge wrote:

> *Tinker* in no way suggests that students may be required to announce their intentions of engaging in certain conduct beforehand so school authorities may decide whether to prohibit the conduct. Such a concept of prior restraint is even more offensive when applied to the long-protected area of publication [Id. at 1358].

10. *Baughman* v. *Freienmuth*, 478 F.2d 1345 (4th Cir. 1973).
11. *Williams* v. *Spencer*, 622 F.2d 1200 (4th Cir. 1980).
12. *Sullivan* v. *Houston Independent School District*, 333 F.Supp. 1149 (S.D. Tex. 1971). The name of this case is taken from a 1969 decision involving another Houston student, Dan Sullivan, who was suspended because he distributed an underground newspaper that criticized school officials. As a result of a class action brought by Sullivan, a federal district court issued a permanent injunction prohibiting the Houston School District from unreasonably restricting the distribution of student papers. *Sullivan* v. *Houston Independent School District*, 307 F.Supp. 1328 (S.D. Tex. 1969). The case described here has the same legal title because Paul Kitchen, the student who initiated this case, asked the same federal court to hold the Houston School District in contempt for violating the 1969 permanent injunction the court had issued after the first *Sullivan* case.
13. *United States* v. *Head*, 317 F.Supp. 1138, 1143 (E.D. La. 1970).
14. As one 15-year-old female student testified about the use of words like "fuck": "To young people, it's more or less accepted. I mean, it's an everyday

happening. And ordinary people, they just aren't used to it, and they were raised up to believe that it was wrong." *Sullivan* at 1165.

15. Id. at 1167. In addition Judge Seals quoted with approval a 1965 statement printed in *Christianity and Crisis,* which observed:

> For Christians the truly obscene ought not to be the slick-paper nudity, nor the vulgarities of dirty old or young literati. . . . What is obscene is that material, whether sexual or not, that has as its basic motivation and purpose the degradation, debasement and dehumanization of persons. The dirtiest word in the English language is not "fuck" or "shit" in the mouth of a tragic shaman but the word "Nigger" from the sneering lips of a Bull Connor [Ibid.].

16. *Miller* v. *California,* 413 U.S. 15 (1973).
17. The problem with the old test, according to Justice Burger, is that it required the prosecution "to prove a negative, i.e., that the material was *utterly* without redeeming social value—a burden virtually impossible to discharge under our criminal standards of proof."
18. *Roth* v. *United States,* 354 U.S. 476 (1957).
19. *Sullivan* v. *Houston Independent School District,* 475 F.2d 1071 (5th Cir. 1973). This is the same appeals court that decided the *Shanley* case examined earlier in the chapter.
20. *Quarterman* v. *Byrd,* 453 F.2d 54 (4th Cir. 1971).
21. This was similar to the *Shanley* case discussed above. *Quarterman* also pointed out that the application of the First Amendment "may properly take into consideration the age or maturity of those to whom it is addressed." Thus some publications may be protected when directed to adults but not when made available to minors. Similarly, a difference may exist between publications distributed in a secondary school and those distributed in a college. Therefore a high school student's right to freedom of expression may be curtailed by regulations "reasonably designed to adjust these rights to the needs of the school environment."
22. *Scoville* v. *Board of Education of Joliet Township,* 425 F.2d 10 (7th Cir. 1970).
23. In a dissenting opinion Judge Castle wrote that the "admitted action" by Breen and Scoville in calling upon their fellow students "to flaunt the school's administrative procedures by destroying, rather than delivering to their parents," materials given to the students for that purpose justified the school's disciplinary action. Judge Castle did not believe more evidence was necessary to support the district court's decision. "In my view," he wrote, "the students' advocacy of disregard of the school's procedures carried with it an inherent threat to the effective operation of a method the school authorities had a right to utilize for the purpose of communicating with the parents of students."
24. *Jacobs* v. *Board of School Commissioners,* 490 F.2d 601 (7th Cir. 1973); 420 U.S. 128 (1975).
25. Similarly, another appeals court struck down a rule limiting orderly student distribution of leaflets and other nonschool literature to areas "outside" the school. *Riseman* v. *School Committee of Quincy,* 439 F.2d 148 (1st Cir. 1971).
26. *Papish* v. *University of Missouri Curators,* 410 U.S. 667 (1973).

27. A related case raised the question of whether a university could restrict the publication of a story in a college-sponsored literary magazine because the language was so "tasteless and inappropriate" that it would injure the reputation of the university. The court held that the story, which contained much "street language," could not be stifled merely because it might draw an adverse reaction from the majority of politicians or ordinary citizens. To suppress language for this reason "would be to virtually read the First Amendment out of the Constitution." *Bazaar* v. *Fortune*, 476 F.2d 570 (5th Cir. 1973).

28. *Thomas* v. *Board of Education, Granville Central School District,* 607 F.2d 1043 (2nd Cir. 1979). For a thoughtful discussion of the regulation of indecent language, see M. Chester Nolte, "New Pig in the Parlor: Official Constraints on Indecent Words," *Nolpe School Law Journal, 9,* No. 1 (1980), 1–22.

29. *Zucker* v. *Panitz,* 299 F.Supp. 102 (S.D. N.Y. 1969).

30. *Trachtman* v. *Anker,* 563 F.2d 512 (2nd Cir. 1977).

31. One psychologist testified that in more than 25 years of experience he had "*never* encountered a situation in which a child, adolescent or adult had been adversely affected by a questionnaire!" He argued that this was especially true of students in Manhattan, who were constantly bombarded with sexually explicit material and with the harsh realities of city life.

32. *Gambino* v. *Fairfax County School Board,* 429 F.Supp. 731 (E.D. Va. 1977), 564 F.2d 157 (4th Cir. 1977).

33. *Bayer* v. *Kinzler,* 383 F.Supp. 1164 (E.D. N.Y. 1974).

34. *Dickey* v. *Alabama State Board of Education,* 273 F.Supp. 613 (M.D. Ala. 1967).

35. *Joyner* v. *Whiting,* 477 F.2d 456 (4th Cir. 1973).

36. The case also involved the editor's policy that no whites would serve on the staff and no advertising would be accepted from white merchants. Concerning these issues, the court upheld the president's right to prohibit racial discrimination in staffing the newspaper and accepting advertising. But the court did not agree that the appropriate remedy for the paper's discrimination was the permanent cessation of financial support. "To comply with the First Amendment," wrote Judge Butzner, "the administration's remedy must be narrowly drawn to rectify only the discrimination in staffing and advertising." Id. at 462–464.

4
Teacher Freedom of Speech Outside the Classroom

Congress shall make no law . . . abridging the freedom of speech or of press, or the right of the people peaceably to assemble and petition the Government for a redress of grievances.
> —The First Amendment of the Constitution

The Fourteenth Amendment provides that "no State shall . . . deprive any person of . . . liberty . . . without due process of law." It has been held that the freedoms of speech and of the press are among the Fourteenth Amendment "liberties."[1]
> —Charles Black, Jr.

The First Amendment was designed to protect the freedom of speech of citizens in a democratic society. It protects the freedom of an individual to speak and write critically about governmental policies and public officials. Whether the criticism is balanced or biased, careful or sloppy, constructive or destructive, usually it should not jeopardize a citizen's job.

Is a teacher equally free to criticize public officials and government policy? Or does a person give up certain First Amendment rights when he accepts employment in the public schools?

If an employee of a private business were discharged for publicly "blasting" his boss, he would have no constitutional right to reemployment. Should a public school teacher have more freedom than his counterpart in industry?

Does public criticism of educational matters by a teacher carry more weight than similar statements by the average citizen? If so, does a teacher have a greater responsibility to check the accuracy of his public comments? And if he fails to exercise this responsibility, does a school board have the right to dismiss him?

These are some of the questions posed by the cases in this chapter.

We begin by examining the landmark case of *Pickering* v. *Board of Education*. The *Pickering* case not only confronts a wide range of free-speech issues for teachers, but also illustrates one route for legally resolving constitutional conflicts: the local court, the state appeals courts, and finally the U.S. Supreme Court.

THE SCOPE OF FREE SPEECH

The Pickering Case: A Critical Letter to the Editor[2]

Marvin Pickering was a high school teacher in Will County, Illinois. He was critical of the way the superintendent and the Board of Education had tried to raise money for new schools and of their expenditures for athletic purposes. He did not want his opinions to be restricted to the teachers' lounge, so he sent the following controversial letter to the local newspaper:

DEAR EDITOR:

. . . Since there seems to be a problem getting all the facts to the voter on the twice defeated bond issue, many letters have been written to this paper and probably more will follow, I feel I must say something about the letters and their writers. Many of these letters did not give the whole story. Letters by your Board and Administration have stated that teachers' salaries total $1,297,746 for one year. Now that must have been the total payroll, otherwise the teachers would be getting $10,000 a year. I teach at the high school and I know this just isn't the case. However, this shows their "stop at nothing" attitude. To illustrate further, do you know that the superintendent told the teachers, and I quote, "Any teacher that opposes the referendum should be prepared for the consequences." I think this gets at the reason we have problems passing bond issues. Threats take something away; these are insults to voters in a free society. We should try to sell a program on its merits, if it has any.

Remember those letters entitled "District 205 Teachers Speak," I think the voters should know that those letters have been written and agreed to by only five or six teachers, not 98% of the teachers in the high school. In fact, many teachers didn't even know who was writing them. Did you know that those letters had to have the approval of the superintendent before they could be put in the paper? That's the kind of totalitarianism teachers live in at the high school, and your children go to school in.

In last week's paper, the letter written by a few uninformed teachers threatened to close the school cafeteria and fire its personnel. This is ridiculous and insults the intelligence of the voter because properly managed school cafeterias do not cost the school district any money. If the cafeteria is losing money, then the board should not be packing free lunches for athletes on days of athletic contests. The taxpayer's child should only have to pay about 30¢ for his lunch instead of 35¢ to pay for free lunches for the athletes.

In a reply to this letter your Board of Administration will probably state that these lunches are paid for from receipts from the games. But $20,000 in receipts doesn't pay for the $200,000 a year they have been spending on varsity sports while neglecting the wants of teachers.

You see we don't need an increase in the transportation tax unless the voters want to keep paying $50,000 or more a year to transport athletes home after practice and to away games, etc. The rest of the $200,000 is made up in coaches' salaries, athletic directors' salaries, baseball pitching machines, sodded football fields, and thousands of dollars for other sports equipment.

These things are all right, provided we have enough money for them. To sod football fields on borrowed money and then not be able to pay teachers' salaries is getting the cart before the horse.

If these things aren't enough for you, look at East High. No doors on many of the classrooms, a plant room without any sunlight, no water in a first aid treatment room, are just a few of many things. The taxpayers were really taken to the cleaners. . . .

As I see it, the bond issue is a fight between the Board of Education that is trying to push tax-supported athletics down our throats with education, and a public that has mixed emotions about both of these items because they feel they are already paying enough taxes, and simply don't know whom to trust with any more tax money.

I must sign this letter as a citizen, taxpayer and voter, not as a teacher, since that freedom has been taken from the teachers by the administration. Do you really know what goes on behind those stone walls at the high school?

Respectfully,
Marvin L. Pickering[3]

Questions to Consider

1. Did Pickering have the right to publish letters criticizing his superintendent and school board? If so, should he have gone through channels before making his criticism public?
2. Did Pickering have a duty of loyalty to his superiors? Should he have been careful not to damage their professional reputations?
3. If Pickering's public criticism was correct, should this protect him? If some of his criticism was incorrect, does this justify the school board in dismissing him?
4. Are there sometimes reasons for limiting a teacher's right of free speech? Or should a teacher have the same rights as any other citizen?

SCHOOL BOARD ACTION

Angered by the publication of the letter, the Board of Education prepared formal charges against Pickering. The charges stated that his letter to the newspapers contained

> many untrue and false statements and comments which directly and by innuendo and without justification, questioned and impugned the motives, honesty, integrity, truthfulness, responsibility and competence of this Board of Education and the School Administrators of this District in carrying out their official duties . . . seriously involved and damaged the professional reputations of said Administrators and Board and are and will be highly disruptive to the discipline of the teachers and morale and harmony among teachers, administrators, Board of Education and residents of the District.[4]

After a full hearing on these charges, the board dismissed Pickering because it determined that publication of his letter was "detrimental to the efficient operation and administration of the schools of the district." But Pickering contended that the letter was protected by his constitutional right of freedom of speech, and he took his case to court.

THE ILLINOIS COURTS

The local court affirmed the decision of the school board. Pickering then appealed to the Illinois Supreme Court, which found that a number of the statements and charges made by Pickering in his letter were untrue and misleading. The court also pointed out that Pickering "never made a formal or informal protest or report to any of his superiors about the subject matter of his accusations and charges."

The court acknowledged that citizens generally have the right to openly criticize public officials. Moreover, such officials can take no action against members of the public for making false statements if the critics believed their statements were true. But in this case the court said Pickering could not be considered "a mere member of the public." On the contrary, "he holds a position as teacher and is no more entitled to harm the schools by speech than by incompetency, cruelty, negligence, immorality, or any other conduct for which there may be no legal sanction."

The question, said the court, is not whether the public has the right to criticize school officials but whether the school board must continue to employ a teacher who publishes misleading statements which might be detrimental to the schools. The court answered this question negatively. It reasoned that Pickering's acceptance of a teaching position obliged him to refrain from making statements about the operation of the schools that he would have had the right to make had he not been a teacher.

Thus the Illinois court concluded that "a teacher who displays disrespect toward the Board of Education, incites misunderstanding and distrust of its policies, and makes unsupported accusation against the officials is not promoting the interests of his school . . ." Therefore, the court refused to set aside the school board's decision to dismiss Pickering.

THE SUPREME COURT

Despite the ruling of the Illinois court, Pickering still believed his letter was protected by the First Amendment. He therefore appealed to the U.S. Supreme Court.

In its argument before the Supreme Court, the school board contended that a teacher, "by virtue of his public employment has a duty of loyalty to support his superiors" in attaining the goals of education, and that if he must speak out publicly he should do so accurately. Pickering, on the other hand, argued that since teachers have the same rights as other citizens, public officials should be able to take action against a teacher's false statements only if they are defamatory, that is, if the teacher knew they were false or made them with reckless disregard for their accuracy.

In view of these conflicting claims, Justice Marshall wrote on behalf of the Court that the problem was "to arrive at a balance between the interests of the teacher, as citizen, in commenting upon matters of public concern and the interests of the State, as an employer, in promoting the efficiency of the public services it performs through its employees." The Court then examined the two major questions presented by this case.

First, it considered whether Pickering could be dismissed for making critical comments in public. Can public criticism, even if it is true, disrupt discipline and loyalty, and therefore form a basis for dismissal?

The Court found that the statements in Pickering's letter consisted mainly of criticism of the school board's allocation of funds and of both the board's and the superintendent's methods of informing (or not informing) the taxpayers of the real reasons why additional funds were sought for the schools. First, the Court "unequivocally" rejected the board's position that such critical public comments by a teacher on matters of public concern that are substantially correct may furnish grounds for dismissal.

Second, the Court considered whether Pickering could be dismissed if the board found that some of his statements were incorrect. These centered on Pickering's exaggerated claims regarding the costs of the athletic program and the suggestion that teachers had not been paid on occasion. The only completely false statement was his claim that $50,000 a year had been spent to transport athletes; the correct figure was about $10,000. Concerning these statements, the Court wrote:

> The Board's original charges included allegations that the publication of the letter damaged the professional reputations of the Board and the superinten-dent and would foment controversy and conflict among the Board, teachers, administrators and the residents of the district. However, no evidence to

support these allegations was introduced at the hearing. So far as the record reveals, Pickering's letter was greeted by everyone but its main target, the Board, with massive apathy and total disbelief.[5]

The board must therefore have decided that Pickering's statements were harmful to the operation of the schools by equating the board members' own interests with those of the schools. However, the accusation that administrators are spending too much money on athletes cannot be regarded as "detrimental to the district's schools." Such an accusation, wrote Justice Marshall,

> reflects rather a difference of opinion between Pickering and the Board as to the preferable manner of operating the school system, a difference of opinion that clearly concerns an issue of general public interest. In addition, the fact that particular illustrations of the Board's claimed undesirable emphasis on athletic programs are false would not normally have any necessary impact on the operation of the schools, beyond its tendency to anger the Board.[6]

More important, the question of whether a school system requires additional funds is a matter of legitimate public concern in which the judgment of the school administration cannot be taken as conclusive. On such a question, wrote the Court,

> Free and open debate is vital to informed decision-making by the electorate. Teachers are, as a class, the members of a community most likely to have informed and definite opinions as to how funds allocated to the operation of the schools should be spent. Accordingly, it is essential that they be able to speak out freely on such questions without fear of retaliatory dismissal. . . .[7]

In this case Pickering made erroneous public statements on current issues. The statements were critical of his employer but were not shown to have impeded his teaching or to have interfered with the operations of the schools. Therefore, the Court concluded,

> In a case such as this, absent proof of false statements knowingly or recklessly made by him, a teacher's exercise of his right to speak on issues of public importance may not furnish the basis for his dismissal from public employment.[8]

Does the Pickering *case mean that a school board could never restrict a teacher's right to publicize his views?* No. As Justice Marshall wrote,

> It is possible to conceive of some positions in public employment in which the need for confidentiality is so great that even completely correct public statements might furnish a permissible ground for dismissal. Likewise, positions in public employment in which the relationship between superior and subordinate is of such a personal and intimate nature that certain forms of public criticism of the superior by the subordinate would seriously undermine the effectiveness of the working relationship between them can also be imagined.[9]

Although Justice Marshall did not indicate how the Court would rule in these situations, he did note that such cases would pose significantly different considerations from those of the *Pickering* case.

What if a teacher published a letter that had no factual basis? In such a case questions might be raised about his fitness to teach, and the letter could be used as evidence of the teacher's general incompetence. But he could not be dismissed simply for writing the letter. Other evidence of the incompetence would have to be examined.

Would the First Amendment protect a teacher who published statements that he knew were false about an issue of public importance? Probably not. As Justice White pointed out in a separate opinion on the *Pickering* case, "Deliberate or reckless falsehoods serve no First Amendment ends and deserve no protection under that Amendment."[10] And as the Supreme Court stated in a previous case, "The knowingly false statement and the false statement made with reckless disregard of the truth, do not enjoy constitutional protection." [11]

HOW FAR DOES THE PICKERING CASE EXTEND?

Pickering was the first major decision by the U.S. Supreme Court protecting the right of teachers to speak out on public issues. Since a decision by the Supreme Court is binding on all other state and federal courts, *Pickering* has been cited in almost all subsequent cases involving teachers who have been disciplined because of their controversial statements. The following cases should help clarify both the scope and limits of a teacher's First Amendment rights outside the classroom. They also illustrate how various state and federal judges have applied the principle of the *Pickering* decision to resolve related educational controversies.

The Lusk Case: Criticism of Coworkers[12]

In 1973 a federal district court extended the *Pickering* ruling to protect a Texas high school teacher who was fired after his critical statements received wide media coverage, injured his relationship with his principal and led to hostile parent reactions.

Because he feared that school conditions in Dallas might "give rise to massive disorders," Haywood Lusk warned his superintendent (verbally and in writing) about the frequent assaults and robberies on school grounds. He also wrote that the principal and the staff of his school were "mentally and sociologically unqualified to deal with modern, complex, multiracial student bodies." Lusk repeated his criticisms before the Dallas School Board and City Council and added that "in order to survive," students in his school "learn to disobey authority, run, lie, cheat, and steal."

In rejecting Lusk's dismissal for "public breach of ethics," the court wrote that Lusk's criticisms concerned "matters of vital interest to every citizen of Dallas," particularly those who had children in the public schools, and that they were properly brought to the attention "of governing bodies who had the power to act" on them. In this case, Judge Hill concluded that "society's interest in information concerning the operation of its schools far outweighs any strain on the teacher-principal relationship." Furthermore, wrote the court, Lusk's conduct should be judged "in terms of its propriety and not by the impression that may have been created in the minds of the public by the news media." According to Judge Hill, only if the exercise of a teacher's First Amendment rights "materially and substantially impedes the teacher's proper performance of his daily duties in the classroom or disrupts the regular operation of the school will a restriction of his rights be tolerated."

The Givhan Case: Is Private Criticism Protected?[13]

Bessie Givhan was a junior high school English teacher who was dismissed after a series of private encounters with her principal. The principal alleged that Givhan made "petty and unreasonable demands" in an "insulting," "loud," and "hostile" manner. The trial court found that her demands "were neither petty nor unreasonable" because they involved employment practices that she "conceived to be racially discriminatory." Despite this finding, the court of appeals ruled in favor of the school on the grounds that the "privately expressed . . . complaints and opinions to the principal" were not protected under the First Amendment. But in a 1979 decision, the U.S. Supreme Court disagreed and extended the *Pickering* case to apply to private criticism.

The court rejected the notion that the First Amendment does not protect criticism of a principal by a teacher because of their close working relationship. On behalf of the Court, Justice Rehnquist indicated that the First Amendment requires the same sort of balancing test for private expression by a public employee as it does for public expression. This means that the interests of the teacher as a citizen in commenting on matters of public concern "must be balanced against the interests of the State, as an employer, in promoting the efficiency" of the public schools. The Court emphasized that a teacher's freedom of speech is not lost when he "arranges to communicate privately with his employer rather than to spread his views before the public." On the other hand, a teacher's criticism—either public or private—may not be protected when it specifically impedes "the proper performance of his classroom duties" or generally interferes with the regular operation of the schools. In the case of personal confrontations between an educator and his immediate superior, Justice Rehnquist noted that judges may also consider the "manner, time, and place" of the confrontations when balancing the rights in conflict.

If a court finds that constitutionally protected criticism was one of the reasons for a teacher's dismissal, would this guarantee that the teacher would be reinstated? No. Cases concerning controversial expression involve a two-step judicial analysis. First, the teacher must prove that her conduct was constitutionally protected and that it was a "substantial or motivating" factor for dismissal. Then, according to the *Givhan* case, the burden of proof shifts, and the school board is given an opportunity to show "by a preponderance of the evidence that it would have reached the same decision . . . in the absence of such protected conduct." If the board can prove that it would have dismissed the teacher even in the absence of the constitutionally protected statement or writing, the dismissal would be upheld. If not, the teacher would be reinstated and perhaps be entitled to monetary damages.

The Johnson Case: A Right to Complain[14]

Donna Johnson was a "floating" teacher at a Roanoke, Virginia, junior high school for two years. When she learned that she would not be given a permanent classroom for her third year, she complained to the principal. At their first conference, he said there was nothing he could do to change the assignment; and at a second conference, he said that "he didn't want to hear any more about it." Despite this warning, Johnson wrote a letter of complaint to the superintendent and then filed a grievance about her "floating position." Later in the year, the principal recommended and the school board voted not to renew Johnson's contract because she "had been insubordinate and had displayed a poor attitude." Johnson, however, alleged that her contract was not renewed in retaliation for complaining and for filing a grievance.

A federal district court found that Ms. Johnson's complaints were protected by the First Amendment. According to Judge Williams, ". . . the right of a teacher to voice concerns about conditions which interfere with the education of her students falls squarely within the protections afforded by the Constitution." Thus neither her complaints about her assignment nor her grievance to secure a permanent room was permissible basis for terminating her employment.

In sum, the court concluded that Johnson met the Supreme Court test for reinstatement outlined by Justice Rehnquist in the *Givhan* case: (1) She established that the complaints about her room assignment were constitutionally protected and were a "substantial or motivating factor" in the decision not to rehire her. (2) The school board could not show by "a preponderance of the evidence" that it would have reached the same decision in the absence of her complaints. Therefore, the court ordered the school board to reinstate Johnson.

The Aumiller Case: Defending Homosexual Behavior[15]

Richard Aumiller was a lecturer at the University of Delaware, a faculty advisor to the campus Gay Community organization, and a homosexual. During the 1975–1976 school year, three local newspapers printed interviews with him. In the interviews he pointed out that gays had nothing to hide and were seeking acceptance on campus; he also tried to counter several misconceptions about homosexuals; and he argued that gays should admit their homosexuality to themselves and to others. As a result, Aumiller's contract was not renewed because the university president believed the interviews were "evangelistic promotions of homosexuality and would harm and embarrass the university by implying official approval of homosexual conduct. However, a federal district court ruled that dismissing Aumiller because of the interviews violated his First Amendment rights.

Judge Murry Schwartz rejected the notion that Aumiller implied he was speaking on behalf of the university simply because he identified himself as a member of the faculty and as an adviser to the Gay Community. Moreover, he was not trying to convert students to homosexuality; rather his statements were directed toward educating readers to accepting homosexuals as equals and to demythologize homosexual stereotypes.

With reference to the *Pickering* decision, the judge noted that in this case there was no evidence that Aumiller's interviews interfered with his teaching duties, that they disrupted university activities, or breached any close or confidential relationships. The court emphasized that the unpopularity of Aumiller's views "cannot justify the limitation of Aumiller's First Amendment rights" because the fundamental purpose of the amendment is to protect "the free expression of controversial and unpopular ideas" from interference by the government.

Since Aumiller's contract was not renewed because of his public statements, he was reinstated and awarded back pay of $12,454 and compensatory damages of $10.000 "for the mental distress, humiliation and embarrassment" caused by the violation of his rights. In addition, the court ordered the university president to pay $5000 in punitive damages because he maliciously and knowingly disregarded Aumiller's constitutional rights.

Related Issues

Can a teacher be transferred for speaking critically about a school program? *Pickering* protected a teacher from being fired, but what about a teacher who is simply transferred to another school with no loss of pay or status? In Arizona, a Mexican-American guidance counselor, Socorro Bernasconi, publicly opposed the way Mexican-American children were placed in classes for the mentally retarded because they were tested in

English rather than in Spanish. After she suggested that parents could sue to stop this practice, she was transferred to a school with well-to-do children, but very few Mexican-American children. Since Bernasconi had special training in bilingual testing, she felt the transfer violated her rights.

A federal court said that her initial teaching assignment was a matter of administrative discretion and involved no constitutional right. But once she was assigned to work with Mexican-American children, officials could not transfer her out of a position for which she was "uniquely suited" because of her public criticism. The court concluded that the school's "interest in being free from general criticism cannot outweigh the right of a sincere, educational counselor to speak out against a policy she believes to be both harmful and unlawful."[16]

In a related Illinois case, teacher Barbara McGill was transferred because she had publicly complained about school procedures on several occasions and had privately disagreed with some of her principal's decisions and "had brought these disagreements to his attention." School officials charged that she was "stirring up trouble" in the teachers' lounge. McGill argued that her transfer "amounted to a denial of her rights of free speech." Based on the *Pickering* and *Givhan* decisions, a federal court ruled in McGill's favor because it concluded that her speech "did not impede the proper performance of [her] daily duties or interfere with the regular operation of the schools." In this 1979 opinion, the court noted that school officials are likely to "chill the exercise of constitutionally protected speech . . . through an unwanted transfer as well as through outright discharge."[17]

Must a teacher's public criticism of his school system be couched in moderate terms to be entitled to constitutional protection? Not according to the Court of Appeals of New York. The court held that "indiscreet bombast in an argumentative letter," without damage to the operation of the school system and without proof of reckless or intentional error, was not sufficient to sanction disciplinary action. "Otherwise," the court wrote, "those who criticize in an area where criticism is permissible would either be discouraged from exercising their right or would be required to do so on such innocuous terms as would make the criticism seem ineffective or obsequious."[18]

Does the First Amendment protect a teacher's right to circulate controversial petitions on school premises? Generally, it does. Beginning in January 1967 the Los Angeles Teacher's Union circulated the following "Petition for Better California Education":

> To: Governor Ronald Reagan; Max Rafferty, State Superintendent of Public Education; and the Los Angeles City Board of Education: We, the undersigned certificated employees of the Los Angeles City School District, do hereby protest the threatened cutback in funds for higher education and

imposition of tuition at college and university campuses. We further petition you to increase, not cut, the revenues for public education at all levels to meet our soaring enrollments and big city problems—by overhauling our tax structure now, not by violating California's proud claim to free public education for all.[19]

The school board prohibited the circulation of the petition because the subject was controversial, would "cause teachers to take and defend opposing political positions, thereby creating discord and lack of harmony," and would disturb and distract teachers doing lesson planning, since "discussions between petition circulators and off-duty teachers will inevitably involve some disagreements and resultant debates."

The union asked the court to prohibit the Board of Education from interfering with teachers' First Amendment rights. In 1969 the Supreme Court of California issued an opinion that strongly defended the right of teachers to petition for redress of grievances. Such a petition, wrote Justice Peters on behalf of the California Court, "epitomizes the use of freedom of expression to keep elected officials responsive to the electorate, thereby forestalling the violence which may be practiced by desperate and disillusioned citizens."

Furthermore, Justice Peters pointed out, "tolerance of the unrest intrinsic to the expression of controversial ideas is constitutionally required even in the school." For school officials to justify the prohibition of a particular opinion, they must be able to show that the danger rises "far above public inconvenience, annoyance or unrest." Moreover,

It cannot seriously be argued that school officials may demand a teaching faculty composed either [of] unthinking "yes men" who will uniformly adhere to a designated side of any controversial issue or of thinking individuals sworn never to share their ideas with one another for fear they may disagree and, like children, extend their disagreement to the level of general hostility and uncooperativeness. Yet it is precisely the inevitable disharmony resulting from the clash of opposing viewpoints that defendants [Board of Education] admittedly seek to avoid in the present case.[20]

Before issuing the Court's ruling, Justice Peters wrote:

It is imperative that the courts carefully differentiate in treatment those who are violent and heedless of the rights of others as they assert their cause and those whose concerns are no less burning but who seek to express themselves through peaceful, orderly means. In order to discourage persons from engaging in the former type of activity, the courts must take pains to assure that the channels of peaceful communication remain open and that peaceful activity is fully protected.[21]

Thus, the Court concluded that the union's petition in this case

clearly falls within the desirable category of political activity, and their past conduct clearly evidences respect for laws and willingness to challenge them in courts rather than through disruptive channels. Absent a showing of a clear and substantial threat to order and efficiency in the school, such proposed First Amendment activity should not be stifled.[22]

Although this opinion is not binding on courts outside California, it presents a strong case for the protection of teachers' rights to petition for redress of grievances in similar situations throughout the country.*

THE LIMITS OF FREE SPEECH

The preceding cases have expanded and defined the scope of a teacher's freedom of speech outside of school. The following cases indicate some of the limits of this freedom.

Reckless Accusations[23]

In 1969 two Alaska teachers were dismissed for publishing an "Open Letter" to the Seward School Board. The letter alleged that a number of incidents involving the superintendent were "definitely detrimental to the morale of our teaching staff and the effectiveness of the local educational system." Several of the allegations were false; these included the charge that the superintendent ordered a custodian to do electrical work "beyond his skill in a dangerous building" and threatened "to get one-third of the faculty this year and half of the remainder the next year." The letter also charged that the superintendent was "upsetting the school system" and "bringing teachers and others into public disgrace and disrespect."

Although this case appeared similar to *Pickering*, the Alaska court pointed out that it differed in several important ways: (1) The false statements in the Open Letter did *not* concern matters of public record and therefore could not be easily corrected by the school board. (2) Unlike the Pickering letter, which was greeted with "massive apathy," this letter led to intense public controversy involving teachers, the school board, and, the public—a controversy that lasted more than a year. (3) The false accusations in this letter "were not consistent with good faith and were made in reckless disregard of the truth." Thus this situation differed substantially from the *Pickering* case, and the court upheld the dismissal of the Alaska teachers.

---

*In a recent related case, a federal court ruled that a school board could not ban the nondisruptive sale of a teacher organization newspaper in public schools. *Substitutes United for Better Schools v. Rohter*, 496 F.Supp. 1017 (1980).

No Right to Vilify[24]

At a New Jersey school district's orientation for new teachers, the president of the local teachers' association described the district as a "snakepit for young teachers" and characterized the superintendent as a "villain" who did not negotiate in good faith and was "intimately embroiled" in local politics. As a result of the speech, she was dismissed for "conduct unbecoming a teacher."

The president argued that her speech should be protected by the First Amendment. But a state appeals court wrote that "free speech and collective bargaining rights do not endow a teacher, as a school district employee, with a license to vilify superiors publicly." The court acknowledged that teachers clearly do have the right to speak out on educational matters of public interest. Unlike *Pickering*, however, the court found that the president did not speak directly about issues of public concern but "distorted them into a vehicle to bring scorn and abuse on the school administration in general and the superintendent of schools in particular."

Grossly Offensive Remarks[25]

A public university in Texas withdrew an offer to employ Betty Duke as a teaching assistant after she used extensive profanity in blasting school policies and administrators (that "fucked over people") at an unauthorized meeting during freshman orientation. She also gave out leaflets to freshmen saying that the university would educate them to play such roles as "whore—selling your soul for a grade" and "smack-freak—addicted to the heroin of white, middle class values."

In upholding the action of the school officials, a federal appeals court wrote that Duke "owed the university a minimal duty of loyalty and civility to refrain from extremely disrespectful and grossly offensive remarks aimed at the administrators of the university. By her breach of this duty, the interests of the university outweighed her claim for protection."

Beyond Popular Vote[26]

In July 1977 James Swilley, a teacher and union president from Mobile, Alabama, alleged at a closed board meeting that a local principal had endangered the safety of his pupils. Although the board instructed Swilley to withhold further action until its investigation was complete, Swilley disseminated his charges to the local news media and was officially reprimanded. Swilley charged that the reprimand was unconstitutional. A federal district court, however, said that the possible removal of a principal is not a matter of public policy to be resolved by a majority vote;

it is the board's personnel decision. When such problems are made public before they are investigated, they can "interfere with the orderly operation of the school system" Moreover, in the eyes of the public, Swilley's dual position as teacher and union president implied greater knowledge of school operations that made his "premature remarks" to the media more difficult to counter. Therefore, the court concluded that the *Pickering* decision did not protect Swilley's public criticism.

Distribution of False Charges[27]

In 1973, a tenured high school English teacher from Hartford, Connecticut, was dismissed for distributing leaflets prepared by a student revolutionary group. The leaflets charged the principal with imposing a "reign of terror" at the school and falsely alleged that he had refused to reinstate a militant student despite a court order and had used "military riot gas" against the demonstrating students at another school. The court ruled that the distribution of these leaflets was not protected by the First Amendment because their purpose was to cause dissension, they contained serious and damaging accusations against a principal by a coworker, and their false statements had an immediate and harmful impact on the operation of the school.

Breach of Duty[28]

To protest the administration's failure to bargain with the faculty, Roger Shaw violated college policy by refusing to attend a faculty workshop or to march at commencement. As a result he was fired. Shaw argued that his protest was a form of symbolic speech. The court, however, ruled that Shaw's conduct went beyond protected speech "into the realm of breach of the express obligation" of employment. The judge concluded that the college was simply "unwilling to acknowledge the right of its teachers to disregard the rules with impunity."

Noncooperation[29]

In considering whether a teacher was unconstitutionally dismissed, a federal appeals court indicated that "bickering and running disputes" with a department head is not the kind of speech protected by the First Amendment. According to Judge Haynsworth, a school has a right to expect a teacher to follow instructions and to work cooperatively with the head of the department. If a teacher cannot or will not, "he does not immunize himself against loss of his position simply because his noncooperation and aggressive conduct are verbalized."

Summary

In the decades before *Pickering,* teachers were disciplined and even fired for publicly criticizing school policies and personnel. It was assumed that teachers could be prohibited from making critical statements about their schools in order to maintain professional loyalty and good working relationships. In 1968, however, the U.S. Supreme Court rejected this assumption. The *Pickering* case held that the First Amendment protected teachers as citizens and allowed them to speak out freely about educational matters of public concern without fear of retaliatory dismissal. But freedom of speech, like other constitutional rights, is not absolute. This means that there are limits to teachers' freedom of expression when it conflicts with other legitimate values and responsibilities.

How can a judge decide when a teacher's controversial statements should be protected? According to the Supreme Court, judges should balance "the interests of the teacher, as citizen, in commenting upon matters of public concern and the interests of the state, as an employer, in promoting the efficiency" of the schools. In *Pickering* the Court protected a teacher who wrote a sarcastic letter to his local newspaper criticizing the financial decisions of his school board and the administrative style of his superintendent. The Court emphasized that voters should be able to hear the informed opinions of teachers about public educational issues and that teachers should not be punished for expressing their views openly.

Pickering illustrates the way the Court applied the balancing test to resolve a specific school controversy. In subsequent cases, other courts used this test and the principles outlined in *Pickering* to indicate the scope and limits of an educator's freedom outside the classroom. Thus *Lusk* held that a teacher's responsible criticism about matters of "vital public interest" should be protected even if it injures his relations with his principal and coworkers unless it "materially and substantially" impedes his classroom performance or disrupts the regular operation of the school.

Givhan ruled that angry allegations about racial discrimination directed *privately* at a principal, are just as protected as *public* criticism about such assertions. Other cases have held that a teacher cannot be fired on grounds of "poor attitude" because she complains about working conditions related to her teaching and that a faculty member cannot be dismissed for giving interviews to local newspapers that express a highly unpopular viewpoint.

A California court ruled that teachers have the right to circulate controversial petitions on school premises during their free time unless such activity poses a serious and imminent threat to school efficiency. If a teacher's statement is constitutionally protected, she cannot be reprimanded, transferred, or otherwise disciplined for making it.

Other courts have noted the limits of teachers' freedom of expression. *Watts* held that the First Amendment did not protect a letter that contained false and reckless accusations that were not made in good faith and caused substantial disruption. *Swilley* ruled that statements to the press about a personnel matter under investigation may not be protected. Other judges have held that the First Amendment did not protect scornful and abusive public statements, the distribution of false and damaging accusations, noncooperative conduct, or the breach of a contractual obligation.

In short, teachers, like other citizens, have the right to speak freely outside of school on controversial issues unrelated to education. Furthermore, the courts have consistently ruled that the First Amendment applies to teachers and protects them in speaking out publicly and privately about matters of educational concern. In addition, teachers cannot be discharged simply because their statements may be unpopular and unconventional or may contain unintentional errors. On the other hand, the Constitution does not protect accusations that are false and reckless or statements that substantially disrupt school efficiency. Even if a teacher's criticism interferes with his relationship with his principal or coworkers, it might still be protected if it concerns an issue of public importance and the criticism is made responsibly.

NOTES

1. Charles Black, Jr., *Perspective in Constitutional Law*, Englewood Cliffs, N.J., Prentice-Hall, 1963, p. 85. By incorporating the First Amendment protection of free speech into the Fourteenth Amendment, courts have protected citizens against abridgment of their free speech by the states as well as the federal government.
2. *Pickering* v. *Board of Education*, 225 N.E.2d 1 (Ill. 1967); 391 U.S. 563 (1968).
3. 225 N.E.2d 1 at 2–4.
4. Id. at. 7.
5. 391 U.S. 563 at 570.
6. Id. at 571.
7. Id. at 572.
8. Id. at 574.
9. Id. at 570.
10. However, White's opinion suggests that to fire a teacher, a school board might have to prove not only that the teacher's statements were knowingly or recklessly false, but also that they had some harmful impact on the schools. Id. at 583–584.
11. *Garrison* v. *Louisiana*, 379 U.S. 64,75 (1964).
12. *Lusk* v. *Estes*, 361 F. Supp. 653 (N.D. Tex. 1973).
13. *Givhan* v. *Western Line Consolidate School District*, 99 S.Ct. 693 (1979).
14. *Johnson* v. *Butler*, 433 F.Supp. 531 (W.D. Va. 1977); cert. denied 434 U.S. 825 (1977).

15. *Aumiller* v. *University of Delaware*, 434 F.Supp. 1273 (D. Del. 1977).
16. *Bernasconi* v. *Tempe Elementary School District, No. 3.*, 548 F.2d 857 (9th Cir. 1977); cert. denied 434 U.S. 825 (1977).
17. *McGill* v. *Board of Education of Pekin Elementary School District No. 108 of Tazewell County, Illinois*, 602 F.2d 774 (7th Cir. 1979).
18. *Puentes* v. *Board of Education of Bethpage*, 250 N.E.2d 232 (N.Y. 1969).
19. *Los Angeles Teachers Union* v. *Los Angeles City Board of Education*, 455 P.2d 827,828 (Cal. 1969).
20. Id. at 833.
21. Id. at 836
22. Ibid.
23. *Watts* v. *Seward School Board*, 454 P.2d 732 (Ala. 1969).
24. *Pietrunti* v. *Board of Education of Brick Township*, 319 A.2d 262 (N.J. 1974).
25. *Duke* v. *Northern Texas State University*, 469 F.2d 829 (5th Cir. 1973).
26. *Swilley* v. *Alexander*, 448 F.Supp. 702 (S.D. Ala. 1978).
27. *Gilbertson* v. *McAlister*, 403 F.Supp. 1 (D. Conn. 1975).
28. *Shaw* v. *Board of Trustees of Frederick Community College*, 549 F.2d 929 (4th Cir. 1976).
29. *Chitwood* v. *Feaster*, 468 F.2d 359 (4th Cir. 1972).

Chapter 5
Teachers' Academic Freedom

Teachers and students must always remain free to inquire, to study, and to evaluate to gain new maturity and understanding; otherwise our civilization will stagnate and die.
—Chief Justice Earl Warren in *Sweezy* v. *New Hampshire*[1]

A reluctance on the part of the teacher to investigate and experiment with new and different ideas is anathema to the entire concept of academic freedom.
—*Parducci* v. *Rutland*[2]

To impose an intellectual straitjacket on our educational leaders, wrote Chief Justice Warren, "would be to imperil the future of our nation." Since new social, aesthetic, and scientific discoveries can always be made, it is important that teachers remain free to evaluate and criticize the values, styles, and truths of the past and the present. This is the purpose of academic freedom. It includes not only a teacher's right to speak and write freely about her subject but also the right to select appropriate teaching materials and methods.

Academic freedom is based on the First Amendment and on the need, in a democratic society, to protect the freedom of teachers and students to challenge established concepts. It was the process of challenging established concepts that gave rise to the controversies presented in this chapter.

The cases confront such issues as these: May teachers assign books or articles that offend parents or school authorities? May they use teaching methods that are not acceptable to the majority of citizens in their community or to members of their profession? Should they be permitted to express controversial personal views to students in the classroom?

After examining the leading case of *Keefe* v. *Geanakos,* this chapter will consider several related aspects of academic freedom, including teaching methods, controversial material, and the issue of relevance.

The Keefe Case: Offensive Language and Academic Freedom[3]

Robert Keefe taught high school English in Ipswich, Massachusetts. He was a creative teacher who wanted to do more than the curriculum required. He sought to expose his students to relevant and provocative contemporary writing. Therefore, on the first day of school in September 1969 he gave each member of his class a recent issue of *The Atlantic.* He assigned the lead article, entitled "The Young and the Old," which discussed dissent, protest, radicalism, and revolt. The article contained the term *motherfucker* which was repeated a number of times. Keefe explained the origin and context of the term and told the class that any student who considered the assignment distasteful could have an alternative one.

The following excerpt from the controversial article illustrates its language, style, and tone:

> The Columbia rebellion is illuminating. What it lacked in graffiti it more than made up for in its already classic slogan, "Up against the wall, motherfucker!" I make no claim to full understanding of the complete psychological and cultural journey this phrase had undergone. But let me at least sketch in a few steps along the way:
>
> 1. The emergence of the word "motherfucker" to designate a form of extreme transgression. . . .
>
> 2. The use of the word in contemptuous command by white policemen when ordering black (and perhaps other) suspects to take their place in the police lineup, thereby creating the full phrase, "Up against the wall, motherfucker!" . . . .
>
> Finally, Lionel Trilling's pun, in characterizing the striking students (not without affection) as "alma-mater-fuckers," a witty example of an important principle: the mocking of mockery.
>
> In evaluating the significance of the phrase and its vicissitudes, the classical psychoanalytic approach would, immediately and definitively, stress the Oedipus complex. After all, who but fathers are motherfuckers?[4]

Questions to Consider

1. If you were a member of the Ipswich School Board, would you vote to dismiss Keefe for assigning the article? Why or why not?
2. If parents objected to the article and the school board asked Keefe not to use it again but he refused, would the board be justified in firing him?
3. If not, does this mean that a teacher could assign any book or article? Shouldn't school boards have some control over what publications are assigned to students? If so, how much?

RESULTS OF THE ASSIGNMENT

There was no evidence of negative student reaction to the article or the class discussion. However, a number of parents found the "dirty" word highly offensive and protested to the school committee. Members of the committee asked Keefe if he would agree not to use the word again in class. The teacher replied that he could not in good conscience agree. After a meeting of the school committee, Keefe was suspended and proceedings were initiated to dismiss him. Keefe, however, believed this would violate his rights and went to court to stop his dismissal.

The case raises a number of questions regarding controversial speech in a high school classroom. The following is the way one federal appeals court treated them:

Isn't an article that repeatedly uses a vulgar and highly offensive term pornographic and improper? It depends on the article. In this case the judge found the article "scholarly, thoughtful, and thought-provoking." The court said it was not possible to read this particular article as "an incitement to libidinous conduct." If it raised the concept of incest, wrote the judge, "it was not to suggest it, but to condemn it," for the word was used "as a superlative of opprobrium."

Assuming that the article had merit, couldn't the teacher have discussed the article without considering the controversial word? Not in this case. The offending word was not artificially introduced but was important to the development of the thesis and conclusions of the author. Therefore, no proper study of the article could avoid considerations of the offensive word.

Can't a school committee protect students from language that the parents of some students find genuinely offensive? This would depend on the specific situation—the age of the students, the words used, and the purpose of their use. In this instance the word was used for educational purposes. Most high school seniors knew the word, and it has been used nationally by young radicals and protestors. The judge questioned whether quoting a "dirty" word in current use would be a shock too great for high school seniors to stand.

"If the answer were that the students must be protected from such exposure," wrote Judge Aldrich, "we would fear for their future." Thus, he concluded that the sensibilities of offended parents "are not the full measure of what is proper in education."

Does that mean a teacher could assign any book that is legally published? Are obscenity standards the same for students as for adults? No, the court does not go that far. The issue is one of degree. Whether the use of offensive language is proper depends on the circumstances. In fact, Judge Aldrich acknowledged that "some measure of public regulation of classroom speech is inherent in every provision of public education." But the judge concluded that the application of such a regulation in the *Keefe* case "demeans any proper concept of education." Thus, as the Supreme Court has pointed out, the unwarranted inhibition of the free speech of teachers not only affects the teachers who are restricted but also has an "unmistakable tendency to chill that free play of spirit which all teachers ought especially to cultivate and practice."[5]

The concern for the protection of academic freedom, of course, goes beyond the selective protection of offensive language. It is based on a historic commitment to free speech, on the importance of academic inquiry to social progress, and on the need of both teachers and students to operate in an atmosphere that allows free challenge of established concepts.

CONTROVERSIAL METHODS

In the following cases, teachers claim that their academic freedom has been violated after they are disciplined for using controversial teaching methods. The judicial decisions in this section help clarify the scope and limits of academic freedom as it applies to this topic.

The Mailloux Case: Beyond Majority Vote[6]

The *Keefe* case indicated that a teacher cannot be fired merely for assigning an article that contains vulgar language that offends parents. Whether the language used is protected by academic freedom depends on the circumstances of the case—the relevance and quality of the article or story, the opinion of other educators in the field, the age and maturity of the students, and the effect on the class. The problem is, How can a teacher know before he assigns an article or uses controversial language whether he will be fired or protected? In the Mailloux case Judge Charles Wyzanski tried to answer this question.

Roger Mailloux was an eleventh-grade English teacher at a coed high school in Lawrence, Massachusetts. In the fall of 1970 his class was discussing a novel about a young teacher in rural Kentucky and his encounter with conservative local practices such as seating boys and girls on opposite sides of the classroom. During the discussion some students commented that the practice of seating boys and girls separately was ridiculous. Mailloux said that some current attitudes are just as ridiculous. As an example, he introduced the subject of taboo words and wrote the word *fuck* on the blackboard. He then,

> . . . in accordance with his customary teaching method of calling for volunteers to respond to a question, asked the class in general for an explanation. After a couple of minutes, a boy volunteered the word meant "sexual intercourse." Plaintiff [Mailloux], without using the word orally, said: "We have two words, sexual intercourse, and this word on the board; one is accepted by society, the other is not accepted. It is a taboo word." After a few minutes of discussion of

other aspects of taboo, plaintiff went to other matters. At all times in the discussion, plaintiff was in good faith pursuing what he regarded as an educational goal. He was not attempting to probe the private feelings or attitudes, or experiences of his students, or to embarrass them.[7]

The next day the parent of a girl in Mailloux's class complained to the principal. After an investigation by the head of the English department and a hearing before the school committee, Mailloux was dismissed for "conduct unbecoming a teacher." He went to court to seek reinstatement because he believed that the school committee deprived him of his rights under the First and Fourteenth Amendments.

After evidence was presented in court, Judge Wyzanski found that:

The topic of taboo words was relevant to the teaching of eleventh-grade English.

Use of the word *fuck* is relevant to a discussion of taboo words. "Its impact," commented Judge Wyzanski, "effectively illustrates how taboo words function."

Boys and girls in the eleventh grade are sophisticated enough to treat the word in a serious educational manner.

Mailloux's writing the word did not have a disturbing effect on the class.

In the opinion of some educational experts, the way Mailloux used the word *fuck* was appropriate under the circumstances and served a serious educational purpose.

Other qualified educators testified that Mailloux's use of the word was neither reasonable nor appropriate.

With these facts in mind Judge Wyzanski then discussed the prevailing law in such cases. The *Keefe* case, said the judge, upheld two kinds of academic freedom: the "substantive right" of a teacher to choose a teaching method that serves a "demonstrated" educational purpose and the "procedural right" of a teacher not to be discharged for the use of a teaching method that is not prohibited by clear regulation.

In this case the judge ruled that the teaching methods used by Mailloux "were obviously not 'necessary' to the proper teaching of the subject and students, in the sense that a reference to Darwinian evolution might be thought necessary to the teaching of biology."[8]

Should the ruling of the *Keefe* case apply to Mailloux? The *Keefe* case, wrote Judge Wyzanski, "indicated that the use in the classroom of the word 'fuck' is not impermissible under all circumstances—as, for example, when it appears in a book properly assigned for student reading." But when a secondary school teacher chooses a teaching method that is not necessary and is not generally regarded by his profession as permissible, it is undecided "whether the Constitution gives him any right to use the method or leaves the issue to the school authorities."

Judge Wyzanski emphasized that academic freedom is not confined "to conventional teachers or to those who can get a majority vote from their colleagues." Nevertheless, the judge explained that academic freedom in high schools should be distinguished from postsecondary education:

> The secondary school more clearly than the college or university acts *in loco parentis* with respect to minors. It is closely governed by a school board selected by a local community. The faculty does not have the independent traditions, the broad discretion as to teaching methods, nor usually the intellectual qualifications, of university professors. Some teachers and most students have limited intellectual and emotional maturity. Most parents, students, school boards, and members of the community usually expect the secondary school to concentrate on transmitting basic information, teaching "the best that is known and thought in the world," training by established techniques, and to some extent at least, indoctrinating in the mores of the surrounding society. While secondary schools are not rigid disciplinary institutions, neither are they open forums in which mature adults, already habituated to social restraints, exchange ideas on a level of parity. Moreover, it cannot be accepted as a premise that the student is voluntarily in the classroom and willing to be exposed to a teaching method which, though reasonable, is not approved by the school authorities or by the weight of professional opinion. A secondary school student, unlike most college students, is usually required to attend school classes, and may have no choice as to his teacher.[9]

Bearing this in mind, Judge Wyzanski ruled that for a controversial teaching method to be constitutionally protected, it is not enough for a secondary school teacher to prove that it was done in good faith, is relevant to his students, and is regarded by some experts as serving a serious educational purpose. He must also show that the teaching method "has the support of the preponderant opinion of the teaching profession or of the part of it to which he belongs." If this is not shown, the state may suspend or discharge a teacher, "but it may not resort to such drastic sanctions unless the state proves he was put on notice, either by a regulation or otherwise that he should not use that method."

This procedural protection is afforded a teacher because he is engaged in the exercise of "vital First Amendment rights." In his teaching capacity he should not be required to "guess what conduct or utterance may lose him his position."

Since Mailloux did not know that his conduct was prohibited by any regulation or understanding among teachers, Judge Wyzanski ruled that it was a violation of due process for the school committee to discharge him. (The concept of due process is discussed more fully in Chapter 12.) However, the judge noted that despite this ruling school authorities are free "after they have learned that the teacher is using a teaching method of which they disapprove, and which is not necessary to the proper teaching of the subject, to suspend him until he agrees to cease using this method."

The Lawrence School Board appealed Judge Wyzanski's decision to the U.S. Court of Appeals. The appeals court agreed with the trial court's ruling that Mailloux had not received adequate notice informing him that the techniques he used would be considered improper. However, the court rejected the guidelines Judge Wyzanski had devised, believing that "they will introduce more problems than they would resolve." Instead, the court preferred the "balancing test," which requires that the judge consider each case individually and balance all of the circumstances to determine whether a school board's interest in reasonable discipline is "demonstrably sufficient" to restrict a teacher's right to free speech.[10]

The Olicker Case: The Outer Edge of Freedom[11]

Eileen Olicker, a first year reading teacher in an Oakland junior high school, was dismissed for distributing to her pupils stories written by them containing vulgar descriptions of sexual organs and the sex act. The teacher typed the material and made copies for classroom use. The assignment was planned for poor readers who were told they could write about anything they chose and that their stories would be shared with other members of the class. This approach was intended to overcome the students' negative attitude toward writing and to enable them to discuss each others' stories. When she saw the writing dealt mainly with sex, excretion, and menstruation, Olicker considered telling the students that their material was too vulgar to be distributed; but she feared this would make them more hostile and difficult to teach. She was dismissed after a student she had disciplined left a copy of the material in the principal's box a month after the incident.

In a 2 to 1 decision, a California appeals court ruled in Olicker's favor. The majority noted that she had been an unusually sensitive, dedicated, and effective teacher and that this one incident did not produce "any disruption or impairment of discipline."

Two expert witnesses testified that Olicker's teaching method of having her students write about subjects that interested them was "a sound educational approach." The fault was found in the reproduction and distribution of the materials. The court acknowledged that the "'efficacy'" of this approach "may well be questioned by other teachers as well as laymen." However, Judge Molinari noted: "it is not our function to pass upon the academic merits of such a teaching technique"—only to determine whether the approach disrupted discipline or impaired the teaching process. Since the judge found no such disruption, Olicker was protected.

In conclusion, the court explained that teachers should not be disciplined "merely because they made a reasonable, good faith, professional judgment in the course of their employment with which higher authorities later disagreed." And in a concurring opinion, Judge Sims observed: "If standards of taste of future generations are to be elevated, it will not be accomplished by . . . self-embarrassed school trustees who discharge as unfit those who would bring the problem out in the open for discussion."[12]

The Hetrick Case: Stressing the Basics[13]

Phyllis Hetrick was not rehired as an English instructor at Eastern Kentucky University because of her refusal to conform to the teaching style demanded by her department. Hetrick emphasized student freedom to organize class time and to choose their own out-of-class assignments. As a result, she covered only half of the material she had been told to teach.

Hetrick wanted to teach her students "how to think rather than merely to accept and to parrot what they had heard." However, the school administration expected their instructors "to teach on a basic level, to stress fundamentals, and to follow conventional teaching patterns" because they believed the students were generally unsophisticated.

In this case, a federal district court ruled in favor of the school. The court wrote that the First Amendment does not require a school "to tolerate any manner of teaching method the teacher may choose." The issue, said the court, is not which educational philosophy had greater merit, but whether a school "has a right to require some conformity with whatever teaching methods are acceptable to it," and whether it may decline to rehire a teacher whose methods are not conducive "to the achievement of the academic goals they espoused." The trial court said the school had this right and a federal appeals court agreed. The court of appeals wrote that academic freedom "does not encompass the right of a non-tenured teacher to have her teaching style insulated from review by her superiors . . . just because her methods and philosophy are considered acceptable somewhere within the teaching profession." The court rejected the notion that a teacher's method is a "protected form of speech that cannot be considered by a school administration in determining whether a non-tenured teacher should be renewed."*

The Beebee Case: Experimentation Is Vital[14]

In 1976 the Michigan Court of Appeals ruled that a disagreement about "teaching philosophy" was not enough to justify the firing of Louise Beebee, a tenured elementary teacher. The evidence showed that her

---

*In a related case, the Washington Supreme Court recently ruled that two high school teachers had no First Amendment right to team teach an alternative history course, but could be required to teach in a conventional manner contrary to their preferred method. *Millikan* v. *Board of Directors of Everett S.D.*, 611 P. 2d 414 Wash. (1980).

students' achievement level was equal to that of their peers. Testimony indicated that some parents liked the teacher's methods, whereas other parents and the principal did not. In ruling against the dismissal, the court made these observations about controversial methods:

> Should we require tenured teachers to teach alike and to be liked by everyone? We think not. The latter requirement is ridiculous on its face. Some parents will always criticize a teacher, especially one who utilizes methods different from those used when they went to school. . . .
>
> Experience has shown that there is no one "right" way to teach. Different environments and types of students require different teaching methods. Some degree of variance in methods and classroom experimentation is vital to any school that seeks to be flexible . . . [and] adapt to changing circumstances. . . .

The Ahern Case: To Teach as Directed[15]

Frances Ahern, a high school economics teacher, attended a summer institute that led her to change her teaching methods and to allow her students to decide on course materials, discussion topics, and rules for classroom behavior. When Ahern was absent for a week, a substitute became frustrated by student resistance to traditional discipline, and slapped one of the students. The incident became the focus of class discussion. Ahern said her goal was to help students formulate a policy concerning corporal punishment. The principal warned her to stop discussing the incident, to teach economics, and to use more conventional teaching methods. When Ahern ignored the warning, she was dismissed. The teacher defended her action "in the interest of preserving rapport with her students and of guarding her academic freedom to select the method of teaching to be employed in her classroom." But the principal argued that Ahern failed to teach as directed, and instead "continued to discuss with students, students' rights and teachers' rights."

A federal circuit court ruled in favor of the principal. The court concluded that the Constitution does not give a teacher the right either to (1) persist in teaching behavior which violated valid requirements of the school board concerning classroom method or (2) "teach politics in a course on economics."

CONTROVERSIAL MATERIAL

The cases in this section focus on another aspect of academic freedom: the right of faculty to select teaching materials that are appropriate for their students.*

---

*For related cases on the selection and "deselection" of library books, see Chapter 2, pp. 33–37.

The Parducci Case: Controversial Stories and Academic Freedom[16]

In Montgomery, Alabama, Marilyn Parducci assigned her eleventh-grade class a comic satire by Kurt Vonnegut, Jr., entitled "Welcome to the Monkey House." The following day the principal and the associate superintendent expressed their displeasure with the story. They described the content of the satire as "literary garbage" and construed the "philosophy" of the story as "condoning, if not encouraging 'the killing off of elderly people and free sex.'" They advised Parducci not to teach the story in any of her classes.

Parducci was bewildered by their interpretation. She considered the satire a good literary work and, although not meaning to cause trouble, she felt she had a professional obligation to teach it. After a hearing before the school board, Parducci was dismissed for assigning materials that had a "disruptive" effect on the school and for refusing "the counseling and advice of the school principal." Parducci felt that her dismissal violated her First Amendment right to academic freedom and went to court to seek reinstatement.

In considering this case Judge Johnson first summarized the basic constitutional principles involved:

> Although academic freedom is not one of the enumerated rights of the First Amendment, the Supreme Court has on numerous occasions emphasized that the right to teach, to inquire, to evaluate, and to study is fundamental to a democratic society. . . .
>
> The right to academic freedom, however, like all other constitutional rights, is not absolute, and must be balanced against the competing interests of society. . . . While the balancing of these interests will necessarily depend on the particular facts before the Court, certain guidelines in this area were provided by the Supreme Court . . . [which] observed that in order for the state to restrict the First Amendment right of a student, it must first demonstrate that "the forbidden conduct would *materially* and *substantially* interfere with the requirements of appropriate discipline in the operation of the school. . . ."[17]

The first question considered by the court was whether "Welcome to the Monkey House" is appropriate reading for high school juniors. Although the story contains several vulgar terms and a reference to an involuntary sex act, the court, "having read the story very carefully," found "nothing that would render it obscene."

The court's finding that the story was appropriate for high school students was confirmed by the reaction of the students themselves. Rather than disrupting the educational process, the evidence indicated that the story "was greeted with apathy by most of the students." The court therefore found that the conduct for which Parducci was dismissed was not such that "would materially and substantially interfere with reasonable requirements of school discipline."

Since the school board "failed to show either that the assignment was inappropriate reading for high school juniors or that it created a significant disruption to the educational processes of this school," the court concluded that Parducci's dismissal "constituted an unwarranted invasion of her First Amendment right to academic freedom." The court noted:

> When a teacher is forced to speculate as to what conduct is permissible and what conduct is proscribed, he is apt to be overly cautious and reserved in the classroom. Such a reluctance on the part of the teacher to investigate and experiment with new and different ideas is anathema to the entire concept of academic freedom.[18]

Discussing Controversial Issues: The Cases of Sterzing and Cooper[19]

In Stafford, Texas, several parents objected to the way Henry Sterzing taught his high school civics class. They especially objected to his unit on race relations that was alleged to be "propagandistic" and to his response to a student's question indicating that he was not opposed to interracial marriage. As a result, the principal and school board advised him to teach his course "within the text and not discuss controversial issues." But Sterzing explained that it was impossible to teach current events to high school seniors and avoid controversial questions. Sterzing was dismissed for insubordination.

A federal court ruled, however, that Sterzing could not be discharged for discussing controversial issues in class. The court acknowledged that a teacher has a duty "to be exceptionally fair and objective in presenting his personally held opinions and actively and persuasively present different views." In this case, however, the court ruled that Sterzing's "classroom methods were formulated and conducted within the ambit of professional standards" and that his statements in class neither substantially interfered with discipline nor subjected students unfairly to indoctrination.

A recent related case involved a Texas teacher, Janet Cooper, who used a controversial "sunshine simulation" to teach American history during the post-Civil War period. The technique involved role playing by high school students and evoked strong feelings on racial issues. As a result, a number of parents complained to members of the school board, and Cooper was advised "not to discuss Blacks in American history." Because of her use of the simulation, Cooper's contract was not renewed. Cooper argued that her classroom discussions were constitutionally protected activities, and she took her case to court. In a 1980 opinion, a federal appeals court agreed with Cooper's argument, reinstated her, and awarded her back pay and attorney's fees.[20]

The Clark Case: Disregarding the Text and Syllabus[21]

A nontenured undergraduate biology teacher, Verdelle Clark, was warned by his department to stop overemphasizing sex in his health survey course. Clark rejected this warning. He explained that he had surveyed his students' interests and found that "they wanted sex education and mental health emphasized." He agreed to this emphasis and to "only touch on the other topics covered by the assigned text and course syllabus." When Clark was not rehired, he claimed that his First Amendment rights had been violated.

In rejecting Clark's contention, a federal appeals court ruled that he had no constitutional right "to override the wishes and judgment of his superiors and fellow faculty members as to the proper content of the required health course." The court concluded that academic freedom was not "a license for uncontrolled expression at variance with established curricular content."

RELEVANCE

The Brubaker Case: Inappropriate and Irrelevant[22]

Three eighth grade teachers from Cook County, Illinois, were discharged for distributing movie brochures about the 1969 rock festival "Woodstock." These contained various articles, poems, and pictures. One piece, "Getting Together," included the following controversial references to drugs, sexual behavior, and vulgar language:

Woodstock felt like home. A place to take acid. A
place to make love. . . .
Grass smoked together. Stink of our shit;
Music of Laughter. Gathering together.
Bodies naked in the water, touching each
other, opening hearts into greater awareness . . . like a drop of water in the crest of
the tide, moving together we're a big
fucking wave. . . .

The teachers and their expert witnesses argued that the distribution of the flyers should be protected by the First Amendment because they could promote rapport with students, "increase the realism of the classroom," and were a useful, educational "improvisation." But other experts, the trial judge, and the court of appeals disagreed. The majority of the court believed that the flyers were not relevant to the subjects being taught. The three teachers taught French, industrial arts, and language arts. The brochures were given to any students who wanted them, were not prepared for classroom use, and were not approved by school authorities.

Moreover, the court noted that none of the teachers even tried to explain to their students how the brochures related to what they were studying.

The court also found the brochure inappropriate for eighth grade students. Its purpose was to publicize a movie that had been widely criticized for sexual promiscuity and drug use and had clearly been assigned an "R" rating (which provided that persons under 17 could not be admitted alone). Furthermore, the brochure promotes a viewpoint contrary to state law that requires students to be taught about "the harmful effects of alcoholic drink and narcotics."

The court pointed out that academic freedom does not protect conduct that is "both offensive and unnecessary to the accomplishment of educational objectives; . . . such questions are matters of degree involving judgment on such factors as the age and sophistication of the students, relevance of the educational purpose, and context and manner of presentations."

The court rejected the teachers' appeal with these words:

> to the minds of eighth graders, the brochure's poetry can . . . be fairly read as an alluring invitation and a beckoning for them to throw off the dull discipline imposed on them by the moral environment of their home life, and in exchange to enter into a new world of love and freedom—freedom to use acid and grass, freedom to take their clothes off and to get an early start in the use of such vulgarities as "shit," "fucking" and their companions.[23]

The Simon Case: A Narrow View of Academic Freedom[24]

Dan Simon, a black high school teacher with 15 years of experience, was fired for neglect of duty. Among the many charges against him, Simon was found to have made several "irrelevant" statements concerning sex activities between the black and the white races during his World History class.*

Simon claimed that these statements should be protected by his academic freedom. The Louisiana Court of Appeals disagreed. In a conservative opinion, it wrote that courts require "some serious educational purpose underlying the use of a phrase or a word for it to be protected under the auspices of academic freedom." The court concluded that in this case the statements in question were not clearly relevant, "served no serious educational purpose and are therefore not entitled to protection."

---

*Simon noted, for example, that "Integration in churches and classrooms came recently, but in bed for a long time, because if a white man wanted a little loving he would go across the tracks." And he commented that: "The black man has had the idea that only white women could love adequately because of picture shows. Until recently there were no black women in movies."

The Birdwell Case: Clearly Irrelevant Statements[25]

A St. Louis mathematics teacher, Beauregard Birdwell, was dismissed after he told his algebra class that army recruiters had no right to be at the high school and that the students were "4,000 strong" and could push the recruiters, throw apples at them, make them feel unwanted, and get them off campus. Birdwell argued that he should not be dismissed because his comments did not cause substantial disruption and therefore were protected by the First Amendment.

The court did not agree. It ruled that his statements interfered with the educational process, were "infused with the spirit of violent action," were "completely irrelevant" to his duty to teach mathematics, and "diverted the time and attention of both students and teacher from the prescribed curriculum." The judge also observed that Birdwell's "zealous advocacy" in the court of his right of free speech "contrasts sharply with his obvious intolerance of the exercise of such speech by others with whose views he disagrees."

BEYOND ACADEMIC FREEDOM

The Harris Case: Insubordination[26]

William Harris was a tenured high school English teacher from Schenectady County, New York. For several years he had taught J. D. Salinger's *Catcher in the Rye* in his sophomore class. In 1973 parents complained about Harris' use in the classroom of "explicit street language" appearing in the book. To resolve the problem, the superintendent and the principal met with the teacher who "voluntarily agreed to drop the book and find an appropriate substitute." A year later, however, Harris resumed use of the book, "without warning and despite the earlier [written] understanding." As a result, he was dismissed for insubordination.

Harris said his actions should be protected by the Constitution, but the New York Court of Appeals disagreed. In a 1978 decision, the court indicated that it might have defended the teacher's academic freedom had he been charged with "teaching an unacceptable work of literature" and "firmly stood his ground against community pressure in defense of his classroom activities." Instead, Harris agreed not to teach the Salinger book and then "reneged on the understanding."*

---

*Courts usually do not rule on whether a particular school board penalty is appropriate because they consider this to be a matter of administrative discretion. But under the circumstances of this case, the court ordered the school to reduce the penalty since "dismissal of the tenured teacher is so disproportionate to the offense as to shock the court's sense of fairness."

The La Rocca Case: Religious Indoctrination[27]

Joan La Rocca was a tenured art teacher at the Rye Senior High School. She was dismissed after she encouraged students to attend meetings of her religious organization, used classroom facilities during school time to preach her religious beliefs, and used her authority as a teacher to encourage Bible study and recruit students under the guise of guidance. La Rocca said she felt free to express her religious ideas wherever she was because she believed them to be true. Since she failed to stop discussing her beliefs and recruiting for her faith in school, a New York court ruled that her actions clearly violated the religion clause of the First Amendment.

The Celestine Case: Incompetence Not Protected[28]

Allen Celestine had been teaching in a Louisiana school system for 11 years. He had become increasingly concerned about the vulgar language used by his fifth grade students. Therefore, when two girls in his class used the word *fuck*, he required them to write it 1000 times to teach them a lesson. As a result, he was dismissed for incompetence. Celestine claimed that his right to academic freedom protected his choice of punishment. The court, however, ruled that the First Amendment does not entitle a teacher to require young students "to use and be exposed to vulgar words, particularily when no academic or educational purpose can possibly be served."

The Jergeson Case: "Poor Journalism" Not Protected[29]

A Wyoming school district decided not to rehire Raymond Jergeson as a high school journalism teacher and adviser to the school newspaper on grounds of incompetence. As evidence of incompetence, the administration showed that Jergeson failed to advise students of the inappropriateness of a satirical edition of the school paper that criticized the school staff and included a picture of a row of urinals.

The Supreme Court of Wyoming upheld the school's action. The court acknowledged that students may have been exposed to "a more base and filthy humor outside the schools." However, in a conservative opinion, the judge explained that "in the halls of an institution where lofty ideals and examples should be the rule," this type of publication is out of place. According to the court the school board might have legitimately concluded that the controversial articles "did interfere with the discipline of the school and did collide with the rights of others, namely the teachers and administrators of the school." Moreover, the students were not speaking out on a controversial matter of public concern, but were "making personal attacks on members of the faculty." Despite a strong dissenting opinion, the majority said that the school board was justified in concluding that Jergeson's failure to try to stop the paper was· "a demonstration in poor journalism" and an "example of his incompetence."

COMMENT

As the cases in this chapter have indicated, controversial language may be protected under some circumstances and not under others. Often this is due to the age of the students or the relevance of the language. But in some cases, in which reasonable people differ as to what language is appropriate, decisive factors may be the values, age, background, and attitudes of the judge hearing the case.

In *Brubaker,* for example, Judge O'Sullivan seemed to grudgingly acknowledge that "by second or third year high school, most American males have become familiar with" vulgar words such as "fuck." He expressed a forlorn hope, however, "that most of our young ladies will never employ that kind of speech." Similarly, in *Celestine,* Judge Hood refused to write this word in the court's decision, even though it was central to the case. Instead, he awkwardly referred to it as "a four letter word beginning with the letter 'F,' being an extremely vulgar word meaning sexual intercourse." In both cases, the judges were sympathetic to parents and administrators who were disturbed that such language would enter the classroom.

In contrast, consider the way Judge Graves reacted to the protest over the use of the same word in *Harris.* He noted that *Catcher in the Rye* has a chapter or two dealing with the protagonist's sex life in which

> horrible to contemplate, the author indulges several times in a well-known, common vulgarity, the use of the word 'F − − K.' This ancient anglo-saxon four letter obscenity is one not unknown outside the classroom to high school students and to their elders. . . . It is difficult to fathom how the presence in the school curriculum of a book containing such language could possibly have any serious independent impact on the morals and behavior of the students or the orderly administration of the school system.[30]

Summary and Conclusions

Judicial protection for academic freedom is based on the First Amendment, on the importance of intellectual inquiry to social progress, and on the belief that teachers and students should be free to question and challenge established concepts. Like other constitutional rights, however, academic

freedom is not absolute; it must be balanced against the community's right
to determine educational goals and to maintain reasonable discipline.

METHODS AND MATERIALS
Most courts have tended to protect the right of teachers to use controversial
methods or materials that were relevant to the subject. *Keefe* and *Parducci*,
for example, held that teachers cannot be fired simply because they assign a
controversial book or article or use vulgar language in the classroom.
According to most courts, whether such methods or materials are protected
depends on the circumstances of each case. The circumstances that judges
consider include the educational relevance of the controversial language or
publication, the teacher's purpose, the age and maturity of the students,
the quality of the material being used, and the effect on the students.

In a few cases such as *Parducci,* the courts went further in protecting
academic freedom and have ruled that a school board cannot restrict a
teacher's First Amendment rights unless it demonstrates that the teacher's
conduct would "materially and substantially interfere" with reasonable
requirements of school discipline. On the other hand, a few conservative
courts, such as those in Wyoming and Louisiana, have interpreted
academic freedom quite narrowly. Thus the *Simon* case, for example, failed
to protect a history teacher's comments on sex activity between the races
because "they were not clearly relevant" and "served no serious educational purpose."

BEYOND ACADEMIC FREEDOM
Academic freedom, of course, does not protect teaching that is incompetent or irrelevant nor does it protect religious or political indoctrination.
Thus a math teacher's discussion of his views on army recruiting and
political action in an algebra class was not protected, nor was a teacher
protected who used her position to try to "educate" her students
concerning her religious beliefs.

In sum, all courts recognize that teachers are entitled to academic
freedom. Although some judges have interpreted this concept narrowly,
most courts will protect teachers from being fired simply because they
assign a controversial book or article, use vulgar language, try a questionable teaching method, or make an unpopular comment. In determining
whether to protect a teacher's controversial methods or materials, most
courts use a "balancing test," a case-by-case inquiry that balances the
teacher's right to academic freedom against the competing interests of the
community. In most instances, this means that a teacher's use of
controversial methods, language, or materials will be protected by the
First Amendment unless school officials can show that (1) it caused
disruption; (2) it was not relevant; or (3) it was not appropriate to the age and
maturity of the students.

NOTES

1. *Sweezy* v. *New Hampshire,* 354 U.S. 234 (1957).
2. *Parducci* v. *Rutland,* 316 F.Supp. 352 (M.D. Ala. 1970).
3. *Keefe* v. *Geanakos,* 418 F.2d 359 (1st Cir. 1969).
4. Robert J. Lifton, "The Young and the Old: Notes on a New History," pt. I, *The Atlantic, 224,* No. 3 (September 1969), 47.
5. J. Frankfurter, concurring in *Wieman* v. *Updegraff,* 344 U.S. 183, 195 (1952).
6. *Mailloux* v. *Kiley,* 323 F.Supp. 1387 (D. Mass. 1971).
7. Id. at 1388.
8. This refers to the Supreme Court's opinion in *Epperson* v. *Arkansas,* 393 U.S. 97 (1968), in which it ruled that an Arkansas "antievolution" statute was unconstitutional. That statute, which is based on the belief of certain religious groups, makes it illegal for a public school to teach that "mankind ascended or descended from a lower order of animals." It was outlawed because it conflicts with the First Amendment mandate of government neutrality toward religion. And, according to Justice Stewart's concurring opinion, it is also unconstitutional because it "would clearly impinge upon the guarantees of free communication contained in the First Amendment."
9. *Mailloux* at 1392.
10. *Mailloux* v. *Kiley,* 448 F.2d 1242 (1st Cir. 1971).
11. *Oakland Unified School District* v. *Olicker,* 25 C.A.3d 1098 (1972).
12. In a strong dissenting opinion Judge Elkington criticized the majority for establishing "a new high-water mark in judicially permitted licentiousness . . . and of all places, in the classroom of a grammar school." The effect of the majority opinion, wrote the judge, was to declare "beyond school disciplinary redress, a teacher's exposure of grammar school children to a compulsory, sordid, debased and sadistic discussion of the human sexual act." "We should not," he concluded, "allow feelings of compassion to legitimize her conduct, and thus create new and bad law." Id. at 1117–1118.
13. *Hetrick* v. *Martin,* 480 F.2d 705 (6th Cir. 1973).
14. *Beebee* v. *Haslett Public Schools,* 239 N.W.2d 724 (Mich. 1976).
15. *Ahern* v. *Board of Education of School District of Grand Island,* 456 F.2d 399 (8th Cir. 1972).
16. *Parducci* v. *Rutland,* 316 F.Supp. 352 (M.D. Ala. 1970).
17. Id. at 355.
18. Id. at 357.
19. *Sterzing* v. *Ft. Bend Independent School District,* 376 F.Supp. 657 (S.D. Tex. 1972).
20. *Kingsville Independent School District* v. *Cooper,* 611 F.2d 1109 (5th Cir. 1980).
21. *Clark* v. *Holmes,* 474 F.2d 928 (7th Cir. 1972), cert, denied 411 U.S. 972 (1973).
22. *Brubaker* v. *Board of Education, School District 149, Cook County, Illinois,* 502 F.2d 973 (7th Cir. 1974).
23. Id. at 976. In a dissenting opinion, Judge Fairchild acknowledged that school authorities probably had the right to prohibit the "Woodstock" brochures for eighth graders. However, he did not believe that the material was so irrelevant

or offensive that teachers should be fired for electing to use it—especially since most of it simply consisted of factual accounts of the festival.

24. *Simon* v. *Jefferson Davis Parish School Board*, 289 So.2d 511 (La. 1974).

25. *Birdwell* v. *Hazelwood School District*, 491 F.2d 490 (8th Cir. 1974).

26. *Harris* v. *Mechanicville Central School District*, 408 N.Y.S.2d 384 (1978).

27. *La Rocca* v. *Board of Education of Rye City School District*, 406 N.Y.S.2d 348 (1978).

28. *Celestine* v. *Lafayette Parish School Board*, 284 So.2d 650 (La. 1973).

29. *Jergeson* v. *Board of Trustees of School District No. 7*, 476 P.2d 481 (Wyo. 1970).

30. *Harris* v. *Mechanicville*, 382 N.Y.S.2d 251 (1976).

Chapter 6
The Teacher's Private Life

There are certain professions which impose upon persons
attracted to them, responsibilities and limitations on freedom
of action which do not exist in regard to other callings. Public
officials such as judges, policemen and school teachers fall into
such a category.
—*Board of Trustees* v. *Stubblefield*[1]

The private conduct of a man, who is also a teacher, is a proper
concern to those who employ him only to the extent it mars
him as a teacher. . . . Where his professional achievement is
unaffected, where the school community is placed in no
jeopardy, his private acts are his own business and may not be
the basis of discipline.
—*Jarvella* v. *Willoughby* —*Eastlake City School District*[2]

"Today's morals," wrote the California Supreme Court, "may be tomorrow's ancient and absurd customs."[3] Morals certainly vary according to place and time, yet few parents would willingly have their children taught by teachers they consider immoral. And if parents expect teachers to serve as adult models for their children, should a school board have the right to dismiss a teacher who violates the community's moral standards? Moreover, if a teacher holds a special position of trust and responsibility, can parents and administrators expect a higher standard of personal conduct from teachers than the law requires of the average citizen?

These are some of the issues raised in the cases presented in this chapter. They lie on the frontier of public controversy, involving teachers who have violated community norms regarding sexual activity, use of marijuana, excessive consumption of alcohol, and obscene language. The conflicts arise out of a clash of rights: Teachers assert that their private lives are their own business, whereas school boards argue that teachers are models for their students and must meet the moral standards set by the community.

The Sarac Case: Is Homosexuality Immoral?[4]

In 1962 Thomas Sarac was arrested and charged with making a "homosexual advance" to L. A. Bowers at a public beach in the city of Long Beach, California.[5] Sarac was a secondary school teacher, Bowers a police officer. The arrest resulted in Sarac's conviction for disorderly conduct. Sarac was then accused of being unfit for service in the public school system because of his conduct on the beach, the criminal proceedings against him, and Bower's testimony that Sarac admitted to "a homosexual problem since he was 20 years old."

As a result, the state board of education revoked Sarac's secondary school teaching credential. Sarac went to court and argued that the board had acted unconstitutionally "because it failed to establish any rational connection between the homosexual conduct on the beach . . . and immorality and unprofessional conduct as a teacher."

The court, however, did not find Sarac's argument persuasive. It wrote:

> Homosexual behavior has long been contrary and abhorrent to the social mores and moral standards of the people of California. . . . It is clearly, therefore, immoral conduct within the meaning of [the] Education Code.[6]

In view of Sarac's duty to teach his students the principles of morality and his necessarily close association with children, the court found "a rational connection between his homosexual conduct on the beach and the consequent action of respondent [Board of Education] in revoking his secondary teaching credential on the statutory grounds of immoral and unprofessional conduct and evident unfitness for service in the public school system of this State."

The Morrison Case: Teaching and Homosexuality Reconsidered[7]

Marc Morrison was another California teacher who engaged in homosexual activity that became public and resulted in the revocation of his teaching credentials. Morrison also took his case to court, but for him the results were different from Sarac's.

Morrison had been a public school teacher for a number of years before becoming friendly with Fred Schneringer, another teacher. As a result of this friendship, the two men engaged in a physical homosexual relationship during a one-week period. About 12 months later

Schneringer reported the incident to Morrison's superintendent; this led Morrison to resign. More than a year later the Board of Education conducted a hearing concerning the revocation of Morrison's life diploma, which qualified him as a secondary school teacher in California. Morrison admitted that he had engaged in homosexual acts with Schneringer in his apartment. He also stated that he did not regard his conduct as immoral. He testified, however, that he had engaged in no other homosexual acts before or after this single incident. There was no evidence presented to contradict Morrison's testimony. The board concluded that the incident with Schneringer constituted immoral and unprofessional conduct that warranted revocation of Morrison's life diploma. But Morrison went to court to set aside the board's action.

Questions to Consider

1. What arguments would you use to support the board's action? To support Morrison's case for reinstatement?
2. What constitutes immoral conduct that would justify revoking a teacher's license? Any immoral conduct? Any sexual immorality? Any immoral conduct that might affect his teaching?

THE CASE AGAINST MORRISON
The board used the following arguments to support its action:

A teacher stands *in loco parentis.* His students look up to him as the person taking the place of their parents during school hours and as an example of good conduct.

State law requires all teachers "to endeavor to impress upon the minds of the pupils the principles of morality."

Morrison was a potential danger to his students not only because of his immoral acts, which he admitted, but also because he did not regard such acts as immoral.

Homosexual behavior is contrary to our moral standards and constitutes unprofessional conduct, which need not be limited to classroom misconduct or misconduct with children.

THE OPINION OF THE COURT
Despite the arguments of the board of education, a majority of the California Supreme Court ruled in favor of Morrison for the following reasons:

It is dangerous to allow the terms *immoral* and *unprofessional* to be broadly interpreted. To many people, "immoral conduct" includes laziness, gluttony, selfishness, and cowardice. To others, "unprofessional conduct" for teachers includes signing petitions, opposing majority opinions, and drinking alcoholic beverages. Therefore, unless these terms are carefully and narrowly interpreted, they could be applied to most teachers in the state.

The Board of Education should not be empowered to dismiss any teacher whose personal, private conduct incurs its disapproval. A teacher's behavior should disqualify him only when it is clearly related to his effectiveness in his job. When his job as a teacher is not affected, his private behavior is his own business and should not form a basis for discipline.

The court therefore stated that the board cannot abstractly characterize Morrision's conduct in this case as "immoral" or "unprofessional" unless that conduct implies that he is unfit to teach. But how can a Board of Education determine whether a teacher's behavior indicates his fitness to teach? In making this determination the court suggested that the board consider the circumstances surrounding the case.

In this instance there was no evidence to show that Morrison's conduct had affected his performance as a teacher. "There was not the slightest suggestion that he had ever attempted, sought or even considered any form of physical or otherwise improper relationship with any student. Furthermore, there was no evidence that Morrison failed to teach his students the principles of morality required by law or that the incident with Schneringer affected his relationship with his co-workers."

For a school board to conclude that a teacher's retention in the profession presents a danger to students or fellow teachers, its conclusion must be supported by evidence. In this case the court ruled that the board had not presented adequate evidence to support its decision to revoke Morrison's life diploma.

The board relied heavily on the *Sarac* case and argued that its reasoning should apply to Morrison. But most of the justices disagreed. Thus, Justice Tobriner wrote on behalf of the majority, "The facts in *Sarac* are clearly distinguishable from the instant case; the teacher disciplined in that case had pleaded guilty to a criminal charge of disorderly conduct arising from his homosexual advances toward a police officer at a public beach; and the teacher admitted a recent history of homosexual activities." This was not the case with Morrison.

In sum, the California Supreme Court's decision does not mean that homosexuals must be permitted to teach in the public schools. It does mean that in California:

An individual can be removed from the teaching profession only upon a showing that his retention in the profession poses a significant danger of harm to either students, school employees, or others who might be affected by his actions as a teacher.[8]

Additional Questions

1. Do you think the *Morrison* decision would have been different if Morrison's single homosexual incident had been with a consenting high school senior? Why or why not?
2. Would you feel differently about the *Morrison* case if Morrison had admitted *frequent* homosexual activity with consenting adults in private?
3. Should a different standard be applied to heterosexual activity? Do you think a male teacher should have his teaching credential revoked for making a sexual advance (without force) toward a woman on a public beach?
4. A dissenting opinion indicated that Morrison's "unrepentent" attitude toward his homosexual conduct made him a greater danger as a classroom teacher. Do you agree?
5. What, if any, private conduct that the majority of the community considers immoral would justify a school board in dismissing a teacher?
6. Do laws that encourage school boards to fire teachers for immoral conduct promote good education? Is it possible that "immorality laws" are unconstitutional?

Commenting on Morrison's contention that a ban on immoral conduct might conflict with a constitutionally protected right to privacy, Justice Tobriner wrote:

> An unqualified proscription against immoral conduct would raise serious constitutional problems. Conscientious school officials concerned with enforcing such a broad provision might be inclined to probe into the private life of each and every teacher, no matter how exemplary his classroom conduct. Such prying might all too readily lead school officials to search for "telltale signs" of immorality in violation of the teacher's constitutional rights.[9]

Justice Tobriner's concern about investigating teachers' private lives and protecting their privacy are issues confronted in the following cases.

The Andrews Case: Disqualifying Unwed Mothers[10]

Fearing that the presence of teachers with illegitimate children would endanger his school's reputation, a Mississippi superintendent established a rule that "parenthood of an illegitimate child would automatically disqualify an individual" from employment with the school system. Pursuant to this policy school officials began investigating the backgrounds of present and prospective teachers. As a result, the district declined to hire one teacher and failed to renew the contract of another. Officials offered several reasons for their policy: Unwed parenthood is proof of immoral conduct, unwed parents are improper role models for students, and such parents contribute to the problem of student pregnancy.

In 1975 a federal appeals court rejected these reasons. First, Judge Simpson indicated that "present immorality" does not necessarily follow from unwed parenthood. Under the superintendent's policy, "a person could live an impeccable life yet be barred as unfit for employment for an event . . . occurring at any time in the past." The policy "equates the single fact of illegitimate birth with irredeemable moral disease. Such a presumption is not only patently absurd, it is mischievous and prejudicial, requiring those who administer the policy to 'investigate' the parental status of school employees and prospective applicants. Where no stigma may have existed before, such inquisitions by overzealous officialdom can rapidly create it."

The court also rejected the notion that unwed parents would be improper models. The judge doubted that students would seek information about the private family life of teachers and then try to emulate them. Moreover, the school district offered no evidence, beyond speculation, that the presence of unwed parents in school contributed to student pregnancy. Finally, the court noted that "unwed mothers only, not unwed fathers" were penalized by the policy. For these reasons, Judge Simpson ruled that the policy violates the constitutional right to equal protection and due process.

The Sullivan Case: An Evolving Right[11]

Kathleen Sullivan was an elementary teacher in a small, rural South Dakota town when a male friend came to live with her. When parents, students, and school board members learned that the couple was not married, Sullivan's principal advised her to discontinue her living arrangement; otherwise it would jeopardize her job. Sullivan replied that whom she lived with was her personal business and not a school matter. When no compromise could be worked out, Sullivan was fired.

The board concluded that her conduct violated local mores, was a "bad example" for her students, and that community disapproval would prevent her from getting parental cooperation and support. Sullivan claimed that her dismissal violated her rights to privacy and freedom of association, and she sued the board for damages.

Although the court noted that the case posed "very difficult constitutional issues," it ruled in favor of the school board. First, it indicated that the scope and limits of the "newly evolving constitutional right to privacy" is not clear. Courts have not yet determined whether "the right of a couple to live together without benefit of matrimony" falls within the scope of such a right. Second, even if the Constitution does protect Sullivan's lifestyle, this does not necessarily resolve the case. A court would still have to balance the teacher's privacy interests against the board's legitimate interests in promoting the education of its students. The court concluded that board members could not be held liable for violating Sullivan's "clearly established constitutional rights" because no such right had clearly been established.

The Thompson Case: Insufficient Evidence[12]

Diane Thompson had been a Missouri elementary teacher for ten years when her boyfriend Cal moved in with her in 1979. Two months later, school officials informed Diane that she could either resign (in which case she would be given a favorable recommendation) or be fired (and have her teaching credential taken away). Four days later she married Cal and told school officials of her marriage. Nevertheless, the next day the school board suspended her on grounds of immorality. The board explained that several parents objected to Diane teaching their children and that publicity about her cohabitation had undermined her effectiveness. However, a federal court disagreed.

In this 1980 decision, the judge wrote: "The mere fact that some parents may have an adverse attitude towards plaintiff is not sufficient evidence in the court's view to demonstrate that an attitude would prevail *in the classroom* that would undermine the learning environment." The court noted that before she was fired, most people in the community were unaware that Diane was cohabiting with Cal. Therefore the court felt it was unfair of the board to publicize Diane's conduct through its actions and then conclude that she was unfit "based upon its speculation of unfavorable community reaction" to Diane's prior conduct that was of brief duration and was terminated by getting married. The court distinguished this case from Sullivan who lived in a home furnished by the school that was near the school and frequently visited by students. In contrast to Diane's situation, over 140 residents of Sullivan's community petitioned for her dismissal, thereby indicating widespread community hostility.

The Acanfora Case: Free Speech and Misrepresentation[13]

When Joseph Acanfora filled out his application for a teaching position in Maryland's Montgomery County Schools, he intentionally failed to indicate that he had been a member of the Homophiles, an organization that promoted public understanding of homosexuality. He omitted this information because he thought it would decrease his chances for employment. Acanfora was hired as a junior high school science teacher. When school officials learned that he was a homosexual, they transferred him to a nonteaching position. Following his transfer, Acanfora granted several press and television interviews concerning the difficulties that homosexuals encounter. School officials felt these interviews "exhibited an indifference to the bounds of propriety governing the behavior of teachers." As a result of these events, Acanfora's contract was not renewed, and he took his case to court.

A federal appeals court considered whether Acanfora could be penalized for either his media interviews or his false application. Concerning his interviews, Judge Butzner found that he sought community acceptance of homosexuality but did not advocate it, that he stressed he would not discuss sexuality with his students, and that the interviews did not disrupt the school or impair his capacity as a teacher. Therefore, the court held that these press, radio, and television interviews were protected by the First Amendment and did not justify the nonrenewal of his contract.

However, the court ruled differently about Acanfora's conscious omission from his teaching application of belonging to the Homophiles. The court acknowledged that Acanfora may have had a right to challenge some of the questions on the school application. Nevertheless, Judge Butzner rejected the notion that his misrepresentations should be ignored. "Acanfora wrongfully certified that his application was accurate to the best of his knowledge when he knew that it contained a significant omission," wrote the court. The judge noted that Acanfora "purposely misled the school officials so he could circumvent, not challenge, what he considered to be their unconstitutional employment practices." The court concluded that when a citizen "undertakes to mislead" school officials by false statements, he cannot then assert that the school operation he was trying to mislead is unconstitutional.

The Pettit Case: Lacking Normal Prudence[14]

Elizabeth Pettit taught mentally retarded children in California's elementary schools for 13 years. She was also a member of "The Swingers," a Los Angeles club that promoted diverse sexual activities among members. Pettit was arrested and fined after an undercover policeman attended a club party at a private residence and observed that the teacher engaged in sexual activity with three different men. (In addition, Pettit and her husband had previously appeared on television programs in disguises and discussed nonconventional sexual behavior.) After her arrest, her teaching credential was revoked on grounds of moral turpitude based on testimony from the policeman and three school superintendents who testified that Pettit's conduct "disclosed her unfitness to teach."

Because of her long record of consistent service and evidence that she would not repeat her indiscretions, Pettit asked the court to restore her teaching credential. She argued that the *Morrison* ruling should support her position. But the California Supreme Court disagreed.

The court distinguished this case from *Morrison*. In *Morrison*, the board acted without sufficent evidence, whereas in this case, the board

heard expert testimony asserting Pettit's unfitness to teach. More important, Morrison's conduct "occurred entirely in private," whereas Pettit's
indiscretions took place in the semipublic atmosphere of a club party, were
witnessed by several strangers, and involved three different partners. Her
performance, wrote Justice Burke, reflected "a total lack of concern for
privacy, decorum, or preservation of her dignity and reputation" and
indicated "a serious defect of moral character, normal prudence and good
common sense." A further indication that Pettit lacked that "minimum
regard for propriety expected of a public school teacher" is disclosed by her
television appearances that gave notoriety to her unorthodox sexual views.

In a strong dissenting opinion, Justice Tobriner criticized the majority
for holding teachers to a higher standard of conduct than other professionals. Will a skilled attorney be disbarred or a surgeon lose his license for
committing a consensual sexual act that deviated from traditional norms?
"The danger of the majority's doctrine becomes especially onerous," wrote
the justice, "when we know that a large proportion of the younger
generation do engage in unorthodox sexual activities deemed anathema by
some members of the older generation." Will we frustrate productive
careers by castigating conduct that is widely practiced by some but is
regarded by judges as "immoral"? The dissent concluded that the
commission of a consensual sex act "clandestinely observed by means of a
surreptitious intrusion" not disclosed to students or to teachers and not
adversely affecting Pettit's teaching should not have supported revocation
of her license "even though the act is labelled 'criminal' on the books."

The Brennan Case: Teachers and Marijuana[15]

Barnet Brennan was the teaching principal of a California school when
one of her friends was arrested and convicted for possessing marijuana.
Her friend argued that the laws making the possession and use of
marijuana illegal were unconstitutional. Brennan agreed. She therefore
executed an affidavit in support of her friend that said, in part:

> Marijuana is not harmful to my knowledge, because I have been using it since
> 1949 almost daily, with only beneficial results. . . . I have been a teacher for 30
> years and at present am the teaching principal of a public school. During
> school hours I never feel the need of using *cannabis sativa* [i.e., marijuana],
> however, each recess is eagerly awaited for smoking tobacco cigarettes. I do
> not consider marijuana a habit forming drug, but to me nicotine is . . . .[16]

Brennan urged the court "to set aside these unconstitutional laws"
depicting marijuana as addictive and harmful, and "setting forth harsh and
cruel penalties for its possession, sale and use."

Her affidavit immediately attracted publicity, and her students soon
learned of its content. As a result, the board of the school district notified
Brennan that she would not be reemployed. Since she believed her

dismissal was unconstitutional, she went to court to compel the board to reemploy her. The court pointed out that Brennan's sworn statement was an admission that she had for many years used marijuana in defiance of state law. She did not merely advocate change of the law but declared her belief that violation of the law was appropriate, despite the fact that it might constitute commission of a felony. And although it was not Brennan's intention that her affidavit should receive wide publicity, it certainly was reasonable to anticipate that this would happen.

Brennan argued that she should not be penalized when there was no evidence that her statement had a negative effect on students. The court responded that the school board acted so promptly after learning of the affidavit that there was little time for any effect to develop. Here, said the court, there was "competent evidence" on the "likely" effect of Brennan's conduct on the students. One witness testified, "I would be inclined to believe that the pupil would be thinking 'If my teacher can gain her ends by breaking the law, then I, too, can gain my ends by breaking the law!' " Although witnesses were not unanimous, the court found there was adequate evidence to support a finding of unfitness to teach.

The court recognized that Brennan's desire to express disapproval of a state law does not render her unfit to teach. But the point in this case, said the court, is that Brennan,

> . . . has intentionally and knowingly violated the law, because she does not personally agree with that law, and then publicly declared that fact in such a way that it would reach and affect her pupils. It is not the affidavit which is the basis of this action against appellant [Brennan]. The affidavit is merely evidence of appellant's competence or lack of competence to teach.[17]

Would the court have ruled differently if Brennan had publicly filed her affidavit opposing marijuana laws but said nothing about using marijuana? Apparently it would have. The court commented that another teacher in Brennan's school had filed an affidavit in the same criminal case and had also advocated a change in the laws regulating marijuana, which he felt were unconstitutional. The other teacher, however, "did not say he ever used marijuana." The court noted with approval that the board not only took no action against the other teacher because of his affidavit but even promoted him to replace Brennan.

In a later California case, a state appeals court ruled that a teacher could not be discharged after being convicted for cultivating a marijuana plant. This ruling resulted because testimony indicated that the teacher would probably not repeat his crime, that his return to the classroom would not have a negative effect on the school, and that firing him for possessing a single marijuana plant would be an "excessive reaction." Moreover, the court noted that "marijuana related offenses need not necessarily always be crimes of moral turpitude . . . measured by the morals of our day."[18]

RELATIONS WITH STUDENTS

Before upholding teacher dismissals on grounds of immoral or unprofessional conduct, courts usually require some direct evidence that the controversial conduct interferes with teaching effectiveness. Should the same evidence be required when the alleged immoral behavior relates to students? As the following cases indicate, courts tend to be more strict in this area.

The Stubblefield Case: Unfitness to Teach[19]

Joseph Stubblefield was a certified teacher in a California public junior college. After teaching a class one night, he drove a female student to a dark street near the college and parked. A little later a Los Angeles County deputy sheriff patroling the area spotted the teacher's automobile. Because he could see no occupants, the deputy thought it was abandoned. He shined his flashlight into the car and found Stubblefield apparently involved in a sexual relationship.[20] When he recognized that the person with the flashlight was a deputy sheriff, Stubblefield shouted, "Get the hell away from me you dirty cop." He then knocked the deputy to the ground with his car door and quickly drove away. The deputy chased him at speeds of 80 to 100 miles per hour until Stubblefield's car finally pulled over.

Because of these events, Stubblefield was dismissed on grounds of immoral conduct and unfitness to teach. Stubblefield, however, contended that the *Morrison* case should prohibit his discharge because the evidence against him concerned only his out of school conduct and did not demonstrate that this conduct affected his teaching.

Questions to Consider

1. Should a male teacher be dismissed because of a single, private sexual relationship with a consenting junior college student? What about a consenting high school senior?
2. Should a teacher be dismissed for such a relationship only if it affects his classroom teaching?
3. If Stubblefield had been polite to the deputy, would the case for dismissing him have been substantially weakened?
4. Does the reasoning of the *Morrison* case apply here? Or can this case be distinguished from *Morrison?*

THE OPINION OF THE COURT

The California Court of Appeals ruled that Stubblefield's actions constituted immoral conduct indicating unfitness to teach. The court pointed out that in the public school system a teacher is regarded as a person whose words and actions are likely to be followed by his students. Therefore, responsible conduct by a teacher should exclude "meretricious relationships with his students" and assaults on duly constituted authorities.

The clear import of the *Morrison* decision, said the Court, is that a teacher may be discharged on evidence that his behavior indicates potential for misconduct with a student or has gained such notoriety that his on-campus activities would be impaired. The fact that Stubblefield and his companion were easily discovered "demonstrates the tenuous security from public attention provided by the front seat" of an automobile. Stubblefield's assault upon the officer and attempt to escape at high speeds ultimately insured further public attention. Finally, "unfitness to teach," in the sense that Stubblefield was more likely than the average man to engage in improper conduct with a student, "can be inferred from the very conduct itself." The evidence that was lacking in *Morrison* "was overtly manifested here." In conclusion, the Court wrote:

> The integrity of the educational system under which teachers wield considerable power in the grading of students and the granting or withholding of certificates and diplomas is clearly threatened when teachers become involved in relationships with students such as is indicated by the conduct here.[21]

The Jarvella Case: Use of Vulgar Language[22]

A dedicated and enthusiastic high school teacher from Ohio named Jarvella was fired for "immorality" because he wrote two private letters to a former student, Ben Nicholas, who had graduated from high school the previous year.

Nicholas' mother found the letters among his personal effects. Because she was angered by the language in the letters, she turned them over to the police department. Local newspapers learned of the letters and wrote several stories about them, and the prosecuting attorney was quoted as saying that he considered them hard-core obscenity and that "it seemed obvious that a person who would write letters of this kind is not fit to be a school teacher." Subsequently the school board terminated Jarvella's contract on the ground of "immorality." Jarvella went to court to appeal the board's decision.

After a hearing, Judge Simmons ruled in Jarvella's favor. Concerning the letters the judge wrote: "They contain language which many adults would find gross, vulgar, and offensive and which some 18 year old males would find unsurprising and fairly routine."

The term *immorality*, said Judge Simmons, must refer not to "immoral conduct" in the abstract but to that which is "hostile to the welfare of the school community." The private writings of a teacher not contrary to that welfare "are absolutely immaterial" and cannot be used to justify discharging the teacher.

THE TEACHER'S PRIVATE LIFE   125

There was no evidence that the writing of these letters adversely affected the welfare of the schools—except after public disclosure. And this, wrote Judge Simmons, "was the result, not of any misconduct on [Jarvella's] part, but of misconduct on the part of others. . . ."

The court concluded that a teacher's private conduct is a proper concern of his employer only when it affects him as a teacher; "his private acts are his own business and may not be the basis of discipline" so long as his professional achievement is not affected.

The Urso Case: Discussing Sex[23]

A 1978 Pennsylvania case involved a teacher who was dismissed on grounds of immorality because of two separate incidents involving the proposed "spanking" of two of his female high school students that each perceived as sexual advances. The teacher admitted that he had sexual fantasies about spanking girls and that he did not know whether he could control his fantasies in the future. Nevertheless, the teacher claimed that since his *conduct* was not immoral, he should not be penalized for discussing the proposal or for his fantasies.

The court acknowledged that a teacher "cannot be found guilty of immorality based solely on his admitted fantasies." However, the discussion of sexual subjects is a matter of particular sensitivity in our society. "Where teachers engage in such discussions with children, the problem is exacerbated because of the significant influence teachers exert." When such discussions occur outside the curricular setting, a school board can reasonably conclude that the conduct is improper. Such a conclusion, wrote the court, is an adequate basis for dismissing a teacher "on the grounds that his conduct offended the moral standards of the community and set a bad example to the youth under his charge."

RELATED CASES
A number of other teachers have been dismissed for using "inappropriate" language or for talking with their students about sex in school. In Florida, for example, a court upheld the firing of a high school instructor for immorality because he talked about virginity and premarital sex during a band class. According to the judge, teachers "should not be permitted to so risquély discuss sex problems in our teenage mixed classes as to cause embarrassment to the children or to involve in them other feelings not incident to the courses."[24] Similarly, a Wisconsin court upheld the dismissal of a Milwaukee high school speech teacher who discussed houses of prostitution, told stories about intercourse with a cow, and seemed to approve of premarital sex.[25] And in Pennsylvania a tenured language teacher was dismissed for immoral conduct after he called a 14-year-old student a "slut" and implied that she was a prostitute. In upholding this

action, a state court wrote that the teacher's behavior reflected "totally inappropriate language and conduct in the context of the teacher-student relationship."[26]

The Denton Case: Inherently Harmful Conduct[27]

Gary Denton was a Washington teacher who began dating a high school student after obtaining permission from her parents. As a result of their relationship, the student became pregnant and Denton was discharged when he admitted being the father. Because his girlfriend was not a student at his school and because there was no evidence that their relationship affected his teaching, Denton claimed his discharge was improper. But a state appeals court disagreed.

Although Judge Pearson acknowledged that "immorality" is not a ground for discharge without evidence of unfitness to teach, the court declined to set such a requirement when the sexual misconduct "directly involves a teacher and a minor student." The court ruled that in such a situation a school board may properly conclude that "the conduct is inherently harmful to the teacher-student relation, and thus to the school district."

The Weissman Case: Positive or Sordid?[28]

A popular, "nontraditional" Colorado teacher was fired because of his behavior on a four-day field trip. On the trip he engaged in what he called "horseplay" in the back of a van with several female high school students. This consisted of tickling them all over their bodies and in carrying on a "vulgar" and sexually "suggestive" dialogue. The teacher viewed his behavior as a "positive educational experience" and as "a situational response," an attempt to act his "natural self to gain rapport" with his students. In contrast, the court viewed his conduct as "sordid," found it had "no legitimate professional purpose," and upheld his dismissal.

IS ILLEGAL CONDUCT IMMORAL?

In past decades teachers were automatically denied employment if they had any criminal record, and they were quickly dismissed if they were convicted of a crime. Today these policies and practices are being reexamined by educators and judges.

Questions to Consider

1. Would you favor dismissing teachers for illegal rather than immoral conduct?
2. Should schools be able to dismiss teachers for *any* illegal conduct? Or

should teachers be dismissed only for serious crimes? Or for crimes involving "moral turpitude?"

3. Does it make any difference when or where the crime was committed or against whom? Or how much publicity it received?

Theft and Assault: The Skripchuk Case[29]

In 1975 Leon Skripchuk was named "outstanding industrial arts teacher" in the state of Delaware. During that year he also pleaded guilty to charges of theft and aggravated assault with a gun. This led to his dismissal for immorality. Since this was the only blemish in his 20-year teaching career, he went to court to block his dismissal.

Despite experts who testified that "it is most unlikely" that Skripchuk would ever again be involved in similar criminal conduct, the judge sustained his dismissal. The Delaware court ruled that the teacher's actions were "unquestionably immoral." Moreover, school officials believed that these criminal convictions, which received widespread local publicity, would make parents fearful and would impair his effectiveness as a teacher. Therefore, the court concluded that Skripchuk's termination was not arbitrary but was a reasonable exercise of discretion.*

Driving While Intoxicated: The Watson Case[30]

Joseph Watson was a California teacher who had been convicted of six offenses involving the use of alcohol during the ten years preceding his application for a general secondary diploma.[31] The state Board of Education denied Watson's application. Since Watson believed he was a good teacher, he took his case to court. Relying on the *Morrison* ruling, Watson argued that because there was no evidence showing that his convictions affected his classroom performance, the action of the board should be reversed.

The court acknowledged that the only evidence against Watson was his convictions involving consumption of alcohol. Nevertheless, it held that this amply demonstrated his unfitness to teach for the following reasons:

First, one of the main concerns of parents, administrators, and legislators is "the effect of the use and overindulgence in alcohol on their youngsters." Since the court found that Watson's use of alcohol had gotten entirely out of his control, he could not have "the proper concerned attitude necessary for successfully counseling and directing young students away from the harmful effects of alcohol."

Second, Watson's conduct was public. Being arrested as a "public

---

*In a recent related case, a Pennsylvania court upheld the dismissal of a teacher for immorality after she admitted engaging in shoplifting at a local supermarket. *Lesley* v. *Oxford Area School District*, 420 A.2d 764 (Pa. 1980).

drunk" or for driving under the influence of alcohol did not create in Watson "the example young people at an impressionable age need." In contrast to Morrison, whose conduct received no publicity before the board's action, Watson had persistently and publicly violated important community values and jeopardized the welfare of his students and the public.

Finally, Watson's apparent disregard for law and order was a serious concern. The court emphasized that an important part of education is the teaching "by example as well as precept of obedience to properly constituted authority." By contrast, Watson's behavior clearly indicated that he is unfit to teach and work with young people. "I don't know," said the trial judge, "what better evidence there could be of immorality than a series of criminal convictions."

On the other hand, the Montana Supreme Court ruled that convictions for driving while intoxicated were not enough to discharge a teacher for immorality. In overruling school authorities, the court held that "violations for driving under the influence of intoxicating liquor" are not in themselves "tantamount to immorality." To sustain the dismissal of such a teacher, the court indicated that school officials would have to present evidence indicating that the convictions would affect the teacher's professional performance.[32]

Dismissal for Illegal Conduct: The Case of Jack M[33]

In 1977 the liberal California Supreme Court considered the questions of when it is legitimate to dismiss teachers for illegal conduct and when it is reasonable to fear that students might emulate such conduct. In answer, the court wrote that dismissal for illegal conduct is reasonable "only under two conditions." First, the teacher's conduct must be "sufficiently notorious" that students know or are likely to learn of it. Second, "the teacher must continue to model his past conduct." The court went on to add the following provocative comment:

> The teacher who committed an indiscretion, paid the penalty, and now seeks to discourage his students from committing similar acts may well be a more effective supporter of legal and moral standards than the one who has never been found to violate those standards. Since these conditions will vary from case to case, proof that one has at some past time committed a crime should not in itself suffice to demonstrate that he is not now and never will be a suitable behavior model for his students.

Factors to Consider: The Lujan Case[34]

Vidal Lujan was an exceptionally able teacher of retarded children in Sunnyvale, California. During a 1976 teachers' strike, while students were being taught by substitutes, he became upset and phoned a false bomb report to the police. At the time he believed that a visual count of the students evacuated from the school would challenge "the incorrect attendance figures" announced by the district and thereby cause the district to "negotiate more earnestly" and shorten the strike. He later acknowledged that his action was "unjustifiable, shameful, and immoral," and was convicted of a misdemeanor and served seven days in prison for "false report of planting a bomb." These events received wide publicity, and the district tried to fire Lujan for immoral conduct. A state court, however, ruled in his favor.

The court noted that a decision on the fitness of a teacher must be based on "*all* the evidence" and "may not consider a single act alone, reprehensible as it may be." Among the factors that should be considered are (1) the likelihood of recurrence of the questioned conduct; (2) the extenuating or aggravating circumstances; (3) the effect of notoriety and publicity; (4) impairment of teachers' and students' relationships; (5) disruption of the educational process; (6) motive; and (7) proximity or remoteness in time of conduct.

The trial court considered each factor and found that Lujan had the continued support of the community, students, and teachers; he maintained good classroom performance after the incident; his teaching effectiveness was not impaired in spite of the publicity; he "is not a present threat of harm" to students or teachers; his continued presence in the school was not disruptive; and the possibility of repetition was extremely remote. On the basis of this evidence, the court ruled that "Lujan's unfitness to teach was not demonstrated" by the school district. In 1980 an appeals court "reluctantly" upheld this ruling because it felt bound by the California Supreme Court's decisions in the *Morrison* and *Jack M.* cases, which prohibited firing teachers solely for a single criminal act.

NOTE: An increasing number of courts are considering a variety of factors (such as the seven listed in *Lujan*) in assessing whether a teacher deserves to be fired for illegal or immoral conduct.* But it is uncertain whether courts in other states would prohibit the dismissal of a teacher under the circumstances of this case.

THE TREND OF DECISION

After the 1969 *Morrison* decision, many teachers' rights advocates hoped that courts would soon rule that schools could not discriminate against competent teachers because of their sexual preferences and that statutes allowing teachers to be dismissed for immorality would be held unconstitutional. In 1973 the case of *Burton* v. *Cascade School District* seemed to support these hopes.

*A 1980 federal opinion indicates that courts are in agreement on eight similar factors "to be considered in determining if a teacher's immoral conduct renders her unfit to teach." *Thompson* v. *Southwest School District*, 483 F.Supp. 1170 (W.D. Mo. 1980).

The Burton Case[35]

After Peggy Burton acknowledged that she was a "practicing homosexual," she was dismissed as a high school teacher on grounds of immoral conduct. Her dismissal was pursuant to an Oregon statute that empowered school boards to dismiss teachers for "immorality." But a federal judge declared the statute "unconstitutionally vague." Because the statute did not define immorality and because it means different things to different people, "its definition depends on the idiosyncracies of the individual board members." It may be applied so broadly, wrote Judge Solomon, "that every teacher in the state could be subject to discipline." A statute so broad makes board members "the arbiters of morality for the entire community." In so doing, "it subjects the livelihood of every teacher in the state to the irrationality and irregularity of such judgments." Judge Solomon concluded that the statute is unconstitutionally vague because (1) it fails to give warning of what conduct is prohibited; (2) it permits erratic and prejudicial exercise of authority; and (3) it does not require a connection between the alleged conduct and teaching.

Thus *Burton* protected a practicing homosexual and declared a state immorality statute unconstitutional. Despite Judge Solomon's decision, most courts have not gone this far. The following cases illustrate the way many judges tend to rule on these issues.

The Kilpatrick Case[36]

In 1976 school officials in Montgomery County, Alabama, obtained evidence that one of their teachers, Howard Kilpatrick, made "sexual advances towards female students." As a result of this behavior, he was discharged because of immoral conduct. The teacher, as in *Burton*, claimed that the term *immoral conduct* was unconstitutionally vague, overbroad, and could include innocuous activity that some school officials considered improper. The court acknowledged that the "ultimate reach of the term immorality" was not clear. In this case, however, Judge Johnson did not feel that there was any problem about vagueness. Any teacher, wrote the judge, could be "expected to know" that actions such as these "cannot be condoned in the classroom setting." The court concluded that a person to whom a rule or statute may be constitutionally applied cannot challenge the law on the ground that "it may conceivably be applied unconstitutionally to others, in other situations not before the court."

The Gaylord Case[37]

James Gaylord had been an excellent high school teacher in Tacoma, Washington, for over 12 years when he was discharged for immorality after he became known as a homosexual. His sexual status was reported to his principal after he counseled a former student about homosexual problems. Gaylord did not deny that he was a homosexual, but he never tried to flaunt it. Therefore, he felt his discharge was grossly unfair and at his trial said: "I quite frankly find it rather galling to have sat through . . . this trial and hear administrators say that. . . . I've been a very good teacher, and yet to be without a job, particularly when I see other people who still hold their jobs who haven't read a book or turned out a new lesson plan, or come up with anything creative in years."

Despite extensive testimony concerning his good teaching, a majority of the Supreme Court of the state of Washington upheld his dismissal. In this 1977 decision, Justice Horowitz pointed out that a teacher's efficiency is determined by his relation with students, their parents, fellow teachers, and school administrators. The judge noted that "at least one student" plus several administrators, teachers, and parents publicly objected to Gaylord remaining on the teaching staff and testified that his continued presence on the faculty "would create problems." According to the court, this evidence supported the school's concern that the continued presence of Gaylord after he voluntarily became known as a homosexual would result in confusion, fear, and parental concern that would impair his efficiency as a teacher.

Eight years after *Morrison*, the Washington court wrote that "homosexuality is widely condemned as immoral" and that if Gaylord was retained, students could treat his retention as approval of homosexuality. To say that school officials must wait for "specific overt expression of homosexual conduct before they choose to prevent harm," concluded Judge Horowitz, is to ask them "to take an unacceptable risk."

Teachers Defended

RUMORS, CHURCH, AND APPEARANCE
Annabel Stoddard was a divorced mother who taught in a small, isolated, religiously oriented Wyoming community. Although she was a competent teacher, her contract was not renewed. Despite the official written reasons given for her nonrenewal, the evidence indicated that the real reasons were because of "rumors that she was having an affair," because she did not attend church regularly, and because of her unattractive appearance. In 1979 a federal court found that the school officials were "motivated by constitutionally impermissible reasons" in recommending her nonrenewal and Stoddard was awarded $33,000 in compensatory damages.[38]

OBESITY NOT ENOUGH
Elizabeth Blodgett was a 41-year-old physical education teacher who was not rehired on grounds of "obesity." Her principal explained that because of her weight, she was unable to serve as "a model of health and vigor" or to

demonstrate certain aspects of the physical education program. Blodgett's lawyer argued that obesity should not be a reason for terminating her unless it impaired her ability to teach, and he presented ample evidence to prove that she was a very successful teacher and coach. The court agreed. As to her inability to serve as a "model of health," the court wrote: "Any requirement that the teachers embody all the qualities which they hope to instill in their students will be utterly impossible of fulfillment." As for the contention that the teacher set a bad example that her students might imitate, the court observed that "obesity, by its very nature, does not inspire emulation." Because there was no evidence that Blodgett's weight had a negative effect on her teaching, the court concluded that her termination was arbitrary and ruled in her favor.[39]

THOUGHTS NOT PENALIZED

A Kansas teacher, David Bogart, was charged with possession of marijuana because of drugs his son kept in his room. Although Bogart was cleared of the charge, he was dismissed for "conduct unbecoming an instructor." Before the school committee, Bogart admitted that he considered trying to protect his son and taking the blame himself, although he did neither. A federal court held that this was not a lawful basis for dismissal. "It is fortunate," wrote the court, "the state is not allowed to penalize its citizens for their thoughts, for it would be the rare and either mindless, supine or super-saintly citizen who has not at some time contemplated and then rejected the illegal."[40]

COMMITTING ADULTRY

The Iowa Board of Educational Examiners revoked the teaching certificate of Richard Erb because he had been discovered committing adultery. However, a state court ruled that a person who commits adultery is not automatically unfit to teach. In this case, Erb had an excellent record, and the court found this "isolated incident" was not grounds for revocation when there was no evidence to indicate that it would have an adverse affect on his teaching.[41]

POSSESSION OF MARIJUANA

A California teacher had his teaching credentials revoked solely because he had been convicted of possession of marijuana. The court reversed this action since there was no evidence that the conduct might adversely affect students or teachers, that the conduct received publicity, that it was likely to recur, or that there was any other evidence indicating unfitness to teach.[42]

Beyond the Limits

PUBLICIZING A HOMOSEXUAL MARRIAGE

Librarian James McConnell applied for a license to marry a homosexual friend. The event was widely publicized on television and in several newspaper articles (e.g., "Prospective Newlyweds Really in a Gay Mood" and "Two Homosexuals Plan to Wed"). As a result, McConnell's appointment at the University of Minnesota library was disapproved. Since McConnell was well qualified for the job, his lawyer argued that the decision not to employ him was a clear example of "unreasoning prejudice" and was an unconstitutional deprivation of his right to equal protection of the law. But a U.S. Court of Appeals did not agree.

"This," said the court, "is not a case in which an applicant is excluded from employment because of a desire clandestinely to pursue homosexual conduct." Instead, it is a case in which a prospective employee demands the right "to pursue an activist role in *implementing* his unconventional ideas" concerning homosexuals and thereby "to foist tacit approval of this socially repugnant concept" upon his employer. "We know of no constitutional fiat," concluded the court, "which requires an employer to accede to such extravagant demands."[43]

OBSENITY NOT PROTECTED

A Chicago teacher, Mark Weissbaum, was an editor and part owner of a magazine, *Sasha's World*, that featured suggestive photographs and drawings of naked persons being abused. Weissbaum was fired for conduct unbecoming a teacher after school officials received a copy of the magazine that pictured him with a partially nude woman. The teacher claimed that the school violated his First Amendment rights by dismissing him for his appearance and participation in the publication of the magazine. But a federal district court disagreed. The court found that the dominant theme of *Sasha's World* was a morbid interest in nudity, sex, and sadomasochism, that it depicts sexual conduct in a patently offensive way, and lacks serious literary or artistic value. Since the magazine is legally obscene and not entitled to First Amendment protection, the teacher's dismissal did not violate his constitutional rights.[44]

ENCOURAGING TRUANCY
A Nevada teacher was dismissed for unprofessional conduct after he encouraged his daughters not to attend school and said he would continue to allow them to be truant. In defense, the teacher said that his daughters' conduct was a family matter and that he never advised his students to break the law. A state court acknowledged that the teacher had a right to disagree with the compulsory attendence laws, but it denied he had a right to carry that view into effect. By encouraging his own children to violate the law, his conduct had harmful consequences among students and teachers at his school and throughout the system. The court concluded, "A teacher's influence upon his pupils is not limited to what he says and does in the classroom, and a teacher's right to teach cannot depend solely upon his conduct in the schoolroom."[45]

SEX CHANGE
In New Jersey, a male, tenured music teacher, Paul Monroe Grossman, was dismissed after he underwent "sex-reassignment" surgery that changed his external anatomy to that of a female (called Paula Miriam Grossman). "She" began to live and dress as a woman. Although there was conflicting testimony about Grossman's probable future effectiveness, the court supported her dismissal due to "incapacity" because of "potential psychological harm to students" if the teacher were retained.[46]

STRIP POKER
An Illinois court upheld the dismissal of a Peoria teacher, Stephen Yang, because he was discovered by police partially undressed playing strip poker in his automobile with a female high school student.[47]

Summary and Conclusion

Whether a teacher can be dismissed for conduct that is generally considered immoral or illegal depends on the circumstances of the case. Circumstances that appear to be especially important are: (1) whether the conduct was personal and private, (2) whether it was likely to become public, and (3) whether it involved students.

PERSONAL AND PRIVATE ACTIVITY
Morrison and subsequent cases have held that teachers cannot be dismissed for immoral conduct simply because it is contrary to the mores of a community. Thus, the fact that a teacher has done something that most people regard as immoral (e.g., homosexual activity, smoking marijuana,

excessive drinking, committing adultery, bei[n]
vulgar language) is not by itself sufficient ground[s]
a teacher it must be demonstrated that his "imm[
specific conduct that affects his ability to teach. As long [
as a teacher is not affected, most courts hold that his priv[
own business.

PERSONAL CONDUCT LIKELY TO BECOME PUBLIC
Generally, courts uphold the dismissal of teachers if their immoral conduct
becomes known through the teacher's fault *and* has a negative impact on
the teacher's effectiveness. Examples include publicly admitting to
frequent drug use, encouraging truancy, or living openly as an unmarried
couple in a small, conservative community. However, in cases of notori-
ously illegal or immoral behavior, some courts allow teachers to be
dismissed even without evidence that the conduct impaired their teaching.
In cases such as repeated convictions for drunken driving, conviction for
armed assault, or appearing in a pornographic magazine, judges may say
that the negative impact of such behavior is "apparent."

Whether working as a bartender in a controversial establishment,
being publicly known as a homosexual, committing a crime, or directing a
nudist camp could result in dismissal might depend on a variety of factors
such as the size, sophistication, and values of the community, the notoriety
of the activity, when the activity took place, and whether it occurred in the
community where the teacher is employed.

IMMORAL CONDUCT WITH STUDENTS
In such cases the courts can be expected to be quite strict. Thus, evidence
of a single homosexual relationship between a teacher and a student would
probably be enough to sustain a teacher's dismissal, even if the relationship
had occurred years before and even if no other students, parents, or
teachers knew about it. Similarly, a public school teacher who participated
with his students in smoking marijuana, drinking excessively, or using
obscene language would probably receive no protection from the courts.

In some situations, however, the age and maturity of the students
might make a difference. Hence, the use of vulgar language or perhaps
even a discreet sexual relationship between a junior college teacher and a
19-year-old student might be regarded far differently from such language
or relationship between a junior high school teacher and his students.

EVIDENCE TO SUPPORT DISMISSAL
In the case of personal and private conduct, a teacher cannot be dismissed
unless competent evidence is presented to support the charge of unfitness
to teach. Where personal conduct has become public through the teacher's
intention or indiscretion, evidence of the actual negative effect of his

g an unwed mother, or using
for dismissal. To dismiss
orality" is related to
s his competence
competence
e acts are his

ally not necessary; competent
on the students is probably
uct with a student, there is no
to have any negative effect on
e develops concerning a single
a student, the teacher could be
hough he is an excellent teacher
ent has affected his teaching.

removal of a teacher for immoral
here are no recent opinions of the
and decisions in different states
rtheless, most courts recognize that a
his private actions unless they relate
tions and have a clear impact on his

NOTES

1. 94 Cal. Rptr. 318, 321 (1971).
2. 233 N.E.2d 143, 146 (1967).
3. *Morrison* v. *Board of Education*, 461 P.2d 375 (Cal. 1969).
4. *Sarac* v. *State Board of Education*, 57 Cal. Rptr. 69 (1967).
5. Sarac was specifically charged with having "rubbed, touched, and fondled the private sexual parts of one L. A. Bowers, a person of the masculine sex, with the intent to arouse and excite unnatural sexual desires in said L. A. Bowers." Id. at 71.
6. Id. at 72.
7. *Morrison* v. *State Board of Education*, 461 P.2d 375 (1969).
8. Id. at 391.
9. Id. at 390.
10. *Andrews* v. *Drew Municipal Separate School District*, 507 F.2d 611 (5th Cir. 1975).
11. *Sullivan* v. *Meade Independent School District No. 101*, 530 F.2d 799 (8th Cir. 1976).
12. *Thompson* v. *Southwest School District*, 483 F.Supp. 1170 (W.D. Mo. 1980).
13. *Acanfora* v. *Board of Education of Montgomery County*, 491 F.2d 498 (4th Cir. 1974).
14. *Pettit* v. *State Board of Education*, 513 P.2d 889 (Cal. 1973).
15. *Governing Board* v. *Brennan*, 18 C.A.3d 396 (1971).
16. Id. at 399−400, footnote 1.
17. Id. at 402−403.
18. *Board of Trustees of Santa Maria Joint Union High School District* v. *Judge*, 123 Cal. Rptr. 830 (1975).
19. *Board of Trustees of Compton Junior College District* v. *Stubblefield*, 94 Cal. Rptr. 318 (1971).
20. In the words of the court, the deputy observed that Stubblefield's "pants were

unzipped and lowered from the waist, exposing his penis. The student was nude from the waist up, and her capri pants were unzipped and open at the waist." Id. at 320.

21. Id. at 323.

22. *Jarvella v. Willoughby—East Lake City School District*, 233 N.E.2d 143 (Ohio 1967).

23. *Penn-Delco School District v. Urso*, 382 A.2d 162 (Pa. 1978).

24. *Pyle v. Washington County School Board*, 238 So.2d 121 (Fla. 1970).

25. *State v. Board of School Directors of Milwaukee*, 111 N.W.2d 198 (Wisc. 1961).

26. *Bovino v. Board of School Directors of the Indiana Area School District*, 377 A.2d 1284 (Pa. 1977).

27. *Denton v. South Kitsap School District No. 402*, 516 P.2d 1080 (Wash. 1973).

28. *Weissman v. Board of Education of Jefferson County School District No. R-1*, 547 P.2d 1267 (Colo. 1976).

29. *Skripchuk v. Austin*, 379 A.2d 1142 (Del. 1977).

30. *Watson v. State Board of Education*, 22 C.A.3d 559 (1971).

31. These included four convictions for drunken driving. Watson was again arrested for drunken driving while his application was pending before the state board. Id. at 561.

32. *Lindgren v. Board of Trustees High School District No. 1*, 558 P.2d 468 (Mon. 1976).

33. *Board of Education of Long Beach Unified School District v. Jack M.*, 139 Cal. Rptr. 700 (1977).

34. *Board of Education of the Sunnyvale Elementary School District v. Commission on Professional Competence of the Sunnyvale Elementary School District*, 162 Cal. Rptr. 590 (1980).

35. *Burton v. Cascade School District Union High School No. 5*, 353 F.Supp. 254 (D. Ore. 1973); affirmed, 512 F.2d 850 (9th Cir. 1975).

36. *Kilpatrick v. Wright*, 437 F.Supp. 397 (M.D. Ala. 1977).

37. *Gaylord v. Tacoma School District No. 10*, 559 P.2d 1340 (Wash. 1977).

38. *Stoddard v. School District No. 1, Lincoln County, Wyoming*, 590 F.2d 829 (10th Cir. 1979).

39. *Blodgett v. Board of Trustees, Tamalpais Union High School District*, 97 Cal. Rptr. 406 (1971).

40. *Bogart v. Unified School District No. 298 of Lincoln County, Kansas*, 432 F.Supp. 895 (D. Kan. 1977).

41. *Erb v. Iowa State Board of Instruction*, 216 N.W.2d 339 (Iowa 1974).

42. *Comings v. State Board of Education*, 100 Cal. Rptr. 73 (1972).

43. *McConnell v. Anderson*, 451 F.2d 193 (8th Cir. 1971).

44. *Weissbaum v. Hannon*, 439 F.Supp. 873 (N.D. Ill. 1977).

45. *Meinhold v. Clark County School District*, 506 P.2d 420 (Nev. 1973).

46. *In Re Grossman*, 316 A.2d 39 (N.J. 1974).

47. *Yang v. Special Charter School District No. 150 Peoria County*, 296 N.E.2d 74 (Ill. 1973).

Chapter 7
Freedom of Religion and Conscience

> If there is any fixed star in our constitutional constellation, it is that no official, high or petty, can prescribe what shall be orthodox in politics, nationalism, religion, or other matters of opinion or force citizens to confess by word or act their faith therein. If there are any circumstances which permit an exception, they do not now occur to us.
>
> —Justice Jackson in *West Virginia* v. *Barnette*[1]

FREEDOM OF RELIGION—STUDENTS

The Gobitis Case: Compulsory Flag Salute

In thousands of schools children stand each morning and, with hands on their chests, recite: "I pledge allegiance to the flag of the United States of America and to the Republic for which it stands; one nation, under God, indivisible, with liberty and justice for all." This is a relatively simple, routine type of patriotic exercise—less than what is expected of public school children in most countries of the world.

In 1940 in Minersville, Pennsylvania, Lillian Gobitis, age 12, and her 10-year-old brother William were expelled from school because they refused to salute the flag as part of the daily opening ceremonies. Participation was mandatory for both teachers and students, as prescribed by the local Board of Education. Having been denied tax-supported education, the Gobitis parents enrolled the children in private schools. In order to avoid the financial costs of private education, the father went to court seeking an injunction to eliminate the requirement of participation in the flag salute as a condition for his children's attendance at the Minersville school.[2] He argued that compulsory flag salute in the schools violated the freedom of religion provisions of the First Amendment.

To support its case for expulsion, the Board of Education presented the following arguments.[3]

1. The expulsion of the children did not violate any constitutional rights, because their refusal to salute the flag was not founded on a religious belief.
2. The act of saluting the flag is not, by any stretch of the imagination, a "form of worship." The salute has no more religious implication than the study of history or civics or any other act that might make a pupil more patriotic as well as teach him "loyalty to the State and National Government."
3. The act of saluting the flag is only one of many ways in which a citizen may evidence his respect for the government. Every citizen stands at attention and men remove their hats when the national anthem is played; yet such action cannot be called a religious ceremony. The same respect is shown the American flag when it passes in a parade; yet that is not a religious rite.
4. The act of saluting the flag does not prevent a pupil, no matter what his religious belief may be, from acknowledging the spiritual sovereignty of Almighty God by rendering to God the things that are God's.

On behalf of the Gobitis children it was argued that the flag salute requirement violated their freedom of religion because they were Jehovah's Witnesses and relied on the following verses from chapter 20 of Exodus: "Thou shalt have no other gods before me. Thou shalt not make unto thee any graven image, or any likeness of anything that is in heaven above, or that is in the earth beneath, or that is in the water under the earth; Thou shalt not bow down thyself to them, nor serve them." The following points were made by Gobitis:

1. Although many people believe that saluting the flag has nothing to do with religion, the Supreme Court has repeatedly held that the individual alone is privileged to determine what he shall or shall not believe. The law therefore does not attempt to settle differences of creeds and confessions or to say that any point or doctrine is too absurd to be believed.
2. The saluting of the flag of any earthly government by a person who has promised to do the will of God is a form of religion and constitutes idolatry.

Questions to Consider

1. Does saluting the flag violate religious freedom?
2. Does saluting the flag engender patriotism and national unity?

3. Which of the arguments do you find more convincing, those for the school board or those for the Gobitis children?

THE OPINION OF THE COURT

The U.S. District Court and the U.S. Circuit Court of Appeals both decided in favor of the Gobitis children, but the Supreme Court reversed the rulings. In explaining the opinion of the Court, Justice Frankfurter recognized the grave responsibility of the Court when it has to reconcile a conflict between religious liberty and state authority. He noted the centuries of strife over religion that led our founding fathers to include a guarantee of religious freedom in the Bill of Rights. Thus Justice Frankfurter wrote that the First Amendment

> sought to guard against repetition of those bitter religious struggles by prohibiting the establishment of a state religion and by securing to every sect the free exercise of its faith. So pervasive is the acceptance of this precious right that its scope is brought into question, as here, only when the conscience of individuals collides with the felt necessities of society.[4]

No right, however, is absolute, not even the right to practice one's religious beliefs. Any liberty when carried to an extreme is likely to deny some other right. As Justice Frankfurter phrased it, "Our present task, then, as so often is the case with courts, is to reconcile two rights in order to prevent either from destroying the other. But, because in safe-guarding conscience we are dealing with interests so subtle and dear, every possible leeway should be given to the claims of religious faith."[5]

Cases before the court generally involve a central issue, and in this case the issue was whether legislatures and local school boards may determine the appropriate means to develop certain common, basic attitudes on the part of schoolchildren.

The Court asserted that the goals of patriotism and loyalty were clearly legitimate. It is proper for a state, through its schools, to attempt to develop "a common feeling for a common country"; consequently, the disagreement, as the Court saw it, centered on the legitimacy of the means selected to attain this end. In discussing the question of the appropriateness of the means (compulsory flag salute), the Court exhibited restraint from entering what it considered to be the educator's arena:

> The wisdom of training children in patriotic impulses by those compulsions which necessarily pervade so much of the educational process is not for our independent judgment. . . . The courtroom is not the arena for debating issues of educational policy. It is not our province to choose among competing considerations in the subtle process of securing effective loyalty to the traditional ideals of democracy, while respecting at the same time individual idiosyncrasies among a people so diversified in racial origins and religious allegiances. So to hold would in effect make us the school board for the

country. That authority has not been given to this Court, nor should we assume it.[6]

In the final paragraphs of the opinion, the Court acknowledged the need for an ordered society symbolized by the flag, but attempted to balance this with strong protection of freedom of religion.

> The preciousness of the family relation, the authority and independence which give dignity to parenthood, indeed the enjoyment of all freedom, presuppose the kind of ordered society which is summarized by our flag. A society which is dedicated to the preservation of these ultimate values of civilization may in self-protection utilize the educational process for inculcating those almost unconscious feelings which bind men together in a comprehending loyalty, whatever may be their lesser differences and difficulties. That is to say, the process may be utilized so long as men's right to believe as they please, to win others to their way of belief, and their right to assemble in their chosen places of worship for the devotional ceremonies of their faith, are all fully respected.[7]

Then the Court called attention to the role of the legislature in altering or eliminating "foolish legislation."

> Judicial review, itself a limitation on popular government, is a fundamental part of our constitutional scheme. But to the legislature no less than to courts is committed the guardianship of deeply-cherished liberties. Where all the effective means of inducing political changes are left free from interference, education in the abandonment of foolish legislation is itself a training in liberty. To fight out the wise use of legislative authority in the forum of public opinion and before legislative assemblies rather than to transfer such a contest to the judicial arena, serves to vindicate the self-confidence of a free people.[8]

A DISSENT

Eight of the Supreme Court justices upheld the compulsory flag salute, but the ninth, Justice Stone, wrote a powerful dissenting opinion. He recognized the right of governments to ensure their survival, even if in so doing they must suppress religious practices, dangerous to morals, public safety, health, and good order. However, he saw no such dangers involved in the refusal of two children to participate in a school ceremony contrary to their religious convictions. In his words:

> The Constitution may well elicit expressions of loyalty to it and to the government which it created, but it does not command such expressions or otherwise give any indication that compulsory expressions of loyalty play any such part in our scheme of government as to override the constitutional protection of freedom of speech and religion. And while such expressions of loyalty, when voluntarily given, may promote national unity, it is quite another matter to say that their compulsory expression by children in violation of their own and their parent's religious convictions can be regarded as playing so important a part in our national unity as to leave school boards free to exact it despite the constitutional guarantee of freedom of religion.[9]

The Supreme Court, then, in an 8 to 1 decision, upheld the Minersville Board of Education in its requirement that students, as a condition of school attendance, must salute the flag.

The Barnette Case: Gobitis Overruled

After the Court upheld the mandatory flag salute, the West Virginia legislature passed a law requiring its schools to teach civics, history, and the Constitution "for the purpose of teaching, fostering and perpetuating the ideals, principles and spirit of Americanism, and increasing the knowledge of the organization and machinery of the government." The West Virginia Board of Education followed such legislation with various regulations including a compulsory flag salute. The regulations ordered the following:

> Failure to conform is "insubordination" dealt with by expulsion. Readmission is denied by statute until compliance. Meanwhile the expelled child is "unlawfully absent" and may be proceeded against as a delinquent. His parents or guardians are liable to prosecution, and if convicted are subject to fines not exceeding $50 and jail term not exceeding thirty days.

This led to the case of *Barnette* v. *West Virginia.*[10]

In *Barnette* children of Jehovah's Witnesses refused to comply with the law, although they did offer to give the following pledge in place of the official one:

> I have pledged my unqualified allegiance and devotion to Jehovah, the Almighty God, and to His Kingdom, for which Jesus commands all Christians to pray. I respect the flag of the United States and acknowledge it as a symbol of freedom and justice to all. I pledge allegiance and obedience to all the laws of the United States that are consistent with God's laws, as set forth in the Bible.[11]

Since only three years intervened between the *Gobitis* ruling and the *Barnette* case, we would expect the Court to follow precedent. *Barnette*, however, overruled *Gobitis* and protected the religious freedom not to salute the flag. The Court split 6 to 3 in favor of the children who were Jehovah's Witnesses. There had been some changes in the membership of the Court after the *Gobitis* decision, and some of the judges changed their minds in the interim, pursuant to extensive and careful deliberations. The three dissenting judges would have reaffirmed *Gobitis*, including Justice Frankfurter, who wrote a long and scholarly dissent.

Although respecting the states' desire to build national unity and their use of schools toward that end, the Court struck down compulsion in the expression of sentiment or belief as illegitimate. In the words of the Court,

> the state may "require teaching by instruction and study of all in our history and in the structure and organization of our government, including the guarantees

of our civil liberty, which tend to inspire patriotism and love of country."
Here, however, we are dealing with a compulsion of students to declare a
belief. They are not merely made acquainted with the flag salute so that they
may be informed as to what it is or even what it means. The issue here is
whether this slow and easily neglected route to arouse loyalties constitutionally may be short-cut by substituting a compulsory salute and slogan.[12]

Speaking to this issue, Justice Jackson wrote this often quoted
paragraph:

> If there is any fixed star in our constitutional constellation, it is that no official,
> high or petty, can prescribe what shall be orthodox in politics, nationalism,
> religion, or other matters of opinion or force citizens to confess by word or act
> their faith therein. If there are any circumstances which permit an exception,
> they do not now occur to us.

He then applied these principles to the *Barnette* case.

> We think the action of the local authorities in compelling the flag salute and
> pledge transcends constitutional limitations on their power and invades the
> sphere of intellect and spirit which it is the purpose of the First Amendment to
> our Constitution to reserve from all official control.[13]

Justice Jackson also disagreed with the notion that the remedy to
wrong legislation is through new legislation or through the political
process.

> The very purpose of a Bill of Rights was to withdraw certain subjects from the
> vicissitudes of political controversy, to place them beyond the reach of
> majorities and officials and to establish them as legal principles to be applied
> by the courts. One's right to life, liberty, and property, to free speech, a free
> press, freedom of worship and assembly, and other fundamental rights may
> not be submitted to vote; they depend on the outcome of no elections.[14]

Justice Jackson made it clear that First Amendment freedoms are
preferred freedoms. Whereas some rights can be restricted if the government has a legitimate end and chooses reasonable means, preferred rights
receive more protection. If a right is a preferred, or a *fundamental*, one,
then the state must show a *compelling* need before such a right can be
restricted.* Applying this to the controversy surrounding the compulsory

*For example, in order to cut down on pollution and congestion our right to commute to work
or school daily by car can be restricted by the government through reasonable means, such as
issuing stickers that permit us to drive only on Mondays and Wednesdays, thus forcing us to
use public transportation or car pools. The end (reducing pollution and congestion) is
legitimate and the means (restricting the use of private cars) is reasonable. By contrast, the
government may not prevent an individual from making speeches in public parks even if the
government proclaimed the goal of creating parks as quiet, peaceful places for people to enjoy.
Although the goal is legitimate and the means reasonable, the preferred, or fundamental,
right of free speech receives a higher degree of protection. The state must show a compelling
need before the right to free speech can be restricted.

flag salute, the state has a legitimate purpose in seeking to gain social unity and patriotism. Saluting the flag is one reasonable means to attempt to accomplish this end. However, religious freedom is a preferred right. Consequently it cannot be restricted unless the state can show a compelling need for the flag salute requirement. Thus in the *Barnette* case, in which rights were in conflict, the state could not show sufficiently powerful interest to override a fundamental right of private citizens.

Justice Frankfurter's dissent explained his views concerning the constitutional protection of religious freedom:

> Its essence is freedom from conformity to religious dogma, not freedom from conformity to law because of religious dogma. . . . Otherwise each individual could set up his own censor against obedience to laws conscientiously deemed for the public good by those whose business it is to make laws. . . .
>
> The essence of the religious freedom guaranteed by our Constitution is therefore this: no religion shall either receive the state's support or incur its hostility. Religion is outside the sphere of political government. This does not mean that all matters on which religious organizations or beliefs may pronounce are outside the sphere of government. Were this so, instead of the separation of church and state, there would be the subordination of the state on any matter deemed within the sovereignty of the religious conscience. Much that is the concern of temporal authority affects the spiritual interests of men. But it is not enough to strike down a non-discriminatory law that it may hurt or offend some dissident view. It would be too easy to cite numeous prohibitions and injunctions to which laws run counter if the variant interpretations of the Bible were made the tests of obedience to law. The validity of secular laws cannot be measured by their conformity to religious doctrines. It is only in a theocratic state that ecclesiastical doctrines measure legal right or wrong.[15]

A close reading of the case indicates that the dissent used the "reasonableness" test to uphold the school board regulation, whereas the majority applied the "compelling interest" test. Thus the current law is that in public elementary and secondary schools, school boards or legislatures may not require participation in saluting the flag for students who have religious objections to such practices.

The Schempp and Murray Cases: Must Students Pray or Read the Bible?

Pennsylvania passed a law in 1959 requiring that "at least ten verses from the Holy Bible shall be read, without comment, at the opening of each public school on each day. Any child shall be excused from such Bible reading, or attending such Bible reading, upon the written request of his parents or guardian."[16] Roger, Donna, and Ellory Schempp were Unitarians from Germantown, Philadelphia, who attended the Abington Senior High School. There, as in many other high schools throughout the state, opening exercises were conducted each morning, pursuant to the statute. Ten verses from the Holy Bible were broadcast over the intercommunications system to all homerooms, where the students stood and repeated them in unison. Students could absent themselves from the classroom if they wished; or they could remain and not participate. After the Bible reading came the salute to the flag and school announcements.

The district court ruled that the Pennsylvania statute violated the First and Fourteenth Amendments and ordered the schools to discontinue the practice it required. The school district, together with the attorney general of Pennsylvania, appealed to the Supreme Court.

Questions to Consider

1. Do you find the practice described desirable or objectionable? On what theory do you base your opinion?
2. What section of the Constitution is relevant to the situation?
3. Is there anything coercive in the situation described?
4. Can a small minority prevent a practice the majority sees as desirable? Should it be able to do so?

A COMPANION CASE

In the meantime another controversy involving similar issues was working its way up the court hierarchy. This controversy was based on a 1905 rule of the Board of School Commissioners of Baltimore, Maryland, which provided for the "reading without comment, of a chapter in the Holy Bible and/or the use of the Lord's Prayer."

William J. Murray, III, and his mother, Madalyn Murray, were professed atheists who objected to this rule and asked for its cancellation. At their insistence the rule was amended to permit children to be excused from the exercise on their parents' request. The Murrays, not satisfied with permission to be excused, went to court to rescind the entire rule. As serious atheists they claimed that the rule violated their rights

> in that it threatens their religious liberty by placing a premium on belief as against non-belief and subjects their freedom of conscience to the rule of the majority; it pronounces belief in God as the source of all moral and spiritual values, equating these values with religious values, and thereby renders sinister, alien and suspect the beliefs and ideals of your Petitioners, promoting doubt and question of their morality, good citizenship and good faith.

The Maryland courts found in favor of the school practices and against the request of the Murrays, who then appealed to the Supreme Court. As in other instances in which the legal issues are substantially the same, the Court ruled on the *Schempp* and *Murray* cases in one opinion.* In a

---

*For this reason, the citation for *Murray* case is the same as in *Abington* v. *Schempp*, 374 U.S. 203 (1963).

landmark decision the Court declared that Bible reading and prayers in the schools were unconstitutional. It did so only after a careful review of previous cases and after making clear that the Court has consistently through the years taken a position of neutrality toward religion, and "while protecting all, it prefers none, and it disparages none."

In probing the intent and meaning of the principle of separation of church and state, Justice Clark, a devout Catholic, wrote:

> The First Amendment's purpose was not to strike merely at the official establishment of a single sect, creed or religion, outlawing only a formal relation such as had prevailed in England and some of the colonies. Necessarily it was to uproot all such relationships. But the object was broader than separating the church and state in this narrow sense. It was to create a complete and permanent separation of the spheres of religious activity and civil authority by comprehensively forbidding every form of public aid or support for religion.[17]

After examining the sequence of previous cases that interpreted the religious freedoms of the First Amendment, the Court concluded that in the *Schempp* and *Murray* cases the

> exercises are prescribed as part of the curricular activities of students who are required by law to attend school. They are held in the school buildings under the supervision and with the participation of teachers employed in those schools . . . such as opening exercises in a religious ceremony. Given that finding, the exercises and the law requiring them are in violation of the establishment clause.[18]

The Court rejected the argument that since students may absent themselves from the exercises, no coercion is involved and therefore Bible reading and prayers are legitimate.[19]

Schempp, in an 8 to 1 decision, reviewed with painstaking scholarship the legal history of the church-state relationship in America. It firmly prohibited religious exercises, Bible reading, and prayers in the public schools, both compulsory and voluntary. The Court also made it clear that hostility toward religion is also unconstitutional and that nothing in the law prohibits studying religion, comparative religion, or the history of religion.

In spite of the clear language of the *Schempp* case and the overwhelming agreement of the justices (8 to 1), various schools and even state legislatures have continued with practices, policies, and even laws that violate the First Amendment's call for a "separation of church and state."

For example, the school board of Orange City, Florida, allowed the distribution of Gideon Bibles and, as part of morning exercises, encouraged prayers over the loudspeaker system. Parents objected to these practices as well as to a Florida law which, among other values, mandated the teaching of "every Christian virtue." A federal appeals court agreed with the parents and held that each of these practices as well as the state law were contrary to the First Amendment.[20]

The Supreme Court also declared unconstitutional a Kentucky statute requiring the posting of a copy of the Ten Commandments, purchased with private contributions, on the wall of each classroom in the public schools of the state. Although the state courts upheld the law, the Supreme Court found that it served no secular legislative purpose. The Court applied its three-part test: (1) the statute must have a secular legislative purpose, (2) its principal or primary effect must be one that neither advances nor inhibits religion, and (3) the statute must not foster excessive entanglement of government and religion. [21]

In a 1979 case that arose in Sioux Falls, South Dakota, the courts reaffirmed that schools may teach about religion as a significant part of our culture and our history. In a challenge to school board policies related to Christmas programs in public schools, the courts warned that religious ceremonies must not be performed in schools "under the guise of 'study'," yet the performance of religious art, literature, or music does not necessarily invalidate the activity if the primary purpose served is secular and not religious. [22]

SILENT MEDITATION

If prayers in school are unconstitutional, what about meditation? Massachusetts students and their parents challenged a law that required teachers "in all grades and in all public schools" to observe a minute of silence "for meditation or prayer." [23]

To decide the case, the judge applied a three part test developed by the Supreme Court to test the constitutionality of any law that might be in conflict with the First Amendment's prohibition against the "establishment of religion." (1) Does the law have a secular purpose? (2) Does it have a primary effect that neither advances nor inhibits religion? (3) Does it avoid excessive government entanglement with religion?

Applying this test, Judge Murray ruled that since the Massachusetts law is stated in the disjunctive, thus permitting meditation *or* prayer, and since meditation refers to silent reflection on any subject, be it religious or secular, it does not violate the First Amendment. There is no entanglement between church and state when teachers merely provide a moment of silence that students use as they see fit. Judge Murray, although upholding the state law, reminded us that "the line that separates the permissible from the impermissible in this area is elusive." Although cases have used the phrase "a wall of separation between church and state," they have also recognized that in some areas of contact between religion and state-sponsored activities, the separation has never been absolute. Consequently, disagreements are likely to arise and find their way to court.

In another case related to prayers in schools, a federal district court ruled against "Students for Voluntary Prayer," denying them the right to use the public school building for communal praying prior to the start of school, as a violation of the establishment clause of the First Amendment. [24]

TRANSCENDENTAL MEDITATION IN SCHOOLS?

Although in Massachusetts a law provided for silent meditation, in New Jersey a school introduced some elective courses in transcendental meditation. Parents went to court to eliminate the courses on the ground that they violated the First Amendment.[25]

The court found that the goals and objectives of the courses were clearly secular, that is, the reduction of stress and other beneficial physical effects. The means used, however, were held to be religious, according to the publicly accepted meaning of the term. Some teachers, students, members of the clergy, and even some professors testified that in their opinion the courses were not religious. However, the judge rejected their "subjective characterizations," regardless of their sincerity. After considering the texts used, the ideas propagated, and the assignment of a "mantra"* at an out-of-school religious ceremony called the "puja," the judge held that the means used were religious for purposes of the First Amendment. Thus, since public funds were used for the courses, the arrangement constituted an "excessive government entanglement in religion."

FREEDOM OF CONSCIENCE

The Spence Case: ROTC and Religious Freedom[26]

In 1972 John Spence, Jr., was a student at Central High School in Memphis, Tennessee, where, according to state law, every student was required to take one year of either physical education or ROTC training. Since no physical education was offered for male students at Central High School, although facilities were available nearby, ROTC was the only alternative.

Retired army officers taught ROTC using materials developed by the U.S. Army. Once a week the students wore military uniforms, studied military drill and tactics, and worked with firearms. Spence refused to attend the ROTC classes on the grounds that he was a conscientious objector, stating:

> By reason of religious training and belief, I am conscientiously opposed to participation in war in any form and am opposed to being subjected to combat training for the purpose of being prepared to enter war. As stated above, my convictions are based upon religious training and belief which is in turn based upon a power or being or upon a faith to which all else is subordinate and upon which all else is ultimately dependent. This sincere and meaningful belief occupies in my life a place parallel to that filled by the Supreme Being, God.

Spence's request was denied and, because he refused to attend ROTC classes, he was not awarded his diploma, although he had fulfilled all other requirements.

---

*A *mantra* is a meaningless sound repeated regularly to help a person meditate.

Questions to Consider

1. Is the ROTC requirement a reasonable condition attached to high school attendance? Should the requirement be waived on the grounds of conscientious objection?
2. Should all requirements be subject to such objections? If so, would this nullify the laws requiring compulsory schooling?
3. Is there a distinction between high school ROTC training as a substitute for physical education and serving in the armed forces?

THE OPINION OF THE COURT

In an earlier case the Supreme Court held that a state college or university can require ROTC training as a condition of attendance.[27] The arguments in behalf of Central High School relied heavily on this case, in which the Court said:

> Instruction in military science is not instruction in the practice or tenets of religion. Neither directly nor indirectly is government establishing a state religion when it insists upon such training. Instruction in military science, unaccompanied here by any pledge of military service, is not an interference by the state with the free exercise of religion when the liberties of the Constitution are read in the light of a century and a half of history during the days of peace and war.[28]

Judge Clark, formerly of the Supreme Court,* however, distinguished the case of Spence, a high school student, from the earlier *Hamilton* case on the grounds that high school attendance was not a matter of choice. The *Hamilton* case had ruled that if a state university requires ROTC as a condition of attendance, a student who voluntarily attends the university cannot insist on being excused from the prescribed course. The court found crucial the distinction between voluntary and compulsory attendance. In upholding Spence's right to be excused from ROTC, Justice Clark recognized that the sincere beliefs of a conscientious objector must receive the same constitutional protection as traditional religious beliefs. Without a compelling state interest, such beliefs cannot be violated.

> As the trial judge aptly observed, the ROTC course requirement forced John to choose between following his religious beliefs and forfeiting his diploma, on the one hand, and abandoning his religious beliefs and receiving his diploma on the other hand. The State may not put its citizens to such a Hobson's choice consistent with the Constitution without showing a compelling state interest . . . within the State's constitutional power to regulate.[29]

Judge Miller, dissenting in the *Spence* case, found the distinction between compulsory and voluntary attendance "to be unpersuasive" and

---

*After Mr. Clark resigned from the High Court when his son became U.S. Attorney General, he served on other federal courts by assignment.

would have followed the *Hamilton* ruling. He saw serious dangers if the majority doctrines were broadly applied:

> The conscientious objector, if his liberties were to be thus extended, might refuse to contribute taxes in furtherance of any other end condemned by his conscience as irreligious or immoral. The right of private judgment has never yet been so exalted above the powers and the compulsion of the agencies of government. One who is a martyr to a principle—which may turn out in the end to be a delusion or an error—does not prove by his martyrdom that he has kept within the law.[30]

Judge Miller in his dissent made it clear that *he* would extend the protection of the First Amendment only to groups whose religious views and convictions have been firmly established over long periods of time. This would exclude the "mere subjective evaluation" of conscientious objectors.*

It is clear, however, that the courts extend the protection of the First Amendment not only to established religions but to newer ones as well. Furthermore, the amendment applies to sincere conscientious objectors whether they are religious or not. In each case, however, the particular issues must be considered, because even First Amendment rights are not absolute. The particular rights in conflict must be examined and the relative importance of the state interests and those of the individuals considered. Since freedom of and from religion are among the preferred rights of our Constitution, governments must show a compelling state interest before their actions will be upheld over the rights of individuals.**

The Banks Case: Pledge of Allegiance and Freedom of Conscience[31]

Andrew Banks, a senior at Florida's Coral Gables High School, refused to stand during the Pledge of Allegiance. He claimed that the school board regulations requiring him to stand during the salute to the flag violated his constitutional right of free speech and expression.

The board policy stated that "students who for religious or other deep personal conviction, do not participate in the salute and pledge of allegiance to the flag will stand quietly." The school officials denied that Banks's refusal to stand was an exercise of his constitutional right to free

---

*More recently, however, it has been questioned whether a compulsory ROTC requirement would be upheld even at the college level in state institutions. See, for example, *Anderson* v. *Laird*, 466 F.2d 283 (2nd Cir. 1972), which strikes down compulsory chapel attendance at the United States service academics. The opinion (in note 80 on p. 295) raises questions about the continued validity of the *Hamilton* holding.
**Such a compelling state interest, for example, upheld the requirement of polio immunization for all schoolchildren over the religious objections of some.

speech and expression. They also claimed that a compelling governmental purpose required students to stand during the pledge. When Banks was suspended from school for his refusal, he went to court to challenge the policy.

Questions to Consider

1. May student objection to saluting the flag be based on freedom of conscience, or must it be based on freedom of religion?
2. Is it reasonable to require students who do not wish to salute the flag to stand quietly?
3. Is standing at a flag salute a form of speech or expression? Is refusing to stand a form of expression?

THE OPINION OF THE COURT

The District Court of Florida relied on the *Barnette* and *Tinker* cases in reaching its decision. It noted an interesting distinction between the two cases, indicating that the tenor of *Barnette* was negative, whereas that of *Tinker* was positive. *Barnette* was negative in that it prohibited the state from compelling individuals to act in a manner that would violate their convictions in "politics, nationalism, religion, or other matters of opinion." By contrast, *Tinker* positively asserted that students carry their constitutional rights into the schools.

The conduct of Andrew Banks was scrutinized by the court in light of the "material disruption test" proclaimed in *Tinker*. Evidence showed that Banks caused no disturbance by refusing to stand, that he did not attempt to influence other students, and that he was not conspicuous in his behavior. His testimony showed that his refusal to stand was based on his own Unitarian beliefs as well as being a "simple protest against black repression in the United States."

The court recognized that "standing is an integral portion of the pledge ceremony and is no less a gesture of acceptance and respect than is the salute or the utterance of the words of allegiance." It went on to recognize Banks's right to express his opinion by refusing to stand and participate in the Pledge of Allegiance as a right protected by the First Amendment.

A RELATED CASE

Results similar to those in the *Banks* case were reached on somewhat different facts in a New York case during 1969. School officials insisted that students who refused to participate in the Pledge of Allegiance should stand quietly or leave the room.[32] Three students involved in the lawsuit objected to the pledge because they did not believe that the words "with liberty and justice for all" were true in America today. One of them, an atheist, also objected to the phrase "under God." They refused to leave the room and wait in the hall during the ceremony "because they considered exclusion from the room to be a punishment for their exercise of constitutional rights."

The reasoning of the New York court was substantially the same as in the *Banks* case. The court upheld the right of the students not to participate in the flag salute for reasons of conscience. Their right to remain quietly in the room was also protected.

When school officials pointed out that others had joined the protesting students in sitting out the pledge, the court noted that "the First Amendment protects successful dissent as well as ineffective protests."

RELIGIOUS OBJECTIONS TO SCHOOL ATTENDANCE

A growing minority of critics of education have begun to argue that the changes needed in our system are so great that they cannot take place within the present framework of compulsory education. Some call for an end to required education and urge free choice by parents and students. Such critics see the *Yoder* case, which involved a legal exemption from compulsory education for a group of Amish children, as a first step in that direction.

Others—those who favor community control and alternative schools—also see the *Yoder* case as supporting their position. In this vein the editors of *Of Education and Human Community* wrote that the Supreme Court's *Yoder* decision "indicates strong support for community control of schools where the values and life styles of a community are threatened by the rules and regulations of the larger community."[33]

Is the *Yoder* case the first step toward "a deschooled society"? Does it challenge our traditional acceptance of compulsory education? Will it lead other groups to follow the Amish example and request exemptions from state educational statutes? These are the questions raised by the landmark case of *Yoder* v. *Wisconsin*.

The Yoder Case: Who Has a Right Not to Go to School?[34]

Jonas Yoder, Adin Yutzy, and Wallace Miller were sincere and committed members of the Amish community in Green County, Wisconsin. Because they believed that high school attendance was contrary to the Amish religion—namely, that it would endanger their own salvation and that of their children—they decided not to send their 14- and 15-year-old children to school after they had graduated from the eighth grade. In so doing they violated Wisconsin's compulsory school attendance law (which requires attendance until age 16). As a result, the parents were charged, tried, and convicted of violating the law and fined $5 each by the local county court. The Amish parents believed that the compulsory attendance law abridged their rights under the First and Fourteenth Amendments, and they appealed their conviction.

In support of their position the parents presented expert witnesses on religion and education who testified about the tenets of the Amish religion and the impact that high school attendance could have on the Amish communities. The Amish, for example, deemphasize material success, reject the competitive spirit, and believe that salvation requires life in a church community separate from worldly influence. They object to high schools because the values they teach conflict with the Amish way of life. The high schools tend to emphasize intellectual and scientific accomplishments, self-distinction, competitiveness, worldly success, and social life with other students. In contrast, Amish society emphasizes informal learning-through-doing, a life of "goodness" rather than a life of intellect, wisdom rather than technical knowledge, community welfare rather than competition, and separation rather than integration with contemporary society.

The Amish argued that high school education is contrary to their beliefs, not only because of its emphasis on competition in classwork and sports and its pressures of peer group conformity, but also because it physically and emotionally removes Amish children from their community during formative adolescent years, a time when they need to acquire the attitudes and skills to carry on the roles of Amish farmers or housewives. These roles can best be learned through example in the Amish community rather than in non-Amish schools that tend to develop values that "alienate man from God."

One expert witness testified that "compulsory high school attendance could not only result in great psychological harm to Amish children because of the conflicts it would produce" but could "ultimately result in the destruction" of the Amish church community. Another educational expert described the Amish system of learning-through-doing the skills relevant to their adult roles in the Amish community as "ideal" and "perhaps superior to ordinary high school education."

The Amish do not object to elementary education because they believe their children must know the three Rs in order to read the Bible, to be good farmers and citizens, and to deal with non-Amish people when necessary. They accept such basic education because it does not "significantly expose their children to worldly values or interfere with their development in the Amish community."

Questions to Consider

1. Do you agree that compulsory high school attendance would endanger the religious values of Amish children? Would it endanger the values of youngsters of other religions?

2. Should Amish children be exempt from high school attendance? Are there others who should also be exempt?
3. What criteria should be used to determine who should and should not be required to attend school? Who should make this decision— the student, the parents, the school board, or the courts?

THE OPINION OF THE COURT

After reviewing the evidence, the Supreme Court turned to the constitutional principles and substantive issues in the *Yoder* case. First the Court noted that "there is no doubt" that a state has power "to impose reasonable regulations for the control and duration of basic education." On the other hand, the state's interest in universal compulsory education is not absolute; when it impinges on other fundamental rights, such as those protected by the First Amendment freedom of religion clause, then the rights in conflict must be balanced by the court. Thus in order for Wisconsin to compel school attendance against a claim that such attendance interferes with the practice of the Amish religion, the state must show either that it does not significantly deny the free exercise of religious belief by its requirement or that its interest in compulsory education is "of sufficient magnitude to override the interest claiming protection" under the freedom of religion clause.

Based on the unchallenged testimony of experts in education and religious history and strong evidence of a sustained faith pervading the Amish way of life, the Court concluded that compulsory secondary schooling "would gravely endanger if not destroy" the free exercise of Amish religious beliefs. The Court reached this decision because it found such schooling exposes Amish children "to worldly influences in terms of attitudes, goals, and values" contrary to their beliefs and interferes with the religious development of the Amish child and "his integration into the way of life of the Amish faith community at the crucial adolescent state of development." The Wisconsin compulsory attendance law undermines the Amish religion by requiring the Amish to "either abandon belief and be assimilated into society at large, or be forced to migrate to some other and more tolerant region." Thus the law carries with it "precisely the kind of objective danger to the free exercise of religion which the First Amendment was designed to prevent."

Wisconsin claimed that even if the compulsory education law did conflict with Amish religious practice, the state's interest in such a law is paramount. The state argued the law should be upheld for two reasons: Education prepares individuals to be self-reliant members of society, and it is necessary to prepare citizens to participate effectively and intelligently in our open political system. Moreover, Wisconsin attacked the Amish position as one "fostering 'ignorance' from which the child must be protected by the State." In addition, Wisconsin claimed that without additional schooling, Amish children who wished to leave their religious community would be ill equipped for life.

The Court was not persuaded by these arguments. On the contrary, the evidence in this case, wrote Justice Burger, "is persuasively to the effect that an additional one or two years of formal high school for Amish children in place of their long established program of informal vocational education" would do little to serve compelling state interests. He further noted: "Whatever their idiosyncrasies as seen by the majority, this record strongly shows that the Amish community has been a highly successful social unit within our society even if apart from the conventional 'mainstream.'"The Amish are "productive law-abiding members of society"; they provide for their own dependents and accept no public welfare. According to the Court:

> The Amish alternative to formal secondary school education has enabled them to function effectively in their day-to-day life under self-imposed limitations on relations with the world, and to survive and prosper in contemporary society as a separate, sharply identifiable and highly self-sufficient community for more than 200 years in this country. In itself, this is strong evidence that they are capable of fulfilling the social and political responsibilities of citizenship without compelled attendance beyond the eighth grade at the price of jeopardizing their free exercise of religious belief. . . . There can be no assumption that today's majority is "right" and the Amish and others like them are "wrong." A way of life that is odd or even erratic but interferes with no rights or interests of others is not to be condemned because it is different.[35]

Wisconsin also argued that if the Court exempted Amish children from compulsory attendance, it would fail to recognize the individual Amish child's right to a secondary education. Such an exemption would take no account of a possible conflict between the wishes of parents and children and "might allow some parents to act contrary to the best interests of their children by foreclosing their opportunity to make an intelligent choice between the Amish way of life and that of the outside world."

In response Justice Burger observed that the same argument could apply to all students in church schools and that there is no evidence "that non-Amish parents generally consult with children up to ages 14–16 if they are placed in a church school of the parents' faith." Furthermore, if the state is empowered to "save" a child from his Amish parents by requiring an additional two years of a formal high school, the state will in effect influence the religious future of the child. Therefore this case involves "the fundamental interest of parents, as contrasted with that of the State, to guide the religious future and education of their children." In addition, the Court noted that this primary role of parents in the upbringing of their children "is now established beyond debate as an enduring American tradition."

This does not mean the power of the parent may not be subject to limitation if it appears that parental decisions will jeopardize the health or safety of the child, or have a potential for significant burdens for society. But the evidence in this case indicated that accommodating the religious objections of the Amish by foregoing one or two additional years of compulsory education for Amish children would not impair the physical or mental health of the children or result in their inability to be responsible citizens.

In sum, Justice Burger wrote that the Amish in this case have "convincingly demonstrated" (1) the sincerity of their religious beliefs; (2) the interrelationship of their belief and their way of life; (3) the vital role that belief and daily conduct play in the continued survival of the Amish religious communities; (4) "the hazards presented by the State's enforcement of a statute generally valid as to others"; and (5) "the adequacy of their alternative mode of continuing informal, vocational education." In light of this evidence and "weighing the minimal difference between what the State would require and what the Amish already accept," Wisconsin was unable to show "how its admittedly strong interest in compulsory education would be adversely affected by granting an exemption to the Amish." For these reasons the Court held that the First and Fourteenth Amendments "prevent the State from compelling respondents [Jonas Yoder, Adin Yutzy, and Wallace Miller] to cause their children to attend formal high school to age 16."

A DISSENTING OPINION

In a lone dissent Justice Douglas disagreed with the Court's opinion, which considered only the interests of the Amish parents on the one hand and the state of Wisconsin on the other. Instead Justice Douglas argued that:

> No analysis of religious liberty claims can take place in a vacuum. If the parents in this case are allowed a religious exemption, the inevitable effect is to impose the parents' notion of religious duty upon their children. Where the child is mature enough to express potentially conflicting desires, it would be an invasion of the child's rights to permit such an imposition without canvassing his views. . . . And if an Amish child desires to attend high school and is mature enough to have that desire respected, the State may well be able to override the parents' religiously motivated objections.[36]

There was no evidence that the 14- and 15-year-old children in the *Yoder* case testified concerning their educational views. But, in the opinion of Justice Douglas, a child of this age should have the right to be heard on the matter of education. "He may want to be a pianist or an astronaut or an ocean geographer." To do so, observed Douglas, "he will have to break with the Amish tradition."

It is the future of the student not the parent that is "imperiled" by the decision not to attend high school. If a parent keeps his child out of high school, the child will be "barred from entry" into today's "new and amazing world of diversity." The child may rebel or prefer the course of his parents, but this should be decided by the student "if we are to give full meaning to what we have said about the Bill of Rights and of the right of students to be masters of their own destiny."

Viewing the Amish religious tradition as less positive than did the majority, Justice Douglas concluded that if the student "is harnessed to the Amish way of life by those in authority over him or if his education is truncated, his entire life may be stunted and deformed."

THE IMPLICATIONS OF YODER

Could the Court's decision in this case lead people to attempt to escape the reach of compulsory education by organizing into a community and calling themselves a religious group? Could it lead sensitive humanists who reject material values or radical educators who oppose state-regulated education to seek exemptions for their children? Not according to the Court. For such groups, despite the sincerity of their beliefs, would not be able to use the religion clauses of the First Amendment to support their case. As Justice Burger wrote:

> A way of life, however virtuous and admirable, may not be interposed as a barrier to reasonable state regulation of education if it is based on purely secular considerations. . . . Thus, if the Amish asserted their claims because of their subjective evaluation and rejection of the contemporary secular values accepted by the majority, much as Thoreau rejected the social values of his time and isolated himself at Walden Pond, their claim would not rest on a religious basis. [37]

To further insure that the Court's opinion would not be interpreted too broadly, Justice Burger returned to this question a second time in the opinion when he indicated that the decision in this case was a narrow exemption that applied only to a special religious group and was not an attack on the Wisconsin program of compulsory education. Furthermore, he wrote: "It cannot be overemphasized that we are not dealing with a way of life and mode of education by a group claiming to have recently discovered some 'progressive' or more enlighted [sic] process for rearing children for modern life."

Despite these disclaimers by Justice Burger, the Supreme Court in this case allowed a group of parents to defy a state's compulsory education law. Whether other groups will find other arguments to support similar challenges, only time and future litigation will tell.

RELATED CASES AND ISSUES

Other issues relate to the religious freedom of students, some of which have led to court cases and community controversies.

• **Church School at Home?** Early in 1973, in Duval County, Florida, two children were adjudged to be "in need of supervision as persistent truants from school." The parents of the children appealed this school board decision to the Florida District Court of Appeals.[38]

The facts showed that the children were not attending public schools because of their parents' religious belief that "race mixing as practiced in public schools was sinful." Instead, they were taught in their home "school," called the Ida M. Craig Christian Day School, where their mother was the only teacher. She was not certified to teach and did not meet the state-prescribed regulations for private tutors. Furthermore the Covenant Church of Jesus Christ, under whose aegis the "school" operated, was not a regularly established church in Florida. The principal tenet of this church is that of racial segregation. Its members believe "that blacks and Orientals were conceived through the copulation of Eve and Satan, who was disguised as the serpent in the Garden of Eden, and it is therefore sinful and evil to associate with people of those races."

The compulsory school attendance law of Florida could be satisfied by attending (1) a public school; (2) a parochial or denominational school; (3) a private school supported by tuition, endowments, or gifts; or (4) an at-home school with private tutors who meet the qualifications specified by the state Board of Education. But the court ruled that the home teaching arrangements in this case did not satisfy the Florida law and that, clearly, the Ida M. Craig Christian Day School "is neither a parochial nor denominational school within the generally accepted meaning of those terms."

• **The Right to Attend Private Schools.** The *Yoder* case and the Florida case are interesting recent controversies related to the issue of who has the right not to attend public schools. Such controversies are best viewed against the backdrop of an important historical decision. The Supreme Court ruled as early as 1925 in *Pierce* v. *Society of Sisters of the Holy Name*[39] that it was unconstitutional for the state of Oregon to require all children to attend *public* schools for the first eight grades. Although the Court upheld the right of the state to require school attendance, such attendance could be satisfied in private schools, both parochial and secular, as well as in public schools.

• **Religion and Folk Dancing.** The physical education programs of many schools include folk dancing and at times even social dancing. Vigorous folk and square dancing are often part of the daily schedule of elementary schools and is justified in two ways: It is claimed that it has value as an integral part of physical exercise that is healthy for growing young bodies and that properly timed physical exercise will enable children to concentrate better on the academic tasks of the schools.

What action should a school take if certain children believe that dancing of any kind, violates their religious convictions? If such an objection is respected, could it not also be raised against science instruction, the learning of history, foreign languages, or any other segment of the curriculum? What does compulsory schooling mean if any part of it can be vitiated by claiming it to be repugnant to one's religious beliefs?

A California case centered on religious objections to social and folk dancing that were part of the school's physical education program.[40] In the *Hardwick* case the court upheld the objection and exempted the student from the requirement of dancing. The court reached its decision on two grounds: (1) that freedom of religion must be protected against abridgement by school officials and (2) that the schools could not interfere with the rights of parents to control the upbringing of their children, as long as the views of the parents were not "offensive to the moral well-being of the children or inconsistent with the best interests of society."

Other courts have reached similar conclusions in cases involving religious objections to school-required dancing. When courts apply the balancing test, they conclude that protecting religious freedom outweighs the social interests entailed in the dance segment of a physical education program. It is quite probable that the benefits gained from dancing can be reached in ways that do not violate the students' religious convictions. Courts have also ruled in favor of students who, on religious grounds, refused to participate in coed physical education classes in what they believed to be "immodest attire." According to their religious beliefs, exposure of parts of the body to others may cause adultery to be committed in the heart of the viewer, violating their conviction that "the body is the temple of the spirit."[41]

The limits of religious objections to curricular content have not yet been completely established. Perhaps the *Yoder* case provides the most useful basis for predicting future judicial behavior.

• Religious Objections to Sex Education. In many communities parents have objected to sex education in the schools. While some of the objections were based on genuine differences in secular values held by protesting parents, some parents claimed that such instruction violates their freedom of religion.

When such a case arose in New Jersey, the Commissioner of Education ruled that a requirement that high school students attend a course on family living, wherein some sex education was included, does not violate freedom of religion.[42] A California court reached a similar conclusion, particularly since a state law permitted children to be excused from participating in such classes.[43]

• Offensive Antireligious Texts. A controversy that received national publicity arose during the 1974–1975 school year in Kanawha County, West

Virginia. Some parents objected to a series of textbooks and claimed that these books contained matter that is "offensive to Christian morals . . . defames the Nation . . . encourages the use of vile and abusive language," and encourages the violation of both the Ten Commandments and civil law.[44]

Although finding that the materials were indeed offensive to the parents, the court ruled that no constitutional rights were violated. Judge Hall observed that freedom of religion "does not guarantee that nothing offensive to any religion will be taught." Instead, the Constitution requires schools to be neutral between religions and between religion and nonreligion, and it prohibits schools from encouraging or discouraging any religion. Parents or students who object to texts should not go to court, but should pursue their concerns "through boards of education proceedings or ultimately at the polls on election day."

• Skullcaps in the School. A conflict that never reached the courts occurred in Fall River, Massachusetts, in 1971.[45] A 12-year-old junior high school student in that city was sent home by the principal because he insisted on wearing a *yarmulke*, a skullcap worn by orthodox Jewish men. The principal, also a Jew, contended that anyone entering a public building such as a school should remove his hat. The student, on the other hand, claimed that his religious beliefs required him to wear his skullcap and that his action was therefore protected by the First Amendment.

Many school-related legal controversies do not reach the courts. They are resolved by accepting the legal opinion of the city attorney, the city corporation counsel, the attorney general, or other legal source that acts in an impartial advisory capacity. Schools constantly rely on such advice.

In the controversy at hand, the city corporation counsel ruled that the school authorities acted illegally in suspending the youth because he was wearing the skullcap. His religious freedom was protected and prevailed over whatever minor annoyances his wearing a skullcap might have occasioned.

It is interesting to speculate just what other grooming or clothing practices would or would not be so protected. Does a teacher have the right to wear a skullcap? What would be the reaction if followers of Hare Krishna insisted on attending school in peach-colored flowing robes with heads shaved except for pigtails? Would the *Tinker* test be appropriate in these situations?

• Black Armbands on the Football Team. In 1972 several black members of the University of Wyoming football team planned to wear black armbands during a game against Brigham Young University. They wanted to protest what they believed to be racist views of the Mormon Church, which supports Brigham Young University. The athletes claimed that the First

Amendment protected their right to free expression and that wearing the armbands is protected by symbolic speech.

The Wyoming coach, backed by the board of trustees of the university, forbade the wearing of the armbands. In the dispute that ensued, the football players were dismissed from the team. The coach and the university officials claimed that the First Amendment required complete neutrality on religious matters on the part of state institutions. They claimed that the display of black armbands by a state university team would be an expression of opposition to certain religious beliefs and therefore a violation of the principle of neutrality.

This situation presented conflicting claims under the First Amendment. Both sides claimed the protection of the amendment—one for free expression, the other for religious freedom. Furthermore, both claimed the *Tinker* case to support their position.

How would you rule in this conflict? Why? Does *Tinker* apply, and for which party to the conflict?

The U.S. Court of Appeals for the Tenth Circuit ruled in favor of religious neutrality.[46] It carefully considered the facts of the case as well as the *Tinker* principles. It also emphasized earlier Supreme Court pronouncements on religious freedom that "the government is neutral, and while protecting all, it prefers none, and it *disparages* none." The court explained that the decision of the trustees prevented a hostile expression by members of the university team, and thus "it was in furtherance of the policy of religious neutrality by the State."

This case illustrates two major principles. First, it clearly shows a conflict between two powerful constitutional freedoms, those of speech and religion. This conflict calls for an incompatible resolution of a dilemma. Both rights cannot be protected; thus a difficult balancing test must be attempted by the court to reach a resolution not between a right and a wrong but between competing constitutional rights. The second principle illustrated is that the courts tend to give strong protection to religious freedom. One way that this is expressed is through the principle of official neutrality, whereby agents of the government, including schools, may not favor or disfavor religious beliefs and expressions. The armband case should also remind us that although the constitutional principles seem to be clear and bold in the abstract, they become less clear and more difficult to apply in the complex affairs of education.

FREEDOM OF RELIGION—TEACHERS

A careful look at the history of schooling in America shows that the rights of teachers to freedom of religion were often violated. Many communities inquired into the religious beliefs of applicants for teaching positions, and it was not uncommon to require Sunday School teaching and/or church attendance as a condition of employment. Some subtle violations of the freedom of religion of teachers and administrators continue to this day, particularly in relatively isolated, religiously homogeneous communities. Nationwide, however, significant gains have been achieved on behalf of such freedom. Still, some controversies arise and find their way to court.

Compulsory Flag Salute

Many states require by law that every school day begin with the recitation of the Pledge of Allegiance and some specify that teachers must lead the class in such recitation. Massachusetts enacted such a law in 1977, which specifies that: "Each teacher at the commencement of the first class of each day in all public schools shall lead the class in a group recitation of the Pledge of Allegiance to the Flag."

When the governor requested the highest court of the state to render an advisory opinion* on the proposed new law, the majority of the justices advised that such a law violates the First Amendment rights of teachers, whether or not there were criminal penalties for the violation. The Massachusetts court based its opinion on the *Barnette* case discussed earlier, indicating that the rationale of that case applied to teachers as well as to students.[47]

According to the Massachusetts court, "Any attempt by a governmental authority to induce belief in an ideological conviction by forcing an individual to identify himself with that conviction through compelled expression of it is prohibited by the First Amendment."

If a statute impinges on the First Amendment, it will be upheld only if the state has a "countervailing interest which is sufficiently compelling to justify its action." The state of Massachusetts has a legitimate interest in instilling patriotism in its students. The court held, however, that other ways must be found to achieve this goal, ways that do not violate the teachers' right to remain silent. Teachers' freedom of expression, which includes the right to remain silent, can be restricted only "to prevent grave and immediate danger to interests which the state may lawfully protect."

Earlier cases have reached similar conclusions. A case arising in New York,[48] for example, upheld the right of a teacher not to salute the flag when her objections were held as a matter of conscience and not necessarily based on religion. A teacher who respectfully abstains while others salute the flag is not necessarily disloyal. As the U.S. Court of Appeals said, "We ought not impugn the loyalty of a citizen . . . merely for refusing to pledge allegiance, any more than we ought necessarily to praise the loyalty of a

---

*Although the U.S. Supreme Court renders no advisory opinions and rules only on cases involving genuine controversies, many state supreme courts give such advice to their respective governors, on request.

citizen who without conviction or meaning, and with mental reservation, recites the pledge by rote each morning."

In sum, clearly, teachers cannot be compelled to salute the flag or to lead a class in a flag salute if they object either because of religious beliefs or as a matter of personal conscience. However, just as students must be respectful of the rights of others to salute the flag and partake of other patriotic exercises, even more so teachers are obligated to respect such ceremonies and to insure that those who do wish to have opportunities to participate in them.

Personal Leave for Religious Holidays

California, like many states, provides a certain number of days per year for "personal necessity leave" for teachers which can be used against accumulated sick leave. As in many states, "personal necessity" is not defined, and local schools have authority to adopt rules controlling such leaves.

Ms. Waldman, a high school teacher, requested a personal necessity leave to observe Rosh Hashanah, a Jewish holiday. When her school district denied her request and the trial court upheld the school district, Waldman appealed.[49]

The California District Court of Appeals affirmed the lower court decision, but did not consider it necessary to rule on the constitutionality of the issue.* The court held that Waldman was in no way hampered from or disciplined for observing the religious holidays. She could take a leave but not a paid leave. It was within the discretion of the school board to decide whether or not to consider such a leave a "personal necessity." If the court imposed such a rule on the schools, "the results would be chaotic. Every school teacher belonging to every sect, whether a legitimate religious group or not, would forthwith be entitled to 6 days of paid holidays. It appears reasonable, therefore, to limit the definition of personal necessity in a way which allows for effective supervision."

This case holds that a school district may, but need not, allow personal necessity leaves to be used for the observance of religious holidays. But what if a teacher wants to take religious holidays without pay? May a school district set limits on the number of such holidays a teacher may take?

Excessive Absence and Religious Freedom

Mr. Byars, a competent teacher, was employed by his school district in 1969. After he joined the Worldwide Church of God in 1971, he requested certain days off for religious holidays. Although permission was not

---

*In general, courts do not pass on constitutional questions if a decision can be reached on alternative, nonconstitutional grounds.

granted, he was absent for 31 days between 1971 and 1975 for religious observations. In 1973 he was notified that the district disapproved of his absences and would dismiss him for "a persistent failure to abide by the rules of the District" if he continued.

The teacher insisted that he had a constitutional right to observe the holidays of his church. When he continued to assert this right and to act on it, the board voted to dismiss him. In due course his case reached the California Court of Appeals.[50]

Questions to Consider

1. Do you believe that a teacher has right not to work on a religious holiday?
2. Do children suffer from repeated use of substitutes?
3. If both the teacher and the school district have serious interests involved and they clash, how would you rule? Why?

THE OPINION OF THE COURT

The court found that Mr. Byars was a competent teacher and that the church he joined and its holidays were legitimate in all respects. It also found that substitute teachers could not replace Byars "without diminishing the educational benefit to the students." Thus, after noting the difference between holding religious beliefs, which is an absolute right, and acting on them, which cannot be, the court ruled in favor of the school board. Attempting to reconcile the conflicting interests present in the case, the court observed:

> While the free exercise clause prevents any governmental regulation of religious beliefs, in this case we are concerned not with . . . [the teacher's] beliefs but only with his practices in leaving his teaching duties for the purpose of religious observances while under contract with the district.

When Mr. Byars entered into a contract with the district, his obligations were made clear. He has a right subsequently to affiliate with a new religion, but he cannot avoid his legitimate contractual obligations. The teacher's freedom of religion was respected, but it was outweighed by a compelling state interest in maintaining a proper educational program.

On appeal, however, the California Supreme Court reversed the decision and ruled in favor of the teacher. The court based its decision on the California Constitution's provision protecting freedom of religion. It was also influenced by the fact that the total number of days the teacher missed was no more than the number of days of paid leave the state provided teachers. The court noted that teachers' religious beliefs must be accommodated despite the inconvenience and some disruption it might cause the schools.[51]

Refusal to Participate in Some School Activities

Ms. Bein, a probationary teacher, in her second year of teaching a kindergarten class, informed the parents that she could no longer lead certain "religiously-oriented activities or make specific religious projects" because such would violate her newly acquired religion as a Jehovah's Witness. She could not sing "Happy Birthday," recite the Pledge of Allegiance, decorate the room on holidays, or coordinate gift exchanges during the Christmas season.

Some parents, administrators, and the board of education wanted to dismiss her, but Ms. Bein claimed that she was competent and that she had a right not to participate in the activities listed.[52]

The New York Commissioner of Education found that although Bein would not participate in the flag salute, gift exchanges, or other activities she considered religious, she made other provisions for such activities in her classroom. Through the cooperation of some parents, older students, and other teachers, such activities continued as a regular part of the children's schooling. Thus he ruled that the discharge of the teacher was a violation of the establishment clause of the First Amendment.

By contrast, a probationary teacher in Chicago lost her job when she refused, for religious reasons, to follow the prescribed curriculum. Ms. Palmer, also a member of Jehovah's Witnesses, claimed that she would not be able "to teach any subjects having to do with love of country, the flag, or other patriotic matters in the prescribed curriculum." She also considered it idolatry to observe the birthdays of former presidents. The U.S. Court of Appeals ruled in favor of the school board and said that "the First Amendment was not a license for uncontrolled expression at variance with established curricular content. Although Palmer's rights to her religious beliefs are to be protected, she may not impose her views on the students, who have a right to pursue the agreed-upon curriculum.[53] (The U.S. Supreme Court upheld this decision.)

Summary and Conclusions

Conflicts over the proper relationship between church and state seem to be perennial. They were among the most important reasons for the migration of people to the United States, yet the conflicts continued here. Just as most cultural conflicts find expression in our schools, differing interpretations of the proper relationship between religion and public education have led to bitter disagreements and lawsuits.* From among these conflicts,

*These controversial issues involve significant policy matters. Students not acquainted with the issues might read some of the many available books or pamphlets. See, for example, Lawrence Byrnes, *Religion and Public Education*, New York, Harper & Row, 1975, and *Religion in the Public Schools*, Washington, D.C., American Association of School Administrators, 1964.

those selected for analysis in this chapter were ones that centrally involved the rights of students and teachers.

The issues in these cases arose out of compulsory flag salute in the schools, Bible reading and prayers, religious objections to sex education and to ROTC, objections to compulsory schooling, policies related to leaves for teachers, and to teachers' objections to participating in certain school activities.

Although the law on this subject is still changing, authoritative cases have ruled as follows:

1. Courts have held that students and teachers may be exempted from saluting the flag if they object as a matter of religion or of conscience.
2. School requirements that students stand during the pledge have been rejected by courts since standing is "a gesture of respect and acceptance." Refusal to stand in such a situation is protected by the First Amendment. Furthermore, students who refuse to participate in the flag salute or to stand during it may not be removed from the classroom, for that would constitute punishment for the exercise of a constitutional right.
3. The state or a school district may require that schools foster patriotism and respect for the symbols of our nation, including the flag. When a flag salute, or other patriotic exercises are in progress, objecting students or teachers must behave responsibly and respect the rights of those who wish to participate in such activities.
4. The practices of Bible reading or prayers in the public schools violate the establishment clause of the First Amendment and therefore are unconstitutional, whether or not students must participate in such exercises or are excused from them. The activities themselves are unconstitutional when carried on in a public school.
5. A student who attends school pursuant to a compulsory attendance law may not be required to participate in ROTC if he objects to it as a matter of conscience or religion. A 1934 case held that a state college or university may require ROTC participation as a condition of attendance, since students choose to go to college and are not forced by law to do so. Whether this distinction would be applied by the courts today is an open question.
6. The Supreme Court ruled that Amish children do not have to attend public high schools because the curriculum would conflict with their religious beliefs and way of life. This decision, which seems to challenge state-required high school attendance, was carefully limited by the Court and is not likely to be applied to religious groups of more recent origin. The Court emphasized the

unique characteristics of the Amish, including their close-knit communal living for over 300 years.

7. Teachers' leave of absence policies are governed by state laws and local rules. Although these must be reasonable and consistent with the Constitution, boards of education must have discretion in order to conduct schools in the best interest of children. Thus, courts have held that schools may, but do not have to, allow paid personal necessity leaves to be used for the observance of religious holidays. Another case held that even unexcused "excessive" absence by a teacher might be justified when taken for religious reasons.

8. If a teacher has genuine religious objections to certain common primary school activities, such as birthday celebrations, holiday decorations, and gift exchanges, she does not have to participate in them. However, she is responsible to provide for such activities with the help of others, such as cooperating parents, other teachers, or older students.

It is clear from the analysis of relevant cases that the First Amendment's rights to freedom of religion apply to students and to teachers. They are among the preferred or fundamental rights of our Constitution and a public school may restrict them only by showing that a compelling state interest must take precedence over the individual's right. This is a significant change from earlier practices when the religious rights of students and teachers could be curtailed if the schools had any reasonable grounds to do so. The current legal test favors the civil rights of students and teachers as long as they exercise their rights in a responsible way.

NOTES

1. 319 U.S. 624 (1943).
2. *Minersville* v. *Gobitis*, 310 U.S. 586 (1940). Note: The phrase *"under* God" was not in the pledge when this case arose, having been added by an act of Congress in 1954.
3. These arguments are paraphrased from the case. Id. at 587–588.
4. Id. at 593. The Court also noted that "the affirmative pursuit of one's convictions about the ultimate mystery of the universe and man's relation to it is placed beyond the reach of law. Government may not interfere with organized or individual expression of belief or disbelief. Propagation of belief—or even disbelief—in the supernatural is protected, whether in church or chapel, mosque or synagogue, tabernacle or meeting house. Likewise the Constitution assures generous immunity to the individual from imposition of penalties for offending, in the course of his own religious activities, the religious views of others, be they a minority or those who are dominant in government."
5. Id. at 593–594.
6. Id. at 598.

7. Id. at 600.
8. Id. at 600.
9. Id. at 605.
10. 319 U.S. 624, 629 (1943).
11. Id. at 628.
12. Id. at 631.
13. Id. at 642.
14. Id. at 638.
15. Id. at 653, 654.
16. *Abington School District* v. *Schempp*, 374 U.S. 203, 205 (1963).
17. Id. at 31−32.
18. Id. at 223.
19. For authority it simply referred to a case it had adjudicated the year before; *Engle* v. *Vitale*, 370 U.S. 420 (1962).
20. *Meltzer* v. *Board of Public Instruction of Orange City*, 548 F.2d 559 (5th Cir. 1977).
21. *Stone* v. *Graham* 101 S.Ct. 192 (1980).
22. *Florey* v. *Sioux Falls School Dist.*, 49−5, 619 F.2d 1311 (1980), cert. denied Nov. 10, 1980.
23. *Gaines* v. *Anderson*, 421 F.Supp. 337 (1976).
24. *Brandon* v. *Board of Education of Guilderland*, 487 F.Supp. 1219 (N.D. N.Y. 1980).
25. *Malnak* v. *Yogi*, 440 F.Supp. 1284 (1977).
26. *Spence* v. *Bailey*, 465 F.2d 797 (6th Cir. 1972).
27. *Hamilton* v. *Regents*, 293 U.S. 245 (1934).
28. Id. at 265−266.
29. *Spence* at 800.
30. Id. at 801.
31. *Banks* v. *Board of Public Instruction of Dade County*, 314 F.Supp. 285 (S.D. Fla. 1970).
32. *Frain* v. *Baron*, 307 F.Supp. 27 (E.D. N.Y. 1969).
33. James Bowman et al., eds., *Of Education and Human Community:* Lincoln. University of Nebraska Press, 1973, p. 106.
34. *Wisconsin* v. *Yoder*, 406 U.S. 205 (1972)
35. Id. at 1537−1538.
36. Id. at 1546.
37. Id. at 1533.
38. *F. and F.* v. *Duval County*, 273 So.2d 15 (Fla. 1973).
39. 268 U.S. 510 (1925).
40. *Hardwick* v. *Board of School Trustees*, 54 Cal. App. 696, 205 P.49 (1921).
41. *Moody* v. *Cronin*, 484 F.Supp. 270 (C.D. Ill. 1979).
42. *"J.B." and "B.B." as Guardians and Natural Parents of "P.B. and J.B."* v. *Dumont Board of Education,* Dec. N.J. Comm'r of Educ. (1977).
43. *Citizens for Parental Rights,* v. *San Mateo City Board of Education*, 124 Cal. Rptr. 68 (Cal. App. 1975).
44. *Williams* v. *Board of Education of County of Kanawha*, 388 F.Supp. 93 (S.D. W.Va. 1975).
45. Reported in the "Daily Collegian," University of Massachusetts, February 9, 1971.

46. *Williams* v. *Eaton*, 468 F.2d 1079 (10th Cir. 1972).

47. *Opinions of the Justices to the Governor*, 363 N.E.2d 251 (Mass. 1977).

48. *Russo* v. *Central School District No. 1*, 469 F.2d 623 (2nd Cir. 1972).

49. *Cal. Teachers Association* v. *Board of Trustees*, 138 Cal. Rptr. 817 (Cal. App. 1977).

50. *Rankins* v. *Commission On Professional Competence*, 142 Cal. Rptr. 101 (Cal. Ct. App. 1977).

51. *Ranking* v. *Commission On Professional Competence*, 154 Cal. Rptr. 907 (1979).

52. *Matter of Bein*, 15 Educ. Dept. rept. 407, N.Y., Comm'r Dec. No. 9226, (1976).

53. *Palmer* v. *Board of Education of City of Chicago*, 603 F.2 1271 (7th Cir. 1979).

Chapter 8
Student Freedom of
Association

> While the last thing we would wish to do is to interfere with the
> right of freedom of association or the civil rights of the students
> involved, we must maintain an orderly system of
> administration of our public schools.
>
> —*Passel* v. *Fort Worth School District*[1]

> When they ask for change, they, the students, speak in the
> tradition of Jefferson and Madison and the First Amendment.
> The First Amendment does not authorize violence. But it
> does authorize advocacy, group activities, and espousal of
> change.
>
> —*Healy* v. *James*[2]

"Among the rights protected by the First Amendment," wrote Supreme
Court Justice Lewis Powell, "is the right of individuals to associate to
further their personal beliefs." Although freedom of association is not
explicitly set out in the First Amendment, the Supreme Court has long
held the right to be "implicit in the freedoms of speech, assembly, and
petition."[3]

What behavior is protected by this right? Courts have held that
freedom of association allows Americans the right to organize popular and
unpopular social and political groups if their purposes are legal. Thus the
Constitution protects adults who wish to organize and promote the goals
of the Ku Klux Klan, the Communist party, or the Black Panther party, as
well as homosexual, sexist, and racist social organizations.

Do students attending public schools have similar rights? Should
students be able to organize fraternal or secret clubs that promote
undemocratic practices? Should they be able to form radical political
organizations that promote a revolutionary philosophy and discuss illegal
behavior? Are such groups entitled to official recognition by school
authorities? Should they be allowed to use school facilities? Do student
groups have a right to demonstrate on school grounds? Can officials

prohibit students from inviting controversial speakers to school? These are some of the questions confronted by the cases in this chapter.

FRATERNITIES, SORORITIES, AND SECRET CLUBS

Historical Perspective: Can Secret Societies Be Prohibited?[4]

In 1909 the California legislature declared it unlawful for any public elementary or secondary school student "to join or become a member of any secret fraternity, sorority or club." After the adoption of this act, Doris Bradford, a student at San Francisco's Girls High School, joined a "secret, oathbound Greek letter sorority" known as Omega Nu. As a result Doris was suspended. She took her case to court, arguing that the law was unfair in allowing fraternities and sororities at public colleges but prohibiting them among precollege students.

Questions to Consider

1. Should school boards be able to prohibit secret student organizations? What are the reasons for upholding or prohibiting such regulations?
2. Should schools be able to regulate off-campus student organizations? Under what circumstances would such rules be reasonable?
3. Should a school's power to regulate student organizations depend on the age of the students? Should different standards be applied to high school (or elementary) students than to college students?
4. Should schools be able to prohibit "undemocratic" organizations? Could honor societies, leadership fraternities, or charity clubs be prohibited?

THE OPINION OF THE COURT

In the *Bradford* case the legislation prohibiting secret societies was upheld. Explaining the California appeals court's decision, Judge Kerrigan reviewed the history of Greek letter societies before 1912 and wrote:

> In time many educators came to believe that whatever good might be claimed for college fraternities was not shared by secret fraternities organized among boys and girls attending the preparatory schools whose characters are yet unformed. It has been said of such societies that they tend to engender an undemocratic spirit of caste, to promote cliques, and to foster a contempt for school authority. Doubtless these organizations have many redeeming features. . . . Nevertheless, in order to curb what is said to be their evil effects in secondary schools, rules and regulations have recently been adopted by boards of education in many of the cities of the country . . . and courts have uniformly held valid reasonable rules adapted by school authorities to prevent the establishment and development of those secret societies.[5]

HISTORY REPEATED

After the *Bradford* decision the Omega Nus reorganized themselves into a club called K.Ts, and another high school sorority, Alpha Sigma, became the Manana Club. Other Greek letter organizations followed the same pattern. During the following decades these "new" clubs abandoned their secret handshakes, Greek letter names, and much of the "ritualistic nonsense which had been part of their progenitors."[6] However, many educators believed that there was no real difference between them and the original fraternities and sororities that had been their parent organizations. Therefore, in 1959 the California legislature enacted a revised antifraternity law, and various school districts adopted rules designed to implement the new statute.

On the basis of this law the Sacramento Board of Education resolved that it was "detrimental and inimical to the best interests of the public school" and to the "government, discipline, and morale of the pupils" for any student to belong to any fraternity, sorority, or nonschool club that perpetuates its membership by the decision of its own members. The board determined that such organizations "engender an undemocratic spirit in the pupils." The regulation, however, was not intended to prohibit membership in nationally known movements "organized for citizenship training," such as the YMCA, the Girl Scouts, or youth groups sponsored by recognized churches and service clubs.

The Case of the Manana Club: Are Undemocratic Clubs Unconstitutional?[7]

When the Sacramento Board of Education began to enforce its rule against the Manana Club, one of its members, Judy Robinson, went to court to have the rule declared unconstitutional. She argued that the club was not a secret society and submitted to the court a copy of the club's constitution and bylaws, which described its objectives as being "literature, charity and democracy." The trial court agreed with Robinson's position. However, a California appeals court "looked beyond" the club's stated objectives, found that it had very different purposes, and upheld the rules of the school board.

In regard to Robinson's contention that only secret organizations were prohibited, the appeals court wrote that when the legislature referred to "secret" fraternities, sororities and clubs, it spoke generally of those social organizations that (1) derive their membership principally from the public schools; (2) use a selection process designed to create a membership composed of the "socially elite"; and (3) try to maintain class segregation and distinction by "self-perpetuation, rushing, pledging," and admitting a "select few" from the total student body. Those were the practices that the legislature considered harmful and that it sought to stamp out. "And those were the practices," wrote Judge Pierce, "which these clubs, the offspring of the fraternities and sororities, have carefully nurtured and perpetuated over the years."

The practices and rules of the Manana Club belied its stated democratic objectives. Only 20 girls throughout the entire Sacramento school system could be "rushed" each semester, each candidate had to be sponsored by three members, and new members were chosen through a secret process by an admissions committee that investigated each candidate.

The court pointed out that statutes in over 20 states outlawed high school fraternities and organizations such as the Manana Club;[8] that numerous cases over the past 50 years had upheld such legislation;[9] and that only a 1922 Missouri case had held that such prohibitions by a school board went beyond its authority.[10]

The court acknowledged that adults have the right to form clubs ("secret or nonsecret") and the right to be "as snobbish as they choose." Moreover, any attempt to interfere with that right by the legislature would be "arbitrary, unreasonable, and therefore in violation of the First Amendment." But the court emphasized that the constitutional right of free assembly as applied to adults (or even college students) was not involved in this case. Here we are not dealing with adults "but with adolescents in their formative years."

The court also acknowledged that high school fraternities, sororities, and clubs undoubtedly accomplish some good—"mostly to those who belong to them, giving them a sense of security, a feeling of being wanted." But the school board had said that the harm these societies do outweighs the good. School boards are professional in the field; the courts are laymen. "Under these circumstances," wrote Judge Pierce, "we cannot superimpose our judgment over theirs."

Here the school board was not dealing with activities that occurred only within the home. It was dealing "under express statutory mandate" with activities that reached into the school and that were believed "to interfere with the educational process." Thus Judge Pierce concluded that the activities of these prohibited organizations were designed "not to foster democracy (as the Manana Constitution preaches) but to frustrate democracy (as the Manana Club by its admitted activities practices)."

Charity Clubs: Conflicting Views

Janie Passel was a high school student who lived in Fort Worth, Texas, and belonged to a "charity club." The club was prohibited by school board policy because new members were admitted by secret ballot of the old members, and all students were not free to join. The board policy was authorized by state legislation similar to the California statute in *Robin-*

son. Although Passel claimed that the policy and statute unconstitutionally interfered with her freedom of association, the Texas Supreme Court
refused to overrule the board or the legislature.[11] One of the justices,
however, strongly disagreed.

In a dissenting opinion, Justice Smith emphasized that the organization to which Janie Passel belonged was a "charity" club whose purpose
was to "promote friendship" among its members. The dissent pointed out
that no club meetings were to be conducted during school hours or on
school property. The objective of the club (and others that belonged to a
council of charity clubs) was "to contribute to local charitable institutions
through proceeds from various non-professional entertainments and to
promote loyalty, congeniality, lofty ideals and character among high
school students, girls and boys." There was "no hint in the evidence" that
the charity clubs were charged with subversive or any other improper
activity, except in the selection of members contrary to the rule of the
school district. On the other hand, the evidence showed that certain clubs
had raised as much as $4000 for such organizations as the Mental Health
Association and the Fort Worth Children's Hospital.[12]

The dissent pointed out that the legislature had only authorized
school boards to regulate organizations "in" the public school system.
Justice Smith therefore argued that since these charity clubs were not in
the schools, they could not be regulated by school boards. (On the other
hand, if the statute had been intended to apply to clubs that were outside
the schools, then it was unconstitutional.) "In my opinion," wrote the
justice, "the statute is unconstitutional not only because of deprivation of
freedom of association, but also because of discrimination in favor of those
clubs or organizations specifically exempted," such as Boy Scouts, Hi-Y,
De Molay, and similar educational organizations. Justice Smith concluded: "I cannot conceive of any justification for a requirement that these
clubs be disbanded or that the children be suspended from the school of
their choice."

This dissent would seem to be in accord with the principles of *Tinker*
and a trend of decisions expanding student rights. However, most judges
have consistently refused to overturn 50 years of judicial opinion upholding state legislation prohibiting fraternities, sororities, and secret societies
among public school students.

THE RIGHT TO ORGANIZE AND USE SCHOOL FACILITIES

The Healy Case: Can Radical Groups be Denied Recognition?[13]

In 1969 a climate of unrest prevailed on many campuses in this country.
There had been widespread civil disobedience at some colleges, accompanied by the seizure of buildings, vandalism, and arson. During that

time local chapters of SDS (Students for a Democratic Society) had engaged in disruption and violence on some of those campuses. During the 1968–1969 academic year, 850 demonstrations were reported, resulting in over 4000 arrests, 125 students injured, and more than 60 arson incidents.[14] It was in this climate of unrest that a group of students attending Central Connecticut State College (CCSC) began to organize a local chapter of SDS in September 1969.

The Supreme Court case of *Healy* v. *James* was a result of these SDS efforts. Although college cases are not always applicable to high school students, we have included this one because there is no recent Supreme Court case on this topic involving high school students and the principles laid down by the Court in *Healy* have been applied to public school situations.

FACTS OF THE CASE

A group of students at Central Connecticut requested official recognition for a local SDS chapter. The request specified three purposes for the proposed organization: (1) it would provide "a forum of discussion and self-education for students developing an analysis of American society and institutions"; (2) since "ideas without parallel in deeds are empty," it would serve as "an agency for integrating thought with action so as to bring about constructive changes in the university, in American life and the world"; (3) "because of the responsibility of all peoples for the welfare of others, SDS would provide a coordinating body for relating the problems of leftist students and other groups."

The Student Affairs Committee was satisfied with the statement of purposes, but was concerned over the possible relationship between the local group and the national SDS. Representatives of the proposed group, however, stated they would not affiliate "with any national organization" and they accepted some but not all of the aims of the national SDS. The committee approved the application, but the college president, Dr. James, rejected it for these reasons:

1. The statement of purpose to form a local chapter of SDS "carries full and unmistakable adherence to at least some of the major tenets of the national organization."
2. The aims and philosophy of SDS, "which includes disruption and violence," are contrary to the college policy that states: "Students do not have the right to invade the privacy of others, to damage the property of others, to disrupt the regular and essential operation of the college, or to interfere with the rights of others."
3. If the proposed group intends to follow this established college policy, they have not clarified why they wish to become a local chapter of an organization that openly repudiates such a policy.
4. Freedom of speech, the right to establish a forum for the exchange

of ideas, and the right to organize public demonstrations and protests in an orderly manner are all "freedoms on which we stand." But to approve any local organization that joins another organization that "openly repudiates those principles" threatens the freedoms of both students and faculty.

Shortly after the president's rejection, SDS members called a meeting in the Student Center to discuss further action. However, the meeting was disbanded by two of the college's deans on the president's order, since nonrecognized groups were not entitled to use such facilities. As a result of these events, they filed suit on the grounds that the denial of recognition violated their First Amendment rights of expression and association.

The district court dismissed the suit. This decision was approved by a divided U.S. Court of Appeals, and the students appealed to the U.S. Supreme Court.

Questions to Consider

1. If you were the president of the college, would you have approved the local SDS chapter? Under what circumstances, if any, would you disapprove of a student organization? Would nonrecognition of a student group violate any constitutional rights?
2. Can a school administration deny recognition to a local group because of its affiliation with a national organization that has caused campus violence? Because the proposed group refuses to affirm its willingness to adhere to school rules?
3. Can nonrecognition be based on a proposed organization's philosophy that is in basic conflict with the goals of the school? On an administration's honest fear that the student organization would be a disruptive influence on campus?

LEGAL PRINCIPLES

At the outset of its opinion the Supreme Court outlined the constitutional principles applicable to the case. Justice Powell pointed out that public colleges "are not enclaves immune from the sweep of the First Amendment." At the same time, these rights must always be applied "in light of the special characteristics of the environment in the particular case." Despite the recognized need for order in the schools, Justice Powell noted that "the precedents of this Court leave no room for the view that . . . First Amendment protections should apply with less force on ᵢcollege campuses than in the community at large." On the contrary, as the Court has repeatedly emphasized, "the vigilant protection of constitutional freedoms is nowhere more vital than in the community of American schools." And among the rights protected by the Constitution is the right of individuals to associate to further their personal beliefs.

• **Is Nonrecognition a Constitutional Question?** The lower courts held that President James's denial of official recognition "cannot be legitimately magnified and distorted" into an unconstitutional interference with the rights of the students. The circuit court pointed out that the SDS students could still meet as a group and distribute materials off campus and meet together informally on campus as individuals. According to this view, all that was denied was the "administrative seal of official college respectability." The Supreme Court, however, disagreed.

"There can be no doubt," wrote Justice Powell, "that denial of official recognition, without justification, to college organizations" abridges their constitutional right of association. In this case nonrecognition denied the students the use of campus facilities, bulletin boards, and the school newspaper. Since this clearly limited the organization's "ability to participate in the intellectual give and take of campus debate and to pursue its purposes," nonrecognition could not be viewed as "insubstantial."

• **Burden of Proof.** According to the Supreme Court the lower courts also erred in assuming that the students had the burden of proving that they were entitled to recognition by the college and that President James's rejection could rest on the students' failure to convince the administration that their organization was unaffiliated with the national SDS. In this case the students should not have had the "burden of proof." Once they filed an application in conformity with the college requirements, the burden should have been on the administration to justify its decision of rejection. Although a school has a legitimate interest in acting to prevent disruption, a "heavy burden" rests on the college to demonstrate the appropriateness of that action.

CRITIQUE OF THE PRESIDENT'S DECISION

Two fundamental errors required the Supreme Court to reverse the lower court rulings. The errors were discounting the First Amendment implications of nonrecognition and misplacing the burden of proof. In addition to ruling on these questions Justice Powell wrote a detailed analysis of President James's decision, examining four possible justifications for the action and considering whether any of them were constitutionally adequate.

• **The Relationship with National SDS.** Because some SDS chapters had been associated with disruptive and violent campus activity, President James apparently considered that an affiliation between the students and national SDS was sufficient justification for denying recognition. The Supreme Court, however, "has consistently disapproved governmental action . . . denying rights and privileges solely because of a citizen's association with an unpopular organization." In numerous cases it has been established that "guilt by association" is an impermissible basis upon which to deny First Amendment rights. To restrict such rights the government has the burden of establishing not only "a knowing affiliation with an organization possessing unlawful aims" but also "a specific intent to further those illegal aims."[15]

SDS is a loosely structured organization with various factions that promote diverse social and political views, only some of which call for unlawful action. The students in this case proclaim their independence from national SDS. Therefore the Court concluded that this relationship was not an adequate ground for denial of recognition.

• **The Philosophy of SDS.** President James had characterized the local SDS group as adhering to a philosophy of violence and disruption. He wrote that he was unwilling to "sanction an organization that openly advocates the destruction of the very ideals and freedoms upon which the academic life is founded."

The Court, however, ruled that "the mere disagreement of the President with the group's philosophy affords no reason to deny it recognition." As repugnant as these views might be to a college president, the mere expression of them would not justify the denial of First Amendment rights. Whether the students did or did not advocate "a philosophy of destruction" is immaterial. A public college "may not restrict speech or association simply because it finds the views expressed by an group abhorrent." To support this point, the Court quoted a 1961 opinion by Justice Black: "The freedoms of speech, press and assembly guaranteed by the First Amendment must be accorded to the ideas we hate, or sooner or later they will be denied to the ideas we cherish."[16]

• **A Disruptive Influence.** A third reason for President James's decision was his conclusion that the local SDS group was likely to be a "disruptive influence" at the college. If this conclusion was based on the organization's activities rather than its philosophy, and if it was factually supported by the evidence, there might have been a basis for nonrecognition. As the Court pointed out, "associational activities" need not be tolerated where they "infringe reasonable campus rules, interrupt classes, or substantially interfere with the opportunity of other students to obtain an education."

Justice Powell emphasized the importance of distinguishing between speech and action, between the permissible discussion of *any* question (including violence and disruption) and impermissible advocacy "directed to inciting or producing imminent lawless action." Thus, if there had been adequate evidence to support the conclusion that the proposed SDS chapter posed "a substantial threat of material disruption," the president's decision could have been affirmed.

In this case, however, there was no substantial evidence to indicate that these students acting together would constitute a disruptive force on campus. Therefore "insofar as non-recognition flowed from such fears, it constituted little more than the sort of 'undifferentiated fear or apprehension of disturbance which is not enough to overcome the right to freedom of expression.'"

• **Refusal to Follow School Rules.** At a campus hearing, representatives of the proposed SDS group had stated that they did not know whether they might respond to "issues of violence" as had SDS chapters on other campuses or whether they might ever "envision interrupting a class." If these remarks were read as announcing the students' "unwillingness to be bound by reasonable school rules governing conduct," it suggested to Justice Powell a fourth reason for nonrecognition. Although students may advocate amending or even doing away with any or all campus regulations, they may not ignore such rules.

In schools, as in the general community, individuals must respect reasonable regulations concerning the time, place, and manner in which groups may conduct their activities. As the Court indicated, a school administration may require that a group seeking official recognition "affirm in advance its willingness to adhere to reasonable campus law." Such a requirement "does not impose an impermissible condition on the students' association rights." It would not infringe their freedom to speak out, assemble, or petition for changes in school rules.

In this case it was unclear whether the college had such a rule and if so whether the proposed group intended to comply with it. Assuming the existence of a rule such as this, the Court emphasized that "the benefits of participation in the internal life of the college community may be denied to any group that reserves the right to violate any valid campus rules with which they disagree."

CONCLUSION

In sum, the Court held that nonrecognition by the college deprived the students of their constitutional rights and that the college had the burden of proving that nonrecognition was justified. Furthermore, in discussing the possible grounds for the president's action, it outlined the criteria and principles to be applied by schools and courts in other cases similar to this. In conclusion, Justice Powell observed:

> The wide latitude accorded by the Constitution to the freedoms of expression and association is not without its costs in terms of the risk to the maintenance of civility and an ordered society. Indeed, this latitude often has resulted, on the campus and elsewhere, in the infringement of the rights of others. Though we deplore the tendency of some to abuse the very constitutional principles they invoke, and although the infringement of rights of others certainly should not be tolerated, we reaffirm this Court's dedication to the

principles of the Bill of Rights upon which our vigorous and free society is founded.[17]

CONCURRING CRITIQUE

In an unusual concurring opinion, Justice William O. Douglas presented a personal analysis of the current confrontation between students and faculty and a strong defense of student demands for change:

> Many inside and out of faculty circles realize that one of the main problems of faculty members is their own re-education or re-orientation. Some have narrow specialities that are hardly relevant to modern times. History has passed others by, leaving them interesting relics of a by-gone day. More often than not they represent those who withered under the pressures of McCarthyism or other forces of conformity and represent but a timid replica of those who once brought distinction to the ideal of academic freedom.
>
> The confrontation between them and the oncoming students has often been upsetting. The problem is not of choosing sides. Students—who by reason of the Twenty-sixth Amendment become eligible to vote when 18 years of age—are adults who are members of the college or university community. Their interests and concerns are often quite different from those of the faculty. They often have values, views, and ideologies that are at war with the ones which the college has traditionally espoused or indoctrinated. When they ask for change, they, the students, speak in the tradition of Jefferson and Madison and the First Amendment.
>
> The First Amendment does not authorize violence. But it does authorize advocacy, group activities, and espousal of change.
>
> The present case is miniscule in the events of the 60's and 70's. But the fact that it has to come here for ultimate resolution, indicates the sickness of our academic world, measured by First Amendment standards. Students as well as faculty are entitled to credentials in their search for truth. If we are to become an integrated, adult society, rather than a stubborn status quo opposed to change, students and faculties should have communal interests in which each age learns from the other. Without ferment of one kind or another, a college or university (like a federal agency or other human institution) becomes a useless appendage to a society which traditionally has reflected the spirit of rebellion.[18]

The Beresh Case: Patently Unconstitutional[19]

The Mumford Young Socialist Alliance and the Mumford Committee to End Stress asked to become recognized student organizations at Mumford High School. However, the principal, Myer Beresh, turned them down because of a school policy that forbids recognition to student groups that advocate "controversial" ideas or that "stress one side" of issues. Beresh also argued that the operation of the schools would be impaired if "any number and type" of student organization were allowed to "proliferate." However, a federal district court in Michigan was not persuaded by these arguments and ruled in favor of the students.

There was no evidence that the student groups planned or advocated disruptive activities, and they complied with all school rules concerning recognition. Under these circumstances the court ruled that it is "patently unconstitutional" to deny recognition to a student group because it advocates controversial ideas or because of the speculation that it might lead to the proliferation of other organizations. Therefore the judge ordered that the two student groups "are to be granted recognition immediately" and that the school should pay for the court costs and attorney fees.

Homosexual Organizations: Must Gay Groups Be Recognized?

When the Virginia Commonwealth University refused to approve the Gay Alliance of Students (GAS) as a "registered organization," the students went to court. GAS was a prohomosexual political group that advocated liberalizing the laws against practicing homosexuals. The university rejected the application because it believed that recognition would increase homosexual activity on campus and attract homosexuals to the university. However, a federal appeals court ruled in favor of the students.[20]

The court said that registration would not imply approval of GAS's aims just as it does not imply approval of the other 95 registered campus organizations. The judge noted that individuals "of whatever sexual persuasion have the fundamental right to meet, discuss current problems, and to advocate changes in the *status quo*" as long as they do not advocate unlawful activity. If, however, GAS members engaged in illegal homosexual activity, then the university could restrict such conduct. As *Healy* pointed out, the critical line must be drawn "between advocacy which is entitled to full protection, and action which is not." There was no evidence that GAS was devoted to illegal sexual practices and *being* a homosexual is not a crime. Although the university could punish homosexuals who engaged in illegal conduct or who caused substantial disruption, it could not suppress the associational rights of homosexuals.

In a provocative concurring opinion, Judge Markey pointed out the futility of trying to influence student ideas by not recognizing or not registering student organizations. He noted that, according to the prevailing law, groups advocating "any idea, any change in the law" are as entitled to registration as the GAS. Thus, he wrote, associations devoted to "social acceptance of sadism, euthanasia, masochism, murder, genocide, segregation, gambling, or voodoo" must be registered if they properly apply. Therefore, the denial of registration "is a weak, if not impotent, tool" in a school's effort to control student conduct. Even though the ideas of some associations may be abhorrent or sickening, the judge wrote that "the stifling of advocacy is even more abhorrent, even

more sickening" because "it rings the death knoll of a free society."
Schools, he concluded, "cannot inculcate values by unlawfully impeding
the exercise of a fundamental value, the right to speak."*

Questions to Consider

1. Should homosexual organizations be as broadly protected in high
   school as in college? Should courts protect them as fully as political
   organizations?
2. Should religious organizations or Bible study clubs be able to carry on
   their activities in high schools just like any other student group?
3. What are some of the reasons for protecting or for limiting freedom of
   association in the public schools?

A DISSENTING OPINION

In 1977 a divided federal appeals court ruled that the University of
Missouri could not withhold formal recognition of Gay Lib, a student
group that advocated homosexual rights.** In a dissenting statement,
Judge Gibson expressed a view that might be persuasive to many courts if
a case such as this arose in a public high school:

> These institutions are populated by young, often impressionable students;
> school officials have a responsibility to shield students from exposure to
> probable illegal conduct on campus. Missouri has criminalized sodomy. . . .
> Under these circumstances it was permissible for school officials to withhold
> recognition of Gay Lib. Requiring the school to recognize Gay Lib places
> school officials in the unseemly position of officially sanctioning this conduct
> and making school funds and facilities available for the use of a homosexual
> organization, whose members will likely engage in criminal activity, a
> situation not mandated by the First Amendment.[21]

A Bible Study Club: Should Religious Groups Be Recognized?

At California's Edison High School, over 100 students petitioned school
officials to recognize a voluntary Bible study club who wanted to meet on
campus during lunch hour. When their petition was rejected, the

---

*In a related case, another Federal appeals court protected the right of the Gay Students'
Organization of the University of New Hampshire to hold dances and other social functions
as long as they are not substantially disruptive and do not promote illegal behavior. *Gay
Students' Organization of the University of New Hampshire* v. *Bonner*, 509 F.2d 652 (1st
Cir. 1974).

**The university appealed this decision to the U.S. Supreme Court. A majority of the Court
decided not to review the case. But in a strong dissenting opinion, Justice Rehnquist argued
that the Court should consider this controversial issue and indicated his support for the
University's position. *Ratchford, President, University of Missouri* v. *Gay Lib*, 434 U.S.
1080 (1978).

students sued to gain official recognition that was necessary for using classrooms, bulletin boards, and having access to the school newspaper. May a public school permit a Bible study group to meet on campus during the school day like any other student organization? In 1977 a California appeals court answered "no."[22]

The court wrote that if the Bible group was recognized as an official student club, "state financial support would flow directly to the club." Without charge it would be entitled to a paid faculty sponsor and to use classroom space, heat and light, and auditing assistance. As a school-"sponsored" group, it would be able to use the school name and the school newspaper and be able to solicit contributions on campus. This then would "place school support and sponsorship" behind the religious objectives of the club, which would meet at a time when students are compelled by law to attend school. For these reasons, the court ruled that permitting the Bible study club to operate on campus would violate the Constitution because it would "foster excessive state entanglement with religion." The court concluded that the First Amendment does not permit a group "to use the prestige and authority of the school" to proselytize their beliefs among students who are compelled to be on campus and "may be vulnerable to the pressure of an officially recognized student organization."

In a strong dissenting opinion, Justice McDaniel wrote that the majority decision was unfair and unreasonable. On the basis of *Healy* and *Tinker*, he argued that public schools may not discriminate against voluntary student religious groups and solely on that basis deny them recognition. The dissent denied that "recognition" implied "approval." Justice McDaniel noted that the First Amendment protected the right of student groups to discuss "recreational, educational, political, economic, artistic, moral, or even agnostic" subjects. Therefore, he concluded that it was illogical for the majority to interpret the Constitution, ("which includes a guarantee of religious liberty") so "that religion is the one subject not protected" in the public schools.

THE RIGHT TO PROTEST AND DEMONSTRATE

The Gebert Case: Are Sit-ins Protected?[23]

Thirty-six students who attended Pennsylvania's Abington High School participated in sit-in demonstrations during and after school. On the second day of the sit-in the students were cleared from the high school and were suspended for participating in the demonstrations. Evidence indicated that (1) the students attempted to conduct their sit-in "with respect" for orderly school operations; (2) the demonstrations attracted a crowd that congregated in the hallways; (3) school officials could not attend to their normal duties because they had to keep close watch on the sit-in; and (4) some of the demonstrators did not attend classes, were noisy in the halls, and forced the rescheduling of a few classes.

The students claimed that the sit-in was an activity that should be protected under the First Amendment, and they took their case to court.

Questions to Consider

1. Was this sit-in protected by the First Amendment? Was the suspension of these students a violation of their constitutional rights?
2. Should sit-ins or other demonstrations be permitted in school? If so, when and under what circumstances?
3. What should justify the prohibition of a demonstration? The response of curious or angry students? A substantial disruption in the duties of school officials? Missing classes by demonstrators? Noise in the hallways? The need to reschedule classes?
4. Should the intention of the demonstrators to be peaceful and nondisruptive be a significant factor in determining whether or not to punish them?

Since the sit-in interfered with the operation of the school, the question before the court was whether the interference was so "material and substantial" as to justify the suspension of the student demonstrators.

In deciding this issue, should school officials consider the disruptive reaction of the nonparticipating students? Not according to Judge Joseph Lord. In cases such as this, courts and administrators should only consider "the conduct of the demonstrators and not the reaction of the audience." Therefore, the fact that the demonstrations attracted a crowd that congregated in the hallways "cannot be a basis for punishing the demonstrators' exercise of their First Amendment rights."

Was the fact that school officials could not attend to their normal duties an adequate basis for suspending the students? Again the court answered "no." According to Judge Lord, if demonstrations could be stopped simply because some observers overreact or the demonstration requires special administrative supervision, then "all forms of constitutionally protected activity could be barred from the schools." Therefore the court emphasized the importance of distinguishing between "evidence that administrators left scheduled duties in order to keep an eye on potentially disruptive conditions in the schools from evidence that disruptive activity by demonstrators actually occurred."

Did the conduct of the sit-in participants themselves substantially interfere with appropriate school discipline? The court found that it did. "Appropriate discipline," wrote the judge, "certainly requires students to attend their scheduled classes and to refrain from preventing other students from attending classes in their scheduled location." The court recognized that the students involved in the sit-in did not intend to be disruptive, but the evidence indicated that student demonstrators did not attend classes, forced some classes to be relocated, and moved noisily through the halls. Based on such facts, the court found that the demonstrations did substantially disrupt the educational program, and, therefore, the action of the school officials in terminating the sit-in by suspending the students did not violate First Amendment rights.

In sum, the *Gebert* case held that a student sit-in was not illegal merely because it was in school, because other students gathered to watch, or because school administrators could not attend to their regular duties. The court, however, found that these demonstrators did substantially interfere with school activities because they were noisy, missed scheduled classes, and required others to be relocated.

The Sword Case: Prohibiting In-School Demonstrations[24]

Although Judge Lord ruled against the students who brought the *Gebert* case to his court, his opinion indicated a flexible attitude concerning student demonstrations. However, as *Sword* v. *Fox* illustrates, other judges have not been as liberal or as flexible in their approach.

The *Sword* case involved the rules of a public college in Virginia that categorically prohibited all student demonstrations inside any school building. Pursuant to these rules, a group of students were disciplined for taking part in a sit-in demonstration in the administration building. The students challenged the regulation as an unconstitutional restraint on their freedom of speech and assembly.

In upholding the regulation a federal court pointed out that the rule did not restrict "the *right* to protest but the *place* of protest." Although the court acknowledged that "a flat ban on campus demonstrations would be manifestly invalid," it emphasized that students do not have an "unlimited right to demonstrate." Hence schools may place "reasonable, non-discriminatory" restrictions on demonstrations "to protect safety and property" and "maintain normal operations." The court held that this regulation was reasonable since it was not used to deny students the right to protest; it only denied the right to protest in college buildings "where order and study" are expected. "It can scarcely be argued," wrote the court, "that demonstrations in a classroom or administration building during the day would not create a disruption in the education activity of the institution." Demonstrations in such buildings at night could also be banned since they offer "too many opportunities for vandalism, and, in some instances, lawlessness." The court held that the regulation prohibiting demonstrations in school buildings was a reasonable exercise of the school's authority.[25]

The Grayned Case: Regulating Demonstrations near School[26]

This Supreme Court case involved Richard Grayned, a high school student who participated in a demonstration in support of minority student grievances on a public sidewalk about 100 feet from a school building. He was convicted of violating a city "anti-noise" ordinance that prohibited any demonstrations on or near school grounds that disturbed classes. Grayned argued that the restriction was unconstitutional.

In upholding the ordinance Justice Thurgood Marshall noted that the constitutionality of a restriction may depend upon what is being regulated and where. "Although a silent vigil may not unduly interfere with a public library, making a speech in the reading room almost certainly would." That same speech, however, would be perfectly appropriate in a park. "The crucial question," wrote the Court, "is whether the manner of expression is basically incompatible with the normal activity of a particular place at a particular time." Just as *Tinker* made clear that "school property may not be declared off-limits for expressive activity by students, we think it clear that the public sidewalk adjacent to school grounds may not be declared off-limits for expressive activity by members of the public." But in each case protected expression may be prohibited if it "materially disrupts classwork."

The Court recognized that public schools are often the focus of significant grievances and that picketing or handbilling near a school "can effectively publicize those grievances" to pedestrians, teachers, administrators, and students "without interfering with normal school activities." On the other hand, "schools could hardly tolerate boisterous demonstrators who make studying impossible, block entrances, or incite children to leave the schoolhouse." The Court concluded that the antinoise ordinance went no further than *Tinker* said a city may go to prevent interference with its schools.

CONTROVERSIAL SPEAKERS

The Vail Case: Can School Officials Prohibit Controversial Speakers?[27]

Prior to the 1972 New Hampshire presidential primary, Democratic and Republican candidates spoke at Portsmouth High School. Shortly thereafter two students attempted to secure permission for Andrew Pulley, vice-presidential candidate of the Socialist Workers party, to speak in school. School policy provided that "candidates seeking political office who are bona fide candidates are given equal time." In this case the superintendent denied the student request on the grounds that Pulley was not a bona fide candidate since he was not 35 years old and therefore was ineligible to serve as vice-president. But the students argued that the school policy and its application violated the First Amendment.

Questions to Consider

1. Should Andrew Pulley have been allowed to speak?
2. Should candidates generally be given an opportunity to present their views to public school students? Should all candidates for every office be given this opportunity? Or can school officials limit speeches to "major candidates" for certain offices?
3. Can schools flatly prohibit all candidates or all political speakers?

THE OPINION OF THE COURT

The district court noted that this type of case involves the balancing of the rights of students protected by the First Amendment with the responsibilities of school officials to regulate public speaking on school property. Since the election had passed by the time this case was decided, Judge Bownes did not order that Pulley be given an opportunity to address the students at Portsmouth High School. He did, however, clarify some of the constitutional principles to be applied by school officials in future controversies involving outside speakers.

First, the school had argued that the students had no right to sue since Andrew Pulley was not a party to the suit. Judge Bownes rejected this argument. Instead he emphasized that freedom of speech "encompasses the right to receive information and ideas." Since the First Amendment includes the right to hear, its protection extends to listeners as well as speakers. Thus the students of Portsmouth High as well as Andrew Pulley could appropriately take a case such as this to court.

Second, the judge indicated that the school might have the authority to bar "all outside speakers." But he felt this would be an unwise policy since "the interchange of ideas and beliefs that is fostered by providing a forum for outside speakers is healthy and beneficial to the entire educational process."

Third, when a school chooses to provide a forum for outside speakers, as Portsmouth High School had, it must do so in a manner consistent with constitutional principles. According to Judge Bownes, this means that:

1. Access to the podium must be permitted without discrimination.
2. The school may not control the influence of a public forum by censoring the ideas, the proponents, or the audience.
3. The right of the student to hear a speaker cannot be left to the discretion of school authorities "on a pick and choose basis."
4. Freedom of speech and assembly requires that "outside speakers be fairly selected and that equal time be given to opposing views."

The Wilson Case: Prohibiting Political Speakers[28]

In Oregon, Dean Wilson, a high school political science teacher, invited a Democrat, a Republican, a member of the John Birch Society, and a communist to speak to his class. The communist was to be the last speaker. But, before his presentation, 800 people signed a petition opposing his speech, and the school board issued an order banning "all political speakers" from the high school. Wilson and one of his students asked a federal court to declare the board's ban unconstitutional.

Could a school ban the discussion of political subjects or all outside political speakers? Judge Burns ruled that it could not. Although the school could prohibit speakers who would substantially disrupt the educational process, no disruptions had occurred in the political science classes and none was expected. Even if evidence indicated that outside speakers were disruptive, the court ruled that the board could not ban "only outside *political* speakers." Nor could school officials justify their policy by contending that "political subjects are inappropriate in a high school curriculum." On the contrary, the court pointed out that political subjects have been frequently discussed in this high school and in schools throughout the country and that such discussions in fact are "required by law."

Officials could not contend that they were merely excluding incompetent speakers. They acted, observed the court, "under pressure from those who feared, rather than doubted, the speaker's competence by banning all speakers without regard to competence." The board apparently issued its order to "placate angry residents and taxpayers." But according to the judge, "neither fear of voter reaction nor personal disagreement with views to be expressed justified a suppression of free expression."

Did the ban violate the Equal Protection Clause? The court answered "yes" for several reasons: (1) The order discriminated against "political" speakers only by banning them from the school. (2) It discriminated against the teachers of politically oriented subjects by prohibiting only them from using outside speakers. (3) The effect of the order that prohibited the communist from speaking was discriminatory. The court noted that "persons with palatable views could speak; those with less readily digestible views could not."

Judge Burns recognized the difficulty faced by school board members in a community in which many persons "equate Communism with violence, deception, and imperialism." He observed, however, that these evils "have occurred under many flags and in the name of many creeds." Furthermore, he noted that schools would eliminate much of their curriculum if they restricted it to theories and practices of "pacifist, honest, and nonexpansionist societies."

The judge concluded his opinion with this statement about education in a democracy:

> I am firmly convinced that a course designed to teach students that a free and democratic society is superior to those in which freedoms are sharply curtailed will fail entirely if it fails to teach one important lesson: that the power of the state is never so great that it can silence a man or woman simply because there are those who disagree. Perhaps that carries with it a second lesson: that those who enjoy the blessings of a free society must occasionally bear the burden of listening to others with whom they disagree, even to the point of outrage.[29]

Although the *Vail* and *Wilson* cases give some indication of the limits of administrative discretion, the following Mississippi case goes much further in detailing what is and is not proper in the regulations of invited speakers. Although the case involves public institutions of higher education, the reasoning of the court is also relevant to elementary and secondary schools.

Stacy v. *Williams:* Judicial Guidelines for Outside Speakers[30]

During the 1968 presidential campaign, student members of the University of Mississippi Young Democrats were denied permission to invite Charles Evers to campus to speak on behalf of the Humphrey-Muskie ticket. The denial was based on the following regulations that were challenged as unconstitutional:

> No speaker shall be invited or permitted to speak on any campus . . . without first having been investigated and approved by the head of the institution involved. . . .
> No person may be permitted to speak . . . who has announced as a political candidate for public office.
> No person shall be permitted to use the facilities of the state institutions of higher learning whose presence will constitute a clear and present danger of inciting a riot.
> No person shall be invited or permitted to speak . . . who advocates the violent overthrow of the government.
> Any person feeling aggrieved at any adverse ruling . . . may file an appeal within five days [to the Board of Trustees] for a hearing at their next succeeding regular Board meeting.[31]

Questions to Consider

1. Which, if any, of these rules do you believe to be unconstitutional?
2. Is it unconstitutional for school officials to investigate invited speakers? Can administrative approval be required? Under what circumstances can officials legally disapprove speakers?

3. Can schools bar outsiders whose "presence" would constitute a danger
   of riot? If the vast majority of both students and faculty voice strong
   opposition to a proposed speaker, does this justify administrative
   disapproval?
4. Can speakers who advocate the violent overthrow of the government
   be prohibited?
5. Do students have a right of appeal if administrators disapprove of a
   proposed speaker? Does a procedure that provides for appeal at the
   "next regular board meeting" protect student rights?

THE OPINION OF THE COURT

In a long and careful opinion a U.S. District Court analyzed each of the
above regulations challenged by the students, indicated why several were
unconstitutional, and then issued new guidelines for outside speakers.

• **The Prohibition of Speakers Who Are Candidates for Public Office.** Judge
Keady noted that some notification and approval requirements are
constitutional in order to avoid scheduling conflicts, provide adequate
security, and allow authorities to rule on proposed speakers in accordance
with careful standards. But this regulation involved the right of the
campus community to hear and participate in discussions of public policy.
The court explained that a major purpose of the First Amendment was to
protect the free discussion of candidates, governmental operations, and
related political questions. Therefore the judge concluded that so long as
the campus remained open to other outside speakers, "it is patently clear"
that regulations may not exclude all candidates.

• **Prohibition of Persons Whose Presence Will Constitute a Danger of Disruption.** The constitutional difficulty with this provision is that it allows a
person to be barred from campus because his mere "presence" creates a
danger. The court noted that this regulation reflected a misconception of
the "clear and present danger" doctrine. "For it is fundamental," wrote
Judge Keady, "that one may not be barred from speaking merely because
his presence alone provokes riotous conduct among the audience." A
person cannot be restrained from speaking and his audience cannot be
prevented from hearing him unless the feared riot is likely to be caused by
what the speaker himself says or does. In circumstances where the
presence of an invited speaker might cause disruption, "attendant law
enforcement officers must quell the mob, not the speaker." That a
speaker may hold views disliked by a majority of the campus community
is not a permissible basis for the denial of the students' right to hear him.

• **Prohibition of Speakers Who Advocate the Violent Overthrow of the Government.** This regulation is defective in that it bars one who "advocates"

violent overthrow of the government without differentiating between "the mere abstract teaching of the moral propriety for a resort to force and violence and preparing a group for violent action." The distinction is that those to whom the advocacy is addressed must be urged to *do* something rather than merely to *believe* in something. And there must be more than "advocacy to action"; there must also be "a reasonable apprehension of imminent danger."

• **Provision for Appeal at Next Regular Board Meeting.** Since aggrieved persons must be afforded prompt review of an adverse decision, which should be conducted prior to the proposed speaking engagement, they may not be required to await the next regularly scheduled board meeting. "For fundamental constitutional liberties," wrote the court, "may well be lost or substantially diluted by such delay." Hence a prompt, fair, and efficient review is necessary to satisfy the students' right to due process.

A JUDICIAL CODE FOR OUTSIDE SPEAKERS

Since the Board of Trustees failed to develop constitutional rules concerning the regulation of guest speakers, the court took the unusual step of issuing its own regulations. This judicial code emphasized that the freedoms of speech and assembly guaranteed by the Constitution provide an opportunity for students at all institutions of higher education in the state to hear outside speakers. This meant that "free discussion of subjects of either controversial or non-controversial nature shall not be curtailed." However, as "there is no absolute right to assemble or to make or hear a speech at any time or place regardless of the circumstances," the judicial code included the following limitations concerning the invitation of outside speakers:

1. Requests to invite speakers will be considered only when made by a recognized student organization.
2. No invitation shall be issued by an organization without prior written concurrence by the head of the institution or his designee. Any request not acted upon within four days shall be deemed granted.
3. A request may be denied only if the institution determines that "the proposed speech will constitute a clear and present danger to the institution's orderly operation by the speaker's advocacy" of such actions as the violent overthrow of the government; the willful destruction or seizure of the institution's buildings; the forcible interference with classes or other educational functions; the physical harm, intimidation, or invasion of the rights of faculty, students, or administrators; or other violent campus disorders.

4. When an organization's request for an outside speaker is denied, it may appeal and obtain a hearing within two days before a Campus Review Committee composed of three faculty members appointed by the Board of Trustees plus the president and secretary of the student body.
5. When the request for an outside speaker is granted, the administration may require that the meeting be chaired by a faculty member or administrator and that a statement be made that the views presented are not necessarily those of the institution.

COMMENT

Although the judicial code in this case was developed for institutions of higher education, it nevertheless illustrates the way public schools can protect themselves against disruptive speakers and at the same time protect the right of student organizations. Although schools may not be required to have any regulations concerning invited speakers, the case emphasized that any regulations that are developed must be constitutional.

Would courts guarantee the same freedom to students in high schools as to college students? Not necessarily. The answer would depend on the circumstances of each case; and courts have pointed out that many of the circumstances of high school are different from those at most universities. Because of these differences—such as age, maturity, facilities, teacher qualifications, and compulsory attendance laws—public school officials might be allowed to regulate invited speakers more closely.

In *Stacy* Judge Keady used the "clear and present danger" test to determine when an institution of higher education might turn down a proposed speaker. This famous judicial standard has been used for over 50 years to test the limits of permissible speech in the adult community.* In *Tinker* Justice Fortas translated this formula into the "substantial and material disruption" test that is now generally used by courts for determining the limits of permissible expression in public schools and can be expected to be applied in cases involving outside speakers as well.

Related Issues

1. May a school ban "political" speeches but allow "nonpartisan" activities? In 1976 a federal judge said "no."[32] The case arose in Wisconsin

---

*In *Schenck* v. *United States*, 249 U.S. 47, 52 (1919), Justice Holmes wrote that the question in every case is whether the words used under the circumstances "create a clear and present danger that will bring about the substantive evils that Congress has a right to prevent." This opinion also includes his frequently quoted comment: "The most stringent protection of free speech would not protect a man falsely shouting fire in a theatre and causing a panic."

when a group of students tried to rent a high school gymnasium for a lecture by a communist professor, Angela Davis. They were turned down by the school board because of a policy against using schools for "political activities."

The court rejected the policy that allowed nonpartisan but not political activities. Since the purpose of the First Amendment is to protect political speech, Judge Reynolds thought it strange to exalt nonpartisan speech. "Such an inversion of values," wrote the judge, "ill serves the public upon whom falls the serious and challenging business of self-government." The court concluded with this observation:

> Far too frequently the mantle of nonpartisanship is thrown over the shoulders of those who have been successful in obtaining political and economic power in our society, while the pejorative of "political" is reserved for those who have been less successful. . . . What is "political" and what is "nonpartisan" must of necessity—as must beauty—lie in the eyes of the beholder. For that very reason, the Constitution will not allow such determinations to be made by government officials.[33]

2. May schools prohibit varsity athletes from enrolling in summer sports training camps? Texas passed such a rule for football and basketball players to prevent an unfair advantage to schools that might set up a special training program for their teams. But a federal court held that the rule unreasonably interfered with the rights of citizens "to choose their own associates" and make educational decisions for their children. Although the court acknowledged the right of states to adopt narrow rules to prevent unfair competition and discourage overemphasis upon any one sport, it concluded that this Texas rule was too broad and sweeping to stand.[34]

3. Is there a right not to associate? This question was posed by a group of college students who objected to a mandatory fee that was used by student groups to support political causes and speakers they opposed. The court agreed that the students have a "constitutionally protected right to *not* associate with any group" just as they have a right to associate with a group of their choice. Therefore a school cannot compel students to belong to any association that purports to represent all students but that spends money on political causes that these students find repugnant.

The court, however, did not rule that schools cannot require students to pay a mandatory activities fee. This is because a college should be able to use student fees to expose students to a wide range of controversial views and "dissenting students should not have the right to veto every event, speech or program with which they disagree." The court felt that schools should have the discretion to balance the rights of dissenters who must finance controversial programs and the desirability of providing an open forum for wide-ranging ideas.[35]

Summary and Conclusions

Although the right to freedom of association is not explicitly set forth in the Constitution, courts have held the right to be implicit in the First Amendment freedoms of speech, assembly, and petition. As this chapter has illustrated, the freedom encompasses a wide range of issues and is related to earlier chapters on student and teacher freedom of speech. As in the case of other student rights, the law in this area is changing and is sometimes subject to variations in accordance with state statutes. The chapter has been organized around the following four topics.

FRATERNITIES, SORORITIES, AND SECRET CLUBS

Although adults have the right to join secret and undemocratic organizations, courts have refused to grant these rights to public school students. Statutes in over 20 states have outlawed fraternities, sororities, and similar organizations that chose their members in an undemocratic manner. Numerous cases over the past 60 years have upheld such legislation against charges of unconstitutionality. Because these cases seem inconsistent with the principles of the *Tinker* decision, future courts *may* rule that students have a constitutional right to join any out-of-school organization that does not substantially interfere with the operation of the schools. Until then, students should be aware of the risks involved in joining a high school fraternity or sorority, especially in states that have laws prohibiting such organizations.

THE RIGHT TO ORGANIZE AND USE SCHOOL FACILITIES

The *Healy* case established that denial of official recognition to student organizations without justification abridges their constitutional right of association. Therefore, if administrators deny recognition to a student organization, they bear a "heavy burden" to demonstrate the appropriateness of their action.

A relationship between a local student group and an unpopular national organization is not an adequate basis to deny recognition. Furthermore, school officials may not deny recognition because they disagree with the philosophy of a student group.

On the other hand, a school may issue reasonable regulations concerning the time, place, and manner in which student groups may conduct their activities. Hence officials may deny recognition to groups that announce their unwillingness to be bound by such rules. Furthermore, schools need not tolerate student organizations that pose "a substantial threat of material disruption" or that "interfere with the opportunity of other students to obtain an education."

Courts are increasingly protecting the right of *college* students to organize and register controversial political, social, and religious groups on campus. It is uncertain whether courts will rule the same way concerning high school organizations since there are few cases on this issue. However, judges will probably allow administrators greater freedom in regulating high school groups than college groups since their students are younger, are less mature, and are required to attend. They may also give greater protection to radical political organizations than to groups that promote religion or alternative sexual orientations in public schools.

THE RIGHT TO PROTEST AND DEMONSTRATE

1. Generally, courts can be expected to acknowledge the First Amendment right of students to "peaceably assemble"; and most judges probably would hold the categorical prohibition of *all* student demonstrations on school grounds unconstitutional.
2. Most courts will probably not protect student demonstrations *inside* school buildings, especially during school hours. Judges are likely to find that such protests substantially interfere with school activities.
3. A protest *outside* the school building is more likely to be protected than one inside. However, outside demonstrations might not be protected during school hours, especially if protestors are illegally absent from classes or disrupt the classes of others.

CONTROVERSIAL SPEAKERS

Whether controversial speakers invited by student groups can appear before public school audiences involves the balancing of the responsibilities of officials to regulate public speaking on school property with the First Amendment rights of students. Despite these rights, administrators apparently have authority to bar all outside speakers from school. Thus conflicts arise primarily when school authorities permit some outside speakers but not others.

When officials provide a forum for outside speakers, they must give equal time to opposing views and may not discriminate among proposed speakers or censor their ideas. Moreover, officials may not ban all political speakers, all candidates for public office, or prohibit views that most students or teachers find disagreeable.

This does not mean that students have an absolute right to hear a speech at any time or place regardless of the circumstances. Students can be required to notify and request approval of school officials before inviting an outside speaker. If a request is denied, there must be a fair and prompt review procedure that allows students to challenge the administration's decision. A school's denial of a request would be upheld if there is evidence that the proposed speech would substantially disrupt the educational process.

NOTES

1. *Passel* v. *Fort Worth Independent School District*, 429 S.W.2d 917, 925 (Ct. App. Tex. 1968).
2. *Healy* v. *James*, 408 U.S. 169, 197 (1972).
3. Id. at 182.
4. *Bradford* v. *Board of Education*, 121 P. 929 (Ct. App. Cal. 1912).
5. Id. at 931.
6. The quotations in this section are from *Robinson* v. *Sacramento City Unified School District*, 53 Cal. Rptr. 781 (Ct. App. Cal. 1966).
7. Ibid.
8. Judge Pierce noted that the following states have legislation similar to the California statute: "Arkansas, Colorado, Florida, Illinois, Indiana, Iowa, Kansas, Louisiana, Maine, Massachusetts (optional with local boards), Michigan, Minnesota, Mississippi, Montana, Nebraska, New Jersey, Ohio, Oklahoma, Oregon, Pennsylvania, Rhode Island, Texas (limited), Vermont, Virginia, and Washington." Id. at 788.
9. In his opinion Judge Pierce explained the rationale for eight of these cases, including a 1915 decision by the U.S. Supreme Court that upheld a prohibition against Greek letter societies in all Mississippi educational institutions against an attack based on due process and equal protection arguments. *Waugh* v. *Board of Trustees*, 237 U.S. 589 (1915).
10. This was the case of *Wright* v. *Board of Education*, 246 S.W. 43 (Ct. App. Mo. 1922), which held that a St. Louis school board regulation forbidding membership of high school students in secret organizations was not authorized by the legislature and that no rule should be adopted that attempted to control the conduct of pupils out of school hours after they have reached their homes, except such conduct that would clearly interfere with school discipline.
11. *Passel* v. *Fort Worth Independent School District*, 429 S.W.2d 917 (1968); 440 S.W.2d 61 (1969); 453 S.W.2d 888 (1970). This was a long and difficult case that illustrates why citizens sometimes feel frustrated by the procedural and jurisdictional complexities of the law. It began in a Texas District Court and was appealed to the State Court of Civil Appeals in 1968. Both courts ruled in favor of the school board. Passel next appealed to the Texas Supreme Court which reversed (in 1969) for jurisdictional and procedural reasons, and declined to rule on whether the state antifraternity statute was unconstitutional. The case then returned to the district court which again ruled in favor of the school board. This decision was finally affirmed by the Court of Civil Appeals in 1970.
12. The dissent minimized the evidence of two athletic coaches who testified that club members had caused problems in the past. One testified that five or six years earlier some pledging activities had been carried on in the school lunchrooms. Another said that the clubs destroyed school spirit and team unity, but under questioning he admitted that there is "not one scintilla of evidence" that these clubs conduct their meetings or other activities on school grounds.
13. *Healy* v. *James*, 408 U.S. 169 (1972).
14. The increase in campus disturbances during this period was indicated by Jerris Leonard, Assistant U.S. Attorney General, who wrote: "In the first half

of the 1967–68 academic year, 71 demonstrations were reported on 62 campuses across the nation. In the second half of that same year, 221 demonstrations took place on 101 campuses." In 1969–1970 these incidents had increased dramatically: "1,785 demonstrations were reported on campuses across the United States, causing some 462 injuries and eight deaths; 7,200 arrests were made, 246 arson incidents or attempts, and 14 bombings." To the Second Circuit Court of Appeals there was "a nationwide campus atmosphere of ticking timebombs" during this period. *Healy* v. *James*, 445 F.2d 1122, 1131–1132 (2nd Cir. 1971).

15. *Healy* v. *James*, 408 U.S. 169 (1972).
16. *Communist Party* v. *Subversive Activities Control Board*, 367 U.S. 1, 137 (1961).
17. *Healy* at 194.
18. Id. at 196–197.
19. *Dixon* v. *Beresh*, 361 F.Supp. 253 (E.D. Mich. 1973).
20. *Gay Alliance of Students* v. *Matthews*, 544 F.2d 162 (4th Cir. 1976).
21. *Gay Lib* v. *University of Missouri*, 558 F.2d 848 (8th Cir. 1977). In a concurring opinion, one of the judges wrote that the university "will survive even the most offensive verbal assaults upon traditional moral values; solutions to such problems are not found in repression of ideas."
22. *Johnson* v. *Huntington Beach Union High School District*, 137 Cal. Rptr. 43 (1977).
23. *Gebert* v. *Hoffman*, 336 F.Supp. 694 (E.D. Penn. 1972).
24. *Sword* v. *Fox*, 446 F.2d 1091 (4th Cir. 1971).
25. In addition to having authority to regulate the place of demonstrations, school officials appear to be able to prohibit totally demonstrations that take the form of class boycotts or walkouts. Thus the Fifth Circuit Court of Appeals held that a group of black students could be disciplined for walking out of school to conduct a demonstration protesting school policies. In rejecting the claim that such conduct was permissible unless prohibited by a valid regulation, the court said: "No student needs a regulation to be told he is expected and required to attend classes." Hence disciplinary action "with regard to a mass refusal to attend classes" was upheld. *Dunn* v. *Tyler Independent School District*, 460 F.2d 137 (5th Cir. 1972).
26. *Grayned* v. *City of Rockford*, 408 U.S. 104 (1972).
27. *Vail* v. *Board of Education of Portsmouth*, 354 F.Supp. 592 (D.N.H. 1973).
28. *Wilson* v. *Chancellor*, 418 F.Supp. 1358 (D. Ore. 1976).
29. Id. at 1369.
30. *Stacy* v. *Williams*, 306 F.Supp. 963 (N.D. Miss. 1969).
31. Id. at 974–978.
32. *Lawrence University Bicentennial Commission* v. *City of Appleton, Wisconsin*, 409 F. Supp 1319 (E.D. Wisc. 1976).
33. Id. at 1326. Similarly, a federal appeals court held that a high school policy that denied recognition to student clubs that expressed a "partisan" point of view was inconsistent with student First Amendment rights. *Garvin* v. *Rosenau*, 455 F.2d 233 (6th Cir. 1972).
34. *Kite* v. *Marshall*, 454 F.Supp. 1347 (S.D. Tex. 1978).
35. *Good* v. *Associated Students of the University of Washington*, 542 P.2d 762 (Wash. 1975).

Chapter 9
Freedom of Association for Teachers: Loyalty, Politics, and Union Activity

A teacher who is bereft of the essential quality of loyalty and devotion to his government and the fundamentals of our democratic society is lacking in a basic qualification for teaching.

—a New Jersey Court[1]

. . . Government should leave the mind and spirit of man absolutely free. Such a governmental policy encourages varied intellectual outlooks in the belief that the best views will prevail.

—Justice Hugo Black[2]

In the first half of this century, a "proper" teacher did not belong to a union or any other controversial organization, was not active in partisan politics, and did not hesitate to swear her allegiance to the state and federal governments. The cases in this chapter were brought by teachers who challenged this traditional image, an image that is still supported by many parents, administrators, and educators. The four sections of the chapter deal with teachers who have been penalized for (1) failure to take loyalty oaths; (2) membership in controversial organizations; (3) taking an active part in politics; and (4) activities related to teacher organizations.

LOYALTY OATHS

In 1956 Robert Hamilton, Dean of the Univerity of Wyoming's College of Law, published a book entitled *Legal Rights and Liabilities of Teachers.* The book included a discussion of teachers' loyalty oaths, which had then been enacted by about half of the states. Professor Hamilton praised the legislatures that had passed loyalty oath laws for being "commendably concerned with the protection of the schools from the influence of subversive teachers."[3]

He then quoted with approval a court opinion upholding a New Jersey loyalty oath that reflected the attitudes and beliefs of many legislators, administrators, and judges:

> The school system affords the opportunity and means for subtle infiltration. There is no intrusion upon personal freedoms when the government intervenes, as here, to avert this peril to its very existence. A teacher who is bereft of the essential quality of loyalty and devotion to his government and the fundamentals of our democratic society is lacking in a basic qualification for teaching. . . . In the current struggle for men's minds, the state is well within its province in ensuring the integrity of the educational process against those who would pervert it to subversive ends.[4]

In addition, many citizens believed that teachers' oaths should promote such values as "respect for the flag," "reverence for law and order," and "undivided allegiance" to the government. As the following case indicates, the Washington legislature wanted to use teachers' loyalty oaths to accomplish all of these purposes.

But are loyalty oaths a good way to insure loyal teachers? Or is their main effect to restrict free speech and inhibit academic freedom? Are "investigations by higher authority" a good way to eliminate disloyal teachers? Or are there better ways to achieve this purpose? These are some of the questions raised by the cases in this section.

The Baggett Case: A Danger to Conscientious Teachers[5]

In 1931 legislation was passed in the state of Washington requiring teachers to subscribe to the following loyalty oath:

> I solemnly swear (or affirm) that I will support the Constitution and laws of the United States of America and the State of Washington, and will by precept and example promote respect for the flag and institutions of the United States of America and the State of Washington, reverence for law and order, and undivided allegiance to the government of the United States.[6]

In 1955, another statute was passed requiring that each state employee also swear that he does not teach others to overthrow or alter the constitutional form of government by revolution or violence. In 1962, the president of the University of Washington notified all employees that they would be required to take the oath of allegiance as provided in the 1931 act and also swear that they were not subversive persons pursuant to the 1955 statute.

In response, a group of Washington teachers, staff, and faculty brought a class action asking that the two statutes requiring these oaths be declared unconstitutional.* In 1964, the U.S. Supreme Court heard their

*A *class action* is a suit brought on behalf of other persons similarly situated. Thus, in this case, the class action was probably brought on behalf of all Washington teachers and state employees who were required to take the oath.

arguments and ruled in their favor. Here is some of the reasoning underlying the Court's decision.

• **The 1955 Oath.** Does the oath prohibit teachers from supporting a communist candidate for office? Does it reach anyone who supports any cause that is also supported by communists? Is it subversive to participate in international conventions with communist scholars? Because the answers to these questions are uncertain, the Court said that the oath disclaiming subversive activity goes beyond prohibiting the overthrow of the government by force. It extends to altering the government by "revolution," which could include any rapid or fundamental change. By this definition any person supporting or teaching peaceful but far-reaching constitutional amendments might be engaged in subversive activity. Or, if a teacher supported U.S. participation in world government, he might be considered subversive. Therefore, this part of the oath is unconstitutionally vague, broad, and uncertain.

• **The 1931 Statute.** This law exacts a promise that the teacher will "promote respect for the flag and institutions" of the United States and the state of Washington. The Court noted several problems.

How wide, for example, is the range of activities that might be deemed inconsistent with this promise? Would a teacher who refused to salute the flag because of his religious beliefs be accused of breaking his promise? Even criticism of the design or color of the state flag could be deemed disrespectful and therefore in violation of the oath.

The Court also wondered about the national and state "institutions" for which the teacher is expected to "promote respect." Do they include every significant practice, law, and custom of our government or of our culture? Do they consist of those institutions to which the majority of Americans are loyal? If so, the oath might prevent a teacher from criticizing his state's judicial system, the Supreme Court, or the FBI.

Moreover, it is difficult to know what can be done without transgressing the promise to "promote undivided allegiance" to the U.S. Government. "It would not be unreasonable," wrote Justice White, "for the serious-minded oath taker to conclude that he should dispense with lectures voicing far-reaching criticism of any old or new policy followed by the Government of the United States." He could hesitate to join a special-interest group opposing any current national policy, for if he did he might be accused of placing loyalty to the group above allegiance to the United States.

As Justice White noted, the uncertain meanings of the oaths require teachers to "steer far wider of the unlawful zone" than if the boundaries of those zones were clearly marked. The result is that teachers with a conscientious regard for what they solemnly swear and sensitive to the dangers posed by the oaths' indefinite language can avoid risk "only by restricting their conduct to that which is unquestionably safe. Free speech may not be so inhibited." Whenever statutes place limits on First Amendment freedoms, they must be "narrowly drawn to meet the precise evil the legislature seeks to curb," and the conduct prohibited must be "defined specifically" so that the persons affected remain secure in their rights to engage in activities not clearly prohibited.

• **Objection by the State.** The attorney for the state of Washington labeled "wholly fanciful" some of the activities the Court suggested might be prohibited by the two oaths. This may be correct; but it only emphasizes the difficulties caused by the two statutes. If the oaths do not include the behavior suggested, what do they cover? "Where," Justice White wondered, "does fanciful possibility end and intended coverage begin?"

It is not enough to say that a prosecutor's sense of fairness would prevent a successful perjury prosecution for some of the activities apparently included within these sweeping oaths. The hazard of being prosecuted for guiltless behavior remains. "It would be blinking at reality," wrote the Court "not to acknowledge that there are some among us always ready to affix a Communist label upon those whose ideas they violently oppose. And experience teaches us that prosecutors too are human." According to the Court, measures that define disloyalty must allow public employees to know exactly what conduct is prohibited by the oath. Because the majority of the Court found both oaths unduly broad, vague, and uncertain, they were held to be unconstitutional.

• **A Dissenting Opinion.** In a sharp and sometimes sarcastic rebuttal to the majority opinion, Justice Clark wrote:

> It is, of course, absurd to say that, under the words of the Washington Act, a professor risks violation when he teaches . . . a class in which a Communist Party member might sit. To so interpret the language of the Act is to extract more sunbeams from cucumbers than did Gulliver's mad scientist. And to conjure up such ridiculous questions, the answers to which we all know or should know are in the negative, is to build up a whimsical and farcical straw man which is not only grim but Grimm.[7]

The Whitehill Case: "Negative" Oaths and Academic Freedom[8]

Several years after the Baggett case, a "negative" loyalty oath aimed at eliminating "subversive" teachers came before the Supreme Court. It concerned a lecturer at the University of Maryland who refused to sign the state loyalty oath stating that he was not "engaged in one way or another in the attempt to overthrow the Government . . . by force or violence."

The majority of the Court was concerned that Whitehill could not

know, except by risking a perjury prosecution, whether as a member of a
"subversive" group he would "in one way or another" be engaged in an
attempt to overthrow the government. The law requiring the loyalty oath
provided for the discharge of "subversive" persons and called for perjury
action against those who violated the oath. Regarding these provisions,
the Court commented that "the continuing surveillance which this type of
law places on teachers is hostile to academic freedom." The Court held
that the required oath was not precise or clear. Instead it found an
"overbreadth that makes possible oppressive or capricious application as
regimes change." That threat could inhibit academic freedom as much as
successive suits for perjury. Here, concluded the Court, "we have
another classic example of the need for 'narrowly drawn' legislation in this
sensitive and important First Amendment area."

The Monroe Case: Vindicating a Victim of Repression

Albert Monroe was a tenured professor at San Francisco State College in
1950 when a state loyalty oath was enacted.[9] When Monroe refused to sign
the oath, he was dismissed. Since he believed the loyalty oath law was
unconstitutional, he began to challenge it through state administrative
channels. During this process the California Supreme Court upheld the
constitutionality of the oath. Monroe therefore decided it would be futile
to fight his dismissal in court, and he took another job.

Fourteen years later the California Supreme Court reversed itself. It
concluded that the state loyalty oath was unconstitutional and, in the
Vogel case, overruled its earlier decision.[10] On the basis of *Vogel*, Monroe
petitioned the Trustees of the California State Colleges for reinstatement.
The trustees refused, and this time Monroe took his case to court.

On behalf of the California Supreme Court, Justice Tobriner wrote
that failure to reinstate Monroe would have a number of negative
consequences. Its effect would be to continue to punish Monroe for
asserting his First Amendment rights, which had finally been vindicated.
It might "chill" other teachers, preventing them from fully exercising
their rights of freedom of speech and freedom of association. And the "pall
of orthodoxy resulting from earlier exclusionary policies would continue
to inhibit the present educational environment."

On the other hand, Monroe's reinstatement would prevent any
further injury that might flow from his "conscientious adherence to
now-accepted constitutional principles." Furthermore, the reinstatement
of Monroe and others like him would enrich the academic community "by
reintroducing into that community individuals with conscientiously held
beliefs and ideals, beliefs which in the past have been excluded from the
public schools simply because of official disapproval."

In its opinion, the Court not only vindicated Monroe, but also condemned the state loyalty oath. It criticized the oath because it denied to anyone who refused to take it the opportunity to explain his motives and reasons, and because the oath's assumption of guilt by association was automatic and irrefutable.

In conclusion, Justice Tobriner described Monroe as "a victim of the repressive political climate of the post-war era" who had been "forcibly separated by the state from his chosen profession of college teaching for more than 20 years." Thus, the Court ruled, "there now remains no constitutionally permissible grounds for continuing [Monroe's] exile from the state college system."

State v. Lundquist: The Pledge as a Loyalty Oath[11]

In 1971 the Maryland Court of Appeals considered the constitutionality of a state law requiring teachers to salute the flag and to recite the Pledge of Allegiance. In a long, thoughtful, and scholarly opinion, the court considered the pledge as a "sub-species of loyalty oath" that has been expanding in our country since the 1900s. The Maryland law allowed an exception for those who objected to the pledge for religious reasons. But a social studies teacher, August Lundquist, objected to the compulsory salute and pledge because he believed that "such a requirement eliminated his right to freely express his own loyalty to the United States."

The Maryland court supported Lundquist. Relying on prior Supreme Court decisions, Judge Digges noted that schools could certainly teach patriotism and punish teachers who disrupt voluntary patriotic programs. The court, however, held that schools could not punish teachers merely because they refused to participate in the pledge. On the contrary, the First Amendment was intended to prohibit the government from compelling our citizens to participate in any patriotic "ritual."

If teachers did not participate in the pledge, could this cause problems of school discipline and undermine the values of the pledge for students? Although acknowledging the possibility of these dangers, Judge Digges quoted the answer from *Tinker:* "Our Constitution says we must take this risk." In addition, the court expressed serious doubts that the key to patriotism is "compulsory routine" exercises in public schools.

The Ohlson Case: Supporting Affirmative Oaths[12]

A Colorado statute requires that no one may teach in a state public school unless he takes this oath:

> I solemnly swear (or affirm) that I will uphold the Constitution of the United States and the constitution of the State of Colorado, and I will faithfully perform the duties of the position upon which I am about to enter.

A group of teachers from the Denver public schools and the state universities and colleges in Colorado went to court to have this oath declared unconstitutional. They argued that the oath is vague and violates the First Amendment rights of freedom of speech and association, that it deprives teachers of due process of law because it lacks procedural safeguards, and that it violates the Fourteenth Amendment because it does not apply to all public employees.

The U.S. District Court, however, did not agree. On behalf of the court Judge William Doyle wrote that the oath in this case "is not unduly vague." The oath is simply a recognition of our system of constitutional law. It is not overly broad, and it does not constitute a sweeping and improper invasion of a teacher's rights of free association and expression. According to the judge: "Support for the constitutions and laws of the nation and state does not call for blind subservience."

The teachers' second argument—that swearing to "faithfully perform the duties" of their position is unconstitutionally vague—was also rejected by the court. It held that a state can reasonably ask teachers in public schools to subscribe to professional competence and dedication. "It is certain," wrote Judge Doyle, "that there is no right to be unfaithful in the performance of duties."

The teachers' third argument was that the statute violated due process in not providing a hearing upon dismissal for refusal to take the oath. The court, however, ruled that a teacher who is dismissed for refusal to take the oath has no need to cross-examine his accuser, since no hearing can change the fact that he refused to take the oath. His reasons for refusal are irrelevant as long as the oath is simple, direct, and unambiguous.

Finally, the teachers claimed that the statute deprived them of equal protection under the Fourteenth Amendment by arbitrarily requiring teachers and not other employees to take the oath. On the contrary, wrote Judge Doyle, the oath is "an almost universal requirement of all public officials, including lawyers and judges, and it cannot be truthfully said that teachers are being picked on." True, the oath does not apply to all state employees. But as long as the oath is reasonable as applied to teachers, who work in a sensitive and influential area, there is no constitutional requirement that it be applied to all public employees.

In conclusion, Judge Doyle commented that he was "unable to fully discern" why teachers "find the taking of any oath so obnoxious." The oath has roots as deep as the Constitution which requires that government officials take oaths to uphold it. Thus the writers of the Constitution thought the requirement of an oath of loyalty was worth whatever minor deprivation of individual freedom of conscience was involved.

Questions to Consider

1. What factors distinguish constitutional oaths from unconstitutional ones?

2. What do you think are the advantages and disadvantages of loyalty oaths? During normal times? During times of national tension?
3. Do loyalty oaths offer assurance of loyal teachers? Are there any alternative ways of achieving this goal?
4. If you were a state legislator, would you vote for a bill that required teachers to take a clear and simple oath pledging to uphold the Constitution and maintain professional standards? Why or why not?

Judicial Impatience

In the late 1960s and early 1970s, efforts to hunt for disloyal teachers had diminished and some judges seemed impatient with teachers who challenged positive support oaths. In upholding one such oath, a federal judge wrote: "A state does not interfere with its teachers by requiring them to support the governmental systems which shelter and nourish the institutions in which they teach, nor does it restrict its teachers by encouraging them to uphold the highest standards of their chosen profession."[13] Similarly, in 1971, another judge clearly upheld an oath requiring teachers to support the Constitution and discharge their duties to the best of their ability with these words: "The constitutionality of this support oath has been repeatedly sustained by the Supreme Court of the United States against First Amendment attacks by public school teachers."[14]

The Burger Court: Rejecting Literal Notions[15]

In 1972 the Supreme Court ruled on the constitutionality of an oath that required public school teachers and all other Massachusetts employees (1) to swear to uphold the state and federal constitutions and (2) to "oppose the overthrow" of the state or federal government "by force, violence, or by any illegal or unconstitutional method." The first part of the oath was similar to the "support oath" found in the Constitution and was easily upheld by the Court.

The second part concerning promises to "oppose" the overthrow of the government was more controversial. Opponents argued that a literal interpretation of this promise raised the specter of "vague, undefinable responsibilities actively to combat a potential overthrow of the government." Chief Justice Burger, however, rejected such "literal notions" and asserted that the purpose of the oath "was not to create specific responsibilities but to assure that those in positions of public trust were willing to commit themselves to live by the constitutional processes of our system." On behalf of a divided court, Justice Burger wrote that "the second clause does not expand the obligations of the first"; it is merely a commitment not to use illegal force to change the government.

The Chief Justice indicated his hope that the oaths and the intense controversy they caused might someday disappear. "The time may come," he wrote, "when the value of oaths in routine public employment will be thought not 'worth the candle.' " Concerning the fear that these oaths might lead to the prosecution of innocent people, he noted that there had never been a prosecution under the oath statute since its enactment and that none was considered. Therefore, the oath might be considered "no more than an amenity." The Court concluded that those who view the oath in terms of an endless "parade of horribles" should bear in mind that such dire consequences will "not occur while this Court sits."

SUMMARY

The attitude of most judges seems to have changed markedly since the days when a New Jersey court commended the state legislature for trying to protect our schools from the pressures of a "Godless theology" by passing a loyalty oath law. The California Supreme Court illustrated this change in the *Monroe* case, which publicly condemned the excesses of loyalty oaths and vindicated teachers who were injured by them. In the 1960s most courts carefully scrutinized loyalty oaths since they tended to inhibit the exercise of First Amendment rights. If oaths were too broad, uncertain, or vague (such as those broadly disclaiming membership in subversive organizations), they were held to be unconstitutional. Two types of oaths, however, have consistently been upheld: (1) loyalty oaths drawn with precision and prohibiting clearly unlawful conduct and (2) simple employment oaths affirming support for the Constitution or pledging to uphold professional standards. As for the future, the *Cole* case indicates that the Supreme Court under Chief Justice Burger tends not to examine loyalty oaths as critically as it did during the 1960s.

CONTROVERSIAL ORGANIZATIONS AND ASSOCIATIONS

Loyalty oaths are one way that a community can try to exclude teachers who are considered disloyal. This section considers another way: disqualifying teachers who are members of revolutionary or subversive organizations. It also considers whether teachers can be penalized because of the people with whom they associate.

Does a school board have the right to exclude teachers who are members of any revolutionary or subversive organization? Can a board prohibit teachers from sending their children to private, segregated schools? May teachers be penalized because of the controversial behavior of their spouses? These are some of the questions presented in the following cases.

The Adler Case: Guilt by Association Upheld[16]

In 1949 the New York legislature passed the Feinberg Law, which was designed to eliminate members of the Communist Party and other revolutionary groups from the school systems. The preamble of that law made elaborate findings that members of revolutionary groups like the Communist Party have been "infiltrating" into the public schools. As a result, "propaganda can be disseminated among children by those who teach them and to whom they look for guidance, authority and leadership." The legislature also found that members of such groups use their position to teach "a prescribed party line or group dogma or doctrine without regard to truth or free inquiry." This propaganda, the legislature declared, "is sufficiently subtle to escape detection in the classroom; thus the menace of such infiltration into the classroom is difficult to measure." To protect children from such influence, the legislature believed that "laws prohibiting members of such groups . . . from obtaining or retaining employment in public schools be rigorously enforced."

In the *Adler* case the Feinberg Law was attacked as an abridgment of the rights of free speech and assembly of New York public school employees. The majority of the members of the Supreme Court, however, did not believe the law was unconstitutional, and the widely quoted opinion by Justice Minton has frequently been used to justify other restrictions on teachers' rights.

"It is clear," wrote Justice Minton, "that citizens have the right under our law to assemble, speak, think, and believe as they will. It is equally clear that they have no right to work for the state in the school system on their own terms. They may work for the school system upon the reasonable terms laid down by the proper authorities of New York. If they do not choose to work on such terms, they are at liberty to retain their beliefs and associations and go elsewhere. Has the state thus deprived them of any right to free speech or assembly? We think not."

Such persons may be denied the privilege of working for the school system either because they advocate overthrow of the government by force or because they are members of organizations known to have that purpose; for the classroom is a sensitive area. There, said Justice Minton, the teacher

> shapes the attitude of young minds towards the society in which they live. In this, the state has a vital concern. It must preserve the integrity of the schools. That the school authorities have the right and the duty to screen the officials, teachers, and employees as to their fitness to maintain the integrity of the schools as a part of ordered society, cannot be doubted. One's associates, past and present, as well as one's conduct, may properly be considered in determining fitness and loyalty. From time immemorial, one's reputation has been determined in part by the company he keeps. In the employment of officials and teachers of the school system, the state may very properly inquire into the company they keep, and we know of no rule, constitutional or otherwise, that prevents the state, when determining the fitness and loyalty of such persons, from considering the organizations and persons with whom they associate.[17]

THE DOUGLAS DISSENT

Three justices wrote opinions dissenting from the majority of the Court. The strongest of these was that of Justice Douglas, who presents a disturbing picture of the way the Feinberg Law could destroy academic freedom, lead to guilt by association, and result in fear and orthodoxy pervading the schools. Because this opinion not only presents a powerful argument for freedom in the classroom but also foreshadows the future trend of judicial thinking, we quote from it extensively.

> The Constitution guarantees freedom of thought and expression to everyone in our society. All are entitled to it; and none needs it more than the teacher. . . .
>
> The present law proceeds on a principle repugnant to our society—guilt by association. A teacher is disqualified because of her membership in an organization found to be "subversive". . . . Any organization committed to a liberal cause, any group organized to revolt against an hysterical trend, any committee launched to sponsor an unpopular program becomes suspect. These are the organizations into which Communists often infiltrate. . . . A teacher caught in that mesh is almost certain to stand condemned. Fearing condemnation, she will tend to shrink from any association that stirs controversy. In that manner freedom of expression will be stifled.
>
> But that is only part of it. . . . The law inevitably turns the school system into a spying project. Regular loyalty reports on the teachers must be made out. The principals become detectives; the students, the parents, the community become informers. Ears are cocked for tell-tale signs of disloyalty. The prejudices of the community come into play in searching out the disloyal. This is not the usual type of supervision which checks a teacher's competency; it is a system which searches for hidden meanings in a teacher's utterances.
>
> What was the significance of the reference of the art teacher to socialism? Who heard overtones of revolution in the English teacher's discussion of *The Grapes of Wrath?* What was behind the praise of Soviet progress in metallurgy in the chemistry class? . . .
>
> What happens under this law is typical of what happens in a police state. Teachers are under constant surveillance; their pasts are combed for signs of disloyalty; their utterances are watched for clues to dangerous thoughts. A pall is cast over the classroom. There can be no real academic freedom in that environment. Where suspicion fills the air and holds scholars in line for fear of their jobs, there can be no exercise of the free intellect. Supineness and dogmatism take the place of inquiry. A "party line"—as dangerous as the "party line" of the communists—lays hold. It is the "party line" of the orthodox view, of the conventional thought, of the accepted approach. Fear stalks the classroom. The teacher is no longer a stimulant to adventurous thinking; she becomes instead a pipeline for safe and sound information. A deadening dogma takes the place of free inquiry. Instruction tends to become sterile; pusuit of knowledge is discouraged; discussion often leaves off where it should begin. . . .

We need be bold and adventuresome in our thinking to survive. A school system producing students trained as robots threatens to rob a generation of the versatility that has been perhaps our greatest distinction. The Framers knew the danger of dogmatism; they also knew the strength that comes when the mind is free, when ideas may be pursued wherever they lead. We forget these teachings of the First Amendment when we sustain this law.

Of course . . . the classrooms need not become forums for propagandizing the Marxist creed. But the guilt of the teacher should turn on overt acts. So long as she is a law-abiding citizen, so long as her performance within the public school system meets professional standards, her private life, her political philosophy, her social creed should not be the cause of reprisals against her.[18]

Despite the power of this dissent, a majority of the members of the Supreme Court in 1952 voted to uphold the Feinberg Law.

The Keyishian Case: Guilt by Association Rejected[19]

In 1962 Harry Keyishian was an English instructor at the Buffalo campus of the State University of New York. To comply with the state's Feinberg Law, Keyishian was asked to sign a certificate stating that he was not a communist. The law disqualified any teacher or administrator in New York's public educational system who advocated the overthrow of the government by unlawful means or joined any organization, particularly the Communist Party, advocating overthrow of the government.

Keyishian refused to sign the certificate, and as a result his contract was not renewed. He went to court to challenge the constitutionality of the law that led to the nonrenewal of his contract.

Questions to Consider

1. What arguments could be used to support the Feinberg Law? Does not the community have a right to exclude revolutionaries from the classroom?
2. Should a community be able to exclude members of the John Birch Society or the American Nazi Party? What about members of the Black Panther Party or a gay rights organization?
3. What arguments could be used to support Keyishian's case? What constitutional provisions apply?
4. Can a teacher be a member of a political party without supporting all of its purposes? Could he be a member of a militant organization without supporting its unlawful activity? Should the law take these distinctions into account?

THE OPINION OF THE COURT
The majority of the justices of the Supreme Court held that it is unconstitutional to disqualify a teacher merely because he is a member of

the Communist Party or any other subversive organization without also showing that the teacher has the specific intent of furthering the unlawful aims of that party or organization. These were some of the reasons for their decision:

A law that bars employment of any person who "advises or teaches" the doctrine of forceful overthrow of the government is unconstitutionally vague. "This provision is plainly susceptible of sweeping and improper application." It could even prohibit the employment of a teacher who "merely advocates the doctrine in the abstract" without any attempt to incite others to unlawful action.

"Our nation is deeply committed to safeguarding academic freedom, which is of transcendent value to all of us and not merely to the teachers concerned. That freedom is therefore a special concern of the First Amendment, which does not tolerate laws that cast a pall of orthodoxy over the classroom. . . . The nation's future depends upon leaders trained through wide exposure to that robust exchange of ideas which discovers truth out of a multitude of tongues rather than through any kind of authoritative selection."

"Scholarship cannot flourish in an atmosphere of suspicion and distrust. Teachers and students must always remain free to inquire, to study, and to evaluate, to gain new maturity and understanding; otherwise our civilization will stagnate and die."

New York has a legitimate interest in protecting its educational system from subversion. But that interest cannot be pursued by means that broadly stifle fundamental liberties when the end can be achieved by less destructive means.

"Under our traditions, beliefs are personal and not a matter of mere association, and men in adhering to a political party or other organization do not subscribe unqualifiedly to all of its platforms or asserted principles. A law which applies to membership, without the specific intent to further the illegal aims of the organization, infringes unnecessarily on protected freedoms. It rests on the doctrine of guilt by association which has no place here."

Even the Feinberg Law—applicable to public school teachers, who have young captive audiences—is subject to constitutional limitation in favor of freedom of expression and association, for the curtailment of these freedoms has a stifling effect on the academic mind.

Those who join an organization but do not share its unlawful purposes and do not participate in its unlawful activities surely pose no threat, either as citizens or as public employees. Therefore, mere membership in the Communist Party, without a specific intent to further the unlawful aims of that organization, is not a constitutionally adequate basis for excluding Keyishian from his teaching position.

When the U.S. Supreme Court declares a state law unconstitutional as it did in *Keyishian,* similar statutes in other states are not automatically voided. They remain "on the books" and are sometimes enforced unless the state legislature repeals them or until they are challenged in court. This was the situation in Arkansas in the 1970s when a university professor challenged a statute that prohibited membership in subversive organizations for state employees.

The Cooper Case: Facing Judicial Reality[20]

Grant Cooper was an assistant professor of history at the University of Arkansas. He was also a member of the Progressive Labor Party which was affiliated with the Communist Party. Professor Cooper advocated a "revolutionary change of the government of the United States, by violence if necessary." He admitted that he taught these principles to his students and advocated a "communistic point of view." He therefore violated an Arkansas law that prohibits any "member of a Nazi, Fascist, or Communist" organization being employed by the state. As a result, the university refused to pay his salary, and he sued to have the law declared unconstitutional.

In 1975 the Arkansas Supreme Court reluctantly ruled in his favor. After carefully considering U.S. Supreme Court decisions construing similar state statutes, the Arkansas court indicated that it had "no choice but to follow these decisions of the Court which is the final arbiter when constitutional interpretation is in dispute." The court cited *Keyishian* in noting that mere membership in subversive organizations was not an adequate basis for dismissing Cooper. The state, in support of its statute, cited the *Adler* case. Although the Arkansas court seemed sympathetic, it wrote: "However much one might wish to accept *Adler,* . . . one must face the reality that *Adler* has been so thoroughly eroded, if not overruled . . . that we cannot view it as an acceptable precedent to uphold this particular statute." Thus the court ruled that the Arkansas law was unconstitutional and therefore Cooper's membership in the Progressive Labor Party did not disqualify him from state employment.

The Cook Case: *Association v. Integration*[21]

In the wake of public school desegregation, some Mississippi parents established private academies to provide a haven for segregated education. One Mississippi school board ruled that teachers who sent their children to such segregated academies would not be rehired. Three teachers who were not rehired because of this policy challenged it as violating their freedom of association.

On behalf of the board, experts testified that the challenged policy was "significantly related to a teacher's effectiveness and job performance because students in desegregated classes are likely to perceive rejection and experience a sense of inferiority from a teacher whose own children attend a nearby racially segregated school." Relying on this testimony, a divided federal appeals court upheld the school policy. The majority conceded that the policy infringed upon the teachers' constitutional rights. However, the court concluded that because of the importance of desegregation, where the exercise of a teacher's rights "impairs [her] effectiveness or conflicts with the performance of her job, the school board may lawfully refuse to rehire the teacher."*

In a long and thoughtful dissenting opinion, Judge Clark argued that a teacher's right to freedom of association should not be abridged unless evidence clearly demonstrates that the associational activity would substantially and materially interfere with her teaching duties. Since the evidence in this case was speculative and there was no direct proof that the teachers' decisions concerning their children's education had any adverse effect on their teaching, Judge Clark would have ruled in favor of the teachers. He concluded his dissent with this warning:

> Today's case is cast in the appealing garb of reinforcing public school desegregation by suppressing the right to educate one's child in a segregated private school. The problem is that the decisional principle it establishes applies to all forms of personal associations from the Ku Klux Klan to Black Panthers, and from membership in the Citizens Council to membership in the NAACP. Another such victory, bought at the expense of surrendering constitutionally protected rights to the expertise of psychological opinion, and we are undone.[22]

Marital Association: The Randle and Mescia Cases

A teacher's right to freedom of association is relevant not only to controversial political organizations but also to controversial marital associations. This was illustrated in the case of a Mississippi teacher, Rosie Randle.

A middle school principal recommended Randle for a teaching position in his school, but the district superintendent said she was incompetent and refused to approve her. Evidence, however, indicated that the real reason she was not approved was because she was married to a controversial civil rights leader who had once helped organize a boycott

---

*An earlier Alabama case, involving nonteaching employees (a school bus driver and a mechanic), reached a different conclusion. The 1971 case concerned a policy that required all school employees to send their children to public schools to prevent the schools from becoming all black. A federal district court, however, ruled that the employees had a constitutional right to send their children to a private school and that the board's policy violated that right. *Berry* v. *Macon County Board of Education*, 380 F.Supp. 1244 (M.D. Ala. 1971).

of local schools. Randle claimed that the action of the superintendent violated her constitutional right of free association, and a federal court agreed. "Mrs. Randle," wrote the court, cannot be punished "because she elected to become the wife" of a civil rights activist.[23]

There are, of course, limits to this right. These were confronted by a South Carolina teacher, Nicholas Mescia. Mescia's teaching contract was not renewed because of serious "personal problems" with his wife who had a history of violence toward him. She had assaulted him with a bottle and a knife, and on one occasion burst into his classroom and threatened his life. Mescia, however, claimed that he had been "a good influence" on his students and that dismissing him solely because of his domestic problems violated his constitutional right to privacy and marital association. However, a federal judge ruled in favor of the school. He noted that in this case school officials were faced with a "potentially explosive and dangerous" domestic conflict that had disrupted school activities. The court denied that a teacher's right to privacy or to marry whom he wishes gives him the right "to engage in domestic altercations in the classroom of a public high school," thus creating damage to students and teachers alike. Rights and duties, concluded the court, must be weighed, and the board's duty to protect its students is paramount under the facts of this case.[24]

SUMMARY

In 1952, the U.S. Supreme Court upheld the right of states to disqualify teachers who were members of revolutionary or subversive organizations. During the following decade several things changed. First, fears of a communist conspiracy to infiltrate American schools decreased. Second, the courts and the public began to reject the idea of guilt by association. Third, the composition of the Supreme Court began to change. Thus, when the *Keyishian* case came before the Court in 1962, the stage was set for the Court to reverse the *Adler* holding. According to *Keyishian*, schools cannot disqualify a teacher merely because she belongs to a revolutionary organization without specifically showing that she subscribes to the organization's illegal aims and activities.

Since almost two decades have passed since *Keyishian*, could the law change again? Could states pass laws disqualifying members of the American Nazi Party or militant student groups? Would these laws be upheld by a conservative Supreme Court? Although we cannot know with certainty how a future Court would rule, we believe that the principles of *Keyishian* would apply. This means that no school board or state legislature could disqualify a teacher simply because she belonged to an extremist or controversial organization. Similarly, a teacher cannot be penalized merely because of the personal or political activities of a husband or a wife unless competent evidence indicates that such behavior clearly impairs the teacher's classroom effectiveness.

POLITICAL ACTIVITY

In a 1956 survey by the National Education Association (NEA), over 75 percent of the teachers questioned indicated that teachers should not be allowed to campaign for candidates or be active in political parties. Most felt that they should not even work for a presidential candidate. And in a 1968 book entitled *Professional Problems of Teachers*, T. M. Stinnet wrote: "The generally accepted viewpoint has been that . . . teachers should keep out of political activity."[25]

By 1981 this attitude had changed dramatically. The National Education Association (NEA) is now one of the most powerful political organizations in the United States, and its members actively campaign for NEA-backed presidential and congressional candidates.* In its 1978–1979 resolutions, the NEA stated that "every educator has the right and obligation to be a . . . politically active citizen." Furthermore, the association urged its affiliates to seek school board policies guaranteeing educators "their political rights" including participating in party organizations, campaigning for candidates, and contributing to their campaigns, "lobbying, organizing political action groups, and running for and serving in public office . . . without personal loss."[26]

Despite these resolutions, many educators and voters believe that public schools should divorce themselves from political activity and that teachers should be more careful about becoming involved in partisan politics than other professionals. Are they correct? If so, should this limit their political rights? Can teachers, for example, be prohibited from holding or running for public office? Can they express partisan political views in school? These are some of the issues considered in this section.

POLITICS AND SCHOOLS

The Goldsmith Case: Promoting a Candidate in Class[27]

An early California case provides an example of a teacher who went too far in expressing his political views in class. In September 1922 a Sacramento high school teacher, A. L. Goldsmith, made the following remarks in class in support of a candidate for school superintendent:

> Many of you know Mr. Golway, what a fine man he is, and what his hopes are to be elected soon. I think he would be more helpful to our department than a lady, and we need more men in our schools. Sometimes your parents do

*Similarly, the American Federation of Teachers (AFT) is equally active politically. According to a representative of the AFT's Committee on Political Education, "local AFT chapters endorse, support, and work on behalf of candidates at all levels of governm⸀   ⸀vho support the educational and labor goals of our union." Interview with Rachelle Ho⸀⸀⸀itz, AFT, Washington, D.C., November 30, 1979.

not know one candidate from another; so they might be glad to be informed. Of course, if any of you have relatives or friends trying for the same office, be sure and vote for them.[28]

As a result of these comments, Goldsmith was charged with "unprofessional conduct" and suspended by the school board. Goldsmith went to court to seek reinstatement on the grounds that he had been a regular teacher for a number of years and had violated no specific law. Moreover, he argued that the statement he made resulting in his suspension really involved "minor matters."

The court disagreed and supported the action of the board. In its opinion, Judge Hart observed that a teacher's "advocacy" of the election of a particular candidate before students in a public school and attempting to influence students and their parents "introduces into the school questions wholly foreign to its purposes and objectives." Such conduct can "stir up strife" among students over a political contest, and the results would disrupt the discipline of the public school. Such conduct is contrary to "the spirit of the laws governing the public school system."

Questions to Consider

1. Should teachers be free to express their political views in the classroom? What are the risks and benefits of this freedom?
2. What, if any, partisan expression should be protected? Can a teacher wear a political button to class? Can teachers express their personal views about national, state, or local candidates if asked about them by their students during class? Before or after class?
3. Can a social studies teacher assign partisan political readings? Can he express partisan opinions in class if he gives equal time to other views? Can he put political bumper stickers on his car if he parks it in the school parking lot? What about large campaign posters in his car windows?
4. Can a teacher wear a button or armband about controversial political issues such as nuclear power, "forced" busing, or abortion?

The Armband Case: What is Partisan Politics?[29]

In 1969, Charles James, a high school English teacher in New York, wore an armband to class to protest the Vietnam War. As a result, he was briefly suspended and warned against engaging in any other political activity in school. After he again went to class wearing the armband, he was dismissed, and the New York Commissioner of Education supported his dismissal.

Although the Supreme Court had ruled that students have a right to wear armbands to class, the commissioner said that a teacher is in a very different category. Teachers have a responsibility to present a wide range of views on a subject being considered. If the subject involves conflicting opinions, the teacher must present a fair summary of the entire range of opinions so that students may have access to all facets of the subject. By wearing the armband the teacher in this case "was presenting only one point of view on an important public issue on which a wide range of deeply held opinion and conviction exists."

The commissioner then cited the New York Teachers' Association Code of Ethics, which considers it unethical for teachers to "promote personal views on religion, race, or partisan politics." The term *partisan politics,* wrote the commissioner, is not limited to party politics but "embraces any political subject on which differing views exist." Despite the Commissioner's ruling, James, a practicing Quaker, took his case to court. In May 1972 the U.S. Second Circuit Court of Appeals ruled in his favor.

In making this decision Judge Kaufman relied on the Supreme Court opinion in *Tinker,* which noted that neither students nor teachers "shed their constitutional rights to freedom of speech or expression at the school-house gate." Furthermore, the Court held that any limitation on the exercise of constitutional rights can be justified only by the conclusion, based on concrete facts, "that the interests of discipline or sound education are materially and substantially jeopardized, whether the danger stems initially from the conduct of students or teachers."

The Supreme Court did not hold that schools must wait "until disruption is on the doorstep" before they may take protective action. But the Court did emphasize that "freedom of expression demands breathing room." To preserve democracy, wrote Judge Kaufman, "we must be willing to assume the risk of argument and lawful disagreement."

The school board argued that the assumptions of the "free marketplace of ideas" on which freedom of speech rests do not apply to a captive group of children where the word of the teacher may carry great authority. Because students may have no choice concerning school attendance, the Court agreed that there must be some restraint on the free expression of a teacher's views. Thus when a teacher tries to persuade his students that his values should be their values, "then it is not unreasonable to expect the state to protect impressionable children from such dogmatism."

The James case, however, is different. Here the teacher's wearing of an armband did not interfere with his classroom performance, was not coercive, and there was no attempt to proselytize or indoctrinate. Moreover, recent Supreme Court decisions leave no doubt that we cannot allow school authorities to arbitrarily censor "a teacher's speech merely because they do not agree with the teacher's political philosophies." In conclusion, Judge Kaufman commented that it would be foolhardy to shield 16- or 17-year-old students from political issues until they walk into the voting booth after their eighteenth birthday.

The Alabama Case: A Comprehensive Interference[30]

To minimize disruption in the public schools, the Alabama legislature prohibited local school boards from providing raises to any teacher "who participates in, encourages or condones any mass truancy even for a day or any extra-curricular demonstration which is not approved" by the board. A group of teachers argued that these provisions were unconstitutional, and a federal district court agreed.

First, the court ruled that the statute was vague and overboard. Although the state may restrict activities that disrupt schooling, the provision that punishes a teacher who "encourages or condones" demonstrations is not limited to disruptive activities. Teachers are forced by this provision to relinquish their constitutional rights. Thus any comments teachers might make that school officials would construe as favoring a school boycott or strike could cause them to forfeit their pay raise.

Second, the court wrote that "there is no justification for restricting the right of a teacher to engage in non-partisan advocacy of social or political reform" unless such activity interferes with his performance in class or with the operation of the school. Even though officials have a legitimate interest in regulating teacher conduct in the midst of school unrest, "the flat denial of raises to teachers who participate in, encourage, or condone extra-curricular demonstrations . . . constitutes a comprehensive interference with associational freedom which goes far beyond what might be justified in the protection of the state's legitimate interest." Thus the court ruled that the "forfeiture provision is clearly unconstitutional."

The Franklin Case: Political Disruption[31]

Can a school refuse to hire a teacher because of his radical political activity? This was the issue that confronted a federal district court in the case of *Franklin* v. *Atkins*. Bruce Franklin was an outstanding young English scholar; whose appointment at the University of Colorado was not approved because he had participated in campus disruptions and incited students to lawless action while he was a faculty member at Stanford University.

Franklin charged that the reason he was not approved by the Board of Regents after being recommended by the dean and the English Department was that the Regents disapproved of his Marxist speeches and writing and his participation in radical political movements. Judge Arraj acknowledged that a state university may not restrict speech or association by refusing to hire someone simply because it finds the political views expressed to be abhorent. In reviewing the evidence, however, the court found that the primary factor influencing the Regents' decision was not Franklin's views but his "pattern of conduct" and his "definite participation in disruptive activities."

Franklin argued that he never violated any criminal statute. The court, however, noted that school authorities need not tolerate political conduct "materially and substantially disrupting school discipline even though that conduct was perhaps not unlawful." Judge Arraj emphasized that he was not ruling against Franklin because of his "political beliefs, the advocacy of these beliefs, or associations with various political movements." Rather it was because (1) there was "clear and convincing" evidence that Franklin's conduct at Stanford "materially and substantially interfered with University activities" and (2) this was a reasonable basis to conclude that he posed a "substantial threat of material disruption" at the University of Colorado.

THE POLITICAL PROCESS: SEEKING AND HOLDING OFFICE

Questions to Consider

1. Do teachers have the right to campaign actively for any national candidate? For any local candidate?
2. Should teachers be allowed to run for political office? Should they be allowed to run for Congress, for mayor, or for the school committee?
3. What are the probable consequences of allowing or encouraging teachers to be active in politics? What are the probable consequences of discouraging or prohibiting such activity?

The Galer Case: A Leave to Hold Office[32]

In 1976 Professor Mary Jane Galer was elected to the Georgia House of Delegates and requested an unpaid leave of absence from her state college position. Because a Georgia statute prohibited members of the legislature from being employed by any agency of the state government, the college denied Galer's request. As a result, Galer took her case to court. She argued that the statute was unconstitutional because it required her to resign from teaching in order to exercise her First Amendment right to hold public office.

The Georgia Supreme Court assumed that the right to serve in the legislature might be an extension of her rights of political association and expression. Nevertheless, it ruled that state employees can be restricted in exercising these rights to further a significant governmental interest. Here the interest was "to enforce the separation of powers" and to prevent "the obvious conflicts of interest inherent in situations where an individual serves concurrently in two of the branches of state government."

The court noted that the statute strikes an "appropriate balance" between the rights of employees as citizens and the interests of the state. It allows teachers to participate fully in political activities and campaign for public office. The statute merely prohibits a teacher from being employed by the state government while serving in the legislature. Galer, ruled the court, "may hold either position, but she may not hold them at the same time."

Thus the court concluded that a teacher may be required to resign her position if she is elected to public office. Could a rule go further and require a teacher to resign before *seeking* elective office? This is the issue confronted by a Florida court in the following case.

The Jones Case: Running for Office[33]

On February 29, 1960 a Florida lawyer, Thomas B. Jones, filed qualifying papers to seek nomination for the office of circuit judge in the spring primary. At the time, Jones was an associate professor of law at the University of Florida. The day after Professor Jones filed he was called to the office of the president of the university and informed of his dismissal because he had violated a university rule prohibiting employees from seeking election to public office. "Any employee," says the rule, "desiring to engage in a political campaign for public office shall first submit his resignation."

Professor Jones believed that the prohibition against college professors seeking public office encroached on their rights. Therefore, he went to court to have that prohibition declared unconstitutional. But the court held that the rule prohibiting teachers from campaigning for elected office was reasonable because:

> It prohibits no one from teaching, and it does not prohibit a teacher from running for office. It merely says he cannot do both simultaneously.
>
> The demands on the time and energies of a candidate in a "warmly contested" political campaign would necessarily affect his efficiency as a teacher.
>
> Campaigning can have a detrimental effect on the students, not only because of the teacher's inefficiency, but also because of the political influences that might be brought to bear on them.
>
> The potential political involvement of a state university, which depends on public support from all political elements, is a major consideration supporting the reasonableness of the prohibition against teachers running for office.

Jones, however, argued that he could campaign in the evening and on week-ends so as not to interfere with his professional duties. To this, Judge Thornal responded with extreme scepticism:

> Anyone who has ever been associated with a heated political campaign will know that it involves hand shaking, speech making, telephone calling, letter writing, and door to door campaigning from morning well into the night. To anyone familiar with the practical aspects of American politics, it is asking too much to expect him to agree that success in a strenuous political campaign can be achieved merely by appearances at Saturday afternoon fish fries or early evening precinct rallies. The result simply is that it would be extremely difficult for a university professor to conduct his classroom courses with efficiency over a period of eight to ten weeks while simultaneously "beating the bushes" in search of votes to elevate him to the position of a circuit judge.[34]

Despite Judge Thornal's opinion, some courts do not share his view as the following controversy indicates.

The Minielly Case: The First Amendment and Political Activity[35]

In this case an Oregon law prohibiting public employees from running for public office was declared unconstitutional. Although Minielly was a deputy sheriff, the reasoning of the court also applies to teachers. The court recognized that a state has the right to make reasonable regulations for the promotion of efficiency and discipline in the public service. It saw nothing unconstitutional, for example, in preventing a public employee from running for office against his superior, since this clearly would be disruptive to the public service. The problem with the Oregon law, however, was that it went much further than necessary to achieve its goal. Furthermore, it is clear that "running for public office is one of the means of political expression which is protected by the First Amendment. The right to engage in political activity is implicit in the rights of association and free speech guaranteed by the Amendment."

The court then discussed a number of recent First Amendment cases. "It is apparent from these cases," wrote the court, "that a revolution has occurred in the law relative to the state's power to limit federal First Amendment rights. Thirty years ago the statutes now under consideration would have been held to be constitutional. . . ." But in this case the court declared the law prohibiting public employees from running for state, federal, or nonpartisan office "unconstitutional because of overbreadth" and suggested that the legislature pass more narrowly drawn laws. "It cannot be demonstrated," concluded the court, "that the good of the public service requires all of the prohibitions of the present statute."

SUPPORTING CANDIDATES

In 1977 a federal court ruled in favor of two Texas teachers who were not rehired because they supported an unsuccessful candidate in a school board election. In its opinion, the court noted that "a teacher's right of free association is closely akin to freedom of speech," and a teacher cannot be penalized for the exercise of these First Amendment rights. In this case, the court ruled that several individual board members were personally liable for damages since their failure to rehire these teachers "because of their political associations was done in disregard of the teachers' clearly established constitutional rights."[36]

In a related West Virginia case, several school employees were not rehired because they failed to support an influential board member for reelection. In this 1978 decision, the judge wrote that a nonpolicymaking government employee "may not be discharged from a job that he or she is satisfactorily performing upon the sole ground of his [or her] political beliefs or activities."[37]

RESTRICTING POLITICAL ACTIVITY: A NATIONAL PERSPECTIVE

In 1947 the U.S. Supreme Court upheld the Hatch Act which prohibits any federal employee from taking an active part in political campaigns.[38] Although the act does not specifically apply to educators, the Court's decision has been used by local judges to uphold similar state restrictions against teachers.[39]

In response to a majority of the Court, Justice Hugo Black wrote a forceful dissenting opinion that argues against broadly restricting the political activity of teachers and other public employees. After pointing out that the Hatch Act bars millions of federal employees from political action as well as thousands of state employees who work for agencies financed by federal grants, he wrote:

> No one of all these millions of citizens can, without violating this law, "take any active part" in any campaign for a cause or for a candidate if the cause or candidate is "specifically identified with any national or state political party." Since under our common political practices most causes and candidates are espoused by political parties, the result is that, because they are paid out of the public treasury, all these citizens who engage in public work can take no really effective part in campaigns that may bring about changes in their lives, their fortunes, and their happiness. . . .[40]

It is said that the Hatch Act is intended to prohibit public employees from being forced to contribute money and influence to political campaigns and to prevent government employees from using their positions to coerce other citizens. But are such possibilities, asked Justice Black, limited to governmental employer-employee relationships? The same quality of argument would support a law restricting the political freedom of all private employees, particularly of corporations that do business with the government. If the possibility exists that some public employees might coerce citizens or other employees, laws can be drawn to punish the coercers. Justice Black noted that it is inconsistent with our system of equal justice for all to suppress the political freedom of large numbers of public employees because a few might engage in coercion:

> There is nothing about public employees which justifies depriving them or society of the benefits of their participation. They, like other citizens, pay taxes and serve their country in peace and in war. The taxes they pay and the wars in which they fight are determined by the elected spokesmen of all the people. . . . I think the Constitution guarantees to them the same right that other groups of good citizens have to engage in activities which decide who their elected representatives shall be.[41]

Our political system rests on the foundation of a belief "in rule by the people—not some but all the people." Education has been fostered to prepare people for self-expression and good citizenship. In a country whose people elect their leaders, no voice should be suppressed—at least such is the assumption of the First Amendment. "That Amendment," wrote Black, "includes a command that the Government must, in order to promote its own interest, leave the people at liberty to speak their own thoughts about government, advocate their own favored governmental causes, and work for their own political candidates and parties."

The Hatch Act, which the majority held valid, reduces the constitionally protected liberty of millions of public employees "to less than a shadow of its substance." It relegates them to the role of "mere spectators of events upon which hinge the safety and welfare of all the people, including public employees." Finally, wrote Justice Black, "it makes honest participation in essential political activities an offense punishable by proscription from public employment. . . . Laudable as its purpose may be, it seems to me to hack at the roots of a Government by the people themselves."

• **Hatch Act Reconsidered.** Based on arguments such as Justice Black's, the U.S. Supreme Court in 1973 reconsidered whether the Hatch Act unconstitutionally restricted the political rights of government employees. By a 5 to 3 vote, it again upheld the act.[42] It noted that the purpose of the act was "the impartial execution of the Laws." By prohibiting federal employees from taking an active part in partisan politics, the act hopes to reduce the hazards to fair and impartial government, to prevent political parties from using federal employees for political campaigns, and to prohibit the selection for government service being based on political performance.

The Hatch Act does not bar all political activities. Employees are allowed to vote and contribute funds, to express their opinions on political subjects and candidates, to display political stickers and badges, and to take an active part in nonpartisan elections. Thus the act has tried to balance the interests of federal employees as citizens with the government's interest in an impartial civil service. The Court noted that "all 50 states have restricted the political activities of their own employees." It concluded that the Hatch Act's goal of preventing clear, active partisan political activity by government employees is not unconstitutional.

UNCONSTITUTIONAL RESTRICTIONS

• Prohibiting Nonpartisan Politics. Gloria Rackley was a capable and qualified school teacher in Orangeburg, South Carolina. She was also an active member of the National Association for the Advancement of Colored People and a leader in the civil rights movement in her county. She engaged in peaceful demonstrations to end segregation in places of public accommodation. In the fall of 1961 she was arrested for refusing to leave a "white" hospital waiting room. The following spring the superintendent explained to her that her civil rights activities were embarrassing to the school system. Although she continued to be an excellent classroom teacher, she also increased her participation in civil rights activities during the following two years. In September 1963 she was discharged by the school board after leading a group of 200 civil rights demonstrators, some of whom were encouraged to "break the law, jeer at policemen, and disturb good order." Rackley sued to require the school district to reinstate her.[43]

The court pointed out that school boards may consider a broad range of factors other than classroom conduct in determining whether to hire or discharge school teachers. They may not, however, unreasonably restrict the constitutionally protected freedom of political expression and association. Since the Constitution "does not permit a state to make criminal the peaceful expression of unpopular views," Rackley's participation in civil rights activity could not provide a valid basis for her discharge. The court therefore ordered the board to reinstate Rackley.

In similar cases in which competent teachers were dismissed for civil rights activity, the courts have reinstated the teachers. These cases clearly show a pattern of judicial protection for such nonpartisan political activity.[44]

• Prohibiting All Politics. In April 1968 the Tatum School Board in Texas did not rehire Billy Montgomery, partly because of his political activity. The board's action was taken under a regulation prohibiting "all political activity except voting." As a result, Montgomery sued the school board in the U.S. District Court for violating his constitutional rights.[45]

The opinion of the court by Judge Justice explained that the state may protect its educational system from undue political activity that may "materially and substantially interfere" with the operation of the school. On the other hand, the First Amendment to the Constitution guarantees the right of citizens to participate in political affairs. The problem is to arrive at a balance between the interest of the teacher as a citizen in participating in the political process and the interest of the state in promoting the efficiency of the public schools.

Judge Justice then ruled that the regulation enforced by the school board prohibiting teachers from engaging in all political activity except voting was inconsistent with the First Amendment guarantees of freedom of speech, press, assembly, and petition. To support its decision the court cited the arguments of Justice Black in his dissent in the *Mitchell* case. The school board prohibition threatens popular government, wrote Judge Justice, not only "because it injures the individuals muzzled, but also because of its harmful effect on the community" in depriving it of the political participation of its teachers.

• **Related Items.** The following items indicate the changing trend concerning teacher participation in political activity.

> Excerpts from statements by the chairmen of the Republican and Democratic national committees:
>
> The power of example is the teacher's greatest influence. The teacher who runs for office at any level involves his students inevitably in the political process. Any sensitive teacher who becomes a candidate (and we want no insensitive people either in teaching or in politics) does not have to involve his students in any partisan way. But the very fact of his candidacy both enlivens student interest and makes him much more aware of community views about schools. This in turn should make him a better teacher.[46]

> In 1957 the Supreme Court of Oregon ruled that under the state constitution a teacher could not hold his position in the public schools while he was a member of the state legislature. In response, the electorate adopted a constitutional amendment providing that an employee of any school board "shall be eligible to a seat in the Legislative Assembly and such membership in the Legislative Assembly shall not prevent such person from being employed as a teacher."[47]

> In Hawaii, where there had been a prohibition against teachers participating in politics, citizens won a ten-year campaign, when the Board of Commissioners adopted a new ruling saying teachers "are permitted to exercise those political rights and responsibilities

which they share in common with other citizens, such as electioneering for candidates, accepting positions in political campaigns, holding office in political party organizations, and serving as delegates to political party conventions."[48]

SUMMARY

The cases in this section illustrate the conflicting and changing views concerning teacher participation in American politics. Despite these conflicts, however, much of the law on the subject is clear. A school board, for example, may not prohibit teachers from engaging in "all political activity" nor may teachers be punished for wearing political symbols, for supporting particular candidates, or for participating in peaceful demonstrations. On the other hand, teachers have no right to use their position to campaign for a particular candidate, to indoctrinate students, or to urge them to engage in disruptive political activity.

Courts are divided over rules requiring teachers to resign before campaigning for or holding any political office. Some judges believe such rules are broader than necessary to prevent conflicts of interest and to insure an impartial school system. Clearly, however, teachers can be required to take an unpaid leave of absence if campaigning or holding office would substantially interfere with their teaching duties. Although teachers' organizations have become politically powerful, the Supreme Court and some state courts have upheld statutes prohibiting teachers and other public employees from taking an active part in partisan politics. Therefore, during the coming decade, teachers may have more success in changing these laws through the legislature than through the judicial process.

TEACHER ORGANIZATIONS

Since administrators and school boards have great discretion in the management of the schools, can such discretion be used to minimize or eliminate teacher organizations? Can a teacher be dismissed or otherwise disciplined for active participation in union or association causes? (We use the term *organization* to refer to both AFT and NEA affiliates; the word *union* refers to the AFT and its subunits.)

HISTORICAL PERSPECTIVE

The first major case focusing on these issues arose in Chicago a little over 50 years ago.[49] In 1915 the Chicago Board of Education adopted a rule, parts of which follow:

> Membership by teachers in labor unions . . . is inimical to proper discipline, prejudicial to the efficiency of the teaching force and detrimental to the

welfare of the public school system, therefore such membership or affiliation is hereby prohibited. . . .[50]

Suit was brought in the lower court of Cook County, Illinois, to (enjoin prevent) the Board of Education from enforcing this rule. The injunction was granted, the city appealed, and the appeals court reversed the decision, saying:

> The board has the absolute right to decline to employ or to reemploy any applicant for any reason whatever or for no reason at all. The board is responsible for its actions only to the people of the city, from whom, through the mayor, the members have received their appointments. It is no infringement upon the constitutional rights of anyone for the board to decline to employ him as a teacher in the schools, and it is immaterial whether the reason for the refusal to employ him is because of the applicant being married or unmarried, is of fair complexion or dark, is or is not a member of a trades union, or whether no reason is given for such refusal. The board is not bound to give any reason for its action. It is free to contract with whomsoever it chooses.[51]

Questions to Consider

1. Why do many school board members, administrators, and parents object to teachers joining teacher organizations? Why do they object more vigorously to membership in teachers' unions?
2. Are these objections merely expressions of personal preferences, or are there legitimate reasons why teachers as public employees should not organize? If the latter, what are the reasons?
3. Is there a right to strike, guaranteed by the Bill of Rights? Is such a right guaranteed by any other provision in the Constitution?
4. Is it unprofessional for teachers to organize? Is it unprofessional for them to strike?

Although the early cases did not extend constitutional protection to unionization, laws change with changing conditions. It has often been said that the U.S. Constitution would be merely a historic artifact if its provisions were not reinterpreted in light of changing cultural conditions. So it was in this area of the law, where growing acceptance of organizational membership in many walks of life led to new conclusions on the rights of teachers to organize and join associations.

Current Issues

THE RIGHT TO JOIN A UNION

James McLaughlin was dismissed by the Cook County Schools because of his active participation in a local chapter of the American Federation of Teachers. He sued and charged that his dismissal violated his constitutional rights. In 1968 a federal appeals court ruled in his favor. The court wrote: "It is settled law that teachers have the right to free association and unjustified interference with teachers' associational freedom" violates their constitutional rights. "Unless there is some illegal intent," wrote the court, "an individual's right to form and join a union is protected by the First Amendment."[52]

CAN ADMINISTRATORS ORGANIZE?

Just as business and industry did not want its foremen and minor executives involved in employee organizations, school districts have at times passed rules to prevent supervisors, deans, and other administrators from joining teacher organizations. A classic example of this was the Florida statute that prohibited "all persons employed in the Palm Beach County Public School System whose primary employment is in the capacity of administrator or supervisor . . . from participation or membership in any organization or affiliate of any organization the activities of which includes the collective representation of members of the teaching profession with regard to terms, tenure or conditions of employment. . . ."[53]

The district court in declaring the statute null and void said that

> This is a classical example of a Fourteenth Amendment denial of equal protection claim. . . . The defendants have made no effort to demonstrate that Palm Beach County is in any way unique so as to justify placing its educational employees in a class apart from those of other Florida Counties. . . . Similarly . . . (the statute) impinges upon the basic freedoms of expression and association protected by the First and Fourteenth Amendments.[54]

Is There a Right to Strike?

Although the right of all educators to join unions has now been clearly established, courts have felt differently about teacher strikes. Most states have laws restricting or prohibiting strikes by public employees. One reason for denying government employees the right to strike, while affording such a right to private employees, concerns the essential nature of public services. As President Franklin Roosevelt explained: "A strike by public employees manifests nothing less than an intent on their part to prevent or obstruct the operation of Government. . . . Such action, looking forward to the paralysis of Government by those who have sworn to support it, is unthinkable and intolerable."[55]

During recent years, however, many teachers have rejected these traditional views, and they have repeatedly challenged laws that prohibited them from striking. However, they have been uniformly unsuccessful. In California, for example, the United Teachers of Los Angeles asked a state appeals court to rule that teachers have a "constitutional right to engage in a strike as a matter of exercising their fundamental rights of free speech and association."[56] The court, however, impatiently rejected their request. It noted that this question has been determined against the teachers on so many occasions "that we can conceive of no benefit which would result in our reanalysis of the issues" which have been exhaustively treated before. Therefore, the court crisply ruled that "in the absence of legislative authorization, public employees in California do not have the right to strike."

Thus, in most states, the right to join the NEA or the AFT does not include the right to strike. And the fact that many strikes by teachers have occurred in recent decades does not make strikes legal. On the contrary, as one judge clearly warned, participation in an illegal strike "may subject striking employees to a variety of administrative sanctions including dismissal."[57] On the other hand, several states have passed legislation allowing teachers and some other public employees a limited right to strike under certain circumstances.[58]

• Sanctions. Educators tend to disfavor the term *strike* because of its historic association with blue-collar labor organizations. The terms *sanctions* or *withholding of services* are less objectionable to teachers, although the behavior and its consequences might be identical with those of strikes. But the courts are not impressed by the labels used. They cut through verbal camouflage and reach to the heart of an issue or controversy.

In New Jersey, for example, "sanctions" were brought by a teachers' organization against a school system. The "sanctions" constituted collective, concerted action, including massive resignations, blacklisting of the school district, and a campaign to discourage teachers from accepting employment there. The court, in placing a ban on "sanctions," concluded that the net effect of such a practice is the same as that of a strike. It would "accomplish a shutdown, a thrust at the vitality of government, and comes within the same policy which denounces a concerted strike . . . or slowdown or other obstruction of the performance of official duties."[59]

The Winston-Salem Case: Is There a Right to Bargain?[60]

In North Carolina the legislature abolished collective bargaining between public employees and any state or city agency. As a result, the state Association of Educators sued to have the legislation declared unconstitutional. The educators argued that the right of association requires that state governmental units negotiate and enter into contracts with them. In 1974, however, a federal court ruled that there was no such constitutional right.

"The Constitution," wrote Judge Ward, "does not mandate" that the government "be compelled to talk to or contract with an organization." According to the court, the solution from the teachers' viewpoint is to "someday persuade state government of the asserted value of collective bargaining agreements." But this is a political, not a judicial, matter. Where there is a right to bargain collectively, it rests upon national or state legislation and not upon the federal Constitution. Although the First Amendment protects the right of teachers to associate and advocate, it does not guarantee that their advocacy will be effective.

North Carolina, as a matter of public policy, chose not to enter into enforceable contracts with public employee organizations. That decision involves far greater interests than the teachers' right to associate. To the extent that public employees gain power through collective bargaining, "other interest groups with a right to a voice in the running of the government may be left out of vital political decisions." Thus a legislature may choose to give teachers' associations a special status to bargain, or it may place them in no better position than any other group that may try to promote its special interests with the government.

NOTE: Most states have statutes that provide for collective bargaining for teachers and other government employees. But where such laws do not exist and where a school board is unwilling to bargain voluntarily, teachers do not have a constitutional right to bargain collectively.

Related Cases

• **Negotiator Not Protected.** Eskel Norbeck was a high school principal who also served as chief negotiator for the teachers in his district. As a result of his role as negotiator, Norbeck's contract was not renewed, and he sued on grounds that he was punished for exercising his constitutional right of association. The court, however, ruled that "the interest asserted by the school board in efficient school administration is paramount to the right of a school principal to collectively bargain for classroom teachers who he was hired to supervise, discipline, and evaluate." The board members, wrote the court, "were properly concerned with whether the close working relationship among a principal, superintendent, and school board was threatened by Norbeck's role as chief negotiator."[61]

• **Supporting a Strike.** When the Kentucky Education Association proposed a "walkout" of its members, three principals publicly indicated that they supported the association's proposal. Although the principals did not take part in the walkout, they were demoted to classroom teachers. The principals claimed that their demotion was unconstitutional and that they were being punished for exercising their right of free expression and association. The school board argued that since the walkout was held illegal by courts, it had a right to punish employees who supported it.

A trial court agreed with the principals, but a federal appeals court ruled in favor of the school board. The court held that public school principals had no constitutional right to urge or encourage their leaders "to commit illegal acts, or as in the present case to engage in an illegal school strike."[62]*

• **Can Union Activity Protect Incompetence?** In New York, a teacher was told by the board that the quality of her work was not up to the standard the district was trying to achieve. The teacher countered with the charge that her dismissal was in retaliation for activities in behalf of the teacher's union. This claim required a court to determine whether the action of the board was based on constitutionally impermissible grounds, namely organizational activity, or whether it was a legitimate exercise of administrative discretion. The court made it clear that "If the petitioner possesses all the attributes of an excellent teacher, but additionally arouses the displeasure of the School Board merely because she is a union activist, she may not be denied tenure on that ground. On the other hand . . . we do not hold that union activity provides a shelter for a teacher whom the Board decides not to retain for *bona fide*, legitimate reasons. Thus, it will be for the trial court to decide whether to give credence to the Board's claim that it was not motivated by a desire to punish the petitioner for her union activities."[63]

• **Limiting Bargaining.** In New Hampshire the legislature conferred the right to engage in collective bargaining on state employees but denied the right to academic employees of the state university system. The academic employees sued on grounds that the statute violated their constitutional rights. A federal court acknowledged that the First Amendment guaranteed public employees the right to organize collectively and select representatives to bargain. However, the court pointed out that the state does not have a constitutional obligation "to respond to their demands" or enter into a contract with them. Furthermore, the court found a rational basis for the legislature's refusal to extend bargaining rights to academic employees. Although bargaining in education is increasing, there are many who believe that it has negative consequences in higher education on governance, curriculum, and educational policy. Since there is no constitutional right to bargain and since there are detriments as well as

---

*However, a federal appeals court disagreed, ruling that a public school principal has no constitutional right "to encourage teachers under his jurisdiction to commit illegal acts" or engage in an illegal strike. *Bates* v. *Dause*, 502 F.2d 865 (6th Cir. 1974).

benefits to bargaining for academic employees, the court concluded that it was reasonable for the legislature to exclude them.[64]

• **Contracts Limit Freedom.** A group of Colorado teachers went to court when their school district disapproved a list of books they had used in elective high school courses. A federal judge agreed that the selection of books for these courses was "clearly within the protected area recognized as academic freedom." But because of the teachers' collective bargaining that gave the board authority in the choice of instructional materials, the court denied their claim. According to Judge Matsch, "the combination of teachers into bargaining units with the coercive power of group action is a contradiction of the kind of individual freedom protected by the First Amendment." Therefore, the court concluded that teachers who are union members may not seek to avoid their contract by calling upon constitutional freedom when they wish to act independently and individually.[65]*

SUMMARY

The right of educators to organize for the purpose of collective bargaining is now firmly established. Although the Constitution does not require the government to bargain with teachers, most states have legislation that provides for collective bargaining with public employees. On the other hand, strikes by teachers are prohibited in most states. Although legislation in several states gives teachers a limited right to strike, generally such strikes are illegal, and striking teachers may be punished. The many policy questions surrounding the right of teachers to bargain or to strike are issues for legislative bodies, not for the courts.

In the years ahead we expect many controversies over the application and interpretation of collective bargaining agreements and their proper scope and meaning, as well as disagreements concerning the right to strike. There will be significant controversy about the desirability of tenure laws and whether collective negotiation agreements might not in fact provide a more fair and expeditious way of protecting competent teachers.[66] Clearly, major gains have been made by teachers in establishing their right to organize and to freely associate with fellow professionals to pursue matters of mutual interest. It is equally clear, however, that the courts will not protect teachers who are incompetent, immoral, or uncooperative merely because they are also engaged in protected organizational activities.

---

*An appeals court also ruled against the teachers—*not* because they were union members or waived their rights, but because school boards generally have authority to select texts. *Cary* v. *Board of Education,* 598 F.2d 535 (10th Cir. 1979).

• A Disclaimer. There are interesting and difficult problems related to teacher organizations, collective bargaining, and strikes that we do not discuss in this book. We have restricted our presentation of cases and analysis to constitutional rights and have excluded other aspects of labor law as well as the law of contracts and torts, all of which are important for teachers. There is extensive literature on these areas in college libraries throughout the nation.[67]

Conclusions

As recently as the 1950s, teachers were expected to abstain from partisan politics, take loyalty oaths, and be judged by the company they kept. Educators often risked their jobs by joining a radical organization or becoming active in a union. But attitudes have changed dramatically during recent decades.

Today teachers cannot be dismissed solely because they are members of revolutionary or other controversial organizations, or because they associate with political or social extremists. Similarly, teachers cannot be required to take negative loyalty oaths (e.g., swearing that one does not belong to any subversive organization). These oaths as well as those that are vague, overbroad, or ambiguous will generally be held unconstitutional, particularly when there are administrative procedures to "police" and penalize violators. On the other hand, clear, simple affirmative oaths (e.g., pledging to support the Constitution and uphold professional standards) have been consistently upheld for all public employees.

Teachers have the right to join unions or other educational associations to bargain and to lobby for their professional interests. Although most states provide for collective bargaining, they generally prohibit teacher strikes. As teacher organizations have become more powerful, they have become active not only in support of legislation affecting teachers, but also in support of specific candidates. Although individual teachers are no longer prohibited from being politically active, they may not have a right to run for or hold political office—especially when this might cause a conflict of interests or otherwise interfere with their teaching. Such matters will often depend on state legislation and local policy. Thus in some areas teachers are still not as free as lawyers, doctors, and other professionals. But as the cases in this chapter illustrate, a teacher's freedom of association is now much broader than it had been during the first half of the century.

NOTES

1. As quoted in Robert R. Hamilton, *Legal Rights and Liabilities of Teachers*, Laramie, Wyo., School Law Publications, 1956, p. 84.
2 *Adler* v. *Board of Education*, 342 U.S. 485, 497 (1952).

3. Hamilton, op. cit., p. 82.
4. Id. at 84–85.
5. *Baggett* v. *Bullitt,* 377 U.S. 360 (1964).
6. Id. at 361–362.
7. Id. at 382–383.
8. *Whitehill* v. *Elkins,* 389 U.S. 54 (1967).
9. The 1950 oath states in part: ". . . I do not advocate, nor am I a member of any party or organization, political or otherwise, that now advocates the overthrow of the Government of the United States or of the State of California by force or violence or other unlawful means; that within the five years immediately preceding the taking of this oath, I have not been a member of any party or organization, political or otherwise, that advocated the overthrow of the Government of the United States or of the State of California by force or violence. . ." *Monroe* v. *Trustees of the California State Colleges,* 6 C.3d 399, 411 (1971).
10. *Vogel* v. *County of Los Angeles,* 434 P.2d 961 (1967).
11. *State* v. *Lundquist,* 278 A.2d 263 (Md. 1971).
12. *Ohlson* v. *Phillips,* 304 F.Supp. 1152 (D. Colo. 1969).
13. *Knight* v. *Board of Regents of University of State of New York,* 269 F.Supp. 339 (S.D. N.Y. 1967).
14. *Biklen* v. *Board of Education,* 333 F.Supp. 902 (N.D. N.Y. 1971).
15. *Cole* v. *Richardson,* 405 U.S. 676 (1972).
16. *Adler* v. *Board of Education,* 342 U.S. 485 (1952).
17. Id. at 493.
18. Id. at 508–511.
19. *Keyishian* v. *Board of Regents of New York,* 385 U.S. 589 (1967).
20. *Cooper* v. *Henslee,* 522 S.W.2d 391 (Ark. 1975).
21. *Cook* v. *Hudson,* 511 F.2d 744 (5th Cir. 1975).
22. Id. at 757.
23. *Randle* v. *Indianola Municipal Separate School District,* 373 F.Supp. 766 (N.D. Miss. 1974).
24. *Mescia* v. *Berry,* 406 F.Supp. 1181 (D. S.C. 1974).
25. T. M. Stinnet, *Professional Problems of Teachers,* New York, Macmillan, 1968, p. 264.
26. *Resolutions, New Business and Other Actions, 1978–79,* National Education Association, Washington, D.C., pp. 49–50.
27. *Goldsmith* v. *Board of Education,* 225 Pac. 783 (Cal. 1924).
28. Id. at 784.
29. *James* v. *Board of Education of Central Dist. No. 1,* 461 F.2d 566 (2nd Cir. 1972).
30. *Alabama Education Association* v. *Wallace,* 362 F.Supp. 682 (M.D. Ala. 1973).
31. *Franklin* v. *Atkins,* 409 F.Supp. 439 (Colo. 1976); 562 F.2d 1188 (1977).
32. *Galer* v. *Board of Regents of the University System,* 236 S.E.2d 617 (Ga. 1977).
33. *Jones* v. *Board of Control,* 131 So.2d 713 (Fla. 1961).
34. Id. at 718.
35. *Minielly* v. *State,* 411 P.2d 69 (Ore. 1966).

36. *Guerra* v. *Roma Independent School District,* 444 F.Supp. 812 (S.D. Tex. 1977).
37. *Miller* v. *Board of Education of the County of Lincoln,* 450 F.Supp. 106 (S.D. W.Va. 1978).
38. *United Public Workers* v. *Mitchell,* 330 U.S. 75 (1947).
39. Some states have "little Hatch Acts" that restrict the political activities of civil service employees. In addition, there are "solicitation" statutes in over a dozen states that are both restrictive and protective. They prohibit teachers and other public employees from soliciting either funds or services for political purposes. At the same time they also protect these employees from such solicitations.
40. Id. at 106–107.
41. Id. at 111–112.
42. *United States Civil Service Commission* v. *National Association of Letter Carriers, AFL-CIO,* 413 U.S. 548 (1973).
43. *Rackley* v. *School District,* 258 F.Supp. 676 (D. S.C. 1966).
44. E.g., *Johnson* v. *Branch,* 364 F.2d 177 (4th Cir. 1966) and *Williams* v. *Sumter School District,* 255 F.Supp. 397 (D. S.C. 1966).
45. *Montgomery* v. *White,* 320 F.Supp. 303 (E.D. Tex. 1969).
46. As quoted in Stinnet, op. cit., pp. 266–267.
47. NEA Research Memo, Washington, D.C., August 1961, p. 5.
48. Stinnet, op. cit., p. 268.
49. *People ex rel Fursman* v. *City of Chicago,* 116 N.E. 158 (Ill. 1917).
50. Id. at 158.
51. Id. at 160.
52. *McLaughlin* v. *Tilendis,* 398 F.2d 287 (7th Cir. 1968).
53. Florida Laws 1969, ch. 69–1424.
54. *Orr* v. *Thorp,* 308 F.Supp. 1369 (S.D. Fla. 1969).
55. *Norwalk Teachers' Association* v. *Board of Education,* 83 A.2d 482 (Conn. 1951).
56. *Los Angeles Unified School District* v. *United Teachers L.A.,* 100 Cal. Rptr. 806 (1972).
57. *City and County of San Francisco* v. *Cooper,* 120 Cal. Rptr. 707 (1975).
58. Tanimoto, Helene, and Najita, Joyce, *Guide to Statutory Provisions in Public Sector Collective Bargaining: Strike Rights and Prohibitions,* University of Hawaii, 1978, pp. 118–120.
59. *Board of Education* v. *New Jersey Education Association,* 247 A.2d 867 (N.J. 1968).
60. *Winston-Salem/Forsyth County Unit, North Carolina Association of Educators* v. *Phillips,* 381 F.Supp. 644 (M.D. N.C. 1974).
61. *Norbeck* v. *Davenport Community School District,* 545 F.2d 63 (8th Cir. 1976).
62. *Bates* v. *Dause,* 502 F.2d 865 (6th Cir. 1974).
63. *Tischler* v. *Board of Education,* 323 N.Y.S.2d 508 (1971).
64. *University of New Hampshire Chapter of the American Association of University Professors* v. *Haselton,* 397 F.Supp. 107 (D. N.H. 1975).
65. *Cary* v. *Board of Education of the Adams-Arapahoe School District,* 427 F.Supp. 945 (Colo. 1977); 598 F.2d 535 (10th Cir. 1979).
66. For a brief but interesting discussion and prediction for the 1970s, see Myron

Lieberman, "Why Teachers Will Oppose Tenure Laws," *Saturday Review* (March 4, 1972), 55–56.

67. See, for example, Myron Lieberman and Michael H. Moskow, *Collective Negotiations for Teachers: An Approach to School Administration*, Chicago, Rand McNally, 1966; Timothy M. Stinnet, *Turmoil in Teaching: A History of the Organizational Struggle for America's Teachers*, New York, Macmillan, 1968; Newton Edwards, *The Courts and the Public Schools*, rev. ed., University of Chicago Press, 1955; Lee D. Garber and Edmund E. Reutter, Jr., *The Yearbook of School Law*, Danville, Ill., Interstate Printers, published annually; William R. Hazard, *Education and the Law*, 2d ed., New York, Free Press, 1978; Leroy Peterson, Richard Rossmiller, and Marlin Volz, *The Law and Public School Education*, New York, Harper & Row, 1978.

Chapter 10
Racial and Ethnic Discrimination in Education

Racial hatred is an adult rather than a childhood disease.
—Johnson v. *San Francisco Unified*[1]

The only school desegregation plan that meets constitutional standards is one that works.
—U.S. v. *Jefferson*[2]

Our schools have always reflected the racism found in the larger culture. In the nineteenth century, racial discrimination in the schools was often official policy, reflected in separate schools for different races. For many decades these schools were not only separate but unequal; the schooling provided for minorities—blacks, Mexican Americans, and Indians—was clearly inferior.

The twentieth century ushered in the "separate-but-equal" doctrine, which in turn was challenged by the many legal and political attacks on racist practices. This chapter examines racism as it has affected civil rights and schooling. The leading cases are presented so that the reader may come to understand the legal principles related to racially separate schools, the racial aspects of school staffing, "freedom of choice" plans, busing, and related issues.

Historical Trends

CHINESE SCHOOLS FOR CHINESE-AMERICAN CHILDREN?
San Francisco is a city of immigrants as well as a cosmopolitan city and is composed of many ethnic and racial groups. Most of its inhabitants are of

European, African, and Asian ancestry, and they often live and work in ethnic or racial enclaves. The distribution of these groups was due in part to free choice and in part to racial, ethnic, and economic discrimination. The city's schools, particularly the neighborhood elementary schools, tend to reflect the population composition of the surrounding areas that they serve. For example, in an area populated by Chinese Americans, three elementary schools "are filled predominantly with children of Chinese ancestry—in one 456 out of 482, in another 230 out of 289, and in a third, 1,074 out of 1,111."[3]

The San Francisco Unified School District created a plan for the overall desegregation of its schools. The plan included, among its many features, a reassignment of pupils of Chinese ancestry to certain elementary schools away from their neighborhoods in order to "reduce racial imbalance." Busing was to be one of the means used to eliminate segregation. In addition to children of Chinese ancestry, children of other ancestries were to take part in the reassignment plan; these included children of Japanese, Filipino, African, and Spanish ancestry, as well as of various European ethnic backgrounds.

Chinese-American parents objected to the reassignment plans on behalf of their children. In the *Lee* case they requested the school district and the courts to continue the pattern of neighborhood schools that allows children of Chinese ancestry to attend school together. The parents urged that there are important cultural values that cannot be preserved and passed on to future generations if the children are dispersed throughout the city. In addition to the Chinese cultural heritage, the very survival of their language might be in jeopardy if their children could not remain together.

Questions to Consider

1. Does a subculture have a right to perpetuate itself?
2. Should the majority culture force a subculture to accept integration and thus probable assimilation?
3. Do parents have the right to educate their children in a neighborhood school?
4. What parts of the Constitution relate to these issues?

The problem of the Chinese children and parents, briefly stated above, makes it clear that racial and ethnic segregation is not just a problem affecting blacks and whites. Furthermore, it emphasizes the often overlooked fact that minorities do not always wish to integrate with majorities, and it suggests that rather than having solved our problems of racial and ethnic integration, we can expect a variety of new situations calling for novel applications of the Fourteenth Amendment to school-related issues.

The constitutional provision most directly relevant to questions of racial segregation and integration is the following portion of the Fourteenth Amendment: "No State shall . . . deny to any person within its jurisdiction the equal protection of the laws."

The application of the Equal Protection Clause of this amendment to school situations has a substantial history involving hundreds of court cases. For the purposes of this discussion it will be sufficient to examine the landmark decisions of *Brown* I, *Brown* II, and *Swann* and to mention *Plessy* v. *Ferguson* briefly in order to provide historical perspective. After that we will return for a brief look at the issues raised by the Chinese parents in San Francisco.

The Plessy Case: Separate Can Be Equal

In 1890 Louisiana passed a law that in part required

> that all railway companies carrying passengers in their coaches in this state shall provide equal but separate accommodations for the white and colored races, by providing two or more passenger coaches for each passenger train, or by dividing the passenger coaches by a partition so as to secure separate accommodations. . . . No person or persons shall be permitted to occupy any coaches other than the ones assigned to them, on account of the race they belong to.[4]

The statute provided for enforcing the separation of the races by train officials and specified a fine of $25 or imprisonment for no more than 20 days for violators.

Mr. Plessy was assigned by the railroad officers to a coach "for the use of the race to which he belonged, but he insisted upon going into a coach used by the race to which he did not belong." He was forcibly ejected from the coach for white passengers and imprisoned for the violation. His petition asserted that "petitioner was seven-eighths Caucasian and one-eighth African blood." He challenged the constitutionality of the law on various grounds, including the claim that it violated the Fourteenth Amendment.

Although the *Plessy* case did not directly involve the civil rights of students or teachers, it announced a principle that was used in school-related cases to support laws, policies, and practices of racial segregation. The *Plessy* v. *Ferguson* case broadly legitimized the "separate-but-equal" doctrine.

The Supreme Court applied the test of reasonableness to the legislation and concluded that the Louisiana legislature must have broad discretion to decide what was reasonable "with reference to the established usages, customs, and traditions of the people, and with a view to the promotion of their comfort, and the preservation of the public peace and order." Applying this standard, the Court concluded that the law was not unreasonable.

Does separation of the races imply a superior-inferior relationship?

Not in the eyes of the *Plessy* Court in 1896: "We consider the underlying fallacy of the plaintiff's argument to consist in the assumption that the enforced separation of the two races stamps the colored race with a badge of inferiority. If this be so, it is not by reason of anything found in the act, but solely because the colored race chooses to put that construction upon it." The Supreme Court, with only Justice Harlan dissenting, upheld the constitutionality of the Louisiana law, and the case became authority for the principle that "separate-but-equal" is constitutionally permissible.

THE INTERIM YEARS

Separate schools for white, black, Indian, Mexican, and other ethnic children had existed in many parts of the country for years before the *Plessy* case. In fact, the Court in that decision referred to acts of Congress "requiring separate schools for colored children in the District of Columbia." Although logically it was arguable that separate schools can be equal, in fact they were usually not equal. In the years following *Plessy*, various court challenges resulted not in the reversal of the *Plessy* doctrine but in the requirement that schools become more equal. These attempts focused on improving physical facilities and providing better books and instructional materials, as well as upgrading the teaching staff of black and other minority schools.

In the meantime, the separate-but-equal doctrine was being successfully challenged in the courts as it applied to colleges and graduate schools. We will not pursue that line of legal development here, but these cases are alluded to lest the reader infer that the Supreme Court abruptly changed its mind from *Plessy* v. *Ferguson* to *Brown* v. *Board of Education*, the next case to be discussed. During the 58 years separating the two cases, significant developments occurred, which make it clear to knowledgeable observers that the *Brown* case is an evolutionary development rather than an abrupt change.

Brown I

Kansas enacted a law in 1949, which permitted, but did not require, cities with a population of more than 15,000 to maintain separate schools for Negro and white students. Under the authority of this state law the Topeka Board of Education chose to establish segregated elementary schools.

Oliver Brown, a student, and others filed a class suit* challenging the constitutionality of segregated schools, claiming that such an arrange-

---

*A *class suit* is a lawsuit brought by one or more individuals on behalf of a group of people who fall into the same general class or category, for example, a class of consumers, women, and tenants.

ment, when conducted by officials pursuant to law, violated the Equal Protection Clause of the Fourteenth Amendment. The district court found "that segregation in public education has a detrimental effect upon Negro children," but it upheld the arrangement since white and Negro schools "were substantially equal with respect to buildings, transportation, curricula, and educational qualifications of teachers."[5] Brown appealed to the Supreme Court, where his case was heard along with similar cases from South Carolina, Virginia, and Delaware.

School districts and state officials who urged the legitimacy of segregated schooling presented two basic arguments. First, when the Fourteenth Amendment was adopted in 1868 it was not intended to apply to public education. Second, the Court should be bound by the separate-but-equal principle established in the case of *Plessy* v. *Ferguson* in 1896 and followed as precedent in several cases thereafter.

Questions to Consider

1. Did the authors of the Fourteenth Amendment intend it to apply to public education?
2. Can schools be "separate but equal"? How would you determine if two or more schools were equal?
3. Should the Court be bound by the precedent of *Plessy* v. *Ferguson?* When should the Court follow precedent and when not?

THE OPINION OF THE COURT

Chief Justice Earl Warren delivered the unanimous opinion of the Court. He explained that the case must be decided in light of the facts and conditions of contemporary American life and not those of 1868 when the Fourteenth Amendment was adopted. Only by considering the significance of public education in the middle of the twentieth century could it be determined whether segregated schooling deprived children of equal protection of the laws.

In reaching its decision the Court considered the history of public education in America. It noted that the quality of the schools varied by locality and by region and that the South, for various reasons, was slower than the North in its provision for public schools. It also recognized "the low status of Negro education in all sections of the country, both before and immediately after the [Civil] War." The Court quoted Professor Ellwood Cubberley to the effect that "compulsory school attendance laws were not generally adopted until after the ratification of the Fourteenth Amendment, and it was not until 1918 that such laws were in force in all the States."[6]

The Court, after exhaustive consideration of the circumstances surrounding the adoption of the amendment, became convinced that historical considerations by themselves were inconclusive. There was no clear and convincing evidence as to what, if anything, was originally intended for public education by the authors of the Fourteenth Amendment. Furthermore no case prior to this one had raised the direct question of the constitutionality of segregated schooling.

In moving toward its decision, the Court, in an often quoted paragraph, emphasized the centrality of schools in modern life:

> Today, education is perhaps the most important function of state and local governments. Compulsory school attendance laws and the great expenditures for education both demonstrate our recognition of the importance of education to our democratic society. It is required in the performance of our most basic public responsibilities, even service in the armed forces. It is the very foundation of good citizenship. Today it is a principal instrument in awakening the child to cultural values, in preparing him for later professional training, and in helping him to adjust normally to his environment. In these days, it is doubtful that any child may reasonably be expected to succeed in life if he is denied the opportunity of an education. Such an opportunity, where the state has undertaken to provide it, is a right which must be made available to all on equal terms.[7]

Justice Warren then concluded that segregation of public schoolchildren solely on the basis of race deprives minority group children of equal educational opportunity even though the "tangible factors may be equal."*

Why did the Court reject *Plessy* v. *Ferguson?* First, it pointed out that the *Plessy* case involved transportation and not public education. Second, courts do not follow precedents blindly; changing circumstances as well as new knowledge may reasonably lead to new conclusions. This latter factor—namely, a more advanced state of social and psychological knowledge of schooling—had significant influence on the Court. It quoted with approval an earlier Kansas case:

> Segregation of white and colored children in public schools has a detrimental effect upon the colored children. The impact is greater when it has the sanction of the law; for the policy of separating the races is usually interpreted as denoting the inferiority of the Negro group. A sense of inferiority affects the motivation of the child to learn. Segregation with the sanction of law, therefore, has a tendency to [retard] the educational and mental development of Negro children and to deprive them of some of the benefits they would receive in a racial[ly] integrated school system.[8]

The Court also relied on the writing of various psychologists,

---

*In these days of intense efforts to place education on a scientific basis, it is significant to note that the Court considered the intangible, nonmeasurable qualities of schooling as most important. It quoted with approval an earlier case concerning segregated law school education and emphasized the significance of "those qualities which are incapable of objective measurement but which make for greatness in a law school." Id. at 493.

including Dr. Kenneth B. Clark, who analyzed and established the devastating effects of discrimination and prejudice on the personality development of children. Thus, in part as a result of advances in the social sciences, the Court rejected the precedent of *Plessy* v. *Ferguson.* "We conclude that in the feld of public education the doctrine of 'separate-but-equal' has no place. Separate educational facilities are inherently unequal."

The Court, realizing the complexities of desegregating the schools in light of the "great variety of local conditions," requested all parties involved or wishing to be involved to return at a later date and submit arguments for implementation of the *Brown* decision. Thus *Brown* I, within a year, led to *Brown* II.

Brown II

The first *Brown* case declared the fundamental principle that racial discrimination in public education is unconstitutional. In *Brown* II the Court said: "All provisions of federal, state, or local laws requiring or permitting such discrimination must yield to this principle."[9]

Because segregated and discriminatory schooling existed in so many places and under such varied conditions, the Court requested arguments on the question of remedy. In other words, what kind of a legal order should it issue to correct the widespread, massive discrimination?

Questions to Consider

1. What order would you have issued if you had the authority of the Supreme Court?
2. What factors and conflicting interests would you consider before issuing the order?

THE OPINION OF THE COURT

Chief Justice Warren again delivered the unanimous opinion of the Court. He noted that already some steps had been taken toward desegregation as a result of *Brown* I. He also emphasized that local school authorities had the primary responsibility for clarifying, assessing, and solving local educational problems. The local courts, however, must consider whether or not the actions of school authorities constitute "good faith implementation of governing constitutional principles."

Justice Warren recommended that principles of equity and fairness should guide the courts. School districts should consider the interests of minority children in opening the schools as soon as practicable on a nondiscriminatory basis and make a "prompt and reasonable start toward full compliance." "Once such a start has been made, the courts may find that additional time is necessary to carry out the ruling in an effective manner."

The local courts retained jurisdiction over such cases, and the burden of proof was to be on the defendant school district to show that it was proceeding reasonably and in good faith toward "compliance at the earliest practicable date." In its last paragraph the opinion used the now famous phrase "with all deliberate speed" as a general guideline to be used by local school districts in the elimination of unconstitutional racial segregation.

"WITH ALL DELIBERATE SPEED"

What were the reactions to the desegregation decisions of *Brown* I and II? How did school districts and states respond to the call to eliminate racial discrimination with all deliberate speed?

The initial attention focused on the South, where segregation was openly practiced and supported by law. Separate schools existed for blacks and whites, the so-called dual school systems. The North maintained more subtle forms of segregation, often not officially stated or sanctioned. Therefore it was widely believed that the desegregation decisions would apply only to the South. One New Jersey newspaper announced the court ruling with this headline: "It Doesn't Affect Us."

The Griffin Case: The Closing of Schools

In the South, although some school officials urged compliance, resistance was the more typical initial reaction. Such resistance took many forms: governors standing in schoolhouse doors, legislatures passing new laws as delaying tactics, local school boards simply ignoring the decision. One of the most publicized cases arose in Prince Edward County, Virginia, where the supervisors chose to levy no school taxes so that the schools did not reopen in the fall of 1959 when "confronted with a court decree which requires the admission of white and colored children to all the schools of the county without regard to race or color."[10]

The supervisors of Prince Edward County took this action after the General Assembly of Virginia (the state legislature) tried various means of frustrating the intent of the *Brown* decision. When these various efforts were found to violate the Virginia constitution, the "General Assembly abandoned 'massive resistance' to desegregation and turned instead to what was called a 'freedom-of-choice' plan." This plan repealed "Virginia's compulsory attendance laws and instead made school attendance a matter of local option." We can more readily understand the effectiveness of the resistance to integration when we realize that the initial litigation to desegregate the schools of Prince Edward County began in 1951 and the opinion in this case was handed down in 1964!

In this case, *Griffin* v. *Prince Edward County*, the Supreme Court struck down the efforts of state and school officials to avoid or delay school desegregation. The Court carefully considered the reasons for the closing of the schools and found them to be racist and therefore unconstitutional. In its own words:

> But the record in the present case could not be clearer that Prince Edward's public schools were closed and private schools operated in their place with state and county assistance, for one reason and one reason only: to ensure, through measures taken by the county and the state, that white and colored children in Prince Edward County would not, under any circumstances, go to the same school. Whatever nonracial grounds might support a state's allowing a county to abandon public schools, the grounds of race and opposition to desegregate do not qualify as constitutional.[11]

The facts in this case showed that the children of Prince Edward County were treated differently from those in other counties in the state. "Prince Edward children must go to a private school or none at all; all other Virginia children can go to public schools." The result of this is that if children in Prince Edward County go to school, they must go to racially segregated ones, which, "although designated as private, are beneficiaries of county and state support." The Court found that such an arrangement violated the Equal Protection Clause of the Fourteenth Amendment. Furthermore, indicating its lack of sympathy with the variety of delaying tactics, it noted that "the time for mere 'deliberate speed' has run out, and that phrase can no longer justify denying these Prince Edward school children their constitutional rights to an education equal to that afforded by the public schools in the other parts of Virginia."

"FREEDOM-OF-CHOICE"

The phrase "freedom-of-choice" had a broad appeal. It caught on rapidly in the various state legislatures and local school district offices as everyone searched for a palatable way to satisfy the law. Some wanted to use it to abide by the law, whereas others saw in the phrase a new and powerful subterfuge. Some of these issues surfaced in the *Green* case.

The Green Case

New Kent County is a rural area in eastern Virginia with a population of about 4500, half of whom are black. Since there was no residential segregation in the county, persons of both races resided throughout. "The school system has only two schools, the all white New Kent [s]chool on the east side of the county and the all black George W. Watkins school on the [w]est side."[12] Of the 1300 students, 750 were black and 550 were white. Twenty-one school buses traveled overlapping routes throughout the county to transport students, 11 serving the Watkins school and 10 serving the New Kent school.

The segregated schools were initially established and maintained under a 1902 Virginia law that mandated racial segregation in public education. After the *Brown* decisions a State Pupil Placement Board was established under which children were automatically assigned to schools they had previously attended, unless upon their application the board reassigned them to a different school. No student asked for reassignment under this law to a school other than that of his own race. However, while the *Green* case was pending, the school board of New Kent County adopted a new freedom-of-choice plan in order to be eligible for federal financial aid.

Under the freedom-of-choice plan, first and eighth grade students had to choose a school to attend, whereas all other students each year might choose between New Kent and Watkins schools. Students who did not choose were assigned to the school previously attended. The school district argued that such a plan completely satisfied the Fourteenth Amendment since every student, regardless of race, might "freely" choose which school to attend. Charles C. Green and other students argued that the board had not yet satisfied the nondiscriminatory intent of the Fourteenth Amendment, as interpreted in the *Brown* decisions.

Questions to Consider

1. Does freedom-of-choice satisfy the Equal Protection Clause of the Fourteenth Amendment?
2. When is choice really free? Since we all have a history that influences us, are our choices ever really free?
3. Does the Fourteenth Amendment make integration compulsory?

THE OPINION OF THE COURT

Justice Brennan, in delivering the opinion of the Court, expressed serious concern about the long delays in desegregating the schools of New Kent County. He noted that the freedom-of-choice plan was first offered 11 years after *Brown* I and 10 years after *Brown* II "This deliberate perpetuation of the unconstitutional dual system can only have compounded the harm of such a system." Consequently it is not sufficient that the district merely make available some choices to students and their parents. "Moreover, a plan that at this late date fails to provide meaningful assurance of prompt and effective disestablishment of a dual system is also intolerable."

Does this decision mean that the freedom-of-choice plan was illegitimate? Not necessarily, said Justice Brennan. "All we decide today is that in desegregating a dual school system a plan utilizing 'freedom-of-choice' is not an end in itself." Then he incorporated some of the words of Judge Sobeloff of the district court:

"Freedom-of-choice" is not a sacred talisman; it is only a means to a constitutionally required end—the abolition of the system of segregation and its effects. If the means prove effective, it is acceptable, but if it fails to undo segregation, other means must be used to achieve this end.* The school officials have the continuing duty to take whatever action may be necessary to create a "unitary, non-racial system."[13]

In applying the test of effectiveness to this case, Justice Brennan concluded:

The New Kent School Board "freedom-of-choice" plan cannot be accepted as a sufficient step to "effective transition" to a unitary system. In three years of operation, not a single white child has chosen to attend Watkins School and although 115 Negro children enrolled in New Kent School in 1967 (up from 35 in 1965 and 111 in 1966) 85 percent of all the Negro children in the system still attend the all-Negro Watkins School.[14]

The Court concluded that the dual system had not been dismantled. The Court, having declared the arrangement unconstitutional, ordered the school board of New Kent County to formulate a new plan that would desegregate the schools. The case was then returned to the district court "for further proceedings consistent with this opinion."

BUSING

As the years passed, hundreds of desegregation suits were filed as the nation underwent massive readjustments to remedy the unconstitutional arrangements spawned by decades of segregated schooling. First local, then regional, and finally national political figures expressed themselves for and against school desegregation, and busing as a method to combat it, until busing became the most controversial symbol of the struggle.

The Swann Case[15]

The Charlotte-Mecklenburg (North Carolina) school system enrolled over 84,000 students in 107 schools during the 1968−1969 school year. Approximately 24,000 of the students were black, about 14,000 of whom attended 21 schools that were at least 99 percent black. This pupil distribution resulted from a desegregation plan put into effect by the district court in 1965. Pursuant to the *Green* case discussed previously, James E. Swann, a student, and others requested that the school board create a plan that would work more realistically toward removing state-imposed segregation. When the school board's new plans were

*An earlier, lower court case, *U.S.* v. *Jefferson*, 372 F.2d 836 (1966), pronounced a simple, pragmatic test: "The only school desegregation plan that meets constitutional standards is one that works."

found to be unsatisfactory by the district court, the court appointed an expert to submit a desegregation plan. When the expert and the board each submitted a desegregation plan, the district court adopted some elements of each.

The controversial aspects of the plan developed by the expert were described by the district court as follows:

> The plan does as much by rezoning school attendance lines as can reasonably be accomplished. However, unlike the board plan, it does not stop there. It goes further and desegregates all the rest of the elementary schools by the techniques of grouping two or three outlying schools with one black inner city school; by transporting black students from grades one through four to the outlying white schools; and by transporting white students from the fifth and sixth grades from the outlying white schools to the inner city black school.
>
> Under the . . . plan, nine inner-city Negro schools were grouped in this manner with 24 suburban white schools.[16]

The court of appeals affirmed part of the district court's order, but it overruled the district court's plans related to pairing and grouping of elementary schools as placing unreasonable burdens on students and on the board.

The Supreme Court, with Chief Justice Burger writing the opinion, saw four central issues in the *Swann* case:

1. To what extent may racial balance or racial quotas be used to correct a previously segregated system?
2. Must one-race schools, whether all black or all white, be eliminated as a necessary part of desegregation?
3. Are there any limits on the rearrangement of school district or attendance zones?
4. Are there any limits on the use of buses or other transportation to correct segregated schooling?

Questions to Consider

1. What would be your responses to the four issues posed above, in light of the facts of the *Swann* case and applying the legal principles derived from *Brown* I and II and *Green?*
2. Would your answers differ if the issues arose in a community without a long history of racial segregation in the schools?

THE OPINION OF THE COURT

The following summaries represent the Supreme Court's position on each of the major issues of the *Swann* case.

• **On Racial Balance.** Justice Burger relied heavily on the principles of the *Brown* cases and their progeny in his analysis of the facts and applicable law. He emphasized that the application of a "particular degree of racial balance or mixing" would be disapproved. "The constitutional command to desegregate schools does not mean that every school in every community must always reflect the racial composition of the school system as a whole."

He noted that in the *Swann* case the district court had made use of mathematical ratios as starting points in formulating a remedy and not as fixed requirements. A limited use of ratios was within the discretion of the district court in an effort to correct past constitutional violations.

• **One-race Schools.** The Court recognized the widespread phenomenon that in large cities with racial or ethnic ghettos neighborhood schools are often one-race schools. These schools, according to Justice Burger, must be closely scrutinized to determine "that school assignments are not part of state-enforced segregation."

The existence of a small number of one-race or virtually one-race schools was not in itself illegal segregation. However, the legal presumptions were against districts that had one-race schools, and this put the burden on the school authorities to show that such school assignments were genuinely nondiscriminatory. When plans were presented to change the dual system to a unitary one, the schools had to satisfy the courts that their racial composition was not the result of present or past discriminatory action.

• **Altering of Attendance Zones.** In this issue the Court again relied on the more intimate knowledge of local conditions by the district court. A wide variety of arrangements, including "pairing," "clustering," or "regrouping" of schools, might be necessary interim measures to remedy a heretofore segregated school system. At times the results were very awkward and resembled extreme forms of gerrymandering. The Court, speaking through a "conservative" Chief Justice, made this statement about such an arrangement:

> All things being equal, with no history of discrimination, it might well be desirable to assign pupils to schools nearest their homes. But all things are not equal in a system that has been deliberately constructed and maintained to enforce racial segregation. The remedy for such segregation may be administratively awkward, inconvenient, and even bizarre in some situations and may impose burdens on some; but all awkwardness and inconvenience cannot be avoided in the interim period when remedial adjustments are being made to eliminate the dual school systems.[17]

The Supreme Court established no fixed guidelines in this area except to indicate that the objective was to dismantle dual school systems. Thus a "racially neutral" plan would be inadequate. Beyond that, the district courts, which were closest to the schools, could consider such local variables as highways, traffic patterns, and travel time. "Conditions in different localities will vary so widely that no rigid rules can be laid down to govern all situations."

• Busing. Justice Burger expressed a similar need for substantial reliance on the lower courts in the matter of pupil transportation. But he maintained the following:

> Bus transportation has been an integral part of the public education for years, and was perhaps the single most important factor in the transition from the one-room schoolhouse to the consolidated school. Eighteen million of the Nation's public school children, approximately 39%, were transported to their schools by bus in 1969-1970 in all parts of the country.[18]

Therefore, after considering the facts of the *Swann* case, the Court approved the proposed busing plan. It noted that the average time spent on the bus would be less under the new plan then the one previously in operation. Bus transportation was found to be a normal and accepted tool for furthering the development of a unitary school system.

Does that mean that there can be no objection to the busing of schoolchildren to achieve desegregation? Not at all. Justice Burger indicated that valid objections may be raised when "the time or distance of travel is so great as to either risk the health of the children or significantly impinge on the educational process. It hardly needs stating that the limits on time of travel will vary with many factors, but probably with none more than the age of the students."

With the foregoing responses to the key issues, the Supreme Court upheld the initial action of the district court. The principles set forth in the *Swann* case have become very important in the process of desegregating the city schools of the South and the North alike. Thus, in the case involving the Chinese subculture of San Francisco, to which we now turn, the district court relied heavily on *Swann*.

The Johnson and Lee Cases: A City of Immigrants

San Francisco is a city of immigrants, and in 1971, in the *Johnson* case, which involved *all* of San Francisco, the district court ordered the city to put into effect one of two plans that would eliminate segregation.[19] Thereafter the Chinese parents brought suit in the *Lee* case and expressed their disagreement with the overall decision of the federal court in its effort to achieve racial and ethnic balance in the schools of the city.

In the *Johnson* case it had been argued by the defendant school district that earlier decisions of the Supreme Court on behalf of desegregation did not apply to San Francisco for the following reasons:

1. Decisions forbidding segregation applied only to those states "which at an earlier time, had dual school systems" (i.e., states that had separate schools for black and white students).
2. San Francisco's school actions were not unconstitutional because district officials merely drew attendance lines year after year, and there were no rules or regulations segregating racial or ethnic groups.
3. Since the city's population "is more diverse than in other communities, racial segregation in the elementary schools ought to be permitted."

The district court, however, was not favorably impressed by any of these arguments. In rejecting the first, the court admitted that historically it may well have been the case that desegregation orders applied primarily to the dual school systems of the South. That was no longer the case; for "it is shocking, indeed, it is nonsensical, to assume that such practices are forbidden to school authorities in Florida or North Carolina, for example, but are permitted to school authorities in California. Neither the United States Supreme Court nor any other court has drawn a Mason-Dixon line for constitutional enforcement."[20]

In rejecting the second argument of the defendant, the court clarified some confusion about *de facto* and *de jure* segregation.* It made it plain that any action, rule, or regulation "by school authorities which creates or continues or heightens racial segregation of school children is *de jure*." If a school board draws attendance lines that provide for reasonable racial balance, and if solely by virtue of population mobility the racial balance of the school becomes lopsided, that segregation is *de facto*. However, if the school officials were aware of the population shift and drew attendance lines year after year, "knowing that the lines maintain or heighten racial imbalance, the resulting segregation is *de jure*."[21]

In the *Johnson* case no evidence was presented to show that the San Francisco school authorities had ever changed any attendance boundaries for the purpose of eliminating racial imbalance. The court also made it clear, however, that evil or criminal intent was irrelevant to *de jure* segregation. Board members may act in all innocence, yet if their official action "creates or continues or increases substantial racial imbalance in the schools," the action is *de jure*.

Finally, the court rejected the suggestion that racial segregation in the elementary schools of the city should be permitted because the population of San Francisco was more diverse than in other communities.

De jure segregation means segregation by some official action, and it is unconstitutional. *De facto* segregation means segregation through social developments without any official action involved. *De facto* segregation has not been declared unconstitutional. *De jure* means "under color of law" and *de facto* means "as a matter of fact."

After noting that "the law allows no such latitude," Judge Weigel expressed the view that the multiplicity of races made desegregation all the more important. He further indicated that the "evils of racism and ethnic intolerance are not limited to blacks and whites." His comments about the significance of the elementary years are generally shared by educators: "Opposition to desegregation in the elementary schools is particularly ill-advised. It works to prevent the kind of exchange in formative years which can best innoculate against racial hatred. Racial hatred is an adult rather than a childhood disease."[22]

Judge Weigel concluded that *de jure* segregation had been practiced in San Francisco and ordered the school officials to select one of the two alternative plans to achieve a more reasonable racial balance in the elementary schools of the city. Both plans included a certain amount of busing of children as a necessary means to achieve desegregation. He emphasized that no race or ethnic group should be favored in the schools, that high-quality education should be emphasized for all, and that bilingual classes teaching cultural awareness were not to be restricted.

The extent of the court's concerns were stated in its detailed orders to the school district:

The District is directed and ordered:

A. To carry out, effective at the start of the next term of the schools on September 8, 1971, desegregation of the student bodies of each and all of the schools as provided for by the Horseshoe Plan or by the Freedom Plan.*

B. To carry out, diligently and promptly, all other provisions of the Horseshoe Plan or the Freedom Plan provided, however, that if any provision is in conflict with any provision of this Final Judgment and Decree, the latter shall control.

C. To make bona fide, continuing and reasonable efforts, during the next five years, to eliminate segregation in each and every school.

D. To establish and carry out, diligently and promptly, practices for the *hiring* of certificated and classified personnel which will effectively eliminate segregation in the respective staffs, overall, and in each school.

E. To establish and carry out, diligently and promptly, practices for the *assignment* of certificated and classified personnel in a manner which will effectively eliminate segregation in the respective staffs, overall, and in each school.

F. To establish and carry out, diligently and promptly, practices for the assignment of certificated and classified personnel, which will effectively promote *equalization of competence* in all schools.

G. To exercise, at all times, the highest degree of care for the safety and security of all school children at all times during their school attendance and transportation.

*"Horseshoe Plan" and "Freedom Plan" were the names of the two plans submitted as alternative ways of achieving racial and ethnic balance.

H. To provide, to the fullest extent feasible, racial and ethnic balance among students to be bused.

I. To inform all parents in writing, as soon as reasonably possible before the start of the school term this fall (1) of their children's school assignments and (2) of the details regarding bus transportation including, but not limited to, an outline of the safety measures which the District will utilize and of the procedures for enabling parents promptly to reach children in case of emergency.

J. To file with the Court within sixty (60) days after the end of each school year, until the Court may otherwise order, a report showing in reasonable detail all actions taken to comply with this Judgment and Decree. [Italics added.][23]

In addition to the foregoing order, the court issued an injunction permanently restraining the school district from encouraging or supporting segregation in any form in its schools, whether among students, teachers, or other employees.

SELF-SEGREGATION IN CHINATOWN

It was Judge Weigel's order in the *Johnson* case that precipitated the objections of Chinese-American parents discussed earlier (the *Lee* case). In most desegregation cases racial or ethnic minorities seek to eliminate segregation. In the *Lee* case, however, Americans of Chinese ancestry requested the federal appeals court to nullify the order issued in the *Johnson* case.

However, in *Lee*, the appeals court upheld the *Johnson* case as it applied to Chinese-American schoolchildren. It noted that until 1947 California had provided for the establishment of separate schools for children of Chinese ancestry. This type of *de jure* segregation was declared unconstitutional in the 1954 *Brown* case. The *Johnson* case properly ordered the various remedies to overcome the effects of earlier segregationist policies. The court noted that the *Brown* decision "was not written for Blacks alone." Earlier cases were cited to document the fact that the Equal Protection Clause of the Fourteenth Amendment applied to all racial minorities and that among its first beneficiaries were the Chinese people of San Francisco.

The court recognized the interests and concerns of the Chinese parents. It upheld the desegregation plan, however, and noted that the plan made possible bilingual classes as well as courses that taught the "cultural background and heritages of various racial and ethnic groups."

Thus, if we view this controversy as one that involved the interests of the Chinese parents on one hand and those of the entire school district on the other, the courts ruled in favor of the larger district while trying to respect and protect some of the concerns of the parents. Both the *Lee* and the *Johnson* cases relied heavily on the previous decisions of the Supreme Court, particularly the landmark cases of *Brown* and *Swann*.

THE CURRENT STATUS OF THE DE FACTO-DE JURE DISTINCTION

Early in the history of legal efforts to desegregate schools, the distinction between *de facto* and *de jure* segregation became very important. Courts would issue desegregation orders only if constitutional violation had been proven, and only "official" or *de jure* acts of racial segregation were held to constitute violations of the Constitution. Such acts were relatively easy to identify where state constitutions or statutory provisions mandated or explicitly permitted segregated schooling. The most common examples of this were found in southern states.

As more and more desegregation cases were litigated, both North and South, it became clear that school segregation often resulted from school board decisions independently of constitutional or statutory provisions. Was such segregation *de facto* or *de jure*? Although many cases have raised this issue, the *Keyes* case has become a landmark in this area of desegregation law.

The Keyes Case[24]

In a suit filed in a federal district court in Colorado the court found, among other facts, that the school board through the years has engaged in various acts that constituted deliberate racial segregation with respect to a certain section of the city of Denver. Among these acts were the following:

1. The construction of a new, relatively small elementary school in the middle of a black community.
2. The gerrymandering of school attendance zones.
3. The use of so-called optional zones and excessive use of mobile classroom units to help the gerrymandering.

The school board argued on behalf of its policy of creating "neighborhood schools" and also maintained that black and Hispanic students should not be placed in the same category to establish the segregated character of a school. Another important issue in this case raised the question of what significance does an unconstitutional practice in one part of a city hold for other parts or sections of the same city.

On appeal to the Supreme Court, it held that since Hispanics as a group have suffered "the same educational inequities as Negroes and American Indians," for purposes of defining what is a "segregated" school they should be placed in the same category. The Court went on to explain that "the differentiating factor between *de jure* segregation and so-called *de facto* segregation . . . is *purpose* or *intent* to segregate." Furthermore, after it has been shown, as in this case, that school authorities "practiced an intentionally segregative policy in a meaningful or significant segment of a school system," the burden of proof rests on the officials to show that their actions regarding "other segregated schools within the system were not motivated by segregative intent."

The Court, in discussing the "neighborhood school" concept, relied heavily on its earlier decision in the *Swann* case. That is, in a school district with a history of racial manipulation of school attendance, the policy of "neighborhood schools" is not acceptable simply because it only appears to be neutral. Past actions that created or enhanced segregated schooling must be considered together with current plans in order to decide whether or not a proposed policy of neighborhood schooling is genuinely neutral or simply appears to be that way.

Similarly, a California case held that a neighborhood school policy is constitutionally suspect "only where the neighborhoods which define school attendance areas are themselves products of official state discriminatory action."[25] Examples of such actions would be restrictive covenants, discriminatory zoning, or other racially motivated actions shaping the demographic or ethnic makeup of the schools.

Thus the Supreme Court interprets the Constitution to outlaw only *de jure* segregation, whether based on explicit laws and policies or official acts motivated by segregative intent. Such intent can be established by a variety of ways as discussed in the *Keyes* case. Other courts, relying on *Keyes*, indicated that although segregative intent is important, "malevolence or benevolence is irrelevant." A presumption of segregative intent arises when once it is established that school authorities engaged in "acts or omissions, the natural probable and forseeable consequences of which is to bring about or maintain segregation."[26] Such a presumption may be rebutted by school officials by showing that "segregative intent was not among the factors that motivated their actions."

TOWARD A SINGLE STANDARD?

Justice Powell, although concurring in part and dissenting in part, expressed concern about a possible dual standard that was developing toward southern and northern school districts. He said:

> . . . The net result of the Court's language, however, is the application of an effect test to the actions of southern school districts and an intent test to those in other sections, at least until an initial de jure finding for those districts can be made. Rather than straining to perpetuate any such dual standard, we should hold forthrightly that significant segregated school conditions in any section of the country are a prima facie violation of constitutional rights. . . .[27]

Justice Douglas, in a *dissenting* opinion, agreed with Powell and said he would go even further and reject completely the *de jure-de facto* distinction.

. . . I agree with my Brother Powell that there is, for the purposes of the Equal Protection Clause of the Fourteenth Amendment as applied to the school cases, no difference between de facto and de jure segregation. The school board is a state agency and the lines that it draws, the locations it selects for school sites, the allocations it makes of students, the budgets it prepares are state action for Fourteenth Amendment purposes. . . .

I think it is time to state that there is no constitutional difference between de jure and de facto segregation, for each is the product of state actions or policies. . . .[28]

The Columbus and Dayton Cases[29]

In the summer of 1979 the Supreme Court ruled on appeals involving the public schools of two Ohio cities, Columbus and Dayton. In each of the cases, the district court determined that the Board of Education of the respective cities practiced intentional segregation at the time of *Brown* (1954) and has never successfully eradicated the impact of such segregation. In other words, it never "actively set out to dismantle this dual system."

The Court noted in the *Columbus* case that faculty and staff composition may be considered to determine whether or not a dual system exists in addition to the composition of the student body. Relying on its earlier position in *Swann*, the Court noted:

[W]here it is possible to identify a "white school" or a "Negro school" simply by reference to the racial composition of teachers and staff, the quality of school buildings and equipment, or the organization of sports activities, a *prima facie* case of violation of substantive constitutional rights under the Equal Protection Clause is shown.

The Court also held, consistently with *Keyes*, that because the segregative practices of the Columbus Board had a systemwide impact, a systemwide remedy was properly ordered. Thus, purposeful discrimination in a substantial part of a school system furnishes basis to infer systemwide discrimination and therefore a systemwide remedy. The board, of course, may disprove such an inference.

In Dayton, there was no segregative effect or discriminatory purpose proven in the board's actions over the past 20 years with respect to faculty hiring and assignment, the use of optional attendance zones and transfer policies, the location and construction of school facilities, and other school policies. Thus, the board argued that it cannot be held responsible for earlier acts of discrimination. The district court agreed, but the appeals court and the U.S. Supreme Court did not.

The Court held that since there was a history of unconstitutional segregation, the board had an affirmative duty to eradicate all vestiges of a dual school system. This duty continues until a racially neutral or "balanced" school system is achieved. In the words of the Court, . . . "[T]he measure of the post-*Brown* conduct of a school board under an unsatisfied duty to liquidate a dual school system is the effectiveness, not the purpose of the actions in decreasing or increasing the segregation caused by the dual system."

Thus it is not enough for the board to abandon its earlier discriminatory purpose and actions. It has an affirmative responsibility to see to it that school policies and practices are not used "to perpetuate or recreate the dual school system."

Therefore, clearly, the Supreme Court requires proof of *de jure* or intentional segregative policies or practices before it will brand unconstitutional the policies or practices of a school district. The Court has never defined with precision the manner in which such intent is to be proved, but the burden of proof is on the plaintiffs who initiate legal action.

State Constitutions and Laws

Consistent with the Douglas dissent in *Keyes*, some states no longer use the *de jure-de facto* distinction. The California Supreme Court has ruled, for example, that "school boards do bear a constitutional obligation (under the State constitution) to take reasonable steps to alleviate segregation in the public schools, whether the segregation be *de facto* or *de jure* in origin."[30] This places an affirmative obligation on officials to design policies and programs to avoid discriminatory results. The Supreme Courts of Washington and Pennsylvania have reached similar conclusions, whereas state law or policies of state Boards of Education have erased the *de jure-de facto* distinction in Connecticut, Illinois, New Jersey, and New York.

These distinctions were erased, in part, due to the many difficulties in distinguishing *de facto* and *de jure* segregation, including unending factual inquiries and scrutinizing the actions of governmental bodies, and private housing practices. And, in the final analysis, the impact on students is the same under both types of segregation. Thus clearly, several states have gone further in eradicating segregated schooling than mandated by the U.S. Constitution.

Related Issues

RESEGREGATION

Since ours is a mobile population, a school district that desegregates might become resegregated as a result of population shifts. Do school boards have a legal obligation to readjust attendance zones in light of such changing conditions? Not under the federal law, according to a Supreme Court ruling in a case that arose in Pasadena, California.[31]

In 1970 the Pasadena school system was under court order to desegregate so that there be "no majority of any minority in any school in Pasadena." After complying with the order, in the ordinary course of events the city's population changed. By 1974, but not as a result of any official segregative action, several schools had minority children composing the majority enrollment. The Court held that once a school district established a "racially neutral system of student assignment," it is not under continuous obligation to readjust attendance zones if it is not official action that causes the subsequent imbalance.

INTERDISTRICT DESEGREGATION

It is common for our cities to be surrounded by suburbs, with each suburb maintaining its separate school system. For a variety of reasons our core cities have come to contain significantly larger minority populations than the adjacent suburban communities. This pattern tends to be found East and West, North and South. In recent years, the proportion of racial minorities in the core cities has grown to such an extent as to preclude meaningful desegregation of the schools if the desegregation plan were limited by the boundaries of the city. In such situations, does the law require a metropolitan plan or an interdistrict desegregation—one that includes within its scope the suburbs as well as the city? This question arose in a desegregation case in Detroit, Michigan.

Bradley v. Milliken[32]

In 1973 the Detroit school district student population was approximately 64 percent black and 36 percent white. The district, which has existed for nearly 100 years, was surrounded by suburban districts whose population was approximately 81 percent white and 19 percent black. After finding that the Detroit system has practiced unconstitutional racial segregation, the district court considered two desegregation plans: one was limited to the boundaries of Detroit, and the other also encompassed the surrounding suburbs.

The parties urging the metropolitan plan showed that no desegregation plan confined to the city limits would work. As the district court and court of appeals agreed, "any less comprehensive a solution than a metropolitan plan would result in an all black school system immediately surrounded by practically all white suburban school systems, with an overwhelming white majority population in the total metropolitan area." Therefore, the lower courts concluded that the only feasible way to achieve desegregation was by crossing boundary lines separating Detroit from its suburbs. And although there were no claims that the suburban districts violated the Constitution, the courts found that the state of Michigan, along with the city of Detroit, did. Thus, the state committed *de jure* acts of segregation and . . . "the State controls the necessary instrumentalities whose action is necessary to remedy the harmful effects of the State acts." Therefore, concluded the district and appeals courts, an interdistrict remedy was proper.

On appeal, the U.S. Supreme Court, disagreed in a 5 to 4 decision. Chief Justice Burger, writing for the majority, referred to the principle that "the scope of the remedy is determined by the nature and extent of the constitutional violation." Therefore, since the unconstitutional segregation occurred in the city of Detroit, the remedy must be confined to the city limits. The Court will not set aside the boundaries of an autonomous school district and impose a cross-district remedy unless it has been shown that violations of the law in one district "produced a significant segregative effect in another district." Justice Burger also noted that "an interdistrict remedy might be in order where the racially discriminatory acts of one or more school districts caused racial segregation in an adjacent district, or where district lines have been deliberately drawn on the basis of race."

This is precisely what was found in a case in Wilmington, Delaware.[33] The district court found "racially discriminatory acts of the State and local school districts causing interdistrict segregation." What were some of those acts? Prior to the *Brown* decision and for some years thereafter, black and white students were bused across district lines to attend segregated schools; population changes in the metropolitan area were influenced by governmental policies, such as FHA manuals advocating homogeneous neighborhoods, publication of a discriminatory portion of the Realtor's Code of Ethics by a state agency, concentration of public housing within Wilmington and a refusal to rezone in suburban areas to allow public housing and public offices recording of restrictive covenants in deeds; the enactment of a school consolidation law that excluded Wilmington from its coverage; and others. The court held that the facts were sufficient to create "a suspect racial classification" without the presence of a compelling state interest to justify such classification. Furthermore, the facts did not show the infeasibility of an interdistrict remedy. On appeal, the Supreme Court affirmed this decision.

Thus, clearly, the appropriateness of cross-district remedies depend on the particular circumstances of each case. The courts will take into consideration the following: the history of the school district(s) involved, whether or not unconstitutional segregation has occurred, the area of such violation, the laws related to housing, zoning, and financing as well as other actions by public officials that may have contributed to the patterns of racial and ethnic segregation. Even the "conservative" justices will approve cross-district remedies in some situations. Justice Douglas, a liberal judge, was very critical of the Detroit area decision, for he considered the city schools to be not only segregated by race and thus "separate," but also "inferior." In his strong dissent, referring to the 1896 case of *Plessy* v. *Ferguson,* he said, "so far as equal protection is concerned we are now in a dramatic retreat from the 8-to-1 decision in 1896 that Blacks could be segregated in public facilities provided they receive equal treatment."

In his dissenting opinion, Justice Marshall left us with a poignant warning:

> Desegregation is not and was never expected to be an easy task. Racial attitudes ingrained in our Nation's childhood and adolescence are not quickly thrown aside in its middle years. But just as the inconvenience of some cannot be allowed to stand in the way of the rights of others, so public opposition, no matter how strident, cannot be permitted to divert this Court from the enforcement of the constitutional principles at issue in this case. Today's holding, I fear, is more a reflection of a perceived public mood that we have gone far enough in enforcing the Constitution's guarantee of equal justice than it is the product of neutral principles of law. In the short run, it may seem to be the easier course to allow our great metropolitan areas to be divided up each into two cities—one white, the other black—but it is a course, I predict, our people will ultimately regret. I dissent.

TEACHERS, STAFF, AND DESEGREGATION

Although the early desegregation cases focused primarily on the composition of the students, later cases emphasized the importance of looking at the total school environment. Thus, in addition to concerns for racial balance among students, courts began to scrutinize the composition of the faculty, staff, and administrative personnel of schools, as well as policies related to recruitment, hiring, promotion, demotion, tenure, and dismissals.

Courts often refer to the *Singleton* principle, which announced that in districts undergoing desegregation, "principals, teachers, teacher-aids and other staff who work directly with children at a school shall be so assigned that in no case will the racial composition of a staff indicate that a school . . ." is for black or white students.[34] Furthermore, if there is to be a reduction in faculty, staff, or administration, people to be "dismissed or demoted must be selected on the basis of objective and reasonable non-discriminatory standards from among all the staff of the school district."

Similar conclusions were reached in many communities undergoing court-ordered desegregation. Under the broad powers of federal courts, in their formulation of appropriate remedies for past discrimination, some courts have found it necessary to issue detailed, specific orders. A well-known example is one in Boston, where the court ordered (1) the hiring of black and white teachers on a one-to-one basis until the percentage of black faculty reaches 20 percent; (2) an affirmative action program to recruit black faculty until their proportion reaches 25 percent of the faculty; (3) a coordinator of Minority Recruitment and a recruiting budget for 1975–1976 of no less than $120,000; and (4) periodic reports on recruiting and hiring.[35]

It is important to note, however, that the *Singleton* rule, requiring the use of objective criteria in staff reduction decisions, has been applied by courts only in districts undergoing desegregation. The fifth Circuit, for example, addressed this issue directly in a case in which a black teacher was not reemployed and black residents sued, challenging the school district's decision. The court held that *Singleton* is not applicable in the absence of desegregation-related reductions. The *Singleton* case was not designed to "grant a black teacher a job in perpetuity."[36] In such situations the courts apply the principles of due process equally to both black and white teachers and do not emphasize the demanding standards of requiring objective criteria for supporting administrative judgment.

A further complication is added by collective bargaining agreements that usually provide for layoffs by reverse order of seniority in retrenchment or reduction-in-force proceedings. At least one district court held that the constitutional principle requiring desegregation takes precedence over a collective bargaining agreement. Thus, the agreement may be set aside in efforts to reach a certain specified racial balance in a school district undergoing staff desegregation.*

MAY PRIVATE SCHOOLS AVOID DESEGREGATION?

In many communities, parents, wanting to avoid court-ordered desegregation, enrolled their children in existing private schools or created new schools. After years of such practices, black parents brought suit against officials of a private school, claiming that they denied admission to their children, in violation of a federal law that protects the equal right to make contracts. (42 U.S.C. &1981).

The Supreme Court ruled that &1981 prohibits private, commercially operated nonsectarian schools from denying admission to prospective students because they are black.[37] In the words of the Court: "While parents have a constitutional right to send their children to private schools and a constitutional right to select private schools that offer specialized instruction, they have no constitutional right to provide their children with private school education unfettered by reasonable government regulation." Consistently with this ruling, a Court of Appeals held that a private religious school may not expel white female students for romantic association with black students.†

Oliver v. Kalamazoo Bd. of Ed. 498 F.Supp. 732 (W.D. Mich. 1980).
†*Fiedler v. Marumsco Christian School,* 631 F.2d 1144 (4th Cir. 1980).

TITLE VI OF THE CIVIL RIGHTS ACT OF 1964

Although the best-known cases challenging school segregation were based on the Fourteenth Amendment of the Constitution, federal laws and regulations are playing an increasingly important role in this area of school law. Perhaps the most important among these is Title VI of the Civil Rights Act of 1964 that provides, in part, that: "No person in the United States shall, on the ground of race, color, or national origin, be excluded from participation in, be denied the benefits of, or be subjected to discrimination under any program or activity receiving Federal financial assistance."[38] Other sections of this law exempt certain religious organizations from its application, but otherwise broadly prohibit discrimination in all employment except where religion, race, or national origin ". . . is a bona fide occupational qualification reasonably necessary to the normal operation of that particular business or enterprise. . . ."

Thus, today, a person may combat discrimination under the U.S. Constitution and under federal laws as well as state constitutions and state laws.

SUMMARY AND CONCLUSIONS

The history of racial and ethnic segregation in the United States is a long and complex one. Without dealing with all its intricacies in this chapter, we highlighted the key historical cases and indicated what the current law seems to be.

The *Plessy* case, although not directly related to education, was historically accepted as authority for the principle that racially separate-but-equal education was constitutional. *Plessy* was overruled by *Brown* I in 1954, perhaps one of the most important Supreme Court cases related to education. In its now famous opinion, the Warren Court ruled that "in the field of public education the doctrine of "separate but equal" has no place. Separate educational facilities are inherently unequal," and therefore they violate the Fourteenth Amendment.

Within less than a year, *Brown* I was followed by *Brown* II, which set forth the general principles to guide the implementation of the desegregation decision. Because segregated and discriminatory schooling existed in so many communities under such varied conditions, the Court recognized that primary responsibility for desegregation must rest with local school boards. Local courts, of course, would consider whether or not the school authorities had acted in good faith and in a manner consistent with constitutional principles. Compliance was urged "at the earliest practicable date" and school boards were to proceed "with all deliberate speed."

The intentions of the Court were carried out in some communities, but most cities and towns resisted in various forms, ranging from the closing of schools to freedom-of-choice plans. Literally hundreds of lawsuits had to be brought to overcome the noncompliance.

In the *Griffin* case the Court struck down the closing of schools in Prince Edward County, Virginia. It ruled that such action was illegitimate when it was racially motivated. The freedom-of-choice plan suffered a similar fate in the *Green* case, where the Court urged the creation of unitary, nonracial school systems to replace earlier segregated ones. A lower court flatly stated that "the only school desegregation plan that meets constitutional standards is one that works."

In the *Swann* case the Burger Court established four key points: (1) In considering "racial balance" the courts may use mathematical ratios as starting points in formulating remedies but not as fixed quota requirements. (2) One-race schools are not necessarily unconstitutional. School districts will be closely scrutinized to determine whether the one-race schools are part of a plan to segregate children. The presumption is against the existence of such schools; therefore the burden of proof is on the school officials to show that such school assignments are genuinely nondiscriminatory. (3) The altering of attendance zones is a legitimate means to desegregate heretofore segregated school districts. This may include "pairing," "clustering," or "regrouping" of schools to eliminate dual school systems. (4) Busing can be a valid means to integrate the schools. Busing can also be objectionable when the time or distance of travel is so great as to be detrimental to the student's health or education.

There are school districts, however, where racial balance in the schools cannot be achieved by busing. This is true in some of our large cities, like Detroit, where blacks constitute a large majority of the population. Cross-district busing or metropolitan area desegregation (i.e., combining cities and suburbs) has been suggested as a way to achieve a desirable racial balance in such situations. But in 1974 the Supreme Court in a 5 to 4 decision rejected this proposed solution and ruled that Detroit does not have to look beyond its school district boundaries in its efforts to satisfy the Fourteenth Amendment.

The remedy cannot be broader than the constitutional violation, and since the suburbs did not participate in the illegal segregation of the Detroit schools, they cannot be forced to participate in a metropolitan plan of desegregation. Other cases have upheld metropolitanization, including cross-district busing, where the facts showed various actions by city, county, and suburban officials that interacted to contribute to school segregation.

The *Johnson* case involved a northern city, San Francisco. The district court ruled that segregation in a racially and ethnically diverse northern city is as unconstitutional as anywhere else. It held that if the school board creates or continues to draw attendance lines that increase racial imbalance, its action will violate the Equal Protection Clause of the Fourteenth Amendment. The *Johnson* case also provided an example of a court specifically detailing a plan of actions the schools must take to comply with the spirit of *Brown* I and II.

The *Lee* case, in which some Chinese-American parents objected to the court-ordered desegregation, derived from *Johnson.* The case was significant, because it showed that desegregation was not only a "black and white" issue but affected Orientals, Chicanos, Indians, and others as well. Furthermore it was an example of minority parents who did not want integrated schooling. Although the Court upheld desegregation in this case, it respected some of the wishes of the Chinese parents and supported bilingual classes as well as courses that taught about the "cultural background and heritages of various racial and ethnic groups."

The Fourteenth Amendment's Equal Protection Clause has been interpreted to mean that desegregation applies to the faculty, staff, and administration as well as to students. In school districts that have been found guilty of past discrimination, courts have the power to impose detailed plans for integrating the faculty, staff, and administration, including some numerical ratios to overcome past discrimination. Boston is a well-known example of such exercise of judicial power. Furthermore, *Singleton* held that where staff reduction accompanies desegregation, black teachers or administrators cannot be fired without the use of objective criteria.

The *de facto-de jure* distinction continues to be applied by the federal courts. This distinction is easier to apply in southern and border states that historically mandated or allowed segregation by explicit law or state board policy. Since such laws and policies were held unconstitutional, courts may impose appropriate remedies to create "unitary" systems, eliminating all vestiges of earlier "dual" systems. In northern states, however, where no such laws or explicit policies existed, *de jure* segregation is more difficult to prove. The Supreme Court still requires proof of segregative intent on the part of public officials that can be shown to have contributed to segregated schooling. Since such intent is often difficult to prove, and since the impact on students is the same from both *de jure* and *de facto* segregation, many judges, including Supreme Court justices, disagree on the appropriateness of continuing the distinction. The *Keyes* case from Denver is the best-known case highlighting this conflict. The majority of the Court, however, continues the distinction and holds only *de jure* segregation unconstitutional. Several states have gone further, on the basis of state constitutions, state law, or Board of Education policy, and have outlawed segregation in schools whether *de facto* or *de jure.*

Recent decisions have also held that private nonsectarian schools may not exclude black or other minority students, because a federal law provides for the equal right to enter into contracts. Private schools enter into contracts with parents who enroll their children and this right may not be denied on racial grounds.

Hundreds of other decisions could be cited in support of the principles set forth in this chapter. Many other cases are currently under litigation in every part of the country and at every level of schooling. The specific factual conditions call for various situational remedies, but they all must be consistent with the powerful principles enunciated in *Brown* v. *Board of Education of Topeka.* *

NOTES

1. 339 F.Supp. 1315 (N.D. Cal. 1971).
2. 372 F.2d 836 (9th Cir. 1966).
3. *Guey Heung Lee* et al. v. *David Johnson* et al., 404 U.S. 1215 (1971).
4. *Plessy* v. *Ferguson,* 163 U.S. 537 (1896).
5. *Brown* v. *Board of Education of Topeka,* 347 U.S. 483, 484 (1954).
6. Id. at 489.
7. Id. at 493.
8. Id. at 494.
9. *Brown* v. *Board of Education of Topeka, Kansas,* 349 U.S. 294, 298 (1955), commonly referred to as *Brown* II.
10. *Griffin* v. *County School Board of Prince Edward County,* 377 U.S. 218, 222 (1964).
11. Id. at 231.
12. *Green* v. *County School Board of New Kent County, Virginia,* 391 U.S. 430 (1968).
13. Id. at 440.
14. Id. at 441.
15. *Swann* v. *Charlotte-Mecklenburg Board of Education,* 402 U.S. 1 (1971).
16. Id. at 9–10.
17. Id. at 28.
18. Id. at 29.
19. *Johnson* v. *San Francisco Unified School District,* 339 F.Supp. 1315 (N.D. Cal. 1971).
20. Id. at 1318.
21. The distinction between *de jure* and *de facto* segregation has come under increased legal attacks and judicial scrutiny in recent years. Social scientists have now joined this attack. In fact, a well-known sociologist from Harvard University flatly states: "*De jure* segregation is the harsh fact of American society; so-called *de facto* segregation is simply a myth." See Thomas F. Pettigrew, "The Case for the Racial Integration of the Schools," an address delivered at the 1973 Cubberley Conference, Stanford University. (Mimeographed)
22. Id. at 1320.
23. Id. at 1324.

---

*On August 22, 1979, several plaintiffs, including Linda Brown, the original plaintiff in *Brown* v. *Board of Education,* requested the U.S. District Court in Topeka, Kansas, to reopen the 1954 *Brown* case. On November 29, 1979, this request was granted, suggesting that at least a prima facie case has been presented to indicate that the schools of Topeka never achieved full desegregation.

24. *Keyes* v. *School District No. 1, Denver, Colorado,* 413 U.S. 189 (1974).

25. *Diaz* v. *San José Unified School District,* No. C-71-2130 RFD, (N.D. Cal. 1975).

26. *U.S.* v. *School District of Omaha,* 521 F.d 580 (1975). The legal standard of "intent to segregate" continues to be a very difficult one to apply. The several circuit courts have interpreted them differently and even the Supreme Court has changed its language related to the importance of the impact or consequences of a law. The earlier decision in *Griggs* v. *Duke Power Company* 91 S.Ct. 849 (1971) emphasized the racially disproportionate impact of a law that was "neutral on its face," as a violation of Title VII of the Civil Rights Act of 1964. But more recently, *Washington* v. *Davis,* 426 U.S. 229 (1976) held that a law neutral on its face is not infirm "simply because it may affect a greater proportion of one race than of another." In addition to the greater impact on one race, the Court emphasized that "The essential element of *de jure* segregation is 'a current condition of segregation resulting from intentional state action.'" For further insight regarding the complexities and legal difficulties related to this issue, see "Reading the Mind of the School Board: Segregative Intent and the De Facto/De Jure Distinction," *The Yale Law Journal, 86* (December 1976) 317–355; or James E. Phillips, "The Legal Requirements of Intent to Segregate: Some Observations," *Nolpe School Law Journal, 7,* No. 2 (1977), 111–125.

27. *Keyes,* at 567.

28. Id. at 567.

29. *Columbus Board of Education* v. *Penick,* 443 U.S. 449 (1979); *Dayton Board of Education* v. *Brinkman,* 443 U.S. 526 (1979).

30. *Crawford* v. *Board of Education of the City of Los Angeles,* 551 P.2d 28 (1976).

31. *Pasadena City Board of Education* v. *Spangler,* 427 U.S. 424 (1976).

32. 94 S.Ct. 1069 (1974); Bradley, 418 U.S. 717 (1974).

33. *Evans* v. *Buchanan,* 393 F.Supp. 428 (D. Del. 1975).

34. *Singleton* v. *Jackson Municipal Separate School District,* et al., 419 F.2d 1211 (5th Cir. 1970).

35. *Morgan* v. *Kerrigan,* 509 F.2d 580 (1974).

36. *Pickens* v. *Okolona Municipal Separate School District,* 527 F.2d 358 (5th Cir. 1976).

37. *Runyon* v. *McCrary,* 427 U.S. 160 (1976).

38. 42 U.S.C. § 2000(d).

Chapter 11
Sex Discrimination in Education

The pedestal upon which women have been placed has all too often, upon closer inspection, been revealed as a cage.
—California Supreme Court[1]

The Fourteenth Amendment does not create a fictitious equality where there is a real difference.
—Justice Oliver Wendell Holmes[2]

Historically, our schools, like the rest of our culture, have treated girls differently from boys in many respects, and female teachers differently from males. Whether or not the different treatment was discriminatory was a question seldom raised. In recent years, it has been established that sex discrimination is widely practiced in our culture and in the schools. Educators' awareness of such discrimination has been heightened, and various policies and practices are being examined to eliminate sexism. Disagreements have arisen, however, concerning efforts to create non-sexist schools, and some of these disagreements have resulted in lawsuits. In this chapter, cases related to alleged sexist practices in the schools are examined—practices in athletic activities, in admissions, and in curricula, in school policies concerning student marriage, pregnancy, and parenthood, as well as pregnancy leave policies for teachers, sick leave, and differential pay based on sex.

EQUALITY IN SCHOOL SPORTS

The Brenden Case

In 1972 the Northeastern Lawn Tennis Association ranked Peggy Brenden the number one 18-year-old woman tennis player in her area. Since there was very little interest in tennis among the girls of her school, Brenden, a senior at Minnesota's St. Cloud Technical High School, expressed a desire to play on the boys' team. The team had a coach and a schedule of interscholastic matches, neither of which was available for girls. Peggy was informed by the school that she could not participate on the boys' team because of the following rule of the Minnesota State High School League:

> Girls shall be prohibited from participating in the boys' interscholastic athletic program either as a member of the boys' team or a member of the girls' team playing the boys' team.
> The girls' team shall not accept male members.[3]

The *League Handbook,* which contains this rule, has an equivalent regulation for boys. All 485 public schools in the state of Minnesota are members of the League.

Peggy Brenden claimed that her civil rights, specifically her right to due process and equal protection, had been violated. She sought an injunction against the enforcement of any rule that would prevent her from participating in interscholastic athletic events.

The school district contended that the rule was a reasonable one and that its objective was to achieve fair and equitable competition among school athletes. They argued that because there are significant differences in physiology and growth patterns between boys and girls, sex is a reasonable basis of classification in athletic competition.

Questions to Consider

1. Are there significant differences between the sexes that would relate to competitive athletics? What are they? Are these natural or cultural differences?
2. What differences, if any, justify separating boys and girls for purposes of interscholastic competition?
3. What would happen to girls' sports if all teams were open equally to boys and girls?
4. Would you differentiate between contact and noncontact sports?

A COMPANION CASE

The *Brenden* case was joined by that of Tony St. Pierre, a 17-year-old female student at Eisenhower High School, Hopkins, Minnesota. She wanted to compete on the boys' cross-country running and cross-country skiing teams. She too was excellent in these sports and her reasons for wanting to join the boys' team were the same as Peggy Brenden's. Since the legal issues and principles involved were the same, the two cases were decided together by the federal district court in Minnesota.

THE OPINION OF THE COURT

Was the classification arbitrary and thus a violation of the girls' constitutional rights? The district court used the governing principles set forth by the Supreme Court: "A classification must be reasonable, not arbitrary, and must rest upon some ground of difference having a fair and substantial relation to the object of the legislation, so that all persons similarly circumstanced shall be treated alike."[4] Is it then reasonable to differentiate between boys and girls for purposes of interscholastic athletic competition?

The court acknowledged that there are substantial physiological differences between boys and girls:

> As testified to by defendants' expert witnesses, men are taller than women, stronger than women by reason of a greater muscle mass; have larger hearts than women and a deeper breathing capacity, enabling them to utilize oxygen more efficiently than women, run faster, based upon the construction of the pelvic area, which, when, women reach puberty, widens, causing the femur to bend outward, rendering the female incapable of running as efficiently as a male. These physiological differences may, on the average, prevent the great majority of women from competing on an equal level with the great majority of males. The differences may form a basis for defining class competition on the basis of sex, for the purpose of encouraging girls to compete in their own class and not in a class consisting of boys involved in interscholastic athletic competition.[5]

Should these general differences prevent Brenden and St. Pierre from playing on the boys' teams? The court was not bound by statistical abstractions, but looked at the particular individuals at hand and challenged the application of the rules in these instances.

> It must be emphasized in this case, however, that these physiological differences, insofar as they render the great majority of females unable to compete as effectively as males, have little relevance to Tony St. Pierre and Peggy Brenden. Because of their level of achievement in competitive sports, Tony and Peggy have overcome these physiological disabilities. There has been no evidence that either Peggy Brenden or Tony St. Pierre, or any other girls, would be in any way damaged from competition in boys' interscholastic athletics, nor is there any credible evidence that the boys would be damaged.[6]

The school district had also argued that separate competitive programs in interscholastic athletics was desirable and a ruling in favor of the girls would hamper such a development. In rejecting this argument, Justice Lord noted: "There is a vague and undocumented fear on the part of the defendants that the goal of achieving equitable competition will perhaps be hampered. Peggy Brenden and Tony St. Pierre should not be sacrificed upon this altar."

The district court, although ruling in favor of Tony and Peggy, distinguished between the general rule separating girls' and boys' athletics and the application of such a rule to Brenden and St. Pierre. This court's opinion is quite typical of the judicial desire to avoid sweeping decisions and to stay close to the facts at hand.

> This court is not deciding whether the League rules providing that there shall be no participation by girls in boys' interscholastic athletic events is unconstitutional or constitutional. Given the narrow factual situation with which the court is confronted, it is unnecessary and it would be inappropriate to make a determination as to whether the rule would be unconstitutional on its face or in all its applications.[7]

In other words, the court decided only the constitutionality of the application of the League rule to two young women of high skill and achievements as related to the three sports in two high school districts. Judge Lord emphasized these factors to point up the narrowness of the decision.

In sum, the court noted that the two girls had been prevented from participating in interscholastic athletics "on the basis of the fact of sex and sex alone." There were no alternative competitive programs provided for them by the schools. Thus, because the rules as applied to them* were unreasonable and discriminatory, the court declared Brenden and St. Pierre eligible to compete on the boys' teams. It further enjoined the Minnesota State High School League from imposing any sanctions on the two schools on whose teams the girls would compete.

The Bucha Case: Sexually Segregated Swimming[8]

In 1972 Sandra Lynn Bucha was a student in Hinsdale Center Township High School in Illinois. She and another girl were excluded from participating on the boys' swimming team. They filed a class action suit to eliminate or modify the rules of the Illinois High School Association, which regulates interscholastic sports for approximately 790 Illinois high schools.

They challenged the bylaws of the association, which placed limitations on girls' athletic events and not on those in which boys participated; for example, "a prohibition on organized cheering, a one dollar limitation on the value of awards, and a prohibition on overnight trips in conjunction with girls' contests." Although there was an organized athletic program for girls at the high school, the plaintiffs claimed that girls' contests were more like intramural, "multi-sport activities which are devoid of the concentration and competitive emphasis that is characteristic of boys'

---

*Although the rules themselves were not necessarily unconstitutional, their application in these instances was.

extracurricular sports." They also challenged the rule against competition between members of the opposite sex.

Questions to Consider

1. Were the rules of the Illinois High School Association reasonable?
2. Should boys and girls compete against each other? Would most girls and boys be helped by such competition?
3. Should different rules apply to the athletic events of girls than to those of boys?

THE OPINION OF THE COURT

• **Were Plaintiffs Denied Equal Protection?** Judge Austin of the federal court replied in the negative. According to the judge, the "relevant inquiry here is whether the challenged classification is rational." The *Bucha* court then used the same Supreme Court principles as did the *Brenden* court,[9] but based on the facts of this case, it came to a different conclusion.

To determine whether there was a denial of equal protection, a two-step process was used by the court. The first step identified the purposes or objectives of the school activity, and the second asked whether the classification bore any reasonable relationship to any of those purposes. Applying the two-step test to the girls' challenge of the rules of interscholastic competition, what were the results?

Are there legitimate purposes or objectives for interscholastic sports? The court replied in the affirmative; such participation, in its opinion as well as in the opinion of educators, will benefit students both physically and mentally. No one in this case challenged this proposition. The plaintiffs' challenge was aimed at the separation of the sexes and at the different rules applied to the programs of the boys and the girls. The key question was whether or not it was rational to separate girls and boys and to provide different regulations for their contests.

The court quoted with approval an old dictum of Justice Holmes from 1912: "The Fourteenth Amendment does not create a fictitious equality where there is a real difference." It then proceeded to note that "at the pinnacle of all sporting contests, the Olympic games, the men's times in each event are consistently better than the women's." In the case at hand it was also "shown that the times of the two boy swimmers sent to the state championship contest from Hinsdale were better than those ever recorded by either of the named plaintiffs." Expert testimony also pointed up significant physical and psychological differences between male and female athletes.

The court further considered the opinion of women's coaches that "unrestricted athletic competition between the sexes would consistently lead to male domination of interscholastic sports and actually result in a decrease in female participation in such events." These reasons led the court to conclude that the rules and regulations had a rational basis and that therefore the classification was reasonable and did not violate the Equal Protection Clause of the Fourteenth Amendment.

The court noted that a bona fide athletic program existed for the girls as well as the boys, even though some of the regulations governing them differed. Exercising judicial restraint, Judge Austin observed that the issue of what is the best program is for the experts in education and coaching to decide and not for judges. His task was to judge not what is best but whether or not the arrangement was constitutionally permissible. Here, as elsewhere, there may be a difference between what is a wise educational policy and what the law permits. To put it another way, many educational practices are unwise or possibly foolish and damaging to students, even though they are constitutional. Judge Austin made it clear that it is up to educators and legislators to change such situations and that the courts should limit themselves to legal matters.

Although the emphases are different in the *Brenden* and *Bucha* cases, the two are not inconsistent. It is easy to distinguish between them, for in the *Bucha* case there was a program provided for girls as well as boys, whereas there were no such equivalent programs provided in the *Brenden* case. Thus the discriminatory practice was clear in *Brenden*.*

The Reed Case: Is Golf a Right or a Privilege?[10]

In 1972 a case was filed in the U.S. District Court of Nebraska by Debbie Reed, who wanted to be on the school golf team. However, Nebraska's Norfolk High School only had a boys' team, which competed in interscholastic golf meets and tournaments. There was no girls' team at all, and the Nebraska School Association bylaws forbade boys and girls from competing against each other or from being members of the same team.

When Reed sought an injunction that would enable her to play on the boys' team, various arguments were raised against her. It was alleged, for example, that she had no *right* to play golf on the team, that golf, unlike education, is a *privilege* rather than a right.

The court rejected this argument. Justice Urborn explained that even if golf is not educational, the privilege/right distinction is not viable. "The issue is not whether Debbie Reed has a 'right' to play golf; the issue is whether she can be treated differently from boys in an activity provided by the state. Her right is the right to be treated the same as boys unless there is a rational basis for her being treated differently." When the school authorities argued that Debbie was free to play golf even if she

*The *Bucha* case seems to conclude that there is discrimination only if girls have no program whatever. This holding is not consistent with current law.

were not on the team, the court was again unimpressed by the weight of such an argument. It recognized that just like the male golf players, "Debbie Reed seeks the value of local and regional competition, an opportunity to enhance her reputation, and instruction afforded by the coaching staff. Although the defendants argue that she is free to play golf even though she is not a member of the school team, the values she seeks cannot be lightly set aside."

Moreover, Judge Urborn emphasized the requirement of equal access to educational benefits for males and females. He wrote: "The state affords interschool competition and instruction of some expense and effort, surely for the reason that it and the defendant think that the program is of benefit to the participants. If the program is valuable for boys, is it of no value to girls?" The injunction requested by Reed was granted.

TITLE IX AND RELATED CASES

In 1972, Congress passed a law, popularly known as Title IX, that has had and will continue to have a significant impact on sex discrimination in schools.[11] It provides that: "No person in the United States shall on the basis of sex be excluded from participation, be denied the benefits of, or be subjected to discrimination under any education program or act or activity receiving Federal financial assistance." Health, Education and Welfare (HEW) issued regulations implementing Title IX, and many school-related lawsuits have been based on this law. On the other hand, some students and teachers still attempt to enforce their rights under the Equal Protection and Due Process Clauses of the Fourteenth Amendment.

The Hoover Case:[12] Contact Sports

The Colorado High School Activities Association had a rule that forbade coeducational participation in interscholastic contact sports, among them on soccer teams. A high school girl sued when she was denied a chance to participate on the boys' soccer team even though there was no girls' team.

The state association argued that the purpose of the rule was to protect girls from physical harm. The court, however, rejected the argument, and said that "the failure to establish any physical criteria to protect small or weak males from the injurious effects of competition with larger and stronger males destroys the credibility of the reasoning urged in support of the sex classification . . . and there is no rationality in limiting this patronizing protection to females." Furthermore, "Any notion that young women are so inherently weak, delicate, or physically inadequate that the state must protect them from the folly of participation in rigorous athletics is a cultural anachronism unrelated to reality. The Constitution does not permit the use of governmental power to control or limit cultural changes or to prescribe masculine or feminine roles."

The court held the rule to be in violation of the Equal Protection Clause of the Fourteenth Amendment, in that it arbitrarily classified boys and girls according to general physiological differences without regard for the wide range of individual variations within each class. Significantly, the suit was brought under the Equal Protection Clause rather than Title IX. Regulations under Title IX (§ 86.41) allow for separate teams for certain contact sports that include substantial bodily contact.

Similarly, a state association's rule was challenged in Wisconsin,[13] one that prohibited all types of interscholastic activities involving girls and boys competing against each other. The court declared the rule invalid under the Fourteenth Amendment. It held that there is "no governmental objective whatsoever to justify providing boys with the opportunity to participate in varsity interscholastic competition in contact sports while *absolutely* denying the same opportunity to girls." However, the court declined to rule whether "separate-but-equal" teams would be appropriate in contact sports, although it seems to suggest that it might be.

The Yellow Springs Case: Are Parts of Title IX Unconstitutional?

Although some cases have indicated that separate teams for girls and boys will satisfy the law, some courts have gone further. When two Ohio girls challenged the state association's rule against coeducational participation in contact sports, including varsity basketball, separate teams were created for girls. The girls challenged such action and the court ruled in their favor.[14]

According to the Court, the exclusion of girls from contact sports deprives them of liberty without due process of law, unless there is a showing of an important governmental purpose sufficient to justify the infringement. But what of Title IX whose regulations as interpreted by HEW [45 C.F.R. § 86.41(9b)] allow for the separation of the sexes in contact sports? The district court ruled that these regulations "are unconstitutional (under the Fifth Amendment) insofar as they suggest that mixed gender competition, creation of separate teams for girls and boys in each sport, or creation of an all male team in contact sports are independent and wholly satisfactory methods of compliance."

The court held that governmental policies that are based on a presumption that girls are uniformly physically inferior to boys are arbitrary and thus violate due process. The rules cannot bar "physically qualified girls from participating with boys in interscholastic contact sports."

This case seems to go further than others in striking down sex segregation in athletic activities, apparently erasing all distinctions between contact and noncontact sports.

The Impact of State ERA's

Although many states have enacted Equal Rights Amendments (ERA) to their state constitutions, the significance of these amendments for coeducational athletics is yet to be determined. Under such an amendment, a Pennsylvania court ruled that both boys and girls can try out, on an equal basis, for all school teams, including those in contact sports. Its ruling included the sports of football and wrestling, and a Washington Court ruled similarly on football.

When the Massachusetts legislature wanted to enact a law preventing girls from participating with boys in contact sports, that is, football and wrestling, the advice of the state Supreme Court was sought.[15] The justices indicated that under the state's ERA, strict scrutiny would be applied to sex-based classifications. Thus such a law would be inconsistent with the state ERA. However, the court specifically declined to express a view whether such a law would be valid . . . "if equal facilities were available for men and women in a particular sport which was available separately for each sex."

Also in Massachusetts, the state Interscholastic Athletic Association rule was held to violate the state ERA, for it prohibited boys from playing on any girls' team but allowed girls to play on certain boys' teams.[16] By contrast an Illinois case expressly disagreed with the Massachusetts decision and held that a school system could maintain a volleyball team for girls only and that such an arrangement did not violate the Illinois ERA.[17]

SUMMARY AND RELATED ISSUES

Increasingly the schools are reexamining their practices in the area of athletics. Sexist policies are scrutinized and often altered without lawsuits. New York, for example, through a ruling of the state commissioner of education, provided for equal participation in noncontact sports; New Jersey ruled similarly in cases in which there is no separate interscholastic competition for girls. Michigan went further in providing, by law, the opportunity for girls to participate in noncontact sports with boys, even if the schools had all-girl teams.

Other states and districts are currently studying this question to develop fair, nondiscriminatory policies and regulations that will enhance athletic participation by an increasing number of students, whether male or female. Ideologically based solutions do not necessarily optimize such opportunities, even though on paper they seem to provide full equality. Educators must be mindful of relevant educational as well as constitutional principles.

It is generally known that schools and communities value athletic activities for boys more than for girls. Evidence for this abounds in comparing budget allocations as well as interscholastic athletic schedules. Although discriminatory practices are still quite common, the legal trend is against them. In many communities they persist simply because no one has challenged them. Lawsuits are expensive as well as embarrassing for many people. Families prefer to avoid the notoriety and even harassment that accompanies suing the local schools. However, where suits are brought, the courts are likely to give close scrutiny to allegations of unequal treatment in school-related athletic activities.

Although the Fourteenth Amendment continues to be important in fighting sex discrimination, Title IX has become a powerful means for equalizing opportunities for males and females. Among its provisions it requires nondiscrimination in resource allocation, including the supplying of equipment and coaching for both sexes. And although there is controversy concerning some of the HEW regulations implementing Title IX, some legal trends are clear: If team competition is available for boys, it should also be available for girls. In noncontact sports, if there are no teams for girls, they may compete for positions on the boys' team. If there are teams for both, courts tend to respect the separation of the sexes for athletic activities where there are reasonable grounds for such separation. Some courts, however, have declared all such separation to be unconstitutional and some state ERA's have been interpreted to make all athletic competition accessible to boys and girls on an equal and coeducational basis. Most courts and communities have not gone this far and, in contact sports, tend to accept separate-but-equal teams and facilities for boys and girls. Furthermore, contrary to some popular notions, Title IX never provided coed showers or equal financing for all sports.*

SEXIST POLICIES IN THE CURRICULUM

Until recently, many schools denied boys and girls equal access to certain courses.[18] The most obvious examples came from sexist restrictions on courses in metalworking, woodworking, auto shop, cooking, and sewing.

These practices represent such obvious examples of discrimination that policies and rules creating and enforcing them are rapidly crumbling. In some states, such as Massachusetts and New York, specific laws have been passed by the state legislatures prohibiting the exclusion of a student from any course of instruction by reason of that student's sex. In other states, lawsuits are challenging such denial of equal protection. For

---

*Title IX specifically exempts from its application military schools as well as religious schools if the antidiscriminatory policies of the law are inconsistent with the religious tenets of the school. See 20 U.S.C 1681(a) (3 and 4).

example, two suits in California were settled out of court when school authorities agreed to desegregate wood shop[19] and auto shop[20] courses.

When girls are denied equal access to the curriculum by policy or school rule, the law will assist them. There are other types of sexist practices that are more difficult to combat. These are the ingrained customs, values, and attitudes that operate in any social system, including the schools. The informal practices of schools as well as the attitudes of counselors, teachers, parents, and even of other students often deny equal access to the curriculum. These, of course, can only be changed by the difficult processes involved in changing peoples' attitudes, dispositions, and stereotypes. This is an educational and not a legal problem, although court pronouncements also have an educating influence.

UNEQUAL TREATMENT IN ADMISSIONS

Admission to public schools below the college level has generally not presented a problem. The obvious exception has been the racial discrimination discussed earlier. At least one case of discriminatory admissions, however, arose in Massachusetts, the birthplace of public education in America.

The Boston Latin Schools

In 1970 a group of girls took a competitive examination in Boston, Massachusetts, trying to gain entrance into Boston Latin School.[21] Boston Latin, part of the Boston public school system, has two separate schools: Girls Latin School and Boys Latin School. During the 1970 entrance period, in order to be admitted to Girls Latin, a girl had to score 133 or above out of a possible 200 points on the examination. To be admitted to Boys Latin during the same period, a score of 120 or above was required on the same examination. Janice Bray and others filed suit, alleging discrimination against them on the basis of sex.

In order to understand the situation more fully, if should be noted that "the Boys Latin building has a seating capacity for approximately 3000 students and the Girls Latin building has a seating capacity for approximately 1500 students." The Boston School Department, in order to determine the cut-off points on the examination scores, first determined how many vacancies there would be in each building. In this way they arrived at the score of 120 for boys and 133 for girls for the school year beginning in September 1970.

Questions to Consider

1. Was the method used by the Boston School Department to determine cut-off scores reasonable and fair?

2. If you do not think the method was fair, what method would you use?
3. Is building capacity a reasonable basis to determine admission policy?

THE OPINION OF THE COURT

Judge Caffrey of the U.S. District Court struck down the admissions process used by the Boston school authorities. Since the facts were agreed upon by all parties, he readily concluded "that the use of separate and different standards to evaluate the examination results to determine the admissibility of boys and girls to the Boston Latin Schools constitutes a violation of the Equal Protection Clause of the Fourteenth Amendment, the plain effect of which is to prohibit disparities before the law."

Judge Caffrey's analysis indicated that if boys and girls had been admitted on an equal basis, a cut-off point of 127 would have been used on the examination for all students. Thus, if building capacities were to be used to determine total numbers for admission, the schools must use the same cut-off scores for boys and for girls in order to satisfy the constitutional requirement of equal treatment.*

ARE SEX-SEGREGATED SCHOOLS LEGAL?

Although the overwhelming majority of our public schools are coeducational, exceptions exist and some of these have been challenged in lawsuits. If admissions criteria are equal, may a public school system maintain sexually segregated high schools for academically able students?

Yes they may, ruled a federal circuit court when this question arose in Philadelphia in the Vorschheimer case.[22] In effect, the separate-but-equal doctrine was upheld in the area of sex segregation, because school officials and the school board believed it to be an educationally sound policy. The court applied the test of reasonableness to this arrangement and did not want to substitute its judgment for that of school officials. Furthermore, evidence showed the two schools to be equal in size, prestige, and academic quality. An equally split vote by the Supreme Court (4 to 4) affirmed the lower court ruling.

Very different results were reached by the court in a case in which an entire school system maintained sex-segregated student assignments as

---

*Kirstein v. Rector and Visitors of University of Virginia, 309 F. Supp. 184 (E.D. Va. 1970), an earlier case at the college level, reached similar results. A district court held in Virginia that a state university could not exclude women since its special programs were not available in another Virginia school on an equal basis. The fact that the job market might favor males over females is not a legally valid reason to deny admission to females or to impose an unfavorable quota on them. It is common knowledge that professional schools have perpetuated such practices for many years with the support of the rest of society. These practices are being challenged and reexamined in light of current interpretations of the Fourteenth Amendment, and the trend is for courts to strike them down.

part of a racial desegregation plan.[23] Although the district court upheld
the plan, the U.S. Fifth Circuit Court ruled against it on the grounds that
it violated the Equal Educational Opportunities Act 1974 (20 U.S.C §
1703). According to the court, this act "goes beyond the rights guaranteed
children under the Fourteenth Amendment . . . and incorporates a
judgment that a sex-segregated school district is a dual rather than a
unitary school system and results in a similar if not equivalent injury to
school children as would occur if a racially segregated school system were
imposed."

The court distinguished this case from *Vorschheimer* in Philadelphia
in that the *Vorschheimer* case involved a *voluntary* sex segregation
situation in an otherwise coeducational system, whereas this case involved an overall plan of sex-segregated pupil assignment.[24]

What if a student has religious objections to taking certain courses
(such as family life education) in a coeducational class? Such a student may
be excused according to federal regulations.[25]

Rational Basis or Strict Scrutiny?

Although the law that is related to sex-based classification in schooling is
clear in some areas, it is not so clear in others. As we have seen, courts at
different levels and in different places have reached divergent conclusions
on similar issues. One reason for this lack of consistency is that historically, courts once applied the "rational basis" test to such classification,
but they no longer do so. However, although the Supreme Court has
gone beyond the rational basis test in this area, it has not applied the
much more demanding test of "strict scrutiny"; it is applying an intermediate test whereby the Court views with "special sensitivity" or
suspicion sex as a classifying factor.[26]

For example, it was the 'rational basis' test that upheld the
Vorschheimer sex segregation case and continues to uphold, in certain
courts, the separate-but-equal doctrine in sex-based classification. Some
commentators urge that we view with skepticism such arrangements, for
they in fact are seldom equal and . . . "unlike sex-segregated bathrooms or
locker rooms, separate educational facilities seem as likely to contribute to
a myth of male superiority in things academic as to reflect a desire to
perpetuate the mystique of sex."[27]

MARRIAGE, PREGNANCY, PARENTHOOD, AND THE SCHOOLS

It is often said that an unstated goal of our schools is the prolonging of
childhood and adolescence. Since it is generally believed that marriage or
parenthood immediately transforms people into adults, many feel that in

order to prolong adolescence, schools ought to discourage their students from marrying or from becoming pregnant. As we know, however, school success in these endeavors has been less than complete.

Through the years three lines of reasoning were offered by parents and school authorities as justification for school rules related to marriage, pregnancy, or parenthood. Broadly stated these were: (1) sexual relations by teenagers are immoral; (2) the presence of pregnant girls or married students in the schools disrupts educational activities; and (3) pregnant girls and married students should be excluded from the schools for their own physical and psychological well-being.

Questions to Consider

1. Do you believe it is immoral to be unmarried and pregnant?
2. Should pregnant, unwed girls be excluded from regular classes? Should they be in special classes or special schools?
3. Does the presence of pregnant girls or married students disrupt schooling? Do they contribute more than other students to "sex talk" in schools?
4. Do you believe that the embarrassment pregnant girls are likely to suffer in school will do psychological harm to them?
5. Is there any basis for treating expectant mothers and fathers differently in the schools?

The Cooper Case: Marriage and Schooling

An appeals court in Texas had before it the case of a 16-year-old girl seeking readmission to the public school. She had withdrawn from school at the age of 15 and married. After bearing a child, she filed for divorce and also wanted to return to school. A district rule forbade her admission in the following words:

> A pupil who marries can no longer be considered a youth. By the very act of getting married, he or she becomes an adult and assumes the responsibility of adulthood. As a married student he or she shall not serve as an officer of the student body or any class or organization. A married student shall not represent the school in an inter-school contest or activity and shall not participate in school activities other than regular classes. If a married pupil wants to start her family, she must withdraw from public school. Such a pupil will, however, be encouraged to continue her education in the local adult education program and correspondence courses.[28]

When the evidence also showed that Kathy Cooper could not be admitted to the adult education program until she was 21 years old, the Texas court ordered her readmission to high school. It did so by directly relying on a state law that makes public education in Texas available to all persons between the ages of 6 and 21, provided they and their parents or guardians reside in the district. Therefore, the rule quoted above was declared illegal.

The Kissick Case: Marriage and School Football

Jerry Kissick, Jr., was a letterman on the 1958 football team of Garland Public School, Texas. In March 1959, at the age of 16, he married a 15-year-old girl. After his marriage, Kissick received notice barring him from further participation in school athletic activities pursuant to the following school policy: "Married students or previously married students may be barred from participating in athletics or other exhibitions, and not be permitted to hold class offices or other positions of honor. Academic honors such as Valedictorian and Salutatorian are excepted."[29]

Kissick had planned to play football during his remaining years of high school and had anticipated earning an athletic scholarship for college. He therefore filed suit to restrain enforcement of the policy on the grounds that it was unreasonable and discriminatory and that it violated the Due Process and Equal Protection Clauses of the Fourteenth Amendment.

The school officials claimed that the policy was reasonable and well supported by evidence. They argued that it was calculated to discourage "teen-age" marriages, which tend to lead to dropping out of school. Furthermore, they contended that Kissick did not have a right to play football, whereas his right to pursue his academic program was unimpaired.

Questions to Consider

1. Do you consider the school policy to be reasonable?
2. Should early marriages be discouraged?
3. Is barring participation in school athletics if married a reasonable way to discourage early marriages?
4. Is there a right to get married? Where in the Constitution is such a right guaranteed?

THE OPINION OF THE COURT

The school district and its Parent-Teachers Association argued on behalf of the school policy. They pesented the following evidence:

1. That an extensive study of "teen-age" marriages in their community showed ill effects of married students participating in extracurricular activities with unmarried students.
2. That there had been "an alarming increase in juvenile marriages at Garland School."
3. That parents favored the school policy 9 to 1.

4. That of a total of 64 married students during the previous year 24 had dropped out of school.
5. That of those married students who remained in school, at least 50 percent experienced a drop in grades of 10 points or more.
6. That a professional psychologist testified in favor of the school policy.

The court of civil appeals of Dallas, Texas, ruled in favor of the school district. In its reasoning it reflected the historical views of restrictions related to extracurricular activities, restrictions that are still found in some school districts.*

The court in effect ruled that extracurricular activities such as football are distinguishable from the essential programs of the school. Although Jerry Kissick, Jr., certainly had a right to attend school, the Dallas court held that it was not unreasonable to bar him from playing football. The court concluded:

> Boards of Education, rather than Courts, are charged with the important and difficult duty of operating the public schools. So, it is not a question of whether this or that individual judge or court considers a given regulation adopted by the Board as expedient. The Court's duty, regardless of its personal views, is to uphold the Board's regulation unless it is generally viewed as being arbitrary and unreasonable. Any other policy would result in confusion detrimental to the progress and efficiency of our public school system.[30]

The Davis Case

Albert Davis was a senior in Ohio's Fremont Ross High School. He became 18 years old on January 15, 1972, and seven days later he married a 16-year-old girl who was pregnant at the time with his child. He was an honor student, an excellent baseball player, and a member of the varsity for at least two years. Major league scouts were interested in him, and several colleges were willing to grant him an athletic scholarship.

When Davis married, he was aware of the following school rule:

A. Married pupils are permitted to attend school.
B. Married pupils are not permitted to participate in school sponsored extracurricular activities including the Junior-Senior Prom.[31]

After his marriage, he was informed "that the rule would be enforced against him, and his name was not placed on the eligible list for baseball when the list was prepared and filed." Davis went to court to enjoin the

---

*The court's opinion included some discussion of Texas law related to marriages of minors. Although most states have similar laws, our discussion reflects only the relevance of the civil rights provisions of the U.S. Constitution as interpreted by the Dallas court.

school from enforcing the rule. He claimed that he had a constitutional right to get married and that the school rule deprived him of an important part of the school program because of his marriage and had thereby interfered with his civil liberties.

As in the *Kissick* case, the school authorities argued (1) that the rule was intended to discourage early marriages because students who married usually dropped out of school and (2) that after the adoption of the rule, fewer dropped out, and of those who did, a larger number continued their education through home instruction.

A DIFFERENT RESULT

The U.S. District Court in Ohio cited the generally accepted fact that "the right to get married is traditionally a strictly local matter, which each state may regulate as it sees fit." Ohio by law specifies the legal age for marriage; and Albert Davis had acted within it. In various cases the Ohio courts recognized a state policy against "child marriages" whose minor participants are "more to be pitied than scorned." This attitude was a reflection of an understanding that the failure of teenage marriages is appallingly high. Furthermore, the dropout rate of married high school students is also very high, with almost 67 percent of the married girls dropping out in Ohio.

In spite of this, Justice Young recognized that Davis was legally married. Furthermore, evidence showed that the district policy was not successful in discouraging students from getting married. Thus, if the intent of the rule was to deter students from earlier marriage, why punish a student in a case in which the deterrent had not succeeded?

Since Davis' punishment consisted of exclusion from the school baseball team, the question was raised whether extracurricular activities were part of the school program. The court answered affirmatively.[32] Acknowledging the importance of various extracurricular activities, Judge Young specifically recognized the significance to Davis of playing on the baseball team. Any school rule that deprives the student of an important school activity is carefully scrutinized by the courts. The court invoked the *Tinker* case to see whether the school rule was necessary to maintain appropriate discipline or whether it was but part of an "enclave of totalitarianism." Having found that Davis was legally married and that his marriage did not materially or substantially interfere with school discipline, the court ruled in his favor.

The Ordway Case: Unmarried Pregnant Students[33]

Fay Ordway was an 18-year-old pregnant unmarried senior at the North Middlesex Regional High School, Townsend, Massachusetts. On January 28, 1971, she informed Mr. Hargraves, the principal, that she was pregnant and expected her child in June 1971. The principal informed her that she would have to stop attending classes as of February 12, when the school closed for a vacation. His action was based on a policy that provided: "Whenever an unmarried girl enrolled in North Middlesex Regional High School shall be known to be pregnant, her membership in the school shall be immediately terminated."

Pursuant to this policy, the principal wrote a letter to Ordway informing her that she may continue her studies on her own, use all school facilities after school hours and have access to school services, senior activities, games and dances, and free tutoring. Her name would continue on the school roster until graduation in June 1971, but she could not be in regular attendance. Ordway, however, wanted to continue attending school with the other students, and she took her case to court.

Questions to Consider

1. Should Ordway be allowed to continue attending classes?
2. How would you justify the school policy? Do you know people who would support it?
3. Were the provisions offered Ordway in the principal's letter reasonable?

THE OPINION OF THE COURT

Judge Caffrey delivered the opinion of the U.S. District Court. First, he summarized evidence presented by physicians and psychiatrists to the effect that there were no health reasons to exclude Ordway from attending classes. With the exception of "violent calisthenics," she could participate in all normal school activities; in fact, exclusion was likely to "cause plaintiff mental anguish which will affect the course of her pregnancy." According to psychiatric testimony, "young girls in plaintiff's position who are required to absent themselves from school become depressed, and the depression of the mother has an adverse effect on the child, who is frequently born depressed and lethargic."

Social workers also recommended giving students like Ordway the choice of either remaining in class or receiving private instruction after school hours. Fay, whose grades ranged from C pluses to an A, expressed a strong desire to attend regular classes.

Hargraves could not state any educational reasons for Ordway's exclusion, and there were no school disruptions related to her pregnancy. His only rationale for the school policy was the apparent desire on the part of the school committee "not to appear to condone conduct on the part of unmarried students of a nature to cause pregnancy."

Since the school included both junior and senior high school students, there seemed to be a concern that the 12-to-14 age group "might be led to believe that the school authorities were condoning premarital relations if they were to allow girl students in plaintiff's situation to remain in school." This concern, the court pointed out, was inconsistent with the provisions contained in the principal's letter to Ordway.

Considering all the testimony, the court ordered the readmission of Ordway to regular classes. In sum, Judge Caffery found no health reasons to exclude her, no valid educational purpose to be served by her exclusion, and no likelihood that her presence would lead to disruption or interference with school activities or pose any kind of threat to others (the *Tinker* test). Since the court considered public education to be "a basic personal right or liberty" the burden of proof would be on the schools to justify limiting or denying it to a student. Mere pregnancy is not a sufficient reason for such a denial or limitation.

In recent years, courts have increasingly protected students' rights to continue schooling while married and/or pregnant, including their right to participate in extracurricular activities. A Colorado appeals court, for example, decided to follow this recent trend and held that the family responsibilities of married students were not sufficient justification for exclusion from extracurricular school activities.[34]

Separate Schools for Married Students?

Consistently with earlier notions that married students and/or pregnant ones might "contaminate" the others, some school districts provide separate schools for them. Where such separation is optional, as it is in some districts where special curricula are available for pregnant students, students can choose to attend or not attend; therefore no cases exist that challenge such separation. But what about the compulsory segregation of these other students?

Peach County, Georgia, had a policy requiring "students who are pregnant, married, or parents to attend a separate high school." The separate school, two miles from the main high school, had an enrollment of 40 black female students. With its two teachers it had a restricted curriculum, inadequate library, as well as inadequate counseling facilities and extracurricular activities.[35] In declaring this arrangement illegal, the court held that separating these students from others was not done on a rational basis related to a legitimate governmental purpose. Although this situation was so extreme that it would fail even the test of separate-but-equal facilities, it is probable that courts will not allow mandatory segregation of married and/or pregnant students even if the facilities provided them were equal. In our times it would be difficult to argue that an important governmental interest is advanced by such separation; therefore courts are likely to strike these down under the Equal Protection or Due Process Clauses of the Constitution. Interestingly enough, Title IX regulations specify that if a school offers a separate program for pregnant students, it must be comparable to that offered for nonpregnant students. Whether or not such a separate-but-equal program would be constitutional, if mandatory, has not been determined.

REVERSE SEX DISCRIMINATION?

A high school student in Texas challenged a school rule restricting the hair length of male students.[36] He claimed that the rule violated the Texas ERA because it applied only to male students. After going through an analysis of sex-based classification and indicating that such classification will bring about "strict scrutiny" that requires a compelling state interest, the court upheld the school rule. Curiously, it seemed to have applied the rational basis test, although it talked at length about strict scrutiny.

The court held that parents, churches, and schools . . . "may reasonably establish rules of conduct arising out of the relationship (with children) without intervention of the courts. The schools stand somewhat *in loco parentis* to the child. Living by rules, sometimes seemingly arbitrary ones, is the lot of children." Then, urging minimal intervention by courts in the functioning of schools, the court said: "Court intervention is simply not a suitable device with which to enforce some rights. . . . We must be wise enough to perceive that constant judicial intervention in some institutions does more harm than good."

SUMMARY AND COMMENT

Early marriages have been discouraged in our culture, at least since the advent of industrialization. The schools, as significant institutions of social control, have been used by society to help deter "child marriages." One means widely used by schools has been the policy and practice of excluding married students from school. Another has been the denial to such students of the "privilege" of participating in extracurricular activities.*

Although some of these policies are still in effect, their legal legitimacy is doubtful. Since 1929 the reported cases have consistently supported the right of married students to attend public schools[37] Courts have supported this right on the basis of the Equal Protection Clause of the Fourteenth Amendment or simply by reference to state laws requiring or permitting school attendance between certain ages, as in the *Cooper* case in Texas. Public policy is better served by teenagers continuing their schooling, whether married or not.**

---

*Since the *Ordway* case involved an unmarried pregnant girl, the reasons should apply with even more force to married pregnant students.

**We realize that this is a value assertion, current critics notwithstanding. The courts as well as scholarly articles take this position. See, for example, Brian E. Berwick and Carol Oppenheimer, "Marriage, Pregnancy, and the Right to Go to School," *Texas Law Review,* 50 (1972), 1196–1228.

Participation in extracurricular activities by married students had a more complex legal history. Although school rules denying such a "privilege" have often been upheld by the courts, the trend is clearly otherwise. The "right versus privilege" doctrine has been thoroughly discredited and is no longer viable. Even if extracurricular activities were a privilege, a state agency such as a school must not attach arbitrary or discriminatory conditions to participation in the privilege. Thus, increasingly, marriage per se cannot be used to bar membership on an athletic team or participation in school clubs, social functions, or student government, although some courts will probably uphold such a restriction when applied to students who marry *below* the legal age specified by their state.

Many school districts have policies that exclude pregnant students from regular classes and extracurricular activities. These rules are usually justified on moral grounds when the pregnant student is unmarried and on grounds of "contagion" in the case of married girls. Interestingly enough, neither the unwed fathers nor the married fathers are excluded from school under most of these policies. Even the courts that assure the girls' right to continue school seldom speak about the fathers, wed or unwed.

Most pregnant girls who are denied the right to participate in school programs simply drop out of school. Some continue in "home classes" or tutorials. Neither of these arrangements is considered by knowledgeable educators to be on a par with the regular schools. In fact, girls who interrupt their schooling during pregnancy seldom return. On the other hand, those who are given a chance to continue their education during pregnancy are twice as likely to graduate as those denied such an opportunity.[38]

Strong reasons support the right of pregnant girls, married or not, to continue schooling. Not only are their personal and occupational lives likely to be affected by dropping out, but also the lives of their children. Since their ability to support their children will be influenced by their school attendance, they need all the education society is capable of providing.

Are pregnancy exclusion policies racist? Surveys indicate that such policies fall heaviest on members of minority groups—black, Chicano, and others. These girls account for a disproportionate number of pregnancies, which correlate with poverty and unequal access to birth control information, contraceptives, and legal abortions.[39]

As noted above, most instances of exclusion for pregnancy do not reach the courts. When they do, however, the current trend is to protect the right to attend classes and participate in other school activities. Such court holdings are generally based on the Equal Protection Clause of the Fourteenth Amendment, on state laws providing schooling between certain ages, on Title IX, and even on the reasoning of the *Tinker* case.

Applying the principles of *Tinker,* one could argue that before a pregnant student may be excluded, the school authorities would have to show that her presence caused a "substantial and material disruption" of the educational process.

Thus the trend of judicial opinion clearly protects the right to continue schooling despite pregnancy. This development supports individual rights as well as the public policy of having a better educated electorate.

OTHER ASPECTS OF EQUAL PROTECTION FOR STUDENTS

Traditional attitudes toward male-female differences linger in our culture and inevitably affect the schools. New expressions of sexist attitudes appear from time to time, and they may or may not reach the courts, depending upon how aware people are of their rights and how vigorously they protect them.

As indicated in Chapter Twelve, schools may not legally prevent pregnant students from participating in graduation exercises. All the more reason why they may not exclude married students from such participation.

A related question arises concerning the right of pregnant or married students not to attend school. Schools in general have not attempted to enforce compulsory attendance laws against such students. Most schools specifically allow them to drop out though they are within the ages of compulsory schooling. In the rare instances in which schools wanted to enforce compulsory attendance against such students, the courts ruled in favor of the students.[40]

Two legal scholars propose the following policy, which, we believe, is consistent with the cases in this chapter. Although their specific reference is to the state of Texas, there is no reason why the proposal should not apply with equal logic to other states.

> Pregnant and/or married students within the compulsory school age retain their entitlement to a free public education. The Texas Education Code requires school districts to admit them to a full school program of regular classes and activities. The compulsory attendance law continues to apply to them unless they can prove exemption under state statutes.
>
> (a) Punitive action against pregnant students violates state law and the United States Constitution. It is also unwise, because it causes girls to hide their pregnancies from school authorities, who are often the only adults in a position to ensure that they get appropriate medical care. Therefore, it is the policy of the State Board of Education that the public schools shall not make or enforce rules that mandatorily transfer

pregnant girls out of regular classes or to different schools, or that otherwise punish them.

(b) It is both inconsistent with state law and unconstitutional for schools to punish students for marrying. It is the policy of the State Board of Education that the public schools shall not make or enforce rules that bar married students from attendance or participation in extracurricular activities, that restrict their eligibility for academic or other honors, or that otherwise punish them.[41]

PREGNANCY LEAVES FOR TEACHERS

School policies and practices related to teachers that are classified on the basis of sex are increasingly coming under scrutiny. When are they arbitrary? When are they reasonable and thus legitimate? At one point in history it was a common practice for school boards to dismiss women teachers when they married. From today's perspective it seems almost unbelievable that court cases were necessary to declare that marriage is not a reasonable ground for dismissing a woman teacher. Oddly enough, even today some state laws allow individual school districts to provide for such dismissal in their contracts with teachers.[42]

Similarly, most cases have held that it was arbitrary to dismiss a woman teacher who was absent for childbirth; yet, until recently, even this was not a uniformly accepted principle. Cases as recently as 1945[43] have ruled that pregnancy and childbirth constitute "incompetency" or "neglect of duty," thereby justifying dismissal because they render the teacher incapable of carrying on her job. Other courts have dismissed such reasons as absurd.[44]

Recent court rulings have treated marriage and pregnancy as normal events among teachers. However, many state laws required women to take a leave of absence at the fourth or fifth month of pregnancy. Are such rules arbitrary and thus a violation of due process? Or is there a reasonable connection between the rule and some legitimate concern of the state? Courts have held both ways, depending on the circumstances. When a school board demonstrated that before it instituted a maternity leave policy "the teachers suffered many indignities as a result of pregnancy which consisted of children pointing, giggling, laughing and making snide remarks causing interruption and interference with the classroom program of study," the court upheld the leave policy as a reasonable one. In this case[45] the Cleveland, Ohio, Board could show that prior to the leave policy teachers tended to stay on the job far too long. ". . . . And although no child was born in the classroom, a few times it was very close. The evidence showed that in one instance where the teacher's pregnancy was advanced, children in a Cleveland junior high school were taking bets on whether the baby would be born in the classroom or in the hall!" Testimony showed that the purpose of the regulation was to protect the teacher and to maintain the continuity of the classroom program and prevent disruption.

The Cleveland Board also presented evidence that the incidence of violence was steadily increasing in the schools and that physical assaults upon teachers by pupils were increasing significantly. The court further considered the weight changes that occur during normal pregnancies and the fact that frequency of urination increases, agility is impaired, sudden physical exertion is forbidden, and the incidence of toxemia is as high as 10 percent. Other possible complications were discussed, leading the court to conclude that a maternity leave policy is grounded in reason.

Other courts, however, have struck down the typical maternity rule as being arbitrary. An example of this is the Virginia case of *Cohen* v. *Chesterfield County School Board and Dr. Robert F. Kelly,* where the court declared the mandatory maternity leave policy unconstitutional in the following words:

> It is sufficient to say that constitutional protection does extend to the public servant whose exclusion pursuant to a statute (or regulation) is patently arbitrary or discriminatory. The maternity policy of the School Board denies pregnant women such as Mrs. Cohen equal protection of the laws because it treats pregnancy differently than other medical disabilities. Because pregnancy, though unique to women, is like other medical conditions, failure to treat it as such amounts to discrimination which is without rational basis, and therefore is violative of the equal protection clause of the Fourteenth Amendment.[46]

In view of contradictory lower court rulings on this important issue, the Supreme Court accepted the *La Fleur* and *Cohen* cases for review and established some uniform guiding principles in 1974.[47] The Court explicitly recognized the "rights in conflict" in such controversies; on the one hand, the "freedom of personal choice in matters of marriage and family life is one of the liberties protected by the Due Process Clause of the Fourteenth Amendment." On the other, "It cannot be denied that continuity of instruction is a significant and legitimate educational goal."

A policy that requires all pregnant teachers to commence their leaves at the fourth or fifth month of their pregnancy may serve administrative convenience, but it conclusively presumes such women to be unfit to teach past those dates. The Court held such conclusive presumption to be arbitrary and it unduly penalizes female teachers for deciding to bear children. The Court reached the same conclusion on the "return policy." School districts that have pregnancy leave policies generally have policies controlling return to work. School boards offer two justifications for such return rules: to provide for continuity of instruction and to make certain that the teacher is physically able to resume work. Although such rules might seem quite reasonable, noted the Court, the means chosen by school boards unduly infringe upon the teachers' constitutional liberty.

The Court ruled that the ability of a particular woman to continue teaching while pregnant or to return to work after delivery is an individual matter to be determined by her and her physician. Some minimal leave time during the last few weeks of pregnancy might be upheld by the Court; however, the teachers' rights as well as the interest of the school to maintain continuity of instruction can be achieved by a leave policy that allows individualization rather than imposing rigid rules.

Thus a school district may require a notification of pregnancy, together with a statement of intent as to when the teacher desires to begin her leave. A physician's statement may also be required assessing the teachers' health and ability to continue work. Similar statements may be required concerning intent and health status for returning to work after delivery. Most school districts have adopted such individualized maternity leave policies following the ruling of the Court. On the other hand, some districts, emphasizing the need for continuity of instruction, adopted policies that require teachers to commence their leave at the beginning of the school term during which they expect to deliver and not to return to work until the beginning of the term following delivery. Where challenged, lower courts have upheld such policies as reasonable means of insuring continuity of instruction.

A different aspect of sexism is visible in a Georgia policy denying maternity leave to probationary teachers. The court found the policy repugnant to the Equal Protection Clause of the Fourteenth Amendment. The board argued that if untenured teachers were granted maternity leaves it would be impossible to evaluate them for tenure. The court rejected this argument, saying that "the board may extend the probationary period if it desires. Moreover, untenured teachers are permitted to go on study leave, which may be taken for as long as one year, and military leave, which commonly lasts two years."[48] It would be arbitrary and discriminatory to deny equal leave privileges to pregnant probationary teachers.

Sick Benefits for Pregnancy Leaves?

If a teacher takes a pregnancy leave, does she have a right to receive sick pay during that leave?

Payments during a leave due to illness are not a constitutional right. A state might provide it by state law or local school districts might provide it by local policies and regulations. Questions then arise when sick leave pay is provided by state or local law and a teacher claims its benefits while on maternity leave.

The Supreme Court ruled in 1974 that a state may exclude normal pregnancies from its disability insurance coverage program and that such exclusion does not violate the Equal Protection Clause.[49] This exclusion from a disability insurance program does not constitute unconstitutional discrimination even though it applies only to women. In explaining its rationale, the Court used a generally accepted principle: The Equal Protection Clause does not require that a state choose between attacking every aspect of a problem or not attacking the problem at all.

Other efforts were made to secure sick leave benefits for pregnancy leaves under Title VII of the Civil Rights Act of 1964. This act prohibits employment discrimination on the basis of race, color, sex, or national origin. When such efforts failed, Congress enacted a law in 1979 that provides that pregnancies and pregnancy-related disabilities will be treated the same as other disabilities for purposes of sick leaves and disability insurance coverage.

EQUAL PAY FOR MALES AND FEMALES?

Historically, many school districts paid male teachers more than female teachers performing the same or equivalent work. Various justifications were given for such discrepancy, including the desire to attract more men into teaching, paying for extra duties, and providing a "head of household allowance." Are such pay differentials legal?

This question was raised in Texas in 1977, where a school district paid male teachers $300 more per year than female teachers performing equivalent work. When it was found that sex was the primary basis for the higher pay and not a head of household allowance or extra duties, an injunction was granted against such practice. This action was based on the federal Fair Labor Standards Act [20 U.S.C. § 206(d)]. Differential pay could be granted under this law if based on seniority, merit, and additional duties or head of household status, but these would have to apply equally to men and to women.

An important area in which pay disparities abound is the field of coaching. Typically the coaches of women's teams receive lower pay, and although Title IX has been useful to reduce discrimination in the allotment of funds and equipment for female athletics, it has not solved the problem of unequal pay. Courts have been reluctant to apply Title IX to coaches and other employees, holding that the law was intended to benefit students and not the coaches.

The federal Equal Pay Act of 1963 has also been used to attack discrepancies in coaching salaries and so have a variety of state antidiscrimination laws. All states have such laws and under them unequal pay may be challenged in state courts. Several lawsuits in this area have already succeeded and many more have been filed. For example, in Ohio a female junior high physical education teacher sued and alleged discrimnation by school authorities.[50] When the court found the athletic program, facilities, and equipment provided girls to be substantially inferior and her working conditions inferior to those of her male counterparts, it ruled in her favor and awarded her $6000 money damages and $2000 for attorney fees. Similarly, in New York a coach of a female volleyball team was awarded $7800 in back pay and a raise, when it was found that University of Rochester discriminated against her on the basis of sex.

Although the question of "equivalent duties" in the area of coaching is a difficult one to resolve, the widespread discrepancies in pay, based on sex, are under scrutiny everywhere. The Department of Labor is proposing an Equal Pay Policy related to coaching. Its proposed policy claims that coaches generally perform duties that are substantially similar regardless of the sport in question. The department also suggests that although different sports entail different responsibilities, with all factors considered, these demands tend to balance each other out and thus justify substantial equality in pay.

OTHER QUESTIONS CONCERNING TITLE IX

In several cases the question was raised whether a teacher or other school employee can sue under Title IX. Courts have held that the intent of Title IX was to protect students against discrimination and that HEW exceeded its authority in its Title IX regulations related to employment.[51] However, one case held that if sex discrimination against the employee has a direct impact on students, suit may be brought under Title IX.[52]

May an individual bring suit under Title IX, or must the Department of Justice or other official body act to enforce it? The Supreme Court ruled that there is a private right of action and individuals may sue to enforce their rights under Title IX.[53]

Summary and Conclusions

Various school policies and practices have been scrutinized in recent years to eliminate discrimination based on sex. Phrased in terms of constitutional law, claims have been made that "sexist" policies and practices violate the Equal Protection Clause of the Fourteenth Amendment, or, to the extent that such policies and practices are arbitrary and unreasonable, they violate the Due Process Clause of the same amendment. The issues examined can be analyzed under the following headings: (1) equality in school sports; (2) equality in admissions and in the curriculum; (3) restrictions on married and pregnant students; (4) pregnancy leaves and sick benefits for teachers; and (5) equal pay for male and female educators.

EQUALITY IN SPORTS

During recent years, significant strides have been taken toward equality in athletic opportunities for girls and boys. These gains resulted from cases brought under the Fourteenth Amendment of the Constitution, under Title IX, and under state ERA's. Furthermore, as a result of rising consciousness on this issue, sexist policies are often identified and altered without legal action.

The law now requires that schools make available individual and team competitive sports for girls as well as boys. Although schools have no legal obligation to provide interscholastic athletics for any student, but if they do have them, sex must not be the basis for inclusion or exclusion of students. In noncontact sports, such as golf, tennis, or swimming, if there are no teams for girls, they may compete for positions on the boys' teams. If there are teams for both, most courts will respect the separation of the sexes since there are some reasonable grounds for separate athletic competition. Some courts have gone further and struck down all such sex segregation in sports, including both contact and noncontact sports.

State ERA's have influenced some courts to mandate equal access to all sports regardless of sex, even though Title IX allows for the separation of the sexes in contact sports. Title IX has been instrumental in moving schools toward equalizing support for boys' and girls' athletics in finances, equipment, and coaching.

EQUALITY IN ADMISSIONS AND THE CURRICULUM

Historically, there have been relatively few practices of sexual discrimination in admission to public schools. The case involving the Boston schools was found to be one such discriminatory practice, and the court ordered an end to the unequal treatment. In effect, the court ruled that if standardized tests are to be used for admission into a public high school, the same cut-off scores must be used for boys and for girls.

Challenges have also been brought against sex-segregated schooling. Courts have upheld separate academic high schools for boys and girls where the separate schools were genuinely equal and attendance in them was voluntary. A case involving systemwide mandatory sex-segregated schooling was struck down by a lower court.

Sexual discrimination in the curriculum and in admission to classes was rampant until quite recently. These are rapidly disappearing and they are clearly illegal. Many of these policies applied to courses in wood and metal shops, auto shop, cooking, sewing, and home economics. Most school districts are changing such policies voluntarily, some pursuant to Title IX and some as a result of local political pressure. Some have changed in the face of lawsuits. Although sexual discrimination in the curriculum is clearly illegal, informal practices often perpetuate long-held beliefs. Thus girls are all too often counseled not to enroll in physics or algebra, and similar practices discourage boys from taking dance, art, sewing, and, at times, even Latin.

MARRIAGE, PREGNANCY, AND PARENTHOOD

Many school districts have policies related to married students, pregnant girls, or students who are parents. Some of these rules exclude them from school altogether, whereas others only deny participation in student government, athletics, and other extracurricular activities. These policies are aimed at discouraging "teenage" marriages and pregnancies, since adults tend to believe that early marriage leads to dropping out of school or to poor school performance.

The law is clear that students have a right to continue schooling even if they marry. State laws that make attendance compulsory usually do so between specified age limits. Within those limits, students have a right to attend school even if they violate adult values against early marriages. The same rule holds true for pregnant girls, married or not.

The law is not as clear or uniform concerning participation in extracurricular activities by married students. School policies that exclude them from athletic teams have been upheld in some states as exemplified by the *Kissick* case in Texas. Other court decisions are consistent with the *Davis* case from Ohio and rule such policies arbitrary and discriminatory. Perhaps the key distinction between these different holdings is that some courts consider extracurricular activities to be less important than the regular school program and therefore grant the school boards greater discretion in their regulation. Other courts, such as the one in the *Davis* case, hold that extracurricular activities can be very important and might make a significant impact on the life of a student. In our opinion, this will become the dominant judicial view. This view is also shared by many schools which now refer to such activities as cocurricular rather than extracurricular. Thus courts are increasingly extending the right of participation in these activities to married and pregnant students, and to those students with children.

PREGNANCY LEAVES AND BENEFITS FOR TEACHERS

It has been a common practice in public schools to require pregnant teachers to take a leave of absence around the fifth month of pregnancy and not to return until a specified period of months after delivery. Such policies and practices have been declared arbitrary and unreasonable— thus against the Due Process Clause of the Fourteenth Amendment. The Supreme Court has ruled that such policies conclusively presume all women to be unfit to teach after the fifth month of pregnancy. This arbitrarily penalizes female teachers for deciding to bear children. Similar criticism was leveled at fixed and arbitrary "return" policies. Thus pregnant teachers now have the right to decide, with their physicians' advice, when to start their leave and when to return to the classroom. Schools, on the other hand, may require a notification of the pregnancy together with a statement of intent as to when the teacher desires to leave and when she wishes to return.

Following the ruling of the Court, most school districts have adopted a policy of individualized maternity leaves. Some districts, however, emphasizing the need for continuity of instruction, created policies that require pregnant teachers to commence their leave at the beginning of the school term during which they expect to deliver and not to return until the beginning of the term following delivery. Where challenged, lower courts have upheld such policies as reasonable means of insuring continuity of instruction. Serious conflicts also arose concerning sick benefits for teachers on pregnancy leaves. Such benefits are granted by state law or local policy and not by the Constitution. The Court ruled that states may exclude normal pregnancies from their disability insurance coverage. When other efforts failed to secure sick leave benefits for normal pregnancy leaves, Congress passed a law to treat pregnancy-related disabilities the same as other disabilities for purposes of insurance coverage.

EQUAL PAY FOR MEN AND WOMEN

It was not uncommon in the past for schools to pay male teachers more than female teachers. In recent years, such discrepancies have been challenged and courts have established the general principle that equal work merits equal pay. Differential pay may be given for extra duties, for merit, as a "head of household allowance," but not merely for sexual differences. Controversy still abounds concerning the differences in pay of male and female coaches. In this area, although the issues are complex and emotions run high, schools are moving toward substantial equality as a consequence of Title IX as well as of lawsuits based on the Constitution, on the federal Fair Labor Standards Act, and the federal Equal Pay Act of 1963.

There are those who claim that sexual discrimination in schooling will not disappear completely without a national Equal Rights Amendment and without a long period of reeducation of people who create and implement educational policy. Although such estimates might be correct, it is also the case that significant strides have been made in recent years toward reducing and even eliminating sexism in public education.

NOTES

1. *Sail'er Inn, Inc.* v. *Kirby,* 485 P.2d 529 (Cal. 1971).
2. *Quong Wing* v. *Kirkendall,* 223 U.S. 59, 63 (1912).

3. *Brenden* v. *Independent School District*, 742, 342 F.Supp. 1224 (D. Minn. 1972). This case has been affirmed in the Court of Appeals, 477 F.2d 1292 (8th Cir. 1973).

4. *Reed* v. *Reed*, 404 U.S. 71 (1971).

5. *Brenden* at 1233.

6. Ibid.

7. Id. at 1231–1232.

8. *Bucha* v. *Illinois High School Association*, 351 F.Supp. 69 (N.D. Ill. 1972).

9. See *Reed* v. *Reed*, 404 U.S. 71 (1971).

10. *Reed* v. *Nebraska School Activities Association*, 341 F.Supp. 258 (D. Neb. 1972).

11. The complete title of the law is: Title IX of the Education Amendments of 1972, 20 U.S.C. 1681.

12. *Hoover* v. *Meiklejohn*, 430 F.Supp. 164 (D. Colo. 1977).

13. *Leffel* v. *Wisconsin Interscholastic Athletic Association*, 444 F.Supp. 1117 (E.D. Wisc. 1978).

14. *Yellow Springs Exempted Village School District Board of Education* v. *Ohio High School Athletic Association*, 443 F.Supp. 753 (S.D. Ohio 1978).

15. *Opinion of the Justices re House Bill No. 6723*, Mass. Adv. sh., 2728, Massachusetts Supreme Judicial Court (December 22, 1977).

16. *Attorney General* v. *Massachusetts Interscholastic Athletic Association*, 393 N.E.2d. 284 (1979).

17. *Petrie* v. *Illinois High School Association*, 393 N.E.2d. 855 (1979).

18. See, for example, Nancy Frazier, and Myra Sadker, *Sexism in School and Society*. New York: Harper & Row, 1973.

19. *Seward* v. *Clayton Valley High School District*, Civ. Action No. 134173 (Contra Costa Sup. Ct.).

20. *Della Casa* v. *South San Francisco Unified School District*, Civ. Action No. 171–673 (San Mateo Sup. Ct.).

21. *Bray* v. *Lee*, 377 F.Supp. 934 (D. Mass. 1972).

22. *Vorschheimer* v. *School District*, 532 F.2d 880 (3rd Cir. 1976), 430 U.S. 703 (1977).

23. *United States* v. *Hinds County School Board; United States* v. *Amite County School District*, 560 F.2d 610 (5th Cir. 1977).

24. For an analysis of this issue, see Cynthia Lewis, "Comments—*Plessy* Revived: The Separate But Equal Doctrine and Sex-Segregated Education," 12 *Harvard Civil Rights Civil Liberties Law Review* No. 3 (Summer 1977), 585–648.

25. 43 Fed. Reg. 18630 (May 1, 1978).

26. This was first made explicit in *Frontiero* v. *Richardson*, 411 U.S. 677 (1973).

27. Laurence H. Tribe, *American Constitutional Law*. Mineola, N.Y.: Foundations Press, 1978, p. 1065.

28. *Alvin Independent School District* v. *Cooper*, 404 S.W.2d 76 (Tex. 1966).

29. *Kissick* v. *Garland Independent School District*, 330 S.W.2d 708 (Tex. 1959).

30. Id. at 712.

31. *Davis* v. *Meek*, 344 F.Supp. 298 (N.D. Ohio 1972).

32. For authority, the court cited the Supreme Court in *Brown* v. *Board of Education of Topeka, Kansas*, 349 U.S. 294 (1955).

33. *Ordway* v. *Hargraves*, 323 F.Supp. 1155 (D. Mass. 1971).
34. *Beeson* v. *Kiowa County School District*, 567 P.2d 801 (1977).
35. *Hill* v. *A. B. Johnson*, C.A. No. 77-51-Mac. M.D. Ga. (September 14, 1977).
36. *Mercer* v. *The Board of Trustees, North Forest Independent School District*, No. 1302, Tex. Ct. Civ. App. (June 2, 1976).
37. *McLeod* v. *Mississippi*, 122 So. 737 (1929).
38. See Marion Howard, "Pregnant School Age Girls," *Journal of School Health*, *41*, No. 361 (1971), 361−362.
39. Berwick, Brian E., and Oppenheimer, Carol, "Marriage, Pregnancy, and the Right to go to School," *Texas Law Review*, 50 (1972), p. 1214, fn 92.
40. See, for example, *In re Goodwin*, 39 So.2d 731 (1949); and *In re Rogers*, 234 N.Y.S.2d 172 (1962).
41. Berwick and Oppenheimer, op. cit., p. 1228.
42. See *Corpus Juris Secundum*, Vol. 78, pp. 1086−1087.
43. *West Mahonoy Township School District* v. *Kelly*, 41 A.2d 344 (1945).
44. *Corpus Juris Secundum*, op. cit., p. 1087.
45. *La Fleur* v. *Cleveland Board of Education*, 326 F.Supp. 1208 (1971).
46. 326 F.Supp. 1159 (1971).
47. *Cleveland Board of Education* v. *La Fleur; Cohen* v. *Chesterfield County School Board*, 414 U.S. 632 (1974).
48. *Jinks* v. *Mays*, 332 F.Supp. 254 (N.D. Ga. 1971).
49. *Geduldig* v. *Aiello*, 417 U.S. 484 (1974).
50. *Harrington* v. *Vandalia Butler Board of Education*, 418 F.Supp. 603 (S.D. Ohio 1976).
51. *Isleboro School Committee* v. *Califano*, 593 F.2d 424 (1st Cir. 1979).
52. *Caulfield* v. *Board of Education, The City of New York*, 583 F.2d 605 (S.D. N.Y. 1979).
53. *Cannon* v. *University of Chicago*, 441 U.S. 677 (1979).

Chapter 12
Due Process for Teachers and Students

> . . . Nor shall any state deprive any person of life, liberty, or property, without due process of law. . . .
>
> Fourteenth Amendment to the Constitution

> Due process of law is the primary and indispensable foundation of freedom. . . . Procedure is to law what "scientific method" is to science. Under our Constitution, the condition of being a boy does not justify a kangaroo court.
>
> Justice Abe Fortas in *In re Gault*

When Ms. A, a probationary teacher, is not reappointed for the next school year, she claims that her vigorous union activities are the reason for the board's action and alleges a violation of due process of law.

Mr. X, a probationary teacher, is advised to seek a position elsewhere for the next school year. He is told that the quality of his work is "not up to district standards." When he asks for a formal hearing with more specific charges, he is denied it. Mr. X files suit claiming a denial of due process.

Mr. Wilson, a high school teacher, is told by his principal to shave his beard if he wants to be reappointed for the following school year. Mr. Wilson claims that such a requirement violates his constitutional right to due process of law.

Several students are suspended from school after a fight at a school assembly where a controversial speaker addressed the students. The principal had a brief talk with them before the suspension. The students sue, claiming denial of their right to due process.

Priscilla, a high school student, is suspended for three days for violating a school dress code prohibiting the wearing of "provocative clothing." She claims the rule to be so vague as to violate her right to due process.

RIGHTS TO DUE PROCESS

The items cited are but a brief sampling of the wide range of cases in which teachers and students claim that their constitutional rights to due process have been violated. These rights are among the most important yet most complicated ones guaranteed by our federal Constitution. The right to due process, for example, appears in both the Fifth and the Fourteenth Amendments, the former providing that "no person shall . . . be deprived of life, liberty, or property, without due process of law," and the latter specifies that "nor shall any State deprive any person of life, liberty, or property, without due process of law."

"Due process of law" has never been precisely defined. Although it is a generally accepted and powerful legal doctrine, its meaning varies according to the situation, and no general definition of it is applicable to all cases and circumstances. Courts, for example, have said that fair play is the essence of due process[1] or that due process requires only that there be no violation of traditional notions of "fair play" and "substantial justice." Although the exact meaning of "due process of law" cannot be specified in an abstract definition, the courts agree that the phrase has the same meaning in both the Fifth and the Fourteenth Amendments.*

A large body of law is related to the Due Process Clauses of the Constitution. Although our brief treatment focuses on matters related to the rights of teachers and students, we hope the reader will gain some insight into the general principles of this doctrine and its relevance to other constituencies of the school, such as administrators and even parents. Due process (or the ideal of fairness) applies not only to judicial proceedings or acts of the legislature, but also to acts of local agencies or extensions of the state, such as school boards, superintendents, principals, and even teachers.

Popular notions of due process come from the mass media, particularly television, and relate to celebrated criminal cases. The cases involving teachers and students are *civil*, not *criminal* matters. There are various differences between civil and criminal proceedings, the degree of proof required being one of them. A crime is a wrong against society, whereas a civil action involves an individual or a group asserting one's right. Not all the procedural safeguards of criminal proceedings apply to the controversies involving the rights of teachers and students.

---

*Although much has been written about "substantive and procedural due process," for our purposes those categories are not very useful.

As courts have interpreted the Fourteenth Amendment through the years, several important principles have emerged. As general guiding principles, states and other arms of government must provide fair procedures before depriving anyone of "life, liberty, or property," and must not be arbitrary, unreasonable, or discriminatory in their policies or practices. In order to have these principles applied to schools, courts first had to determine whether teaching and going to school were privileges that governments could grant and withdraw at will or whether "life, liberty, or property" was involved in the occupation of teaching or in being a student.

Right or Privilege?

At one point in history, public employment, including teaching, was considered a privilege, not a right. As such it was subject to conditions that could not be attached to the exercise of a right. To illustrate this principle, the following is an extreme example. It is a privilege for a civic group to use your living room for a meeting. You may require, as a condition of receiving such a privilege, that the group begin its meeting with a prayer. You as a private individual may attach such conditions to a privilege you have the power to grant, but a public school that is available for meetings to various civic groups could not attach such a condition to using the facilities because it would violate the First Amendment provision separating church and state.

In the field of public employment, no one has a right to a public position, but unconstitutional conditions may not be attached to such a privilege. In other words, teaching as public employment may not be made conditional on giving up such rights as free speech or assembly.

The question arises as to whether there is a right to any kind of employment. The Constitution does not expressly grant such a right. However, the courts by implication have derived a right to work from the Fourteenth Amendment. In 1923 the Supreme Court declared that the concept of liberty in the Fourteenth Amendment "denotes not merely freedom from bodily restraint but also the right of the individual . . . to engage in the common occupations of life."[2] And if a state denies a person a license or the opportunity to practice his chosen profession, due process requires that he be given a hearing and a chance to respond to charges against him.[3]

However, since there is no constitutionally protected right to *public* employment, due process is not required when the only thing at stake is a *specific* job.[4] For example, if Mr. X, an outspoken campus activist, wishes to be certified as a teacher, the state certification agency may not deny him the opportunity or discriminate against him because of his vigorous, peaceful exercise of his right to speak freely and to organize fellow students. Mr. X, however, does not have a right to a teaching position at Hillside School. Hillside School has wide discretion to select its teachers, although this discretion should not be exercised in violation of constitutional rights.

Although courts have never said that there is a right to public employment, they have recognized the right to "practice a chosen profession," including teaching. Within the meaning of "liberty" one may choose an occupational goal and, if otherwise qualified, pursue it on an equal basis with anyone else. Some courts assert that upon entering an occupation one acquires a "property" right in that occupation that is protected by constitutional provisions against arbitrary or discriminatory action by government officials. At times courts speak of the "expectancy of continued employment" as a right to be protected.

The Supreme Court cut to the heart of the matter when it proclaimed that "We need not pause to consider whether an abstract right to public employment exists. It is sufficient to say that constitutional protection does extend to the public servant whose exclusion pursuant to a statute is patently arbitrary or discriminatory."[5]

Do students have a right to schooling? As we explain more thoroughly in Appendix B, How The System Works, our national Constitution is silent on schooling. Consequently, courts have ruled that there is no federal right to education. Pursuant to the Tenth Amendment, power over schooling is reserved to the states. In principle, a state may choose not to provide public schools for its citizens; however, all states have rejected this alternative. If a state creates a system of public schools, all people within the state have a right to such schooling on an equal, nondiscriminatory basis. Thus public schooling is not merely a privilege controlled at the will or whim of administration or other officials. Courts have protected the right to attend school, during the years provided by state law, under the "liberty" and "property" provisions of the Fourteenth Amendment.

In short, the earlier doctrine that emphasized the distinction between a right and a privilege has been rejected by courts as it might apply to public schools. No unconstitutional reason may be used to prevent one from seeking employment as a teacher or from holding such employment, and no unconstitutional condition may be attached to the right to attend state-supported schools.

Arbitrary and Discriminatory Action

But when is an action arbitrary or discriminatory? Since there is a tendency for each of us to consider any law, rule, or action we dislike as somehow arbitrary or discriminatory, let us turn to some of the cases that have interpreted these terms.

In the *Wieman* case, for example, a loyalty oath of the state of Oklahoma was declared unconstitutional under the Due Process Clause. The oath was based on membership in certain organizations, some of whose members may have been loyal, whereas others were disloyal. The Court indicated that membership in a subversive organization may be innocent, since some people join proscribed organizations while unaware of their activities and purposes. In fact, testimony of J. Edgar Hoover was cited to support this opinion. Consequently, to classify everyone on the basis of mere membership is unreasonable. In the words of the Court, "Indiscriminate classification of innocent with knowing activity must fall as an assertion of arbitrary power. The oath offends due process." In other words, the state may classify people for certain purposes, but the classification must be reasonable and must be related to a legitimate governmental aim.

One obvious example of legitimate classification would be to separate shower facilities for males and females in schools. An illegitimate and therefore arbitrary classification would be to allow only males to vote in school elections or to provide that school administrators will be selected from among the male members of the faculty.

As we have seen in other chapters, some courts have considered it arbitrary to deny teachers the right to have a beard or to teach in pantsuits. Other courts have upheld as reasonable some regulation of grooming and appearance of both teachers and students. Therefore we should keep in mind that what is or is not arbitrary and discriminatory is not always a simple matter. In general, to test a law or a policy for arbitrariness, courts first ask whether there is a legitimate goal for which the law or the policy was created; second, whether there is a reasonable connection between the goal sought and the means chosen; and finally, whether there might not be other, less restrictive ways of achieving the same goals.

Many lawsuits brought under the Equal Protection Clause allege violation of the Due Process Clause as well. This legal move is taken because most cases that involve sexual, racial, and other discriminations are also arbitrary actions and thus violate due process. Most of the cases cited in the chapters on racial and sexual discrimination have involved the Due Process Clause, alleging such discrimination to be arbitrary action as well as a denial of equal protection.

Fair Procedures—Teachers

Lawyers recognize that a right without a process to defend it is no right at all. The basic purpose of procedural due process is to provide fair and useful processes for asserting and protecting whatever rights the laws otherwise provide. The procedures required by due process usually include the right to a hearing, the opportunity to be represented, to present evidence, to question witnesses, and an impartial judge.

Keep in mind that the Fourteenth Amendment does not impose uniform procedures on all of the states. It requires that we follow the Constitution plus the laws of the particular state in which we are located. Thus, what procedural due process requires in Texas is not necessarily identical with the due process provisions of Vermont or Ohio. There are alternative reasonable and fair processes that the states may create and follow, and still meet the requirements of the Fourteenth Amendment. This is illustrated by the different rules concerning dismissal of tenured and nontenured teachers.

TENURED TEACHERS

The laws, rules, or contracts that provide for tenure also specify the process whereby a tenured teacher may be suspended, dismissed, or otherwise disciplined. The courts are strict in their insistence that procedural safeguards provided in the tenure law be meticulously observed. The case of a Michigan teacher illustrates this principle. Mr. Kumph taught successfully in the same school system for nine years. He received a sabbatical year to travel and study abroad, with the requirement that he submit an interim report to the superintendent while on leave. When he failed to meet this condition, he was not offered a contract for the ensuing year. The school system and the lower court agreed that the teacher terminated his relationship with the school district by breaking a requirement of his leave of absence. The Circuit Court of Appeals, however, reversed the decision and protected the teacher. The court insisted that a tenured teacher can be dismissed only by careful compliance with the procedural safeguards of the tenure legislation, including, for example, a 60-day written notice before the end of the school year.[6] This the board had failed to observe.

There is no constitutional provision for tenure. Tenure is granted either by state law or by contract within a school district. There is no civil right that guarantees tenure. In cases of alleged violations one must examine the state laws that provide for tenure and the conditions under which it may be broken. The typical state law provides that incompetence or immorality are grounds for dismissing a tenured teacher. What constitutes incompetence or immorality is a mixed question of fact, community standards, and professional judgment and must be examined in the trial courts. However, neither incompetence nor immorality may be defined in a way that would violate constitutional principles. A school board, for example, may not declare a teacher immoral or incompetent for teaching Darwinian evolution to high school students. Conversely, the assignment of Darwin's original works to a typical fourth grade class would be a piece of evidence of incompetence; additional evidence would have to be introduced. In any event it is clear that some kind of procedural due process is available to tenured teachers whose positions are in jeopardy.

There are those who argue that contracts between teacher organizations and school boards should replace tenure laws. It is argued that such contracts would be more efficient and less expensive to enforce than complex legal procedures.[7] Although some states are reexamining their tenure laws, about three-fourths of them currently have such laws. In states that have no tenure laws, some schools or school districts provide tenure by contract and some by administrative rule.[8] Although many private institutions also grant tenure by contract, our discussion includes only public institutions. With respect to the rights of nontenured teachers, many due process questions are as yet unsettled.

UNTENURED TEACHERS

In recent years some states have enacted laws providing some procedural rights for probationary teachers. In Alaska, Connecticut, Rhode Island, and California, for example, suspension or dismissal may not take place without some elements of due process.[9] In most states there are no such laws. In such states, unless a teachers' contract provides for fair process, we must look to the national Constitution. Courts in some of these states, even in the 1970s, seemed to follow the ringing declaration made by a judge over 50 years ago that:

> The board has the absolute right to decline to employ or to reemploy any applicant for any reason whatever or for no reason at all. The board is responsible for its actions only to the people of the City, from whom, through the Mayor, the members have received their appointments.
>
> It is no infringement on the constitutional rights of anyone for the board to decline to employ him as a teacher in the schools, and it is immaterial whether the reason for the refusal to employ him is because the applicant is married or unmarried, is of fair complexion or dark, is or is not a member of a trades union, or whether no reason is given for such refusal. The board is not bound to give any reason for its action.[10]

This language is so clear and so all-inclusive that further discussion might seem superfluous. But is the case still good law? Look at it in the light of what happened to two teachers in 1969.

Eleanor Pred and Stanley Eteresque were English and mathematics teachers, respectively, in the Miami-Dade County, Florida, Junior College. Each was in the third year of teaching and, if reappointed, would have acquired tenure according to Florida law. The board of Public Instruction of Dade County refused to grant them fourth-year contracts, thereby denying them tenure. The probationary teachers claimed that the action of the board was in retaliation for active participation in the local teachers' association and because Ms. Pred was advancing the "new demands for campus freedom" in her classroom.

Members of the board claimed that the teachers were not being discharged, only that their contracts were not being extended beyond the end of the year. They further claimed that it is essential for the board to have discretionary power over probationary teachers in order to manage the schools properly. The teachers, on the other hand, alleged that they were competent in all respects and that the board was punishing them "solely for the purpose of destroying the Plaintiff's rights of freedom of speech and assembly and for the purpose of curtailing and restricting academic freedom."

The district court upheld the board, and the teachers appealed to the Fifth Circuit Court of Appeals, which reversed the lower court in a powerful opinion. The court was angered by the long delay before the facts of the dispute were established:

> This is another monument to the needless waste of lawyer and judge time and, perhaps more important, client money. For now, 14 months later, the case must go back to start the normal process of discovery leading to the production of facts or the demonstrated lack of them on which, either before or after the conventional trial, the real merits of the case will be determined. [11]

John R. Brown, chief judge of the Circuit Court, quoted extensively from various decisions of the U.S. Supreme Court in explaining his reasons for reversing the lower court. To the argument that there is no right to public employment, he replied: "Equally unpersuasive is the argument that since there is no constitutional right to public employment, school officials only allowed these teacher contracts to expire. . . . The right sought to be vindicated is not a contractual one, nor could it be since no right to reemployment existed. What is at stake is the vindication of constitutional rights—the right not to be punished by the state or to suffer retaliation at its hand because a public employee persists in the exercise of first amendment rights."[12]

He further quoted with approval from three leading cases: "To state that a person does not have a constitutional right to government employment is only to say that he must comply with reasonable, lawful, and non-discriminatory terms laid down by the proper authorities. . . ."[13] . . . "constitutional protection does extend to the public servant whose exclusion pursuant to a statute is patently arbitrary or discriminatory."[14] "The theory that public employment which may be denied altogether may be subjected to any conditions, regardless of how unreasonable, has been uniformly rejected. The protections of the First Amendment have been given special meaning when teachers have been involved. Simply because teachers are on the public payroll does not make them second-class citizens in regard to their constitutional rights. Our nation is deeply committed to safeguarding academic freedom . . . and to impose any strait jacket upon the intellectual leaders in our colleges and universities would imperil the future of our nation."[15]

The court recognized that untenured teachers also have constitutional rights. If the probationary teacher asserts that his dismissal, or nonrenewal of contract, is in retaliation for his exercise of a constitutionally protected right rather than a matter of teaching competence, a fair procedure must be available to determine the facts. If the facts indicate that the dismissal was prompted by the exercise of a right, the courts will apply the "balancing of interests" tests. As the Court explained in a First Amendment case (the *Pickering* case), "The problem in any case is to arrive at a balance between the interests of the teacher, as citizen, in commenting upon matters of public concern and the interests of the State, as an employer, in promoting the efficiency of the public services it performs through its employees." The Board of Education cannot merely speculate that a teacher's activities will be harmful or disruptive to the efficient operation of the school. Administrators may not at their discretion forbid the exercise of a constitutional right. As the *Tinker* case clearly stated, "Certainly where there is no finding and no showing that the exercise of the forbidden right would materially and substantially interfere with the requirements of appropriate discipline in the operation of the school, the prohibition cannot be sustained."[16]

Thus the case of Ms. Pred and her fellow teacher was sent back to the lower court for trial to determine the facts and to apply the balance of interests test to the specific situation. The same result was reached in the case of *Lucia* v. *Duggan* which dealt with personal appearance. This case was particularly significant in Massachusetts, since it was commonly understood that untenured teachers had no right to due process. Under Massachusetts law they were subject to arbitrary, unilateral suspension or dismissal. The *Lucia* case made it clear that procedural due process applies to untenured teachers *if a constitutionally protected right is being threatened*.

Lucia v. *Duggan*, as well as many other cases of due process, was brought to court under the Civil Rights Act of 1871.[17] This law states:

> Every person, who under color of any statute, ordinance, regulation, custom, or usage, of any State or Territory, subjects, or causes to be subjected, any citizen of the United States or other person within the jurisdiction thereof to the deprivation of any rights, privileges, or immunities secured by the Constitution and laws, shall be liable to the party injured in an action at law, suit in equity, or other proper proceeding for redress.

One of the first cases applying the Civil Rights Act of 1871 to an untenured teacher was that of *Bomar* v. *Keyes*.[18] Ms. Bomar was dismissed by the Board of Education because she chose to serve for four weeks on a federal grand jury. When she appealed to the New York

Commissioner of Education, her appeal was dismissed on the ground that she had "not secured permanent tenure. Having been dismissed by the Board of Education during her probationary period, such a dismissal is not subject to review." In other words, the commissioner assumed that a probationary teacher had no right to procedural due process. Bomar pursued her case in court, alleging a violation of the Civil Rights Act of 1871. It was in the U.S. Circuit Court of Appeals that she finally won her case. Judge Learned Hand held that if she had been discharged for having exercised her right to serve on the jury, the decision could not stand and she had a right to a trial to determine the cause of her dismissal. The Civil Rights Act of 1871 is thus used to enforce a variety of constitutional rights.

ORGANIZATIONAL ACTIVITIES

In the face of rising union activity among teachers, administrators, and school boards have often reacted with dismissals and other sanctions. For a variety of reasons, administrators (and many teachers) have looked with disfavor on unionization of teachers. As we have seen, teachers have a right to free association, which includes forming and joining unions. If there is such a right, can an untenured teacher be discharged for exercising such a right? The answer is no.[19] In the McLaughlin case, for example, the court stated:

> It is settled that teachers have the right of free association, and unjustified interference with teachers' associational freedom violates the Due Process clause of the Fourteenth Amendment. Public employment may not be subjected to unreasonable conditions, and the assertion of First Amendment rights by teachers will usually not warrant their dismissal.
>
> Even though the individual plaintiffs did not have tenure, the Civil Rights Act of 1871 gives them a remedy if their contracts were not renewed because of their exercise of constitutional rights.

MIXED REASONS FOR NONREAPPOINTMENT

What will courts do in a situation in which a probationary teacher is not reappointed for complex reasons, some of which relate to competence and professional effectiveness, whereas others are in violation of First Amendment rights?

The Mount Healthy Case

Just such a question arose in Ohio where Mr. Doyle was not recommended for reappointment. When he sued,[20] the evidence indicated that, among other acts, he got into an argument with school cafeteria employees over the amount of spaghetti served him; that he made an obscene gesture to two girls in the cafeteria who disobeyed him; and that he referred to students, in connection with a disciplinary complaint, as "sons of bitches." Evidence also showed that in his capacity as president of the local teachers' association he had called a radio station concerning the principal's memorandum related to teachers' dress and appearance and how these might influence public support for a bond issue.

Granted that Doyle's communication with the radio station was a protected First Amendment activity if it played a "substantial part" in his nonrenewal, should he be reinstated with back pay? Although the District Court and the Court of Appeals so ruled, the U.S. Supreme Court disagreed.

A unanimous Court held that if the school board had sufficient legitimate grounds not to renew the probationary teachers' contract, the fact that protected conduct played a part, "substantial" or otherwise, will not protect the teacher. "A borderline or marginal candidate should not have the employment question resolved against him because of constitutionally protected conduct. But that same candidate ought not to be able, by engaging in such conduct, to prevent his employer from assessing his performance record and reaching a decision not to rehire on the basis of that record, simply because the protected conduct makes the employer more certain of the correctness of its decision."

In short, if there are adequate professional grounds not to renew the contract of a probationary teacher, the fact that the school board also included some wrong reasons in its decision will not save the teacher's job.

Initially, it is the probationary teacher's burden to show that his conduct was constitutionally protected, *and* that this conduct was a substantial or motivating factor in the board's decision not to hire him. Once this is shown, the board has the burden to prove by a "preponderance of the evidence that it would have reached the same decision . . . even in the absence of the protected conduct."

But what about untenured, probationary teachers who make no claims that some constitutionally protected conduct is the basis for their nonrenewal? Can such teachers claim a right to due process simply to find out why they are not being rehired? Can they have a hearing to show that they are competent teachers whose "liberty" or "property" rights are violated without due process of law?

The Roth Case

These are the questions raised by an assistant professor at a state university in Wisconsin.[21] Although this was a college level case, its principles have been applied with equal force to many situations in elementary and secondary schools.

When David Roth, a nontenured assistant professor, was informed that he would not be rehired for the next academic year, he brought suit. He claimed that his Fourteenth Amendment rights were violated because he was not given a notice and a hearing regarding the reasons for his nonrenewal. After examining the meaning of "liberty" and "property" in the Fourteenth Amendment, the Court concluded that the mere non-renewal of a contract, in the absence of other circumstances, does not violate one's "liberty" and does not diminish "property" rights, there being no basis to expect continued employment.

Are there circumstances in which such a teacher would have a right to a hearing? Yes, said the Court, where charges made against the teacher might seriously damage his standing and associations in the community, or so stigmatize him as to make it difficult to secure future employment. Thus, if in the course of the nonrenewal, the school casts a cloud over the teacher's "good name, reputation, honor or integrity . . . a notice and an opportunity to be heard are essential." Similarly, if charges of incompetence, racism, sexism, or other stigmatizing allegations are made as the grounds for the nonrenewal—charges that are likely to influence future possibilities of employment—then notice and a hearing are in order, because . . . "to be deprived not only of present government employment but of future opportunity for it is no small injury. . . ."

The Court specifically did not express an opinion whether or not public schools *should* give reasons, notice, and a hearing in nonretention cases. The wisdom of this is not a judicial matter. Rather, it is for legislatures and school boards to extend these opportunities for proba-tionary teachers; the courts' job is to interpret existing law and not to legislate new policy. Some states and some local boards have enacted laws and policies that provide some modicum of due process to probationary teachers; but these are typically minimal procedures, often nothing more than the right to be told the reasons for the nonrenewal, without any right to challenge those reasons. The main argument for not extending these rights is that the very purpose of a probationary period is to allow a substantial period for administrative discretion to evaluate teachers. Giving full due process rights to untenured teachers, it is claimed, would erase all differences between tenured and probationary teachers.

Of course, if a probationary teacher is terminated *during* the year covered by his contract, he has a right to due process because he has a property right to complete the contract. The foregoing cases relate to *nonrenewal* of a contract, not to terminating a teacher before completing the agreed-upon period of employment.

REDUCTION IN FORCE—("RIF"-ING)
After decades of expanding school enrollments and growing teaching force, the demographic picture of schooling has suddenly changed. Enrollments first leveled off and then began to decline. Many school

districts claimed* to have an oversupply of teachers under contract and sought ways of reducing the teaching force. School finance and other economic factors also influenced communities' efforts to reduce the number of teachers in their schools.

It has been generally understood and accepted that probationary teachers were vulnerable in times of enrollment decline and/or a financial exigency. But what of tenured teachers? Is tenure a protection against a falling enrollment, elimination of programs, or inadequate funds? During recent years these questions have been raised in many communities and are often discussed under the acronym of "RIF"-ing.

The Constitution does not apply to these situations directly. Since tenure is generally granted by state laws, provisions of such laws also specify the conditions under which tenured teachers may be dismissed. Decline in enrollment, termination of programs, or serious financial exigency are usually specified in state laws as grounds for terminating tenured teachers. Furthermore, courts have held that under such circumstances teachers could be terminated even if the state tenure laws were silent on the matter.[22] However, where financial exigency is claimed to be the grounds for terminating a tenured employee, the courts will carefully examine all relevant finances to determine if the reductions are necessary. The burden of proof is on the board to show that there is a financial exigency and that uniform and rational procedures are applied to carry out the reductions.[23]

Increasingly, collective bargaining agreements between teachers' organizations and school boards provide plans for a "uniform and rational" set of procedures to rely upon if local conditions make "reduction in force" unavoidable. Many cases have also gone to court related to dismissals and reassignments of various administrative personnel as school districts consolidate or undergo internal reorganization. In these situations, whenever an educator suffers demotion or salary loss, the principles of due process must be observed.

DUE PROCESS FOR STUDENTS

In this section we discuss some key cases that clarify the nature of fair procedures in student-related conflicts. Do students have a right to a hearing and to have lawyers represent them? Are there different requirements for fair procedures in serious offenses and in minor ones? Are school rules sufficiently clear and specific to provide workable standards for student conduct? Or are they vague and overly broad? All these concerns fall under due process.

*We use the term *claimed* because oversupply is always a function of the student-teacher ratio. A lower ratio in many school districts would eliminate the teacher surplus.

Fair Procedures

If one takes seriously the principle of *in loco parentis*, discussion of due process in the schools seems somewhat odd. For if teachers and administrators act in place of the parents while the child is at school, should we not expect the behavior of educators to be similar to that we find in homes? The concept of *in loco parentis* suggests that disciplinary matters in school are approached with a "guidance" attitude, with care and informality, and not with a legalistic or technical set of mind. In contrast, due process suggests a variety of formal, legalistic procedures that we are not likely to find in homes as parents and children negotiate the daily problems of life.

How many parents have formal hearings, with notice and an impartial judge, before they take Suzy's television privileges away for watching forbidden programs? How many parents grant Johnny a right to counsel before he is spanked for destroying Josi's favorite finger painting? If we do not expect due process in the home, and if we consider schools to be extensions of the home, why should we expect due process in the schools?

Reasoning similar to the above has led to the idea that children and youth *are* different from adults and should be treated differently when they do something adults consider wrong. High motives and enlightened impulses have led to a unique treatment of juveniles that was hoped would be fair and equitable. "The basic right of a juvenile is not to liberty but to custody. He has a right to have someone take care of him, and if his parents do not afford him this custodial privilege, the law must do so."[24]

The ideals embodied in the above quotation, however, have not worked in practice. In the field of juvenile justice, recent court opinions urge that some elements of due process must be accorded to children and youth as well as to adults. "Juvenile Court history has again demonstrated that unbridled discretion, however benevolently motivated, is frequently a poor substitute for principle and procedure.[25] In a leading case involving juvenile courts, the Supreme Court made the following statement on behalf of due process:

> Failure to observe the fundamental requirements of due process has resulted in instances, which might have been avoided, of unfairness to individuals and inadequate or inaccurate findings of fact and unfortunate prescriptions of remedy. Due process of law is the primary and indispensable foundation of individual freedom. It is the basic essential term in the social compact which defines the right of individuals and delimits the powers which the state may exercise.[26]

The *Gault* case, from which this quote was taken, involved a 15-year-old boy accused of using lewd words in an anonymous telephone call to a woman. Does it make sense to use the Court's words from a delinquency proceeding and apply it to the daily life of the school? When children get into a fight on the playground during recess, must due process be used in resolving the conflict? If a 16-year-old is suspected of cheating on a test by two student monitors or a teacher's aide, does due process require a hearing? When and how should the requirements of fair procedures be applied to school matters?

The Tibbs Case: Confronting Witnesses[27]

In Franklin, New Jersey, on October 7, 1970, two sisters were walking home after classes from high school, when they were assaulted by a group of students, mostly girls. They were struck with a stick, pushed to the ground and kicked, and some of their possessions were taken or scattered about. Both had minor injuries, and one had her glasses broken.

They ran back to the school guidance office, crying. Although they could not or would not identify the attackers, some other student witnesses identified about ten of the students involved in the attack, Tanya Tibbs among them. Tibbs claimed that she saw the attack, but did not participate. All ten students identified as the alleged attackers were suspended until an informal hearing was held, and the suspension was lifted from five. The other five were given further hearings and then expelled by the Board of Education.

Tibbs's parents were notified on October 27 that the Board of Education would meet on November 2 for a full hearing to consider the recommendation of the principal and superintendent that their daughter be expelled from school. They were told that they could be represented by an attorney, that the administrators would testify and could be cross-examined, that unsigned written statements of student witnesses would be presented (but that the students would not be there), and that Tibbs could present testimony or statements by witnesses on her behalf.

The hearing was postponed to November 9 at Tibbs's attorney's request. Her lawyer was informed that written statements by student witnesses would not be signed or identified. The administrators explained that the reason for the unsigned statement was that the witnesses feared retaliation if their identities were revealed. The principal testified that "he had received a telephone call from the mother of one of the accused students threatening the life of one of the prospective student witnesses." The situation was seriously aggravated by a history of racial conflict in the schools, and this was considered by the board in its acceptance of unsigned and unidentified statements by student witnesses.

The board found several students guilty, Tanya Tibbs among them. Thereafter, considering her prior poor disciplinary record, she was expelled from school. Her attorney "objected throughout the hearing to the failure to identify and produce and subject to cross-examination any of the accusing witnesses whose statements were read." On appeal to the commissioner of education, it was decided that the action of the local board satisfied due process and "that [the commissioner] was satisfied by the testimony of the principal that school officials had sufficient cause for concern regarding the safety of potential witnesses so as to justify not releasing the students' names or permitting their cross-examination."[28]

Questions to Consider

1. Do you think Tibbs was accorded due process? Were the school procedures fair and reasonable? Were there other ways to get the truth and also protect those who feared retaliation if they testified?
2. Should she or her attorney have had a right to face and cross-examine witnesses against her?
3. If you were a witness in such a racially tense situation, would you volunteer to testify?
4. Would your testimony be influenced by threats or anonymous phone calls attempting to intimidate you?
5. At what age would it be appropriate to have witnesses appear for cross-examination?
6. What procedures are required by due process? Would you require such procedures for *all* school-related offenses?

THE OPINION OF THE COURT

The New Jersey trial court ruled that Tanya Tibbs was not given sufficient due process. The opinion noted that earlier cases generally did not extend due process to school disciplinary cases, not even serious ones. However, with the increasing importance of formal schooling, "when the sanction applied for misconduct was expulsion or suspension of severe duration, especially in college-level cases, the decisions began to speak in terms of hearing requirements of due process."

In the case at hand, the decision for expulsion "constitutes deprivation of a most drastic and potentially irreparable kind. In that setting compromise with punctilious procedural fairness becomes unacceptable." The court recognized differences in the severity of punishment for various kinds of school disciplinary infractions. It stated that for the treatment of school problems in general, formal "due process" is not required. Teachers and administrators must live with those daily problems, and they are best suited to take care of them. However, if the alleged violation is serious enough to bring about long periods of suspension or expulsion, the law requires that school officials follow more careful procedures. High among these procedures is the right to confront and cross-examine witnesses, whenever the decision turns on questions of fact.

> Cross-examination of school children witnesses in proceedings like these should, however, be carefully controlled by the hearing officer or body, limited to the material essentials of the direct testimony, and not be unduly

protracted. Such a proceeding is decidedly not in the nature of a criminal trial nor to be encrusted with all the ordinary procedural and evidential concommitants of such a trial.[29]

Concerning the fears of student witnesses the court noted: "The school community must be content to deal with threats or intimidation of the kind allegedly encountered by invoking the jurisdiction of the law enforcement authorities who must be presumed equal to their responsibilities."

The Goldwyn Case: The Right to Counsel?

Marsha Goldwyn was a senior at Flushing High School in New York. At the beginning of the New York State Regents Examination, yellow scrap paper was distributed with the test papers. During the examination the proctor saw Goldwyn referring to "a piece of scrap paper containing notes on both sides." The paper was confiscated, and after the examination Marsha was taken to the principal's office. According to the acting principal's affidavit:

> Since it seemed impossible for Marsha to have written the notes as she said in a half hour at the beginning of the examination, I challenged her, not to duplicate this feat but just to copy over the notes as fast as she could on the same kind of 6 × 9 paper. In twenty minutes she had not succeeded in copying one-quarter of her notes. . . . I questioned Marsha again and she finally admitted to the cheating, whereupon I tore up her original statement and gave it back to her asking her for a written statement of her new story. This she gave me. All through this Marsha was in a highly excited, emotional state and in tears.[30]

The next-day Goldwyn recanted her confession. However, shortly thereafter, Regents Examination privileges were withdrawn from Goldwyn for a year; after this, if her behavior were exemplary, "consideration will be given to the recommendation of the principal that these privileges be restored."

Marsha Goldwyn's parents retained a lawyer, who complained to the Board of Education that serious punishment was imposed on Marsha without "even a semblance of a hearing." Following this the assistant superintendent suggested a conference that the lawyer could attend, but only as an observer. A lawsuit was brought challenging the procedures that denied Goldwyn the right to be represented by her lawyer.

Questions to Consider

1. Should students have a right to be represented by lawyers in conflicts involving school matters?
2. Can the schools function efficiently if all conflicts with students merit full procedural safeguards?

3. What kinds of conflicts should require more complete procedures and what kinds less?
4. Should we distinguish elementary and secondary schools from colleges in regard to procedural safeguards?

THE OPINION OF THE COURT

The court in part relied on the reasoning of the U.S. Supreme Court in the *Gault* decision,[31] in which procedural due process was required for a 15-year-old youth charged with delinquency before a juvenile court. In that case the high court ruled that the state may not act arbitrarily and without regard for the individual rights of a child.

In the *Goldwyn* case the school officials argued that theirs was but an administrative proceeding, not a criminal matter or a delinquency hearing; thus the same rules should not apply. The New York court disagreed. It saw no reason why fair treatment should not be afforded a student in an administrative hearing when "serious and stringent sanctions may be imposed." Clearly, the punishment in this case was significant. Serious consequences flow from the denial of a right to take the Regents Examination in the state of New York. The withholding of a high school diploma would affect employment opportunities as well as one's chance for scholarships and college entrance. In view of such severe consequences, the court ruled that the Board of Education had deprived Marsha of her right to a hearing "to ascertain the truth of the charges at which she might defend herself with the assistance of counsel."

The court explicitly recognized the difference between the Regents Examination and tests of lesser importance that are conducted almost daily in the schools. It expressed no opinion on what appropriate procedures are for dealing with students suspected of cheating on routine tests. For such situations the *Goldwyn* case would be a weak precedent.

The Dixon Case: Expulsion

A very significant decision in the due process area of students' rights is *Dixon* v. *Alabama State Board of Education.*[32] In this case a number of students were expelled from college for participating in a lunch counter sit-in and civil rights demonstration. When they were expelled without notice, hearing, or an opportunity to defend themselves, they went to court.

The *Dixon* decision, applying a "balancing test," set forth minimal requirements for due process concerning notice and hearing. Since *Dixon* is relied upon quite heavily by other courts, we quote it at length:

> For the guidance of the parties in the event of further proceedings, we state our views on the nature of the notice and hearing required by due process prior to expulsion from a state college or university. They should, we think,

comply with the following standards. The *notice* should contain a statement of the specific charges and grounds which, if proven, would justify expulsion under the regulations of the Board of Education. The nature of the hearing should vary depending upon the circumstances of the particular case. The case before us requires something more than an informal interview with an administrative authority of the college. By its nature, a charge of misconduct, as opposed to a failure to meet the scholastic standards of the college, depends upon a collection of the facts concerning the charged misconduct, easily colored by the point of view of the witnesses. In such circumstances, a hearing which gives the Board or the administrative authorities of the college an opportunity to hear both sides in considerable detail is best suited to protect the rights of all involved. This is not to imply that a full-dress judicial hearing, with the right to cross-examine witnesses, is required. Such a hearing with the attending publicity and disturbance of college activities, might be detrimental to the college's educational atmosphere and impractical to carry out. Nevertheless, the rudiments of an adversary proceeding may be preserved without encroaching upon the interests of the college. In the instant case, the student should be given the names of the witnesses against him and an oral or written report on the facts to which each witness testifies. He should also be given the opportunity to present to the Board, or at least to an administrative official of the college, his own defense against the charges and to produce either oral testimony or written affidavits of witnesses in his behalf. If the hearing is not before the Board directly, the results and findings of the hearing should be presented in a report open to the student's inspection. If these rudimentary elements of fair play are followed in a case of misconduct of this particular type, we feel that the requirements of due process of law will have been fulfilled.[33]

Does the *Dixon* case apply to high school? It probably does. Although the U.S. Supreme Court has never ruled directly on the expulsion of public school students, it has cited *Dixon* with approval on several occasions.* In addition, several other courts, both federal and state, have relied on *Dixon* and extended due process rights to high school students.

Thus the general rule is that in serious disciplinary matters students have a right to due process. But what does due process entail? Even the *Dixon* case indicated that a "full-dress judicial hearing" is not *necessary* in all situations. The following complete standards have been *suggested* by Robert Ackerly for infractions that could result in serious penalties, such as an expulsion or long-term suspension:

1. Notice of hearing, including
    a. the time and place
    b. a statement of the alleged infraction(s)
    c. a declaration of the student's right to legal counsel
    d. a description of the procedures to be followed in the hearing

*See, for example, *Tinker* at 506, fn 2.

2. Conduct a hearing, including
   a. advisement of student's right to remain silent
   b. the presentation of evidence and witnesses against the student
   c. cross-examination of the accusatory evidence
   d. the presentation of witnesses on behalf of the student
   e. the recording (either by tape or in writing) of the proceedings
3. Finding(s) of hearing, including
   a. recommendation(s) for disciplinary action, if any
   b. reporting of findings to appropriate school authorities (e.g., the Board of Education) and to the student
4. Prompt application of disciplinary measure(s), if any, including the right to appeal.[34]

These suggestions are a model for serious disciplinary cases, but they are rarely adopted in their entirety by courts or school authorities.

Goss v. *Lopez:* Suspension and Due Process

Courts have generally recognized that a student has a right to notice and a hearing prior to expulsion or long-term suspension. However, it has not been clear whether a student is entitled to such rights prior to a relatively short suspension. The *Goss* case[35] addressed this issue.

During the 1970–1971 school year, Dwight Lopez and a number of other students were suspended from various schools in Columbus, Ohio, without receiving a hearing. Some were suspended for documented acts of violence, whereas others, like Lopez, were suspended although they claimed to be innocent bystanders of demonstrations and disturbances; no evidence was presented against them, and they were never told what they were accused of doing. Lopez and others, who were suspended for up to ten days, claimed that such punishment without a hearing violated their right to due process of law. A federal district court agreed and the administrators appealed to the U.S. Supreme Court. In a 5 to 4 opinion, the Court ruled on a number of issues that are important to students, teachers, and administrators.

Justice White, writing for the majority, first highlighted the holding of the *Tinker* case, that "young people do not 'shed their constitutional rights' at *the schoolhouse door.*" Then, in extending the holding of *Tinker*, he explained that although the Constitution may not require states to establish public schools, once they do, students have a "property" right in them which may not be withdrawn without "fundamentally fair procedures." The court went on to rule that due process is required even in the cases of short suspensions. A suspension for up to ten days is not so minor a punishment that it may be imposed "in complete disregard of The Due Process Clause," wrote Justice White. "The total exclusion from the educational process for more than a trivial period is a serious event in the life of the suspended child." This is particularly so if the misconduct is recorded in the students' file and is likely to damage his standing with teachers and "interfere with later opportunities for higher education and employment." The opinion suggests that even a suspension for one day merits some modicum of due process.

Questions to Consider

1. Does the *Goss* case turn schools into courtrooms?
2. Does the case place undue burdens on administrators?
3. How can emergencies be handled if the law requires a notice and hearing?

Once the requirement for due process was established, the question still remained as to what process was due the accused students? The Court noted that due process has never required a rigid set of procedures to be applied in all situations; it is a flexible and practical concept. At the very minimum, however, students facing suspension . . . "must be given *some* kind of notice and afforded *some* kind of hearing."

Before being suspended for ten days or less, it is required: "that the student is given oral or written notice of the charges against him and, if he denies them, an explanation of the evidence the authorities have and an opportunity to present his side of the story." Since our basic concern is with fairness, fair procedures, according to the Court, "requires at least these rudimentary precautions against unfair or mistaken findings of misconduct and arbitrary expulsion from school." Clearly, these minimal requirements do not introduce legal technicalities into the schools, technicalities that many of us associate with due process applicable to out-of-school criminal procedures. The *Goss* ruling does not place any more burden on schools than fair-minded educators have themselves accepted and practiced for many years before *Goss*.

The Court also recognizes that emergencies occur in schools where lives and property are endangered. Prior notice and a hearing would not be required in such situations and the law requires only that fair procedures be followed "as soon as practicable" after removal of the danger or disruption.

As indicated above, *Goss* was a close decision (5 to 4) with a strong dissent by Justice Powell. He argued that judges should not interfere with the daily operation of the schools and he disagreed that suspension for a single day threatens any basic constitutional right. His main fear, however, was that the majority opinion would encourage countless lawsuits, related to every routine problem of schooling, including grading, promotions, and classroom assignment. He wanted to have all such matters, including those related to suspensions, referred to the state legislatures, school boards, and educators.

The majority opinion makes it clear, however, that the law does not require elaborate or time-consuming formalities in disciplinary situations that might lead to short suspensions. According to Justice White, "In the great majority of cases the disciplinarian may informally discuss the alleged misconduct with the student minutes after it has occured." The Court sought a balance between the social interest entailed in conducting an effective and efficient school on the one hand and the rights of students on the other.* "It would be a strange disciplinary system," observed Justice White, if an educational institution did not try to inform a student of his misconduct and "let him tell his side of the story in order to make sure that injustice is not done."

The due process requirements of *Goss* have been held to apply when students are transferred from one school to another for disciplinary reasons[36] as well as to suspensions for a three-day period.[37]

The Meyers Case: Freedom from Vague Rules

Fifteen-year-old Gregor Meyers, a student at Arcata High School in California, was suspended because he had long hair. Through his mother, acting as legal guardian, he brought suit against the school authorities for reinstatement.

Meyers had been suspended because the length of his hair violated a portion of the school's "dress policy." This policy, which every student received as part of a *Student Handbook,* read as follows:

> Campus Clothes—Extremes of dress and personal appearance are not conducive to the well being of all. Simplicity, neatness, cleanliness, and good taste are the keynote for school dress. Excessive tightness in clothes as well as extremes in shirt tails and similarly, *extremes in hair styles are not acceptable.*
>
> Girls shall wear skirts and blouses or sweaters or appropriate dresses. Girls (sic) clothes shall fit properly and be in current taste and style.
>
> Boys shall wear conventional slacks or jeans properly adjusted. Shirts shall be buttoned to within one button of the collar. Shirt tails with a square cut or with a soft curve designed for outer wear and in good taste are acceptable wear.
>
> Extremes in dress, in style, and in individual taste are to be avoided.[38]

The grooming rules were to be enforced by the principal or a person designated by him. In practice, he delegated his authority to the vice-principal and the physical education staff who screened the students and identified extremes in hair styles. The vice-principal testified that "he regarded 'extremes of hair styles' as meaning 'deviation from acceptable wear,' and that 'extremes' meant 'deviations' which were not acceptable to him." The vice-principal, as well as teachers, testified that "extremes of

---

*It should be noted in this regard that state statutes often provide procedural rights in addition to those derived from constitutional principles.

hair styling" became focal points for discussion and attention and tended to interfere with classroom learning. On the other hand, Meyers claimed that the regulation was too vague and indefinite and was therefore unconstitutional.

Questions to Consider

1. Do you think that a regulation prohibiting "extremes in hair styles" is too vague? Or do you think that it is sufficiently clear and that it can be understood by most people?
2. Can schools be administered if all policies and regulations must be highly specific?
3. Could you formulate a regulation concerning hair styles that would be clear and specific? Could you formulate such a rule regarding cleanliness, punctuality, or dress standards?

THE OPINION OF THE COURT

In its opinion the California court first recognized that both long hair and beards are entitled to protection as symbolic speech. For such protection, "adulthood is not a prerequisite: the state and its educational agencies must heed the constitutional rights of all persons, including school boys." However, it is also clear that school authorities may impose more limitations upon the rights of minors than upon those of adults. These limitations, however, must stand certain tests:

1. The regulation must rationally relate to an educational function.
2. The public benefits produced by the regulation must outweigh the impairment of the students' constitutional rights.
3. There must be no alternative "less subversive" of the students' rights.

Justice Rattigan for the California Supreme Court explained that the board policy against extreme hair styles failed to meet the requirements of the third test stated above. The regulation was too vague. Since the right to wear one's hair according to one's choice was considered by this court to be protected by the First and Fourteenth Amendments, "in this area, the standards of permissible statutory vagueness are strict and government may regulate 'only with narrow specificity.' "*

The student handbook was not describing facts in its prohibition of "extremes in hair styles." What was extreme was determined by the subjective appraisal of a single school official, the vice-principal. He alone could decide what was acceptable and what was a "deviation." "A 'law' violates due process 'if it is so vague and standardless that it leaves the

---

*The court focused on criterion three without much attention to the first two. This does not necessarily imply that the first two criteria were adequately met.

public uncertain as to the conduct it prohibits or leaves judges or jurors free to decide, without any legally fixed standards, what is prohibited and what is not in each case.'" The "dress policy" in this instance was faulty because it was vague and without clear standards.

Could it be argued that the policy was not a law and therefore not subject to the same requirement? The court simply noted that whereas the "dress policy" is not a law in the same sense as a criminal law, its violation does bring on suspension from school. "The importance of an education to a child is substantial, and the state cannot condition its availability upon compliance with an unconstitutionally vague standard of conduct."

Thus the court struck down the "dress policy" of Arcata High School since the "words 'extremes of hair styles' conveyed no commonly understood meaning, and whether one such style at Arcata High School was 'extreme' was neither determinable nor predictable by anyone except the vice-principal."

A DISSENT

Although the majority of the court struck down the wording of "extremes of hair styles" as overly vague, Judge Christian disagreed. He argued that the day-to-day management of schools should be left to teachers and administrators as long as they acted reasonably. He noted the "almost infinite variety of disciplinary concerns which may arise in a public school: personal sanitation, dress, disorder in the passageways, disruptive speech or conduct in class, and use of bicycles or motor transport, to name a few." Pursuing the requirement of specificity to an absurd degree, he asked: "Must a school specify in a written regulation the minimum allowable frequency of baths before a teacher may require a student to be clean? What kind of specific regulation is required to enable teachers to restrain disruptive speech in classrooms or movement in passageways?" He would leave all such matters to the reasonable control of teachers acting informally and without the technicalities of specific regulations. "So long as the teacher acts reasonably, the Constitution does not require him to work in an atmosphere of litigious contest with any juvenile sea-lawyer who may appear in his class."[39] Although in this case Judge Christian's view was a minority opinion, it is a view that is accepted by many teachers, administrators, and parents.

The Sullivan Case: Overbreadth and Vagueness[40]

"The school principal may make such rules and regulations that may be necessary in the administration of the school and in promoting its best interests. He may enforce obedience to any reasonable and lawful command." This was the only written regulation of the Houston, Texas, school board on which the principal of Sharpstown Junior/Senior High School based his expulsion of Mike Fischer and Dan Sullivan for publishing an underground newspaper. The principal considered the publication of "Pflashlyte" not "in the best interest of the school."

Plaintiffs Sullivan and Fischer alleged that the regulation under which they were expelled was unconstitutional under the "void-for-vagueness" doctrine. Two aspects of this doctrine have been developed by the Supreme Court. The first is overbreadth and the second is vagueness. Under the first, we ask whether a regulation is too broad. "Could a reasonable application of its sanctions include conduct protected by the Constitution?" Second, is it too vague? A regulation "so vague that men of common intelligence must necessarily guess at its meaning and differ as to its application violates the first essential of due process."

The *Sullivan* court was convinced that in serious disciplinary matters, such as those that could result in expulsion or suspension, the fundamental elements of due process must apply. Essential to such due process is sufficient clarity and precision in rules to guide student conduct. In the words of the court:

> School rules probably do not need to be as narrow as criminal statutes, but if school officials contemplate severe punishment they must do so on the basis of a rule which is drawn so as to reasonably inform the student what specific conduct is proscribed. Basic notions of justice and fair play require that no person shall be made to suffer for a breach unless standards of behavior have first been announced, for who is to decide what has been breached?[41]

Applying these principles to the situation at hand, the federal district court found the Houston regulation both vague and overbroad.

> Little can be said of a standard so grossly overbroad as "in the best interests of the school." . . . It cannot be contended that it supplies objective standards by which a student may measure his behavior or by which an administrator may make a specific ruling in evaluation of behavior. . . . It patently "sweeps within its broad scope activities that are constitutionally protected free speech and assembly."[42]

In other words, the regulation was held void for two reasons: (1) because it was too vague to inform students what they could or could not do and (2) because it was so broad that many legitimate activities could fall under its prohibition. As a general rule, then, school policies, rules, and regulations that might bring on serious penalties must be fairly specific and sufficiently clear to inform students affected by them.

Summary and Conclusions

In this chapter we discussed various situations and principles related to due process rights of teachers and students. We have indicated that there is no single formula or set of specific steps that constitutes due process, or fair procedures. Thus the various states, and even school districts, may create different procedures that will satisfy the Constitution.

One of the most complete statements as to what constitutes fair procedure is to be found in the Supreme Court decision in *Goldberg* v. *Kelly*.[43] This case did not involve schools, but we believe the principles would apply to them. The Court indicated that "the minimum procedural safeguards . . . demanded by rudimentary due process" would include:

> The opportunity to be heard at a reasonable time and place.
> Timely and adequate notice giving details of the reasons for the proposed suspension or dismissal.
> An effective opportunity to defend oneself, including oral presentation of evidence and arguments.
> An opportunity to confront and cross-examine witnesses.
> The right to retain an attorney.
> A decision resting solely on the legal rules and evidence adduced at the hearing.
> A statement of the reasons for the determination and the evidence relied on.
> An impartial decision maker.

The above set of general principles would be used as guidelines whenever "life, liberty, or property" is in jeopardy as a consequence of state action. It has also been established in law that a teacher has a "property" right in his contract during the term of the contract and that an applicant for a teaching position has a "liberty" interest in attempting to secure a teaching job or in pursuing any other career. Although there is no right to a *specific* position, one may not be prevented from pursuing an occupation or even from trying to get a specific job without due process of law.

TEACHERS AND DUE PROCESS

It is well-established that tenured teachers have property rights in continuous employment. These rights may not be diminished or in any significant way altered without fair procedures. The laws or contracts that grant tenure generally specify the grounds for breaking tenure as well as the procedures to be followed in any attempt to dismiss tenured teachers. Courts respect and enforce such laws.

In the case of nontenured teachers, until recently there was much ambiguity and conflicting court rulings concerning their right to due process of law. In 1972 the Supreme Court handed down a landmark decision in the *Roth* case that established some guiding constitutional principles. The Court held that an untenured teacher does not have "a constitutional right to a statement of reasons and a hearing on the . . .

decision not to rehire him for another year." The majority emphasized its view that a probationary teacher does not have a property right to continued employment and he cannot claim that his "liberty" was violated without due process "when he is simply not rehired in one job but remains as free as before to seek another."

However, even *Roth* made it clear that if a teachers' reputation, honor, or integrity is damaged in the course of the nonrenewal, or if he is so stigmatized by the reasons for the nonrenewal as to impair his chances for future employment, notice and a hearing are in order to provide an opportunity to refute the allegations.

Furthermore, even nontenured teachers have due process rights, if the grounds for the nonrenewal relate to constitutionally protected activity, such as controversial expression, union activity, one's race, or sex.

In situations in which reduction in force is claimed as the grounds for dismissing teachers, the burden is on the school district to establish genuine need. This might be based on serious decline in enrollment, financial exigency, program elimination, or all these factors. Courts will scrutinize the evidence to insure that such reduction is genuine and not a subterfuge for breaking tenure.

INTERNAL PROCEDURES

Schools and school boards often provide their own internal procedures for handling disciplinary matters among teachers. This is often referred to as "academic due process." The courts tend to respect these internal procedures but will nonetheless scrutinize them for adequacy. Although the courts may impose higher standards of due process, failure by a board to follow its own rules and procedures provides the teacher with a strong claim that his rights have been violated. The same principle applies when collective bargaining contracts provide for procedural safeguards.

The requirement that a school board must follow its procedures applies to both tenured and untenured teachers, even where a board has not officially approved such rules and regulations. For example, in a case in which the board members were aware of a booklet setting forth rules and regulations and a tenured teacher was dismissed without the rules being followed, the court reversed the board and reinstated the teacher.

> It is the court's opinion that the Board should have complied with the procedures set out in the . . . booklet. Even though the booklet may never have had official approval by formal Board action, the members were well aware of its contents.
>
> The promulgation and distribution of the . . . booklet, with the apparent acquiescence and approval of the School Board, without informing those to whom it was distributed that it was not a binding document, when coupled with reliance on it, made the booklet one which should have been followed in terminating the contract. . . .[44]

Concerning procedural due process we can set forth five general rules:

1. A teacher may not be suspended, dismissed, demoted, reduced in compensation, or otherwise deprived of any professional benefit without a fair and open process if the action against him is brought because of his exercise of a constitutional right.
2. In the case of untenured teachers, when a question of professional competence and not a constitutional right is involved, some states by law grant the right to a fair process, whereas others allow the school boards to act unilaterally at their discretion.
3. In the case of untenured teachers, when only the question of nonrenewal of contract is involved, the Supreme Court has ruled that there is no constitutional right to procedural due process.
4. Untenured teachers have a right to due process if the dismissal proceedings stigmatized them and thus reduced their opportunities for further employment or in other ways damaged their honor, integrity, or reputation in the community.
5. Tenured teachers have full due process rights, because they have a property right in their continuous contract.

DUE PROCESS FOR STUDENTS

Until quite recently, teachers and administrators had very broad discretion in matters related to students. Very few people ever raised questions related to the fairness of school procedures, and courts preferred to stay out of controversies related to students. The doctrine of *in loco parentis* was widely accepted and gave educators almost unchecked powers over the school life of students.

In recent years, significant changes have taken place, changes that can be characterized as important gains in the due process rights of public school students. Rights related to schooling were preceded by a general statement in a Supreme Court ruling in the *Gault* case that extended due process protection to all juveniles accused of a crime. Although in-school offenses are seldom criminal matters, courts have increasingly come to recognize that important consequences often flow from school sanctions. Thus, some fair procedures are necessary before a students' "property" right to schooling or "liberty" interests in maintaining a good name and record can be in any way diminished.

In the landmark case of *Goss* v. *Lopez,* the Court made it clear that even short-term suspensions may not be imposed with complete disregard of due process. As a minimum, the student should be faced with the charges, the evidence against him, and, if he denies them, have an opportunity to present his side of the matter. Prior notice and hearing are not required in an emergency situation—one that might entail danger of significant harm to persons or property. School officials may take unilateral action in emergencies, but must follow it with fair procedures as soon as practicable.

Although relatively simple, informal procedures satisfy the law in situations that are likely to result in short suspensions, more serious matters require more extensive and formal procedures. If the alleged infraction might result in long-term suspension or expulsion, the requirements of due process become more rigorous. Although there is no fixed formula for what constitutes due process in serious matters in schools, courts generally require adequate notice, a hearing, the right to challenge the evidence and to cross-examine witnesses, representation by counsel, a fair tribunal, a written statement of the findings, and a right to appeal.

As part of fair procedures, courts have held that school policies or rules must not be too vague or overly broad. A rule that is vague, such as one prohibiting "extremes in hair style," does not provide a clear standard or criterion for students. Therefore, the students cannot predict how the rule will be applied. Overly broad rules, on the other hand, are unconstitutional because they might prohibit conduct otherwise protected by the Constitution. For example, a school policy giving power to the principal to make all rules necessary to promote the "best interest of the school" is overly broad.

In this chapter we focused on certain elements of due process. We have also seen that the principles of due process apply to issues treated elsewhere earlier in this book. Similarly, due process considerations loom large in our next chapter, where we present recent legal developments related to school discipline, locker searches, and school records.

NOTES

1. *Galvan* v. *Press*, 74 S. Ct. 737, 742, 347 U.S. 522 (1954).
2. *Meyer* v. *Nebraska*, 262 U.S. 390, 399 (1923).
3. *Greene* v. *McElroy*, 360 U.S. 474, 79 S. Ct. 1400 (1959).
4. *Cafeteria Restaurant Workers Union, Local 473* v. *McElroy*, 367 U.S. 886, 81 S. Ct. 1743 (1961).
5. *Wieman* v. *Updegraff*, 344 U.S. 183, 192 (1952).
6. *Kumph* v. *Wayne Community School District*, 188 N.W.2d 71 (1971).
7. See Myron Lieberman, "Why Teachers Will Oppose Tenure Laws," *Saturday Review* (March 4, 1972), 55–56.
8. For an excellent discussion of the advantages and disadvantages of the tenure system, see Byse, "Tenure and Academic Freedom," in S. Harris, ed., *Challenge and Change in American Education*, 1965, pp. 313–327.
9. See Frakt, "Non-Tenure Teachers and the Constitution," *Kan. L. Rev.* 27 (1969), 50–53.
10. *People ex rel. Fursman* v. *City of Chicago*, 278 Ill. 318, 116 N.E. 158 (1917), p. 325.

11. *Pred* v. *Board of Public Instruction*, 415 F.2d 851, 852 (5th Cir. 1969).
12. Id. at 865.
13. *Slochower* v. *Board of Higher Education*, 350 U.S. 551, 555 (1956).
14. *Wiemann* v. *Updegraff*, 344 U.S. 183, 191 (1956).
15. *Keyishian* v. *Board of Regents*, 385 U.S. 589, 603 (1967).
16. *Tinker* v. *Des Moines School District*, 393 U.S. 503 (1969).
17. Title 42 United States Code, Section 1983.
18. 162 F.2d 136 (1947).
19. *McLaughlin* v. *Tilendis*, 398 F.2d 287 (1968).
20. *Mount Healthy City School District Board of Education* v. *Doyle*, 429 U.S. 274 (1977).
21. *Board of Regents of State Colleges* v. *Roth*, 408 U.S. 564 (1972).
22. *Ehret* v. *Kulpment School District* 5 A.2d 188 (1939).
23. *Bignall* v. *North Idaho College*, 538 F.2d 243 (9th Cir. 1976).
24. *Ex parte Crouse*, 4 Whart. 9 (Sup. Ct. Penn. 1839); fn. 21 in *In re Gault*, 387 U.S. 1, 17 (1966).
25. *In re Gault* at 18.
26. Id. at 20–21.
27. *Tibbs et al.* v. *Board of Education of Township of Franklin*, 276 A.2d 165 (N.J. 1971); 284 A.2d 179 (N.J. 1971).
28. Id. at 168.
29. Id. at 170.
30. *Goldwyn* v. *Allen*, 281 N.Y.S.2d 899 (Sup. Ct. N.Y. 1967).
31. *In re Gault*, 387 U.S. 1 (1967).
32. 294 F.2d 150 (5th Cir. 1961).
33. Id. at 159.
34. Robert L. Ackerly, *The Reasonable Exercise of Authority*, Washington, D.C.: National Association of Secondary School Principals, 1969, pp. 14–16.
35. *Goss* v. *Lopez*, 419 U.S. 565 (1975).
36. *Everett* v. *Marcase*, 426 F.Supp. 397 (E.D. Penn. 1977).
37. *Hillman* v. *Elliott*, 436 F.Supp. 812 (W.D. Va. 1977).
38. *Meyers* v. *Arcata Union High School District*, 75 Cal Rptr. 68 (1969).
39. Id. at 78.
40. *Sullivan* v. *Houston Independent School District*, 307 F.Supp. 1328, 1345 (S.D. Tex. 1969).
41. Id. at 1344, 1345.
42. Id. at 1345, 1346.
43. 38 U.S.L. Week 4223, March 24, 1970.
44. *Johnson* v. *Angle*, U.S.D.C., Nebraska, No.71-L-222, November 5, 1971.

Chapter 13
Discipline, Unauthorized Searches, and School Records

Not only have the school authorities the right to inspect (school lockers) but this right becomes a duty when suspicion arises that something of an illegal nature may be secreted there.

—*People* v. *Overton*

Survey after survey indicates that discipline in schools ranks first among school-related concerns in the minds of parents and teachers alike. Much has been written about it in both professional and popular magazines and books, yet controversy still abounds. In this chapter we examine the legal aspects of school discipline, the unauthorized search of student lockers and personal belongings, and rights related to school records.

SCHOOL DISCIPLINE

As a general principle, local school authorities may adopt reasonable rules and regulations related to the effective and efficient conduct of the schools. While attending school, educators stand *in loco parentis* to the students. This means that teachers and administrators have the authority to direct, to control, and to discipline students as a parent would at home. This general principle has been and still is important in court determination of reasonableness of punishment. That is, under similar circumstances, would it be reasonable for parents to use the particular punishment used by the school?

Punishment must be reasonable, but the question of reasonableness is always related to the facts of a situation. It must be related to a legitimate educational purpose and not be merely an expression of teacher frustration, anger, or malice. The severity of the punishment should be proportionate to the gravity of the offense and should consider the ability of the child to sustain it. Therefore, the size, age, sex,* and the physical and emotional condition of the student must be considered. Historically, disciplinary practices have been controlled by state statutes or common law principles and it was always understood that punishment must never be cruel or excessive. In recent years, questions have been raised challenging the constitutionality of *any* corporal punishment.

The Ingraham Case: Excessive Punishment

James Ingraham and Roosevelt Andrews, eighth and ninth grade students in Miami, Florida, were severly punished during the 1970–1971 school year. Andrews was beaten for some minor infractions of the rules and Ingraham because he was slow in answering a teacher's questions. At the time of the incident many schools in Dade County used corporal punishment and a Florida law prohibited only punishment that was "degrading or unduly severe" or that took place without prior consultation with the principal or the teacher in charge of the school. County school board policies even prescribed the dimensions of the wooden paddle to be used on students' "buttocks."

Although the normal punishment was limited to one to five blows with the paddle, Ingraham received more than 20 while held over a table in the principal's office. The severe beating caused hematoma requiring medical attention, and he missed 11 days of school. The paddling Andrews received included being struck on his arms, thus depriving him of the use of an arm for a week.**

Questions to consider

1. Do you believe in the use of corporal punishment?
2. Do you believe paddling to be "cruel and unusual punishment" and therefore unconstitutional?
3. Do you believe excessive corporal punishment to be a violation of the Constitution?

---

*It would be interesting to speculate on the future impact of state Equal Rights Amendments on this principle.
**In this analysis we draw substantially on our earlier work, "Discipline and Due Process," *Update on Law-Related Education*, ABA Special Committee on Youth Education for Citizenship, Chicago, Ill. (Fall 1977).

Ingraham and Andrews filed suit in the Florida District Court against several administrators, charging that the severe paddling they received constituted cruel and unusual punishment in violation of the Eighth Amendment, as well as a deprivation of liberty without due process of law in violation of the Fourteenth Amendment. When the district court ruled against them and the court of appeals affirmed this judgment, the students appealed to the Supreme Court.[1]

Is corporal punishment cruel and unusual? To answer this question, the Court examined "the way in which our tradition and our laws have responded to the use of corporal punishment in public schools." It accepted the common law rule that "teachers may impose reasonable but not excessive force to discipline the child." The Court recognized this to be the prevailing rule today, and if "the force is excessive and unreasonable, the educator in virtually all states is subject to possible civil and criminal liability." Only New Jersey and Massachusetts have outlawed the use of corporal punishment in schools. Forty-eight states still authorize its use—21 by statute and 27 by court preservation of the common law rule. (More about the relevance of local law later.)

When is the punishment reasonable and when excessive? All the circumstances must be considered before this question can be answered, including the nature and "seriousness of the offense, the attitude and past behavior of the child, the nature and severity of the punishment, the age and strength of the child, and the availability of less severe but equally effective means of punishment."

After examining common law traditions, current state laws, and school practices, the Court considered the history of the Eighth Amendment and concluded that it does not apply to questions of discipline in public schools. The five-judge majority was satisfied that the original intent behind the Cruel and Unusual Punishment Clause was to control the punishment of criminals. Furthermore, Justice Powell asserted in the majority opinion, schoolchildren need no such protection because in addition to the possibility of civil and criminal suits that may be brought against those who exceed their authority, the very "openness of the public school and its supervision by the community afford significant safeguards against the kinds of abuse from which the Eight Amendment protects the prisoner."

The Court next examined the question of whether due process must precede corporal punishment. The Fourteenth Amendment prohibits any state deprivation of life, liberty, or property without due process of law, and Powell acknowledged that corporal punishment falls under one of these protected categories. He said that punishing a student or inflicting appreciable physical pain implicates the "liberty" interest protected by the amendment.

Granting that a protected interest is involved, the question still remained as to "What process is due"? To answer that question, the Court analyzed the individual interests involved, and the interests of the state in terms of the costs and burdens of additional safeguards.

As to the individual's interests, the Court argued that an ordinary paddling does not threaten any serious right nor cause any grievous loss. The majority then argued that the requirement of additional procedural safeguards would add a significant burden without corresponding benefits.

According to the majority, due process prior to corporal punishment would require "time, personnel and the diversion of attention from normal school pursuits," and educators might well abandon the use of such punishment to avoid the burden of complying with procedural requirements. The question of whether or not to continue corporal punishment in the school is for legislatures and school boards to decide, they argued, and it should not be the by-product of a court decision.

Thus the majority acknowledged that the additional procedural safeguards might marginally reduce the risks of violating a student's rights, "but would also entail a significant intrusion into an area of primary educational responsibility." It therefore ruled that common law remedies will suffice and that the Due Process Clause does not require notice and a hearing prior to administering corporal punishment.

FOUR JUSTICES DISAGREE

In a powerful dissenting opinion, Justice White, joined by Justices Brennan, Marshall, and Stevens, expressed his disagreement with the majority on both major issues: the applicability of the Cruel and Unusual Punishment Clause and the Due Process Clause.

White first considered the Eighth Amendment issue. An examination of the wording of the amendment, as well as its history, led him to conclude that it was meant to apply to all punishment, not only to criminal cases. To illustrate this point, Justice White used an extreme example, often quoted by critics of the decision: "If it is constitutionally impermissible to cut off someone's ear for the commission of murder, it must be unconstitutional to cut off a child's ear for being late to class."

Justice White and his fellow dissenters were not satisfied that the "openness" of public schools is sufficient protection against excessive punishment. Furthermore, they were convinced that if a punishment is barbaric and inhumane, openness to the public and the availability of other remedies do not make it constitutional. White emphasized that he was not suggesting that corporal punishment in the public schools is always a violation of the Eighth Amendment. Rather, he took issue with the view that "corporal punishment in the public schools, no matter how barbaric, inhumane, or severe, is never limited by the Eighth Amendment."

Justice White and the other dissenters also argued the need for due process before corporal punishment. According to them, a key purpose of the due process provision is to protect an individual from erroneous or mistaken punishment that society would not have inflicted had the facts been examined in a more reliable way.

The majority was satisfied that a misuse of corporal punishment could be cured by a subsequent suit for damages or by criminal action. The dissenters, however, contended that "the infliction of physical pain is final and irreparable; it cannot be undone in a subsequent proceeding." They also noted that state laws (including those of Florida) are often inadequate to help students wrongfully punished. Furthermore, they argued that the *Goss* case (discussed in Chapter 12) provides for fairly simple due process requirements that would not be unduly burdensome and time consuming to administer.

In short, the dissent argued that although ordinary corporal punishment does not violate a student's "liberty" interests, excessive or unreasonable punishment does and therefore is protected by the Cruel and Unusual Punishment Clause of the Eighth Amendment. Moreover, the dissenters would require at least some modicum of due process before administering any corporal punishment in public schools.

The Hall Case: A Different Issue

The U.S. Court of Appeals of the Fourth Circuit took a different approach to corporal punishment in a 1980 case. It ruled that excessive corporal punishment might be a violation of "substantive due process." The right to bodily security should not be violated by the state through "brutal, demeaning, and harmful" ways. The court reasoned that the right to such security is a fundamental aspect of personal privacy and is "an attribute of the ordered liberty that is the concern of substantive due process."[2]

Thus, although corporal punishment may not require prior procedural due process and although it may not violate the Eighth Amendment prohibition against cruel and unusual punishment, excessive punishment might violate substantive due process rights embodied in the Fourteenth Amendment.

The Baker Case: Parental Objection

May parents object to corporal punishment in schools? May they exempt their children from such punishment?

Such requests can be made, but schools are not always bound by them. Some states, such as California, have laws that provide for prior written parental approval before corporal punishment may be administered. In the absence of such state law, schools do not have to get approval from parents. In fact, the *Baker*[3] case went further and allowed the school use of corporal punishment over parental objection.

Mrs. Virgina Baker of North Carolina had requested that her son not be spanked or paddled because she opposed such practice in principle. Nevertheless, her sixth grade son was spanked after he violated an announced school rule against throwing balls during certain times. Although the law of North Carolina allows the use of reasonable force "to restrain or correct pupils and to maintain order," Mrs. Baker claimed the law was unconstitutional because it allows such punishment over parental objections. In ruling against her the Court recognized that parents have the basic right to supervise the upbringing of their children, but the Court also recognized "the state's legitimate and substantial interest in maintaining order and discipline in the public schools." Furthermore, since both popular and professional opinions are divided on the question of using corporal punishment, the Court refused to allow "the wishes of a parent to restrict school officials' discretion in deciding the methods to be used in . . . maintaining discipline."

Comments and Related Cases

As indicated before, excessive punishment by teachers or administrators is not protected. Even where corporal punishment is allowed by state law, students can sue for injuries received in the course of such punishment. An Illinois court, for example, acknowledged "the right of a teacher to inflict corporal punishment in the process of enforcing discipline"; but it emphasized that: "he may not wantonly or maliciously inflict corporal punishment and may be guilty of battery if he does so."[4] In this case a teacher struck a 15-year-old boy several times while on duty to keep the crowd away from a fence at a football game.

In a similar case in Tennessee, a district court ruled that a teacher might be liable for damages if the student's injuries were proven to be serious or if the teacher's punitive action was motivated by racial prejudice. In the Tennessee case, it was alleged that the teacher jerked the chair out from under the student in a study hall, causing him injuries and humiliation in the presence of fellow students.[5]

If the state law and board policy allow corporal punishment, there is a presumption that the person who administered it acted reasonably. However, this presumption can be overcome by showing malice or excessive use of force. Whether or not the educator acted out of malice or used too much force is always a question of fact. Medical reports, photographs, statements made in anger, and injuries to the student are useful evidence in trying to prove malicious or excessive force. In such instances the person who abused his limited power to administer punishment may be liable to prosecution for assault and battery as well as for money damages.

Teachers can also be dismissed for violating accepted laws or regulations related to corporal punishment. A New York court, for example, upheld the dismissal of a tenured teacher on grounds of insubordination and the physical abuse of students when the teacher did not adhere to policies and instructions regarding corporal punishment.[6] And in Illinois a sixth grade teacher was fired for using an electric cattleprod as a disciplinary tool.[7] The Illinois law specified "cruelty" as a ground for dismissal of tenured teachers.

The Relevance of State and Local Law

The *Ingraham* case established the proposition that, as a general principle, corporal punishment does not violate the *federal Constitution*. But most of the law related to school discipline is not federal law; it derives from the various state constitutions, laws, and local board regulations, with significant variations among the 50 states.*

In general, the state laws specify the conditions under which serious punishment may be inflicted on public school students. Some states, like Massachusetts and New Jersey, forbid all physical punishment in their public schools. Others, like Montana or Florida, specify the conditions for its administration. Where states permit such punishment, local districts may still choose to ban it. Such prohibitions currently exist in many cities, including New York, Chicago, Washington, D.C., and Pittsburgh.

Expulsion, suspension, or corporal punishment is typically controlled by state statutes. However, if local school authorities are sufficiently innovative and invent a new punishment not yet described in state law, the penalty must not be arbitrary, wholly disproportionate to the offense, or clearly unreasonable. In 1918 Miss Valentine was to be denied her high school diploma for refusing to wear a cap and gown to graduation "by reason of the offensive odor emanating therefrom due to a recent fumigation through the use of formaldehyde by the city health authorities.[8] The Supreme Court of Iowa held that the punishment had "no reasonable relation to educational values" and therefore was not within the authority of the school. She could be denied the right to participate in the graduation ceremony but not to her diploma. Her case illustrates the

---

*One must check the laws of each state as well as the policies and regulations of each school district. Such information is usually available from the office of the local school superintendent, and it is often published in a variety of handbooks.

general rule that school discipline and punishment should be reasonable and related to educational purposes.

Other Aspects of Discipline

School officials and boards have wide-ranging power to make and enforce rules and regulations related to the operation of schools. These powers are either expressly granted by state law or implied as necessary to carry out other educational responsibilities. Courts are reluctant to interfere with the daily operation of the schools and as long as disciplinary rules and procedures are reasonable and nondiscriminatory, judges are not likely to curb the discretionary powers of school officials.

A clear statement of this principle was handed down by a district court in Texas in April 1973. Upholding the long-term suspension of a student for consuming vodka on school grounds, which violated known school rules, the opinion stated these generally accepted principles:

> Among the things a student is supposed to learn at school . . . is a sense of discipline. Of course, rules cannot be made by authorities for the sake of making them but they should possess considerable leeway in promulgating regulations for the proper conduct of students. Courts should uphold them where there is any rational basis for the questioned rule. All that is necessary is a reasonable connection of the rule with the proper operation of the schools. By accepting an education at public expense pupils at the elementary or high school level subject themselves to considerable discretion on the part of school authorities as to the manner in which they deport themselves. Those who run public schools should be the judges in the business of running schools better. . . . Except in extreme cases the judgment of school officials should be final in applying a regulation to an individual case.[9]

If rules, however, are unreasonable, or if there is evidence of excessive punishment, malice, or discriminatory enforcement, the courts are likely to help.

PUNISHMENT FOR CONDUCT AWAY FROM SCHOOL

The law is not clear or uniform regarding discipline imposed by the school for conduct away from it. Early decisions tended to uphold the school officials, particularly if the student's conduct somehow related to the operation of the school. A Connecticut case in 1925, for example, noted: "The conduct of pupils outside of school hours and school property may be regulated by rules established by the school authorities if such conduct directly relates to and affects the management of the school and its efficiency."[10] Courts have reasoned this way under the *in loco parentis* doctrine. However, it is difficult to argue that doctrine when the parent and child are *both* suing the school over punishment administered for conduct while the child was away from school, namely at or near his home.

"DOUBLE JEOPARDY"?

If a student's conduct in or away from school gets him in trouble with the civil authorities, may the school also impose discipline for the same acts? Or is that double jeopardy?

The common-sense notion of double jeopardy is that people should not have to pay twice for the same wrongdoing or mistake. This is an oversimplification of a technical legal concept that was developed in criminal law. In brief, double jeopardy means that a person should not be tried in criminal court more than once for the identical offense.

One can, however, be held liable in both a criminal proceeding and a civil suit for the same behavior. For example, if you drive a car under the influence of alcohol and injure Ms. X, you can be sued by Ms. X for money damages, and the state may prosecute you for drunken driving in a separate action. You may not plead double jeopardy as a defense to the suit by Ms. X because you have already been convicted by the state. Similarly, the teacher who uses excessive force in disciplining a child might be liable for money damages for injuries inflicted, and he also might be prosecuted for assault and battery in a criminal action.

The Howard Case[11]

In March 1969 Robert T. Howard, III, and Douglas Herman were arrested by the police and charged with the "criminal possession of a hypodermic instrument." The arrested high school students were reported to possess some heroin at the time of the arrest. A week later, New Rochelle High School, New York, suspended the two students. The superintendent relied on a Board of Education regulation requiring the suspension of a student "upon his indictment or arraignment in any court . . . for any criminal act of a nature injurious to other students or school personnel."

In this case, as in countless other lawsuits, the court avoided the constitutional issues and based its decision on state law.* The statute, Education Law Section 3214(6)(a), provided that school authorities may suspend a minor from attending school in the following circumstances:

(1) A minor who is insubordinate or disorderly;
(2) A minor whose physical or mental condition endangers the health, safety, or morals of himself or of other minors.

---

*The judicial preference to avoid facing constitutional questions whenever the case can be decided on other grounds is almost universal in our courts.

Did the possession of hypodermic needles and heroin, away from the school, satisfy the conditions of (1) and (2) above? The court ruled in the *Howard* case that it did not. In the words of Judge Grady: "While the *use* of heroin by students off the high school premises bears a reasonable relation to, and may endanger the health, safety and morals of other students, the bare charges against petitioners of *possession* of heroin do not justify suspension on the grounds set forth in section 3214(6)." Thus the court ruled that the school exceeded the powers conferred upon it by state law. Furthermore the court ordered the school to expunge the suspension from the school records.

In this case the students could not be disciplined by the school for alleged criminal behavior away from school. However, the court indicated that although the *mere possession* of heroin away from school could not be grounds for suspension, the *use* of it, even away from school, could be if it were shown to affect other students or the in-school behavior of the users. No double jeopardy issue is involved even though the same behavior would bring on punishment by the civil authorities as well as disciplinary action in the school.

The *Howard* case exemplifies how strictly some judges interpret state laws that grant powers to school officials. It is probable that there are judges in other courts who would have ruled against these students on these same facts. The point is that neither outcome would be vulnerable to the claim of double jeopardy.

An advanced view reflected in few judicial opinions is advocated by the American Civil Liberties Union, and it appears to be consistent with the *Howard* ruling.

> When a student chooses to participate in out-of-school activities that result in police action, it is an infringement of his liberty for the school to punish such activity, or to enter it on school records or report it to prospective employers or other agencies, unless authorized or requested by the student. A student who violates any law risks the legal penalties prescribed by civil authorities. He should not be placed in jeopardy at school for an offense which is not concerned with the educational institution.[12]

Notice that even the ACLU recommendation would permit school disciplinary action for out-of-school violations of law that have demonstrable consequences within the school.

GRADES AND DISCIPLINE

Teachers have been known to lower a student's grade in a course as a disciplinary measure. Schools have also been known to withhold a diploma, prevent or postpone graduation, or even refuse to supply a transcript as punishment for the breaking of school rules. These practices seem to be quite unfair and unreasonable to many people; others urge their use and argue that they are legitimate means to discipline students, keep them learning, and prepare them for responsible citizenship. Where do the courts stand on these issues?

As a general rule, courts will not enter disputes over grades between students and their teachers. Educators have wide discretion in evaluating the quality of student work, and the courts will not supervise the exercise of this discretion. However, if a student claims that his grade was lowered for nonacademic reasons or can show that the teacher acted maliciously or arbitrarily, he will get help from the courts. However, the burden of proof is on the student to establish that the grade received was not related to the quality of the work. This is difficult to prove, and there are no cases reported from elementary or high schools challenging the assignment of grades. But there have been cases involving college students in Florida and Vermont that support the idea that improper conduct or discipline problems may not legally affect academic grades.

High schools and elementary schools today tend to give separate evaluations for academic achievement and for conduct, or "citizenship." Report cards reflect this separation, and some districts even formalize the separation by writing it into policy. In New York, for example, the following is operative:

> Grades are estimates of academic achievement only. Pupils' behavior and attitude do not, in themselves, provide a legitimate basis for calculating grades. Evidences of excellence or deficiencies in character are to be recorded in other ways. . . . Continued absence or lateness should have an effect on the final grade only insofar as it affects actual achievement in the subject.[13]

One reason why it is important to separate academic from disciplinary matters is that courts tend to respect the educator's discretion in academic judgments; however, in alleged violations of school rules, they are more likely to require due process. Thus, by hiding a disciplinary punishment in a lowered grade, teachers can circumvent the constitutional requirement of due process.

Questions to Consider

1. If a grade reflects both achievement and effort, should not disruptive behavior lower the grade?
2. If citizenship training is a legitimate objective of schooling, is it not reasonable to withhold a diploma from students who defy authority and break rules?
3. What do you believe to be the proper relationship between grades, diplomas, graduation, and discipline problems? Why?

DIPLOMAS AND DISCIPLINE

Can students be prevented from participating in graduation ceremonies or receiving a diploma because of some misconduct in school?

We noted previously that as early as 1921 the Supreme Court of Iowa ruled that Miss Valentine, a high school girl who successfully completed all academic requirements but refused to wear a formaldehyde-laden gown to graduation, had a right to receive her diploma. Denying her the diploma had "no reasonable relation to educational values" and therefore was not within the authority of the school. She could not be denied her diploma although she could be excluded from the graduation ceremony.

By contrast, a New York court in 1971 ruled that a student who supposedly threatened and struck the high school principal during a school disturbance could not be barred from graduation exercises.[14] Since the alleged misconduct occurred earlier, and since there was no evidence that the student's presence at the graduation exercises would be disruptive, the court said that excluding her would not be "a reasonable punishment meant to encourage the best educational results. . . . It would indeed be a distortion of an educational process in this period of youthful discontentment to snatch from a young woman at the point of educational fruition the savoring of her educational success." There are several rulings by the New York State Commissioner of Education upholding students' rights to participate in graduation ceremonies in cases where schools attempted to bar them for reasons of pregnancy or for "lack of good citizenship."[15] Other than these, there are no court rulings adjudicating such issues. A due process argument can always be made if the proposed official action is unreasonable in that it has no clear connection to a valid educational propose.

Can the diploma be withheld as a disciplinary measure? The arguments would be similar to the ones proposed above. If a student has fulfilled all academic requirements, it does not seem reasonable to withhold from her the symbol of her accomplishment. Although there are no recent judicial decisions on this issue, a ruling of the chancellor of the New York City schools is instructive.

> Students who violate rules of conduct are subject to disciplinary measures, but the manipulation of a diploma is not a proper or legitimate disciplinary tool in view of the inherent difficulty in defining "citizenship" and the clear danger and impropriety of labeling students as "good" or "bad" citizens. The school system should award the diploma on the basis of carefully defined educational criteria, and not deny or delay the diploma on other than educational grounds or as a means of discipline. In brief, the school is empowered to grant diplomas, not citizenship.[16]

It appears, then, that whereas ordinary grading practices and common disciplinary procedures are within the discretionary powers of educators, extraordinary discipline will be scrutinized by the courts. Excessive measures or those not reasonably related to educational purposes are likely to be struck down as going beyond the authority of schools or as violative of due process. There is a dearth of cases in this area, but it can be suggested with caution that whatever new law exists tends to recognize the expanding rights of students.

UNAUTHORIZED SEARCHES

"A man's house is his castle" is a motto we inherited from the British. Our legal system has generally applied it to the protection of homes from unauthorized search by officials. Public authorities need either a person's consent or a valid court order (a search warrant) to legally search an individual's home, his car, the taxi he is using, the phone booth he temporarily occupies, or even a locker at a train station he is temporarily renting. Does such protection apply to the student's locker at school?

The Overton Case

At Mount Vernon High School, New York, police detectives showed a search warrant to the vice-principal and requested his assistance to search two students and their lockers. In Carlos Overton's locker they found four marijuana cigarettes.[17] It appeared, however, that the search warrant was defective; Overton therefore claimed that the entire search was illegal, invalidating the evidence found. The officials, on the other hand, claimed that the vice-principal consented to the search and that he had a right to do so. They contended that there was no unauthorized search, only one with consent and that therefore the evidence gained was properly used.

Questions to Consider

1. Who owns school lockers?
2. May school officals authorize outsiders to search student lockers?
3. Should authorities be allowed to search student lockers? Can you conceive of some situations in which they should be able to do so? Others in which they should not be able to do so?

THE OPINION OF THE COURT

Carlos Overton, through his lawyers, argued that the protection of the Fourth Amendment against unauthorized searches applies not only to dwellings but also to lockers and desks.* Furthermore, he argued that recent opinions of the Supreme Court have extended constitutional

---

*The Fourth Amendment protects "the right of the people to be secure in their persons, houses, papers, and effects against unreasonable searches and seizures."

protections to students as well as to adults. Thus, since *he* did not consent to the search and since the search warrant was not valid, the search violated his Fourth Amendment rights.

The officials, on the other hand, argued that even if the search warrant was defective, the vice-principal could give consent to search the locker. The court ruled in favor of this position and against the claims of Carlos Overton.

According to Judge Keating, whereas lockers, desks, or cars are also protected from unauthorized searches, there are situations in which someone else is empowered to give consent on your behalf. In this instance the vice-principal gave consent, and the court held that he had he power to do so. "The power of Dr. Panitz to give consent to this search arises out of the distinct relationship between school authorities and students."

The school authorities have an obligation to maintain discipline over students. It is recognized that when large numbers of teenagers are gathered together, their inexperience and lack of mature judgment can create hazards for each other. Parents who surrender their children to this type of environment, in order that the children may continue developing both intellectually and socially, have a right to expect certain safeguards.

The judge went on to discuss the peculiar susceptibility of teenagers to the use of illegal drugs, which places a special obligation on school authorities to investigate charges of possession of narcotics and to take remedial action.

Furthermore, at Mount Vernon High School, as in most schools in the country, the locker combinations were known to the office as well as to the student. Each student had exclusive use of the locker vis-à-vis other students but not in relation to the school authorities. "In fact, the school issues regulations regarding what may and may not be kept in the lockers and presumably can spotcheck to insure compliance." The vice-principal occasionally inspected the lockers.

The New York court went so far as to say that the school had the affirmative duty to retain control over the lockers as part of its overall obligation to supervise students. Thus, when the vice-principal learned of the detectives' suspicion, he had the power to consent to the search by the officials.

On appeal the New York Court of Appeals upheld the decision and specifically quoted this statement from Judge Keating:

> Not only have the school authorities the right to inspect but *this right becomes a duty when suspicion arises* that something of an illegal nature may be secreted there. When Dr. Panitz learned of the detectives' suspicion, *he was obligated to inspect the locker*. This interest, together with the nonexclusive nature of the locker, empowered him to consent to the search by the officers.[18]

Related Cases

State v. *Stein* involved a search of the locker of a high school student who was suspected of having committed burglary, fraud, and larceny.[19] The Supreme Court of Kansas agreed with the *Overton* ruling previously discussed. After recognizing that the status of school lockers "in the law is somewhat anomalous in that it is not like a dwelling, a car, or even a private locker," the court upheld the right of school officials to inspect them. In the words of the court:

> Although a student may have control of his school locker as against fellow students, his possession is not exclusive against the school and its officials. A school does not supply its students with lockers for illicit use in harboring pilfered property or harmful substances. We deem it a proper function of school authorities to inspect the lockers under their control to prevent their use in illicit ways or for illegal purposes. We believe this right of inspection is inherent in the authority vested in school administrators and that the same must be retained and exercised in the management of our schools if their educational functions are to be maintained and the welfare of the student bodies preserved.[20]

New York v. *Jackson*[21] presented an interesting situation related to students' Fourth Amendment rights. In this case, the high school coordinator of discipline received a tip from an informant suggesting that a student named André Jackson was involved with illegal drugs in the school. The coordinator found Jackson in a class and asked him to come with him to the office. Jackson nervously agreed. As they went toward the office, Jackson with a visible bulge in his pocket kept putting his hands there. When they approached the office, Jackson bolted and ran out of the school, with the coordinator in pursuit, yelling to a policeman assigned to the school, "He's got junk and he's escaping." Jackson was caught three blocks away and on him here was a syringe, eyedropper, and other "narcotics works." The policeman took the evidence.

In court, Jackson wanted to exclude the evidence, arguing that it was seized in violation of his constitutional right against unauthorized search and seizure. The New York Supreme Court ruled against Jackson, relying heavily on the doctrine of *in loco parentis*. The court held that school officials stand in place of the parents while children are in school and that their responsibility "did not end abruptly at the school door." By deciding to run out of the school, the student extended the coordinator's authority and responsibility beyond the school property.

Although law enforcement officials might need "probable cause" to secure a search warrant, the court reasoned school officials may act if they have "reasonable suspicion" that illegal or harmful materials are secreted by students. Because a school is a special environment and because school officials have the duty and responsibility to maintain a safe, healthy, and effective learning environment, less demanding criteria are applied by courts to searches conducted by school officials than those by law enforcement agents.

BODY SEARCH

Is there a difference between searching students' lockers or searching their clothing, purses, or even their bodies? Recognizing that the danger of invasion of privacy is greater in some searches than in others, courts have imposed higher standards when searches become more personal. For example, a 17-year-old student underwent a body search when he was observed entering a student bathroom with a fellow student, twice within an hour and exiting within a few seconds. He had been under observation for months on suspicion of drug dealing. Although the search revealed illegal drugs, the New York Court of Appeals excluded the evidence.[22]

The court indicated that a student may expect respect for the privacy of his person even where there are no reasonable expectations of privacy in his locker. As in other cases involving rights in conflict, the court sought a proper balance between "basic personal rights against urgent social necessities." It acknowledged that "the primary purpose of school searches may be to protect the school environment" and recognized the widespread use of drugs. However, the court concluded that even these considerations did "not permit random, causeless searches" that might result in "psychological damage to sensitive children" and expose them to serious consequences such as possible criminal convictions. Although the court gave no formula for determining when there is sufficient grounds for the search, or what constitutes "reasonable suspicion," factors to be considered are "the child's age, history and record in the school, the prevalence and seriousness of the problem in the school (and) the exigency to make the search without delay."

Belliner v. *Lund*[23] exemplifies an almost extreme example of body search in schools. It took place when $3 were reported missing from a coat pocket in a fifth grade classroom. The teacher, aware of prior complaints of "missing money, lunches, and other items," began a search of the class with the aid of other teachers and of school officials. The search, which proved fruitless when it began with coats, pockets, and shoes, ultimately led to the separation of boys and girls and their removal to respective restrooms where they were ordered to strip down to their undergarments and their clothes searched. A two-hour search never turned up the missing money.

In ruling against the school officials, the court noted that school officials need not establish probable cause before a search; however, it found the schools' actions excessive under the circumstances. Although there were facts to suspect that *someone* in the class might have taken the money, there were no facts that pointed suspicion to a *particular* student that would have made a specific search reasonable.

In general, courts tend to respect the discretion of school officials to conduct locker searches if there are reasons to suspect they contain illegal or dangerous materials. Random or arbitrary searches, even if announced in advance, are frowned upon. More personal searches require more substantial grounds because they entail greater invasion of privacy. The full protections of the Fourth Amendment do not apply to ordinary searches by school officials because they are not criminal proceedings, the evidence will not ordinarily be used in courts, and administrators must have some discretionary power to help maintain safe and efficient schools.

Where law enforcement enters the schools, courts increasingly require the use of search warrants. This tends to be the case whether the police act directly or indirectly by asking school officials to do the search and turn the evidence over to them. The "exclusionary rule," a rule developed by the Supreme Court that excludes from use illegally obtained evidence, is the key legal means for discouraging unauthorized searches in violation of the Fourth Amendment. Although not all courts exclude evidence gathered in warrantless or unauthorized searches in the schools, courts and school officials are increasingly sensitive to students' constitutional rights in their area. For example, a 1969 publication of the National Association of Secondary School Principals, entitled "The Reasonable Exercise of Authority," cautions principals against searching of a student's person, desk, or locker" except under extreme circumstances, unless permission to do so has been freely given by the student, the student's parent, and other competent witnesses are on hand.[24]

The Court of Appeals of the Second Circuit also ruled that "reasonable suspicion" might be sufficient for a locker search, but "probable cause" is necessary for highly invasive searches, such as a strip search. As when other clearly established students' rights are violated, the court may award money damages for illegal or unauthorized searches. In this case the district court's award of $7500 damages was upheld on appeal.[25]

SEARCH DOGS

In an unusual case, specially trained dogs were used by the police in a room-by-room search of a high school. In cooperation with school officials, a team of handlers led the dogs on a room-to-room inspection tour of the school while students were kept in their first period classes. Students singled out by the dogs were asked to empty their pockets or purses and some were even strip searched in the nurse's office. Of the 17 students caught with illegal drugs, 12 withdrew from school, 2 were suspended, and 3 expelled.

In a suit challenging the legality of the body searches and the use of dogs, the U.S. District Court ruled that the strip searches were illegal.

Although it saw nothing wrong with using dogs and with the request that students empty pockets and purses when indicated by the dogs' behavior, such "reasonable suspicion," in the opinion of the court, did not warrant a strip search. The court evoked the doctrine of *in loco parentis* to uphold administrative action in using the dogs, if school officials otherwise had reasonable suspicion of drug use in the schools. An interesting aspect of this case was a prior agreement between school officials and the police that any illegal drugs discovered during the search would not be used in criminal investigations or proceedings.[26]

RIGHTS RELATED TO SCHOOL RECORDS

The educational reasons for keeping records of students' progress were summarized by the National Education Association as follows: "Records are kept to assist the school in offering appropriate educational experiences to the student. The interest of the student must supersede all other purposes to which records might be put."

It would be difficult to argue with such a laudable statement. However, the gap between the ideal and the practice is often wide. What is usually in a student's cumulative record (often referred to as a "cum-folder")? Test scores, medical and psychiatric reports, guidance conference summaries, and teachers' comments? Information about a student's health and his parents' education and occupation? Do they contain comments about students such as "a very well adjusted boy," "a troublemaker," "a black militant," "a constructive worker," "disturbs class," "parents drink too much"?

Who has access to a "cum-folder"? Does the student or his parents? Can the local police or FBI see it? What about a prospective employer? Can derogatory information be removed from a folder? Does the Constitution have anything to say about school records?

The Van Allen Case

A faculty member told Mr. Van Allen that his son, a New York public school student, needed psychological treatment and therapy. Mr. Van Allen went to a private physician, who secured a written report from the school guidance personnel. In the meantime, the father requested that the school make all of his son's records, not just the guidance report, available for his inspection. The superintendent of schools refused the request.

The conflict was resolved through court interpretation of the laws of New York. The state law required the records to be kept by the school and to be available for inspection by persons with an *interest* in it. If these were strictly *public* records, then anyone could inspect them. In the eyes of the law, however, school records have an unusual status. They are not public records in the ordinary sense; yet where state law requires them to be kept, the school officials must keep them. Where the state law indicated that a person with an *interest* in then has a right to the records, it would be difficult to argue that parents do not have the requisite "interest." In the words of the court: "It needs no further citation of authority to recognize the obvious interest which a parent has in the school records of his child. We are therefore constrained to hold as a matter of law that the parent is entitled to inspect the records."[27]

STUDENT RECORDS AND THE RIGHT TO PRIVACY

Other cases could be cited, describing denial of access to the students' records to the students and their parents while granting access to others. Furthermore, countless instances could be cited of school records that contained highly questionable and inappropriate comments. For example, one father discovered by chance that his son's school records contained comments that the boy was "strangely introspective" in grade three, "unnaturally interested in girls" at grade five, and had developed "peculiar political ideas" by the time he was 12 years old.[28] By the 1960s, research indicated that the CIA and FBI had access to student files in more than 60 percent of school districts, whereas parents had access in only about 15 percent.[29]

Public reaction to such abuses led, in 1974, to the passage by Congress of the Family Educational Rights and Privacy Act (also known as the Buckley Amendment). In establishing national minimal rights and standards concerning the use of school records, the act has several important features. It protects the confidentiality of school records; it guarantees parents or guardians access to their child's records; and it provides fair procedures to challenge questionable information contained in the records.

Although the federal law provides basic protections related to school records, some states have gone beyond its minimum requirements and regulate the uses and access to school records by state law.

BALANCING COMPETING INTERESTS

The area of school records reflects competing interests of different segments of society. Educators agree that, if competently handled, school records can be of substantial aid in the education of children and youth. Unfortunately, there are too many examples of misuse of school records that work to the detriment of students. The careful use of such records for educational purposes is relatively new and the principle of confidentiality, or "privileged communication," which has been accepted in lawyer-client, physician-patient, priest-penitent relationships, has *not* gained acceptance in the educator-student setting. It is probable that educators will have to demonstrate much greater competence in the professional use of such records before the public and the law will extend the principles of confidentiality and privilege to them.*

Summary and Conclusions

DISCIPLINE

Courts have respected the right and discretion of educators to use various disciplinary methods to maintain an orderly, effective, and efficient school environment. Early in our history the common law principle was established that schools may administer punishment to students, even corporal punishment, provided that it not be excessive or cruel. No formula can be applied to determine whether a particular punishment is reasonable or excessive. Situational factors must be considered in order to make such decisions, and among those factors to be considered are the age, size, sex, and the physical and emotional condition of the student.

Even excessive or brutal punishment may not be unconstitutional. The Court has ruled that the Eighth Amendment's prohibition against cruel and unusual punishment does not apply to schools, for the amendment was intended to apply only to the punishment of criminals in "closed" institutions. Public scrutiny of schools, in the opinion of the majority of the Court, is sufficient to prevent excessive corporal punishment. If such punishment does occur, teachers and administrators may be sued for money damages and they may also be criminally liable for assault and battery. These were the common law remedies developed in the past, and the majority of the Court considers them to be sufficient protection for students. One circuit court held, however, that excessive corporal punishment may be a violation of substantive due process protected by the Fourteenth Amendment.

Although corporal punishment is not necessarily unconstitutional and there is no federal law against it, two states (New Jersey and Massachusetts) and many school districts have prohibited it by state law or local board policy. Therefore, one must check state and local laws applicable to one's school to be fully informed.

---

*For example, too many students' records contain such vague and uninstructive comments as "troublemaker," "Mary is a maladjusted child," "Eric is hostile and aggressive," "parents are uncooperative," or "Joel has trouble with math because he is unmotivated." Teachers might be helped by learning how to draw careful inferences and distinguish facts from opinions, conclusions, and generalizations. The instructional relevance and usefulness of such cum-folder entries must be constantly examined. The latest misuse of cum-folders is its nonuse, guided by the sophisticated copout: "I will not look at the record so that I will not have a 'set' or bias when I work with the student." It would be interesting to propose to well-trained physicians or lawyers that they not become acquainted with their clients' histories as the only way to maintain their objectivity!

Some states, such as California, require prior written parental approval for corporal punishment. In other states, where the law allows such punishment, schools have the discretion to use it even if some parents notify the schools not to use corporal punishment on their children. The Supreme Court also ruled that corporal punishment need not be preceded by notice, a hearing, or other elements of due process.

UNAUTHORIZED SEARCHES

During recent years, scores of cases have been brought by students claiming that the Fourth Amendment protects against the unauthorized search of their school lockers, clothing, and persons. Although the Supreme Court has never ruled on this issue, courts tend to protect administrative discretion to search school lockers if there are grounds for "reasonable suspicion" that illegal or dangerous substances are stored there.

Before a student's clothing or body may be searched, courts require more evidence and a higher degree of probability that the particular student is hiding illegal or dangerous materials. Arbitrary searches or mass searches based on general suspicions are frowned upon by the courts as violating the student's privacy.

When police conduct searches at school, they must have search warrants. Administrative cooperation with the police has led to conflicting court rulings. Some courts exclude evidence found in unauthorized searches, but others have not applied the "exclusionary rule" in student-related cases. Clearly, where school officials collaborate with the police and search for evidence later used in criminal proceedings, the relationship between students and administrators becomes adversary and not what most educators desire. It is therefore increasingly urged that the police should use proper police methods in their work, including search warrants for school-related searches. Such warrants are issued by courts upon showing of "probable cause," whereas a lesser standard, namely "reasonable suspicion," will enable school officials to search a locker as long as school-related disciplinary processes will deal with violators of school rules.

STUDENT RECORDS

School records have been well used by many schools and abused by others. Widespread abuses led to the passage of a federal law in 1974. The Family Educational Rights and Privacy Act strives for balance between a school's "need to know" and families' "right to privacy." It provides minimal requirements for confidentiality of school records, access to them by parents and guardians, and fair procedures to challenge questionable information contained in them.

NOTES

1. *Ingraham* v. *Wright* 430 U.S. 651 (1977).
2. *Faye Elizabeth Hall et al.* v. *G. Garrison Tawney et al.*, No. 78−1553, U.S. Court of Appeals (4th Cir. May 9, 1980).
3. *Baker* v. *Owens*, 423 U.S. 907 (1975).
4. *City of Macomb* v. *Gould*, 244 N.E.2d 634 (1969).
5. *Patton* v. *Bennet*, 304 F.Supp. 297 (E.D. Tenn. 1969).
6. *Bott* v. *Board of Education, Deposit Central School District*, 360 N.E.2d 952 (1977).
7. *Rolando* v. *School Directors of District No. 125, La Salle County*, 358 N.E.2d 945 (1976).
8. *Valentine* v. *Independent School District*, 183 N.W. 434 (1921).
9. *Wingfield* v. *Fort Bend Independent School District* (D.C., S.D., Tex., No. 72-H-232, April 23, 1973).
10. *Rourke* v. *Walker*, 102 Conn. 130 (1925).
11. *Howard* v. *Clark*, 299 N.Y.S.2d 65 (969).
12. ACLU, *Academic Freedom in the Secondary Schools*, New York, 1968, p. 15.
13. Quoted in Alan H. Levine, *The Rights of Students*, New York, Avon, 1973, p. 134.
14. *Ladson* v. *Board of Education, Union Free School District #9*, 323 N.Y.S.2d 545 (1971).
15. See *Matter of Murphy*, 11 Ed. Dept. Rept. 180 (1972); and *Matter of Wilson*, 11 Ed. Dept. Rept. 208 (1972).
16. See *Matter of Carroll*, Decision of Chancellor (December 6, 1971).
17. *People* v. *Overton*, 229 N.E.2d 596 (N.Y. 1967).
18. *People* v. *Overton*, 249 N.E.2d 366 (N.Y. 1969).
19. 456 P. 2d 1 (Kan. 1969).
20. Id. at 3.
21. *New York* v. *Jackson*, 319 N.Y.S.2d 731 (1971).
22. *New York* v. *Scott*, 358 N.Y.S.2d 403 (1974).
23. *Belliner* v. *Lund*, 438 F. Supp. 47 (1977).
24. As quoted in *Student Rights and Responsibilities*, Washington, D.C., National School Public Relations Association, 1972 p. 24.
25. *M. M.* v. *Anker*, 607 F.2d 588 (2nd Cir. 1979).
26. *Doe* v. *Renfrow, Superintendent of Highland Town District*, 475 F. Supp. 1012 (N.D. Ind. 1979).
27. *Van Allen* v. *McCleary*, 211 N.Y.S.2d 501 (1961).
28. "Cumulative Records: Assault on Privacy," in Diana Divoky, *Learning Magazine* (September 1973), 9.
29. "Off the Record: The Emerging Right to Control One's School Files," in Michael Stone, 5 *N.Y.U. Review of Law and Social Change*, 39 (1975).

Chapter 14
Personal Appearance

Each teacher is expected to give proper attention to his personal appearance. A pleasing appearance in dress and manner influences the reaction of students to the teacher and to the general learning environment. . . .

—from a Louisiana School Board Regulation as reported in *Blanchet* v. *Vermilion School Board* (1969)[1]

It comes as a surprise that in a country where the states are restrained by an Equal Protection Clause, a person can be denied education in a public school because of the length of his hair.

—Justice William O. Douglas in *Ferrell* v. *Dallas Independent School District*[2]

I. STUDENTS

Should students have the freedom to choose their dress and hair style? Should there be any limits on that freedom? Should the Constitution protect student grooming and clothing just as it protected Mary Tinker's right to wear her armband? Or is the conflict over personal appearance a less significant issue? Should schools be able to establish dress codes? If so, what criteria should be used to judge whether such codes are constitutional?

The judicial response to these seemingly mundane questions has been quite remarkable: First, the questions have led not only to an extraordinary volume of litigation but also to a large collection of lengthy and lively court opinions. Second, the issues have provoked an unprecedented degree of disagreement—between courts as well as between judges on the same court.[3] Despite the substantial differences among the conflicting judicial rulings on these issues, the Supreme Court has declined to perform its usual role of resolving such differences in constitutional interpretation.

Because the number of controversies has been so great (especially concerning the constitutionality of hair regulations), we will consider only a fraction of the recent decisions. After looking at a 1923 case on cosmetics, we will examine the majority and minority opinions in *Karr* v. *Schmidt*. This 1972 case on the regulation of boys' hair split the Fifth Circuit Court of Appeals and illustrates the detail and determination with which each side supports its view. We will then briefly consider how the other federal appeals courts are divided on this issue. The section concludes with an examination of several cases concerning the regulation of student clothing.

GROOMING

The Pugsley Case: An Historical Perspective[4]

On the opening day of school in Clay County, Arkansas, in 1921 Principal Hicks announced the following rule: "The wearing of transparent hosiery, low-necked dresses or any style of clothing tending toward immodesty in dress, or the use of face paint or cosmetics, is prohibited."

Pearl Pugsley broke this rule by using talcum powder on her face. Her teacher told her to wash it off and not to return with it again. A day or two later she returned with powder on her face and was denied admission to school until she obeyed the rule. Pearl refused and asked a local Arkansas court to set the rule aside. The court dismissed her case, and Pearl appealed. In a split decision the Supreme Court of Arkansas ruled in favor of the school board for several reasons.

First, although the authority of school boards is not without limit, they have "a wide range of discretion," and courts should not interfere with board regulations unless they are illegal or clearly unreasonable.

Second, the question in this case "is not whether we approve this rule as one we would have made" nor "whether it was essential to the maintenance of discipline." On the contrary, "we must uphold the rule" unless we find that the board "clearly abused their discretion."

Third, courts have "more important functions to perform than that of hearing the complaints of disaffected pupils" against school board regulations. It should be kept in mind that board members are usually elected each year and that they are in close touch with the affairs and conditions of their school districts. Therefore courts should hesitate to substitute their judgment for that of school boards.

Fourth, "respect for constituted authority and obedience thereto" is an essential lesson to qualify students for the duties of citizenship, and the schoolroom is an appropriate place to teach that lesson.

Fifth, a rule might be improper if it involved oppression or humiliation, or if it required extensive time or money. But the rule in question does not appear unreasonable in any of these respects.

For these reasons the court was unwilling to say that the rule might not be desirable in aiding school discipline. "We will not annul a rule of this kind," wrote the court, unless there is "a valid reason"; whereas to uphold it, "we are not required to find a valid reason for its promulgation."

NOTE: When Pearl Pugsley was suspended she was 17 years old. In a dissenting opinion Judge Hart wrote: "I think that a rule forbidding a girl pupil of her age from putting talcum powder on her face is so far unreasonable" that the court should say that the board abused its discretion in making it. The dissent concluded: "Useless laws diminish the authority of necessary ones," and the tone of the majority opinion "exemplifies the wisdom of this old proverb."

Whether grooming regulations are useless rules that diminish student respect for all rules is a question that is very much alive today and is reflected in the current controversies that follow.

The Karr Case: A Decision that Divided the Court[5]

In El Paso, Texas, a Committee on Student Grooming and Dress composed of a student, a parent, and an administrator from each of the high schools proposed a code that was adopted by the school board. The code included the following statements:

> In order to help ensure proper acceptable behavior on the part of the students, it becomes necessary to establish certain guidelines to aid parents and students in selecting the proper attire for the school year. . . .
>
> *Guidelines for dress and grooming* . . . : [Boys] Hair may be blocked, but is not to hang over the ears or the top of the collar of a standard dress shirt and must not obstruct vision. . . .
>
> No child shall be admitted to school or shall be allowed to continue in school who fails to conform to the proper standards of dress.[6]

Chelsey Karr attempted to enroll at Coronado High School for his junior year but was denied admission because he was in violation of the regulation limiting the length of boys' hair. After several conferences with school officials proved futile, Karr took his case to court.

Questions to Consider

1. Does the El Paso grooming code seem reasonable? Or does a student have a constitutional right to wear his hair as he pleases?
2. Do you think long hair is a form of symbolic speech? If so, what message does it convey? If it does not communicate that message, is long hair still entitled to protection? How is long hair similar to and different from Tinker's armband?

3. Do the El Paso school regulations violate the Fourteenth Amendment?*
4. Should public school students be able to sue school administrators to protect against *any* infringement of their freedom? Or should courts be expected to protect only those liberties that are important and socially useful?
5. Should a school have to prove that a rule is reasonable to have it upheld? Or should a student be required to prove it is unreasonable to have it declared unconstitutional?

THE OPINION OF THE COURTS

After a four-day trial a U.S. District Court ruled that the denial of a public education to Karr on the basis of the El Paso regulations violated the due process and equal protection guarantees of the federal Constitution. The trial court concluded that the enforcement of the haircut rule "causes far more disruption of the classroom instructional process than the hair it seeks to prohibit." The El Paso School Board disagreed and appealed the decision.

The *Karr* case, wrote the appeals court, presents this question: "Is there a constitutionally-protected right to wear one's hair in a public high school in the length and style that suits the wearer?" A majority of the judges on the U.S. Court of Appeals for the Fifth Circuit said no. On behalf of the court Judge Morgan considered and rejected each of the following theories.

• **The First Amendment.** This is the most frequently asserted basis for the right to wear long hair. It is argued that long hair is a form of symbolic speech by which the wearer conveys his individuality or rejection of conventional values, and it should be protected under the principles of the *Tinker* case.

The problem with this approach, wrote Judge Morgan, is that "it is doubtful that the wearing of long hair has sufficient communicative content to entitle it to the protection of the First Amendment." The court acknowledged that for some the wearing of long hair "is intended to convey a discrete message to the world." But for many the wearing of long hair is simply a matter of personal taste or the result of peer-group influence. Chesley Karr, for example, brought this suit not because his hair conveys a message but "because I like my hair long." Should First Amendment protection extend to those students who intend to convey a message in wearing long hair but not to others? The court felt that such a

---

*Two relevant provisions of the Fourteenth Amendment provide that no state shall "deprive any person of life, liberty, or property, without due process of law; nor deny to any person within its jurisdiction the equal protection of the laws."

rule would be unworkable and that constitutional protection should not depend on the subjective intent of the student in wearing long hair.

• **The Fourteenth Amendment.** Some courts have held that the right to wear hair at any length is part of the individual "liberty" protected by the Due Process Clause of the Fourteenth Amendment. However, Judge Morgan pointed out that individual liberties may be "ranked in a spectrum of importance." At one end of the spectrum are the "great liberties" such as speech and religion that are specifically guaranteed in the Bill of Rights. Of equal importance are liberties such as the right of marital privacy and the right to travel to a foreign country that are so fundamental that "even in the absence of a positive command from the Constitution, they may be restricted only for compelling state interests." At the other end of the spectrum are the "lesser liberties" that may be curtailed by the state if the restrictions are reasonably related to proper state activities. Thus the question posed by this case is not whether hair regulations may restrict a student's liberty but where that liberty should be ranked on the spectrum of importance. Is it so significant that courts should recognize it as a "fundamental" constitutional right? The court concluded it should not.

One reason for this conclusion is that the interference with liberty is a "temporary and relatively inconsequential one." The regulation in question still leaves students a "wide range of personal choice in their dress and grooming." Second, there are "strong policy considerations in favor of giving local school boards the widest possible latitude in the management of school affairs." School administrators, observed Judge Morgan, "must daily make innumerable decisions which restrict student liberty." These range from regulations restricting student parking to a variety of rules regulating student eating and movement during the school day. Each of these rules could also be attacked as a restriction on student liberty. Does it follow that school officials should be called into court and required to demonstrate that these restrictions serve "compelling" state interests and that no "alternatives less restrictive of liberty" are available? Not in cases such as these where "fundamental" rights are not involved.

• **Equal Protection.** The trial court had held that the denial of public education to Karr on the basis of the length of his hair was an "arbitrary classification" that violated the Equal Protection Clause of the Constitution because it discriminated among male students based solely on hair length.

The appeals court, however, found this theory "without merit." In cases such as this, the question is simply "whether the regulation is reasonably intended to accomplish a constitutionally permissible state objective." Moreover, the burden is not upon the school board to establish the rationality of its restriction, but upon the challenger to show that the restriction is "wholly arbitrary."

Based on the record of this case, the court found:

> The school authorities seek only to accomplish legitimate objectives in promulgating the hair regulation here in question. The record nowhere suggests that their goals are other than the elimination of classroom distraction, the avoidance of violence between long and short-haired students, and the elimination of potential health hazards resulting from long hair in the science labs. On a record such as this, we hold that it was clear error to conclude that the school board regulation failed to meet the minimum test of rationality that was properly applicable.[7]

• **Confusion and Burden.** The appeals court was disturbed that different district courts in the circuit have, "on strikingly similar records, reached wholly dissimilar results." Most district judges concluded that grooming regulations are reasonable, whereas some struck them down as "arbitrary." But the validity of these regulations, wrote Judge Morgan, "should not turn on the individual views of the district judges" concerning their "reasonableness."*

What seemed to disturb the court even more was "the burden which has been placed on the federal courts by suits of this nature." This case, for example, required four full days of testimony in the district court. It went to the circuit court with a printed appendix exceeding 300 pages. "Within this circuit alone, there have been numerous other cases" in which students made similar arguments and school boards offered the same justifications. And in each case district courts have been required to hold a "full evidentiary hearing on the issue."

Because of this burden and because these cases do not raise issues of "fundamental" liberty, Judge Morgan announced that henceforth such regulations would be presumed valid. Thus where a student lawsuit "merely alleges the constitutional invalidity" of a high school grooming regulation, district courts would dismiss the case.

The court emphasized that its decision did not indicate indifference to the personal rights of Chesley Karr and other young people. Rather it reflected the "inescapable fact" that neither the Constitution nor the federal judiciary "were conceived to be keepers of the national conscience in every matter great and small."[8]

A DISSENTING VIEW

The opinion of the court was not unanimous. On the contrary, Judge Wisdom, joined by several of his "Brethren," wrote a long, strong

---

*For information on the relationship between district and circuit courts and a description of the federal court system, see Appendix B, How the System Works.

minority opinion. The dissent contains an unusual quantity of social commentary combined with cutting criticism of the majority opinion. It begins with this observation: "Individual rights never seem important to those who tolerate their infringement." Thus the majority ruled that hair length is not a "fundamental right," and "with a few pecks of the typewriter advises the district courts of this circuit that they no longer need distract themselves with lawsuits of the gossamer stuff of this one." Judge Wisdom vigorously dissented for a number of reasons.

First, in determining whether this particular liberty is "fundamental" or not, "the majority and I part company." The majority establishes a spectrum of values along which individual liberties can be ranked. It then places a student's right to determine his hair length among the "lesser liberties" because this interference with liberty is "temporary and relatively inconsequential." For many students, however, hair regulations "will restrict their personal appearance for four or even six years." That is hardly a minimum restriction even if our Constitution can be construed to overlook "small infringements" of constitutionally guaranteed interests. "And I do not think it can," wrote Judge Wisdom.

More important, the range of student choice "is substantially reduced" by today's decision. Speculating on the possible dangers to freedom implicit in the majority ruling, the dissent stated:

> The Court has given the public high schools in this circuit a green light to ban jeans, T-shirts, sandals, wide ties, maxi-skirts, "distractingly" colorful garb of all kinds—in short the chosen attire of many of our young people. Indeed as I read the Court's opinion, it precludes constitutional examination of a public high school requirement of a daily uniform dress.[9]

Second, the majority fears that a parade of school officials will be hauled into court to justify the restrictions they impose on their students. "It is true," notes the dissent, "that the Court's decision aborts the development of potentially far-reaching litigation over the rights of students, but these considerations do not explain the Court's belittling characterization of a young person's right to present himself to the world as he pleases so long as he causes no one any harm." Although Judge Wisdom acknowledged and regretted the overcrowded court dockets, he argued that even "the prospect of exacerbating that condition is no reason to blink at a violation of a liberty which obviously means a great deal to many young people."

To a minority of the court, the right to wear one's hair as one pleases is a "fundamental" right protected by the Due Process Clause. In explaining its rationale, the dissent also presented a strong defense for individual freedom and diversity.

> Like other elements of costume, hair is a symbol of elegance, of efficiency, of affinity and association, of non-conformity and rejection of traditional values.

A person shorn of the freedom to vary the length and style of his hair is forced against his will to hold himself out symbolically as a person holding ideas contrary, perhaps, to ideas he holds most dear. Forced dress, including forced hair style, humiliates the unwilling complier, forces him to submerge his individuality in the "undistracting" mass, and in general, smacks of the exaltation of organization over member, unit over component, and state over individual. I always thought this country does not condone such repression.[10]

Thus, to the minority, hair length regulations "impinge upon the 'fundamental' diversity, freedom and expressiveness of our society, no small portion of which is comprised of students in our public schools."

Third, Judge Wisdom believed that the analysis of the majority was "just dead wrong." The problem with the majority opinion is that it upholds the hair regulation simply because it is "reasonably intended" to accomplish a legitimate educational objective. This means that the majority accept a test for rationality that looks exclusively to the "intentions" of those who issued the regulations. But the failure of a regulation to achieve constitutionally permissible objectives "surely cannot be cured by the good intentions of those who enact it." Thus the majority has not addressed the central question in this case: whether denying an education to a young man "because he has long hair does in fact—not in hope, aspiration or theory—bear a fair and substantial relation to the objectives of the regulation." The lower court found nothing to justify the regulation but "undifferentiated and unrealized fears and speculations."

Finally, the dissent asked: How could the majority of the circuit court uphold a regulation that bears no reasonable relationship to a legitimate educational objective?

By sugaring over with talk of "good intentions" the total failure of this regulation to carry those intentions into effect. I dissent from this novel and unexplained method of writing the Equal Protection clause out of our Constitution even if it threatens to impose on this court the task of bringing to fruition the full spectrum of rights which high school students enjoy with all other Americans. . . .

I submit that under the First and Fourteenth Amendments, if a student wishes to show his disestablishmentarianism by wearing long hair, antidisestablishmentarians on public school boards have no constitutional authority to prevent it.[11]

Related Cases: A Diversity of Judicial Opinion

Just as the judges of the Fifth Circuit were divided over the grooming issue in the *Karr* case, so the various federal appeals courts are also sharply divided among themselves. The Supreme Court has on several occasions refused to review this constitutional question. And as one federal judge complained: "What little guidance we have from the Court in this area is conflicting."[12]

Some circuit courts have upheld the right of local school boards to regulate hair length, whereas other circuits have held such regulations unconstitutional. The rationales used by the courts have varied, and no other issue in the field of student rights has been the subject of so much judicial disagreement.

In *Karr* we examined in detail the conflicting arguments of one circuit court on the question. In the following section we will briefly consider the opinions of several others. These cases illustrate the diversity of judicial reasoning that is found on both sides of the hair length controversy. Moreover, the cases include some of the liveliest legal language that can be found in the *Federal Reporter*. This should challenge the popular concept of judicial writing as dull, colorless, and dispassionate.

UPHOLDING SCHOOL REGULATIONS

King v. *Saddleback:* A Right of School Authorities[13]

In this case, the Ninth Circuit Court of Appeals ruled that long hair was not protected by a "right to be let alone" or "the right of privacy" implicit in the Fifth Amendment. "The conduct to be regulated here," wrote the court, "is not conduct found in the privacy of the home but in public educational institutions where individual liberties cannot be left completely uncontrolled to clash with similarly asserted liberties of several thousand others."

Since the court did not find that the Constitution protected grooming, it held that the burden was on the student to prove that a school's hair regulations were invalid. Although the student in this case caused no disturbance, the court ruled that this fact "does not establish that long-haired males cannot be a distracting influence which would interfere with the educative process the same as any extreme in appearance, dress, or deportment."

The court emphasized that "this is not a question of preference for or against certain male hair styles. . . . The court could not care less." It is a question of the right of school authorities to develop a dress code in accord with their responsibilities.[14]

Jackson v. *Dorrier:* A Problem with the Purple Haze[15]

Michael Jackson and Barry Barnes were members of a combo band known as "The Purple Haze" and grew their hair far longer than permitted by the rules at Nashville's Donelson High School. Evidence indicated that they were a "distracting influence" in several classes and were constantly looking in mirrors, combing and rearranging their hair. One teacher testified that "hardly a day would go by" that she would not have to interrupt her teaching and say: "Put your combs away. This is not a beauty parlor. This is a school classroom."

Based on this evidence, the Sixth Circuit Court of Appeals found that the "deliberate flouting" of school regulations by Jackson and Barnes "created problems of school discipline." The court also found that the students "pursued their course of personal grooming for the purpose of enhancing the popularity of the musical group in which they performed." Neither student testified that his hair style was intended as an expression of any idea or point of view. Hence the court concluded that "the growing of hair for purely commercial purposes is not protected by the First Amendment's guarantee of freedom of speech."

Mercer v. *Board of Trustees:* Courts May Do More Harm Than Good[16]

In a 1976 case, John Mercer challenged his school's hair length regulations on grounds that they applied only to male students and therefore violated the state's Equal Rights Amendment. A state court recognized that any regulation based on sex is "suspect" and is subject to strict judicial scrutiny. Nevertheless, the court refused to hold the school rules unconstitutional.

Chief Justice Brown indicated that having different grooming regulations for men and women was simply "recognizing the facts of life" based on natural physical differences. Despite the *Tinker* case, Justice Brown seemed to feel that the Constitution sometimes should not be applied to public schools. He noted that "Living by rules, sometimes seemingly arbitrary ones, is the lot of children. School is of necessity made up of 'rules.'" Judge Brown concluded with this provocative observation:

> Court intervention is simply not a suitable device with which to enforce some rights. Others, beside the judiciary, are charged with following the dictates of our constitutions. We must be wise enough to perceive that constant judicial intervention in some institutions does more harm than good.[17]

NOTE: Thus far few grooming cases have been based on the growing number of state ERAs. But it is doubtful whether most courts will follow this Texas decision—especially since some have struck down hair length regulations under the less stringent standards of the Equal Protection Clause of the Federal Constitution.[18]

Ferra v. *Hendry County School Board:* Mustache Unprotected[19]

In this 1978 Florida case, a state court upheld a rule requiring students to be "clean shaven." Echoing a theme common to recent cases supporting school regulations, Judge Grimes wrote:

> Had I been on the Hendry County School Board, I doubt if I would have voted to prohibit a high school student from growing a mustache. But . . . I am persuaded that ordinary matters such as these must be left in the hands of the officials who have been duly charged with the operation of our schools. So long as a particular regulation is not "wholly arbitrary," it should be upheld even though it may have the effect of impinging in some small degree upon an individual's freedom. . . . If courts become embroiled in passing on the constitutionality of every conceivable public school regulation, there is a real possibility that persons with serious and legitimate grievances may never be able to get in the courthouse door.[20]

GROOMING AS A CONSTITUTIONAL RIGHT

Richards v. *Thurston:* Embracing Freedoms Great and Small[21]

Bob Richards, a 17-year-old senior from Marlboro, Massachusetts, was suspended for refusing to comply with a school policy against "unusually long hair." In holding the school policy unconstitutional, the First Circuit Court of Appeals commented that the case involved "a very fundamental dispute" over the extent to which the Constitution protects certain "uniquely personal aspects of one's life." The court found that Richards' hair was protected by the Due Process Clause of the Fourteenth Amendment, which "establishes a sphere of personal liberty for every individual" subject to restriction only if exercising that liberty interferes with the rights of others.

The governance of hair length and style, wrote Judge Coffin, may not be so fundamental as some substantive rights already found implicit in the "liberty" that is assured to citizens by the Due Process Clause. "Yet 'liberty' seems to us an incomplete protection if it encompasses only the right to do momentous acts, leaving the state free to interfere with those personal aspects of our lives which have no direct bearing on the ability of others to enjoy their liberty." A narrower view of liberty in a free society might allow a state to require "a conventional coiffure of all its citizens, a governmental power not unknown in European history." For these reasons, the court ruled that "within the commodious concept of liberty, embracing freedoms great and small, is the right to wear one's hair as he wishes."

When can the state restrict a person's liberty? The answer depends on the nature of the liberty and the context in which it is asserted. Judge Coffin noted, for example, that "the right to appear *au naturel* at home is relinquished when one sets foot on a public sidewalk." Similarly, the nature of public school education requires limitations on one's personal liberty in order for learning to take place. The court, however, saw "no inherent reason why decency, decorum or good conduct requires a boy to wear his hair short." Certainly "eccentric hair styling" is no longer a reliable signal of "perverse behavior." Thus the court concluded:

> We do not believe that mere unattractiveness in the eyes of some parents, teachers or students, short of uncleanliness, can justify the proscription. Nor, finally, does such compelled conformity to conventional standards of appearance seem a justifiable part of the educational process.[22]

Bishop v. *Colaw:* **Where a Bromide Is in Order**[23]

The St. Charles, Missouri, school administration suspended Stephen Bishop because his hair style violated the school dress code. Several administrators asserted that male students with long hair "tended to be rowdy, created a sanitation problem in the swimming pool, caused a safety problem in certain shop classes, and tended to make poorer grades than those with shorter hair." The principal even indicated that if boys were allowed to wear long hair so as to look like girls, it might create problems with the continuing operation of the school "because of confusion over appropriate dressing room and restroom facilities."

The Eighth Circuit Court of Appeals rejected these arguments. On behalf of the court, Judge Bright wrote that Stephen possessed "a constitutionally protected right to govern his personal appearance." The court pointed out that this right has been recognized since 1891, when Justice Gray wrote: "No right is held more sacred, or is more carefully guarded, by the common law, than the right of every individual to the possession and control of his own person, free from all restraint or interference of others, unless by clear and unquestionable authority of law."[24] Moreover Judge Bright observed: "It is apparent that the opinion testimony of the school teachers and administrators, which lacks any empirical foundation, likely reflects a personal distaste of longer hair styles, which distaste is shared by many in the older generation." Furthermore, the acceptance of the dress code by the majority of students and parents does not justify the infringement of Bishop's liberty to govern his personal appearance. "Toleration of individual differences," wrote the court, "is basic to our democracy, whether those differences be in religion, politics, or life style."

In concurring opinions, two other judges added these wide-ranging judicial observations:

The connection between long hair and the immemorial problems of mis-directed student activism and negativism, whether in behavior or in learning, is difficult to see. No evidence has been presented that hair is the cause, as distinguished from a possible peripheral consequence, of undesira-ble traits, or that the school boards, Delilah-like, can lop off these charac-teristics with the locks.[25]

I cannot help but observe that the city employee who collects my rubbish has shoulder-length hair. So do a number of our nationally famous Boston Bruins. Barrel tossing and puck chasing are honorable pursuits, not to be associated with effeteness on the one hand, or aimlessness or indolence on the other. If these activities be thought not of high intellectual calibre, I turn to the recent successful candidates for Rhodes Scholarships from my neighboring institution. A number of these, according to their photographs, wear hair that outdoes even the hockey players.[26]

To say that the problem is best left to local authorities demeans the intrinsic constitutional issue involved. Such a rationale could sustain any school prohibition of the recognized constitutional rights of students.[27]

The gamut of rationalizations for justifying this restriction fails in light of reasoned analysis. When school authorities complain variously that such hair styles are inspired by a communist conspiracy, that they make boys look like girls, that they promote confusion as to the use of restrooms, and that they destroy the students' moral fiber, then it is little wonder even moderate students complain of "getting up-tight." In final analysis, I am satisfied a comprehensive school restriction on male student hair styles accomplishes little more than to project the prejudices and personal distastes of certain adults in authority on to the impressionable young student.[28]

It is bromidic to say that times change, but perhaps this is a case where a bromide is in order.[29]

Massie v. *Henry:* In the Style of the Founding Fathers[30]

The student body president of North Carolina's Tuscola High School requested that guidelines be established for student grooming following an incident in which a student with long hair was called a "hippie" and a fight ensued. As a result of his request, grooming guidelines were adopted by the school. Joe Massie and a classmate were suspended for their "deliberate refusal" to conform to the guidelines. Evidence indi-cated that the length of their hair "evoked considerable jest, disgust and amusement," making it difficult to preserve classroom order.

The court in this case considered the students' right to wear their hair as they wished as "an aspect of the right to be secure in one's person" guaranteed by the Due Process Clause. Judge Winter included these rare observations in his opinion:

> . . . there is abroad a trend for the male to dress himself more extravagantly both in the nature, cut and color of his clothing and the quantity and mode of his facial and tonsorial adornment. . . .

With respect to hair, this is no more than a harkening back to the fashion of earlier years. For example, many of the founding fathers, as well as General Grant and General Lee, wore their hair (either real or false) in a style comparable to that adopted by the [student] plaintiffs. Although there exists no depiction of Jesus Christ, either reputedly or historically accurate, he has always been shown with hair at least the length of that of plaintiffs. If the validity and enforcement of the regulation in issue is sustained, it follows that none of these persons would have been permitted to attend Tuscola Senior High School.[31]

Was the evidence that the plaintiffs' long hair had a disruptive effect sufficient to restrict their rights? The Fourth Circuit Court of Appeals ruled that it was not. Judge Winter noted that the administration made little effort to convey to students the "salutary teaching" that "there is little merit in conformity for the sake of conformity" and that one may exercise a personal right any way he chooses "so long as he does not run afoul of considerations of safety, cleanliness, and decency." The court concluded that "faculty leadership in promoting and enforcing an attitude of tolerance rather than one of suppression or derision would obviate the relatively minor disruptions which have occurred."

Crews v. Cloncs: A Denial of Equal Protection[32]

Eugene Cloncs, principal of Indiana's North Central High School, did not admit Tyler Crews to class because he violated the school grooming regulations. Cloncs defended his action with two arguments. First, since Crews's hair distracted other students, the principal considered it disruptive. Second, he argued that it posed a health and safety problem.

To what extent can disruptive conduct of others in response to Crews's long hair be used to justify his expulsion from school? In response to this question, the Seventh Circuit Court of Appeals observed that "it is absurd to punish a person because his neighbors have no self-control and cannot refrain from violence." A similar principle, wrote Chief Judge Swygert, "operates to protect long-haired students unless school officials have actively tried and failed to silence those persons actually engaged in disruptive conduct." Since there was no evidence that school officials tried to punish the students who caused the "relatively insubstantial disruption," the principal failed to justify his action against Crews under his first theory.

The principal's second argument was that short hair was required for health and safety reasons. Testimony indicated the various problems that long hair could cause in the gym, the swimming pool, and the laboratory. The court rejected this theory because health and safety objectives could be achieved through narrow rules directed specifically at the problems created by long hair—for example, by requiring swimming caps in pools and hair nets around machinery or Bunsen burners. Moreover, although girls engage in similar activities, only boys had been required to cut their hair to attend classes, and school officials offered no reasons why health and safety objectives were not equally applicable to girls. The court concluded that the school board's action "constitutes a denial of equal protection to male students" and therefore violated the Fourteenth Amendment of the Constitution.

Arnold v. *Carpenter:* Is a Student-Approved Code Constitutional?[33]

In this final grooming controversy, which occured in Syracuse, Indiana, the Seventh Circuit Court of Appeals went even further in protecting a nonconforming student than it had in the *Crews* case. The controversy was based on the Wawasee High School's dress code that had been carefully prepared by a committee of students, teachers, and administrators and adopted by a vote of 75 percent of the student body. Furthermore, the code included a "consent provision" that authorized noncompliance if, at the beginning of the semester, a parent appeared before the principal and gave written consent for the exception of his child. Nevertheless when school opened, Greg Carpenter chose to violate the code's "long hair provision," and his parents did not request an exception. Carpenter therefore was disciplined as the code provided. He and his father sued to prohibit enforcement of the hair provision.

Questions to Consider

1. Should a grooming code be upheld if elected students participate in its formulation and if it is democratically approved by a student majority?
2. Even if you believe that no code should be enforced upon students against the wishes of their parents, does a code that allows for exceptions based on parental request seem reasonable?

THE OPINION OF THE COURT

In prior cases this appeals court had held that the right to wear one's hair at any length is "an ingredient of personal freedom" protected by the Constitution.[34] In this case, however, the school board argued that previous decisions upholding the right of students to wear long hair did not control "because of the 'unique' democratic formulation of the dress code by Wawasee High School." But the court held that "mere student participation in adoption of the code" did not justify the limitation imposed on Greg Carpenter's constitutional right to wear long hair.

The school board, nevertheless, claimed that the "consent provision" saved the hair regulations since it "places responsibility for noncompliance with the parent where it belongs." In response the court wrote, "the mere failure of the parents to sign the consent form should not be used by the school as a basis for denying Greg the constitutional right to determine his own hair length." Moreover, his appearance at school with long hair was an indication that his parents were agreeable to it. "Not all fathers," observed Judge Kiley, "prefer to have their student sons conform unquestionably to the decision of the majority, or look upon dissent as meriting punishment."

The court ruled that the "consent clause" in the high school dress code "does not cure the fatal constitutional infirmity in the hair provision." A school board cannot require a parent's written consent in order for a student to exercise his legal rights. For these reasons the court declared that the hair length provision of the dress code was "null and void."

A DISSENTING OPINION

In a lively dissent Judge Stevens sprinkled his opinion with the following sociological and philosophic comments:

> The fact that absurd arguments have been advanced to support certain dress codes, or the fact that the older generation has overreacted in its response to the younger generation's desire to do its own thing, should not obscure the fact that society does have a legitimate interest in both the continuity and mutability of its mores.[35]
>
> Since the child has no enforceable right to remain unshorn or unwashed without parental consent, I find nothing offensive in a dress code which merely requires conformity unless excused by a child's parents.[36]

The right which Greg and his parents seek to vindicate in this case does not "warrant invasion" in an area in which other parents, in partnership with the teachers and a majority of the students, have agreed that a measure of conformity to tradition is desirable. "Just as the majority must learn to tolerate the non-conformist, so must he learn to tolerate transient customs of his elders."

The only thing that would be accomplished by invalidating this dress code would be to make it possible for Carpenter both to wear his own hair long and to enable more of his peers to do likewise, "thus enabling him to be more of a conformist." Hence, the decision in this case does nothing to protect any significant interest in nonconformity. Indeed if the slight inconvenience to his father "of evidencing his consent in person has a 'chilling effect' on that interest, our would-be non-conformist might as well get a haircut."

Judge Stevens noted that the decision of the majority "nourishes the pernicious seed of intolerance by encouraging confrontation rather than accommodation." He concluded his dissent with these words: "I would not force Gregory to fast on Saturday when he visits Rome, but I would teach him not to sneer at Romans who do."

Black v. *Douglas:* The Supreme Court and the Grooming Controversy

When federal circuit courts differ in their interpretation of the Constitution, the Supreme Court usually reviews the question, renders a decision, and thus establishes a uniform "law of the land." Despite the sharp differences of opinion among federal courts concerning grooming regulations, the Supreme Court has consistently declined to review circuit court decisions on the issue. Why? The following opinions give us an insight into the probable answer.

TO DISTRIBUTE THE POWERS OF GOVERNMENT: THE OPINION OF JUSTICE BLACK

In 1971 Justice Black reviewed a motion arising out of *Karr* v. *Schmidt.* * The district court had enjoined the enforcement of the El Paso grooming code, and the appeals court had reversed that injunction. Chesley Karr then presented to Justice Black (as the Supreme Court Justice assigned to the Court of Appeals of the Fifth Circuit) an "Emergency Motion" to suspend the action of the circuit court pending appeal to the Supreme Court. In denying this motion, Justice Black wrote:

> The motion in this case is presented to me in a record of more than 50 pages . . . The words used through out the record such as "Emergency Motion" and "harassment" and "irreparable dangers" are calculated to leave the impression that this case over the length of hair has created or is about to create a great national "crisis." I confess my inability to understand how anyone would thus classify this hair length case. The only thing about it that borders on the serious to me is the idea that anyone should think the Federal Constitution imposes on the United States courts the burden of supervising the length of hair that public school students should wear.
>
> . . . . Surely the federal judiciary can perform no greater service to the nation than to leave the states unhampered in the performance of their purely local affairs. Surely few policies can be thought of that states are more capable of deciding than the length of the hair of school boys. There can, of course, be honest differences of opinion as to whether any government, state or federal, should as a matter of public policy regulate the length of haircuts, but it would be difficult to prove by reason, logic, or common sense the federal judiciary is more competent to deal with hair length than are the local school authorities and state legislatures of all our 50 states.[37]

PERMITTING IDIOSYNCRASIES TO FLOURISH: JUSTICE DOUGLAS DISSENTING

In an earlier Texas case, the Fifth Circuit had upheld a grooming code regulating student hair length, and the student had petitioned the

*A motion is a request for a ruling or order that is made to a court or judge.

Supreme Court to review the decision. The court denied the petition, with Justice Douglas writing this lone dissent:

> It comes as a surprise that in a country where the states are restrained by an Equal Protection Clause, a person can be denied education in a public school because of the length of his hair. I suppose that a nation bent on turning out robots might insist that every male have a crew cut and every female wear pigtails. But the ideas of "life, liberty, and the pursuit of happiness," expressed in the Declaration of Independence, later found specific definition in the Constitution itself, including, of course, freedom of expression and a wide zone of privacy. I had supposed those guarantees permitted idiosyncracies to flourish, especially when they concern the image of one's personality and his philosophy toward government and his fellow men.
>
> Municipalities furnish many services to their inhabitants, and I had supposed that it would be an invidious discrimination to withhold fire protection, police protection, garbage collection . . . [or an education] merely because a person was an offbeat nonconformist when it came to hairdo and dress as well as diet, race, religion or his views on Vietnam.[38]

Justice Douglas concluded that he would "grant the petition in this Texas case" and schedule it for argument. Despite a variety of petitions to the Supreme Court from conflicting circuit court cases,[39] most justices have not been willing to grant such petitions, hear the arguments, and establish a national policy on the issue.

LEGAL SUMMARY

Despite the many conflicts over grooming regulations, the law on this subject has become relatively clear as the map on p. 388 indicates. During the 1970s most of the U.S. Circuit Courts of Appeals have ruled on this issue directly, and the others have indicated how they would probably rule. The federal appeals courts have decided that grooming is a constitutional right in the First Circuit (Me., Mass., N.H., R.I., Vt.), the Fourth Circuit (Md., N.C., S.C., Va., W.Va.), the Seventh Circuit (Ill., Ind., Wisc.), the Eighth Circuit (Ark., Iowa, Minn., Mo., Neb., N.D., S.D.), and probably the Second Circuit (Conn., N.Y., Vt.).* In these states, courts will hold grooming regulations unconstitutional unless school officials present convincing evidence that they are fair, reasonable, and necessary to carry out a legitimate educational purpose.

---

*In 1973 the Second Circuit clearly ruled that hair length regulations raised "a substantial constitutional issue." *Dwen* v. *Barry*, 483 F.2d 1126 (2nd Cir. 1973). Although the U.S. Supreme Court overruled that decision as it appled to policemen in *Kelley* v. *Johnson* 425 U.S. 238 (1976), the Second Circuit would probably reaffirm the *Dwen* decision as applied to students because of the important differences between regulating the appearance of students and policemen and the refusal of the Supreme Court to rule on student hair cases.

The law is different in the Fifth Circuit (Ala., Fla., Ga., La., Miss., Tex.), the Sixth Circuit (Ky., Mich., Ohio, Tenn.), the Ninth Circuit (Alas., Ariz., Cal., H.I., Idaho, Nev., Ore.), the Tenth Circuit (Kan., Okla., N.M., Utah, Wyo), and probably in the Third Circuit (Del., N.J., Penn.)* and the Eleventh Circuit (the District of Columbia).** In these states, the circuit courts have decided that grooming is not a significant constitutional issue and that federal courts should not judge the wisdom of codes regulating hair length or style. This does not necessarily mean that there is no legal remedy if a student is disciplined for violating school-grooming regulations. It only means that federal courts will generally not consider these cases. Such grooming restrictions may still be challenged in state courts.

CLOTHING

Jones v. Day: Can School Uniforms Be Required? An Historical Perspective[40]

In 1920 a Mississippi public agricultural high school established a policy that all students must wear a khaki uniform while in school and "when visiting public places within five miles of the school, even on Saturdays and Sundays." One of the students and his father objected. They denied that the school had authority to prescribe student dress "at all times and at all places," and they took their case to court.

The Supreme Court of Mississippi held: (1) the school could require *all* students to wear uniforms at school and while traveling between school and home; (2) it could require *boarding* students to wear uniforms after school hours and on weekends; and (3) it could not require *day* students to wear uniforms after school hours or on weekends while under the authority of their parents. In sum, when students were under the custody of the school, uniforms could be required; when under parental control, their parents' wishes governed. No question was raised concerning the rights of the students.

Bannister v. Paradis: Do Boys Have a Right to Wear Jeans?[41]

Twelve-year-old Kevin Bannister was a sixth grade student in Pittsfield, New Hampshire, who liked to wear blue jeans to school. But the Pittsfield

*Although a recent decision of the Third Circuit held that civilian employees of the National Guard could challenge the guard's hair length regulations, *Syrek* v. *Pennsylvania* 537 F.2d 66 (3rd Cir. 1976), the Third Circuit clearly ruled in 1975 that "the federal courts should not intrude" in the area of school regulation of student hair length and that it would no longer consider school grooming cases. *Zeller* v. *Donegal*, 517 F.2d 600 (3rd Cir. 1975).

**The D.C. Court of Appeals has not ruled directly on the issue of school-grooming regulations, but in a related case it indicated that it agreed with the U.S. Supreme Court and "sees no federal question in this area." *Fagan* v. *National Cash Register Co.*, 481 F.2d 1115 (D.C. Cir. 1973).

School Board passed an elaborate dress code that included this provision: "Dungarees will not be allowed." Although Kevin knew of this provision, he wore jeans to school and was sent home for violating the code. Because he and his parents believed the dungarees prohibition was unconstitutional, they went to court.

• **The Findings.** At the outset the trial court had an interesting problem determining exactly what was prohibited by the no-dungarees rule. The principal defined *dungarees* as "working clothes made of a coarse cotton blue fabric"; the chairman of the school board defined them as "a denim fabric pant used for work," with color of no significance; and the dictionary gave a third definition.[42] But Judge Bownes side-stepped the definitional argument by ruling that for the purpose of this case "blue jeans and dungarees are synonymous" and that Bannister "deliberately violated the school dress code."

• **The Testimony.** The principal of Bannister's school, Mr. Paradis, testified that discipline is essential to the educational process and that proper dress is part of a good educational climate. It was his opinion that if students wear work or play clothes to school "it leads to a relaxed attitude, and such an attitude detracts from discipline and a proper educational climate." Paradis further stated that students with patches on their clothes or with dirty clothes of any type "should be sent home." Although the dress code said nothing about clothing being clean or neat, the principal stated: "I apply the dress code as I see it."

Questions to Consider

1. Does a student have a right to wear dungarees to school? What would be the constitutional basis for such a right?
2. Does a boy have the right to wear any kind of clothing he wishes? Does a girl have the same right? If so, should there be any limit to these rights?
3. Should student rights concerning hair and clothing be treated in the same way by the schools? By the courts? Are there any reasons for treating them differently?

THE RULING OF THE COURT

At the time of this 1970 controversy, the court was unable to find any other reported cases brought under the 1964 Civil Rights Act where clothing was the issue.[43] Judge Bownes noted:

> This dearth of cases relative to wearing apparel in the Civil Rights field may be an indication that neither pupils nor school boards look on clothes with the same emotion and fervor with which they regard the length of a young man's hair or it may indicate, as the Court believes it does, that most school boards are no longer concerned with what a student wears to school as long

as it is clean and covers adequately those parts of the body that, by tradition, are usually kept from public view.[44]

Judge Bownes did not believe that the wearing of blue jeans could be protected under the "right of privacy"; nor did he believe it constituted the kind of expression that is protected by the First Amendment. In fact the court was "tempted to dispose of the matter" on the grounds that there was no deprivation of any constitutional right, except for the precedent of *Richards* v. *Thurston*, a decision of the First Circuit Court of Appeals, which includes New Hampshire.

The language and reasoning of the *Richards* case convinced Judge Bownes that a person's freedom to wear the clothes of his own choosing was a constitutional right protected by the Fourteenth Amendment. "Surely," wrote the judge, "the commodious concept of liberty" invoked in the *Richards* case, "embracing freedoms great and small" was large enough "to include within its embrace the right to wear clean blue jeans to school, unless there is an outweighing state interest justifying their exclusion."

Was there such a state interest that would justify the regulation against wearing dungarees? To answer this question, the court considered (1) the nature of the liberty, (2) the context in which it was asserted, and (3) the extent to which the intrusion on the liberty served the public interest.

Judge Bownes acknowledged that "on the scale of values of constitutional liberties," the right to wear jeans to school "is not very high." However, no evidence was presented to show that the wearing of dungarees inhibited the educational process. Although the judge was "mindful of the testimony" of the principal, he confessed considerable difficulty accepting the proposition that wearing work or play clothes "is subversive of the educational process because students tend to become lax and indifferent."

Does this mean that students can wear anything they wish to school? Not according to Judge Bownes. In fact the judge noted that a school "can, and must, for its own preservation exclude persons who are unsanitary, obscenely, or scantily clad." Good hygiene and the health of others may require that dirty clothing be prohibited, "whether they be dress clothes or dungarees." Nor did the court see anything unconstitutional in a school prohibiting scantily clad students "because it is obvious that the lack of proper covering, particularly with female students, might tend to distract other pupils and be disruptive of the educational process and school discipline." While thus recognizing the school's power to adopt "reasonable restrictions on dress," the court concluded with this observation:

> The standards of appearance and dress of last year are not those of today nor will they be those of tomorrow. Regulation of conduct by school authorities must bear a reasonable basis to the ordinary conduct of the school curriculum or to carrying out the responsibility of the school.[45]

Since Judge Bownes did not believe that the dungaree prohibition was reasonably related to the school's responsibility or curriculum, he ruled that the board had not justified its intrusion on Bannister's personal liberty, "small as that intrusion may be," and that the prohibition was therefore "unconstitutional and invalid."

Scott v. Hicksville Board of Education: Can Girls Be Prohibited from Wearing Slacks?[46]

By a majority vote the students and parents of a New York school district approved a detailed dress code for secondary schools. The code included a prohibition against "girls wearing slacks" except when "permitted by the principal between December 1 and March 31 on petition by the student council when warranted by cold or inclement weather." On two days in October a tenth grade student, Lorri Scott, wore slacks to school. Pursuant to the new code, she was "placed in detention and thereby missed her classes." Lorri believed enforcing the no-slacks rule unlawfully interfered with her right to an education. She therefore went to the local state court to ask that the rule be annulled.

Questions to Consider

1. Is the code's general prohibition against "girls wearing slacks" reasonable? If not, could a dress code that prohibited specific kinds of slacks be upheld?
2. What criteria should be used to distinguish reasonable from unreasonable clothing regulations?
3. If you were a high school principal, what clothing regulations would you establish in your school? Would they be different for boys and girls? If so, would such differences be constitutional under the Equal Protection Clause?

THE OPINION OF THE COURT

To determine whether a school board has the power to proscribe the wearing of slacks by female students, Judge Meyer first turned to the New York State Education Law. He noted that this law gives school boards the power to establish "regulations concerning the order and discipline of the schools," but he found nothing that "deals explicitly with dress." Nevertheless he concluded that school boards have "implied power to regulate dress for reasons of safety, in addition to the express power to do so for reasons of order and discipline." Thus a board has broad discretion concerning what safety, order, and discipline require, but it has no authority to enforce a regulation "which bears no reasonable relation" to these factors. Although the court commended the board for submitting the proposed dress code to referendum, Judge Meyer noted that "such a referendum cannot supply authority that does not otherwise exist."

Does the prohibition of girls wearing slacks fall within the board's authority? "The simple fact that it applies only to female students and makes no differentiation as to the kind of slacks mandates a negative answer." For those facts, observed Judge Meyer, "make evident that what is being enforced is style or taste and not safety, order, or discipline."

Are there clothing regulations that might be within the school's authority to enforce? Although courts generally restrict their rulings to the facts of the case before them, Judge Meyer was unusually expansive in his effort to illustrate the type of clothing prohibitions that might be upheld. In the interest of "safety," for example, a school board can "probably be justified" in prohibiting "the wearing of bell-bottomed slacks by students, male or female, who ride bikes to school." In the interest of "discipline," a regulation against slacks that are "so skintight and, therefore, revealing as to provoke or distract students of the opposite sex" might be valid. And in the interest of "order," a rule against slacks "to the bottoms of which small bells have been attached" would be upheld. Such regulations would be valid because they clearly relate to the school board's "authorized concerns"; the flat prohibition against all slacks is invalid "precisely because it does not."

The school board argued that regulations that differentiated the type of slacks prohibited would be too difficult to administer and might lead to greater controversy because of the individual judgments involved. To that argument the court gave two answers. First, the difficulty of staying within the limits of its authority does not alter those limits. The legislature might extend them, but the school board cannot "lift itself by its bootstraps over them." Second, other provisions in the board's own dress code showed just the kind of proper discrimination in regard to "facial adornment" and "ornamentation" that it argued is impossible in the case of slacks. Thus the code prohibited facial adornment that provoked "so widespread or constant attention as would interfere with teaching and learning" and ornamentation that would make "distracting noises, es- pouse violence, be obscene . . . or call for an illegal act."

In sum, the court annulled the "flat prohibition of girls wearing slacks" and held that a board's regulation of dress was valid only to the extent necessary "to protect the safety of the wearer, male or female, or to control disturbance or distraction which interferes with the education of other students."

Dunham v. *Pulsifer* and *Westley* v. *Rossi:* Grooming v. Clothing

Just as courts differ on whether a student has a right to wear his hair as he pleases, so they differ about clothing regulations. Can we expect a court to rule the same way in clothing cases as in hair controversies? Yes and no. Those courts that do not protect a student's choice of hair style will probably not protect his choice of clothing. But courts that do protect hair style may (or may not) protect student freedom in matters of dress. The *Bannister* case was illustrative of a court that believed that the constitutional liberty that guarded a student's right to wear hair as he wished similarly protected his right to wear the clothing of his choice. Other courts, however, have distinguished hair from clothing and indicated that restrictions on hair style are more serious invasions of individual freedom than are clothing regulations. The *Dunham* and *Westley* cases illustrate the reasoning behind this distinction.

Dunham involved a Vermont high school grooming code for athletes. In this case a federal district court held that the code that restricted the hair length of male athletes was unconstitutional. The Judge ruled that the freedom "to determine one's own hair style" and "personal appearance" is protected by the Constitution. He also noted that "the cut of one's hair style is more fundamental to personal appearance than the type of clothing he wears. Garments can be changed at will whereas hair, once it is cut, has to remain constant for substantial periods of time."[47]

Similarly in the *Westley* case a U.S. District Court in Minnesota struck down a public high school rule requiring boys to have "neat conventional male haircuts."[48] In his opinion Judge Neville questioned whether the length of a boy's hair today is as distracting as "girls scantily clad, for instance" so as to justify the conventional haircut rule. Furthermore, he emphasized that the rule had an effect beyond class hours. "Were a school to prohibit a boy attending school with no shirt," wrote the judge, he could take off his shirt as he leaves the school grounds and "go bare waisted in life at home." But a hair regulation "invades private life beyond the school jurisdiction."

Thus some courts distinguish clothing from hair style on the following grounds: (1) hair style is more fundamental to personal appearance; (2) restrictions concerning hair have a long-term effect; and (3) hair styles today usually do not involve issues of morality and distraction as do some clothing styles. For these reasons, some courts that recognize choice of hair style as a constitutional right do not protect choice of clothing style. Even courts that protect both clothing and grooming give school boards much wider discretion to regulate clothing in the interests of health, safety, order, or discipline.*

II. TEACHERS

If most parents want schools to teach their children conventional standards of dress and grooming, do they have a right to make this part of the

---

*In another clothing case, a federal court upheld rules against "excessively tight skirts and pants" as a reasonable prohibition against immodest clothing, but found rules against frayed jeans, tie-dyed clothes, and shirtails worn outside as having no relationship to discipline. *Wallace* v. *Ford*, 346 F.Supp. 156 (E.D. Ark. 1972).

informal curriculum? If so, isn't it reasonable to ask teachers to be adult models of neatness and good taste?

A bank, a store, or a law firm can require that its employees wear dresses or business suits and ties during working hours. Should a school board be able to make the same type of requirement for its teachers?

An increasing number of teachers argue against these requirements. They say that grooming and dress are personal matters, and that they should be allowed to dress as they like. But many school boards believe it is their responsibility to insure that a teacher's appearance is in accord with the professional standards of the community.

Although teachers and students use similar arguments to oppose personal appearance regulations, courts have ruled that the constitutional rights of the two groups are sometimes different. The cases in this section will illustrate the similarities and the differences between student and teacher dress and grooming decisions and the changes in judicial thinking on this subject during the 1970s.

GROOMING

The Finot Case: The Right to Wear a Beard[49]

Paul Finot taught government to high school seniors in the Pasadena, California, school system for seven years. In September 1963, when Finot arrived at school wearing a recently grown beard, the principal asked him to shave it off. Upon his refusal the Board of Education transferred Finot to home teaching, despite the fact that he was a challenging and effective classroom teacher. Finot branded his transfer "unconstitutional" and went to court.

The board said its action was based on the city's teacher handbook, which called for teachers to practice the common social amenities as evidenced by acceptable dress and grooming, and to set an example of neatness and good taste. This was related to a student handbook prohibiting beards, mustaches, and excessively long hair as "not appropriate dress for male students."

The board's action was also based on the "professional judgment" of Finot's principal and superintendent. They explained that the appearance of teachers had a definite effect on student dress and that student dress had a definite correlation with student behavior—the well-dressed student generally behaved equally well. Their concern was that Finot's beard might attract undue attention, interfere with the process of education, and make the prohibition of beards for students more difficult to enforce. And they felt that wearing a beard did not meet the school's requirement of acceptable grooming or set an example of good taste.

Questions to Consider

1. Do you think the school board was justified in transferring Finot? Was

it justified in expecting its teachers to provide an example of neatness and good taste? Why or why not?

2. If you were a school administrator, what, if any, rules would you issue concerning standards of grooming?

3. Should the wearing of a beard or long hair be allowed under some circumstances and prohibited under others?

COURT DECISION

A California appeals court supported Finot. It said that Finot's right to wear a beard was one of the liberties protected by the Fourteenth Amendment to the Constitution, which prohibits the deprivation of any person's life, *liberty*, or property without due process of law. The court also said that "the wearing of a beard is a form of expression of an individual's personality."

Some people interpret a beard as a symbol of masculinity, authority, or wisdom. Others see it as a symbol of nonconformity or rebellion. In either case, the court recognized that symbols, under appropriate circumstances, "merit Constitutional protection." Thus, although not within the literal scope of the First Amendment, wearing a beard is entitled to its peripheral protection as a form of symbolic speech and a "right of expression." In conclusion, the court ruled that in the absence of evidence that a teacher's wearing a beard has an adverse effect on the educational process, beards on teachers "cannot constitutionally be banned from the classroom."

If wearing a beard is a constitutionally protected personal liberty, does this mean that a school system can set no limits upon these liberties? No. But according to the court, for a school to require a waiver of such liberties as a condition of employment it would probably have to meet three tests. (1) There must be a rational relation between the restriction in question and the effectiveness of the educational system; (2) "the benefits which the public gains by the restraints must outweigh the resulting impairment of constitutional rights"; (3) "no alternatives less subversive of constitutional rights are available."

In the *Finot* case the court held that the school board had failed to meet the second and third tests. It ruled that the benefit in supporting school rules outlawing student beards does not outweigh Finot's right to wear a beard while teaching in a classroom. Furthermore, there are other alternatives open to the school board to deter students from wearing beards that are less subversive of Finot's rights than the policy in question.

The Peek Case: An Instance of Institutional Racism[50]

Ribault Senior High School in Duval County, Florida, had one black teacher. His name was Booker C. Peek, and he wore a goatee as a matter of racial pride. As a French teacher he was considered superior.

Peek's principal repeatedly requested that he remove his goatee, and Peek repeatedly refused. Because of this refusal, Peek was not reappointed to the Duval County School System. Peek believed his constitutional rights were violated by the action and he went to court. The school board claimed that Peek's nonreappointment was based on a reasonable exercise of the principal's discretionary power. However, the court ruled in Peek's favor for the following reasons:

> It referred with approval to the holding in the *Finot* case that the wearing of a beard by a teacher is a constitutionally protected liberty under the Due Process Clause of the Fourteenth Amendment. "The wearer of the goatee here," said the court, "deserves no less protection."
>
> When a goatee is worn by a black man as an expression of his heritage, culture, and racial pride, "its wearer also enjoys the protection of First Amendment rights."
>
> There were no written rules or policy in the school system regulating the discretion conferred upon each principal by the school board in matters of personal appearance. In the absence of such regulations, the action of the principal in requesting the removal of the goatee was "arbitrary, unreasonable and based on personal preference."
>
> The decision to recommend nonreappointment was racially motivated and tainted with "institutional racism," the effects of which were manifested in "an intolerance of ethnic diversity and racial pride." Accordingly, the court ordered the school board to reappoint Booker Peek.*

Miller v. *Cook County Schools:* Latitude to Make Mistakes[51]

Max Miller was a junior high school mathematics teacher from Illinois whose contract was not renewed because of his beard and sideburns. Miller alleged that this violated his constitutional rights. But a federal appeals court disagreed.

Judge Stevens wrote that the members of the court personally regarded "dress and hair style as matters of relatively trivial importance on any scale of values in appraising the qualifications of a teacher." However, school officials may consider an individual's appearance as one of the factors affecting his suitability. The court acknowledged that logically appearance should not be significant and "a teacher should be

---

*In a related case, a federal district court in Mississippi reinstated three black teachers who were fired for failing to comply with a school's grooming regulations. *Conard* v. *Goolsby*, 350 F.Supp. 713 (N.D. Miss. 1972).

able to explain the pythagorean theorem as well in a t-shirt as in a three-piece suit." Nevertheless it noted that "a student's reaction to his teacher is undoubtedly affected by the image he projects."

According to the court, recent cases have raised doubts as to whether grooming choices are protected by the Constitution.[52] Even if such a right exists, it is a relatively minor one. Therefore the court reached two decisions. First, if a school board should *correctly* conclude that a "teacher's style of dress or plumage" has an adverse educational impact and if that conclusion conflicts with a teacher's lifestyle, "we have no doubt that the interest of the teacher is subordinate to the public interest." Second, the court said it would reach the same conclusion even if the school were *incorrect* and the teacher's grooming did not interfere with the educational process. Why? Because the court was persuaded that allowing local boards "the freedom to make diverse choices" and "sufficient latitude to discharge their responsibilities"—and inevitably "to make mistakes from time to time"—outweighs the teacher's interests in these cases.[53]

Morrison v. *Hamilton County:* To Look at Each Other[54]

In upholding a school's antibeard policy for teachers, the Supreme Court of Tennessee wrote:

> The grooming of one person is of concern not only to himself but to all others with whom he comes in contact; we have to look at each other, whether we like it or not. It is for this reason that society sets certain limits upon the freedom of individuals to choose his own grooming.[55]

In a concurring opinion, one of the judges irreverently commented that although the teacher's beard may "provide an unjustified diversion to the class, it could well be that without his beard he would furnish an even more detrimental diversion of attention. Who knows?"

CLOTHING

The Blanchet Case: Enforcing Professional Standards[56]

In September 1967 a Louisiana school board passed the following new policy:

> Each teacher is expected to give proper attention to his personal appearance. A pleasing appearance in dress and manner influences the reaction of students to the teacher and to the general learning environment. A teacher also comes in daily contact with the public, a public which is sometimes very critical of the appropriateness and neatness of the teacher's dress. The teacher who is particular about personal appearances not only contributes to his own acceptance by others, but also influences the attitudes of students and adults toward the teaching profession. The matter of appropriate dress

should be of equal concern of men and women teachers and should reflect accepted standards of good grooming. In the interest of enhancing the image of the teaching profession at school, in the classroom, and in the community, it shall be required that male teachers wear neckties in the official performance of their duties during the course of the school day. Teachers of physical education, industrial arts and vocational agriculture, when teaching outdoor or shop classes, may wear dress appropriate to the teaching of those activities.[57]

When teacher Edward Blanchet refused to comply with the necktie requirement, he was charged with "willful neglect of duty" and suspended until he agreed to comply. Blanchet then filed suit to enjoin the board from enforcing the resolution.

Questions to Consider

1. Is it reasonable for a school board to be concerned with the public image of a teacher? If so, is it reasonable for school boards to require that teachers dress in accordance with "conventional professional standards" in the community? Or does the regulation of a teacher's dress go beyond the authority of a school board?
2. If you were a member of a school board, would you institute a dress code for teachers? If so, what would the code require? Or would you allow complete freedom for teachers to dress as they wished?
3. Would you apply the same principles in judging the constitutionality of dress regulations as of grooming regulations?

THE OPINION OF THE COURT

The Louisiana Court of Appeals was impressed by Blanchet's character and conviction. Thus, Judge Tate wrote:

> From motives all concede to be of the utmost sincerity, this dedicated teacher and father of seven felt the regulation so unreasonably interfered with his personal liberty that, on the strength of this conviction, he chanced his livelihood and the career to which he had dedicated most of his adult life.
> While we might lightly say that, after all, a necktie is only a piece of cloth, nevertheless for the same motives which impelled the Boston merchants not to pay that insignificant little tax on tea just before this nation's independence, Blanchet felt strongly that this regulation impinged on his personal liberty to dress as he wished, without having any reasonable relationship to any educational value.[58]

Despite Blanchet's convictions, arguments, and evidence, the court did not rule in his favor. Here is what happened and why.

Blanchet argued that the rule requiring male teachers to wear neckties during the school day was arbitrary, unreasonable, and unrelated to any educational aim. He introduced evidence indicating that for years most male teachers in rural areas taught without ties, that wearing ties was uncomfortable in the hot months in Louisiana, and that only a small minority of other school boards in the state required teachers to wear neckties. The evidence also indicated that during his 18 years of teaching Blanchet had always dressed neatly, although he usually did not wear a tie. Furthermore, evidence showed him to be "a dedicated and effective teacher, an assistant principal at his school, [and] a sober church-going family man."

In support of its position the school board argued that wearing neckties enhances the image of the teacher as a professional man, increasing the respect accorded him by community and students. There was evidence that most leading citizens and professional men in the community usually wear ties, "representing a conventional attire for those in positions of leadership."

In view of the evidence for and against the board's policy, the court said it would not substitute its judgment for that of the board. Members of school boards are presumably elected or appointed "because of their peculiar fitness for the post." In contrast, judges are chosen because of their legal knowledge, not for their experience in administering a public school system. Therefore, a "presumption of legality attaches to the action" of a school board. Only when evidence shows that the action of such a board is arbitrary or unreasonable is a court justified in interfering. Since in this case the court found that there was a rational basis for the board's policy, it could not be overturned.

Although *Blanchet* may have resolved this issue in Louisiana, the question of teacher attire remained alive during the next decade in other states and in the federal courts. Then in 1977 a federal court of appeals twice reviewed this issue in the following case.

Brimley v. *Hartford:* Trivializing the Constitution[59]

Richard Brimley taught English and filmmaking in an East Hartford public high school. Unlike Blanchet, he wanted to present himself to his students as a person not tied to "establishment conformity," as someone associated with the social outlook of the student generation. Therefore he refused to comply with the school's dress code that required a jacket, shirt, and tie for male teachers in ordinary classroom situations. Like Blanchet, Brimley believed that his "personal integrity" was invaded by the dress regulations, and he also felt that they diminished his effectiveness as a teacher. Therefore he and his union went to court to ask that the regulations be declared unconstitutional. After a federal district court ruled in favor of the school board, Brimley appealed.

Questions to Consider

1. Do you think a court should strike down the Hartford dress code? Why or why not?

2. What are the rights and responsibilities of teachers concerning proper dress? Is there a constitutional right involved? If so, what is the scope and limit of that right?
3. Do you believe there is an important principle involved in this case? If not, are there dangers in courts becoming involved in "trivial" issues? Or are there greater dangers in courts not protecting "minor" rights?

• The Teacher's Interest. A three-judge panel of the Second Circuit Court of Appeals heard this case and a majority ruled in favor of Brimley. Citing history, literature, and philosophy as well as recent cases, Judge Oakes concluded that an individual's appearance involves "a liberty" protected by the Fourteenth Amendment. This liberty interest, wrote the court, includes "freedom from all substantial arbitrary impositions and purposeless restraints."

Brimley also argued that his case involved "the inseparable complex of speech, conduct and character known as teaching" which should be protected from needless regulation by the First Amendment. Judge Oakes agreed. Although schools have wide discretion to decide what is taught, teachers should be free to choose their own methods. According to the court, academic freedom extends "to the particular style of clothing" a teacher wishes to wear—especially when he seems sincere, neat, and reasonable.

• The School's Interest. The school board claimed that its dress code established a "professional image" for teachers, promotes good grooming among students, and helps maintain respect in the classroom. Judge Oakes rejected each argument. He noted that among younger doctors, dentists, clergymen, and engineers "a tie is no longer mandatory and is far from typical." Considering the wide variation in attire worn by professionals today, the board's statement that it wants teachers to wear ties to enhance their "professional image" is almost meaningless and amounts to little more than "it wants its teachers to wear ties because it wants them to wear ties."

The court doubted that there was any significant relationship between the school's tie requirement and the promotion of good grooming among students. Nor did Judge Oakes see any connection between a tie code and classroom respect or discipline. On the contrary, the court observed that "teenagers who are so often rebellious against authority may find a tieless teacher to be a less remote, more contemporary individual with whom they can more easily interact, and hence to whom they are better prepared to listen with care and attention." Judge Oakes concluded that the arguments of the board did not outweigh Brimley's liberty and First Amendment interests.

REHEARING AND REVERSAL

Generally, a decision by a three-judge appeals panel ends the case.* But in this instance, a majority of the judges of the Second Circuit voted to rehear the case because of "the important issue it raised" concerning judicial review of local school board affairs. After a 1977 rehearing before all ten judges, the circuit court voted 8 to 2 to dismiss Brimley's suit.

On behalf of the full court, Judge Meskill wrote that even though school board decisions "may appear foolish or unwise," a federal court should not overturn them unless they "directly and sharply implicate basic constitutional values." Because the court did not believe that this case involved such basic values, it refused to upset the dress code of the school board.

The court was skeptical of Brimley's argument that not wearing a tie was a form of symbolic speech deserving constitutional protection. Unlike those who wore armbands to protest the Vietnam War, what Brimley's refusal meant was vague and unfocused. Because Brimley's message was not clear, it seemed more like conduct than "pure speech" and therefore is entitled to less protection under the First Amendment. Thus the federal courts should restrict themselves to important constitutional issues and not consider this kind of case which is "so insubstantial as to border on the frivolous." "We are unwilling," wrote Judge Meskill, "to expand First Amendment protection to include a teacher's sartorial choice."

The full court balanced the interests of the school and the teacher differently from the three-judge panel. "If Mr. Brimley has any protected interest in his neckwear," wrote the court, "it does not weight very heavily on the constitutional scales." Therefore, the board's regulations should be presumed constitutional unless they can be proved to be irrational and arbitrary. And this Brimley did not do.

Finally, Judge Meskill observed that courts have not been given "a 'roving commission' to right wrongs and impose our notions of sound policy on society." On the contrary, he emphasized the danger in expanding the Constitution to cover cases like this. By bringing "trivial activities" under constitutional protection, "we trivialize the Constitution." The court concluded that "we must be careful not to 'cry wolf' at every minor restraint on a citizen's liberty."

Tardif v. *Quinn:* **Termination for Overexposure**[60]

Claudette Tardif was a 25-year-old high school French teacher whose skirts were shortened according to the youthful style of the late 1960s.

---

*Unlike the Supreme Court, in which all nine judges usually hear the cases, all of the judges of the U.S. Circuit Courts rarely decide cases. The work of the circuit courts is typically done by alternating panels of three judges who decide most cases for the circuit.

Her department head threatened that if she did not change her mode of dress, she would "no longer be in the school system." Tardif made no change; she was therefore not rehired and she sued.

The teacher, observed the court, was terminated because her "image" was "overexposed." Although the court had recognized student grooming as a constitutional right, it refused to extend constitutional protection to teachers' dress. It noted that school dress regulations require less justification than grooming restrictions that affect individuals 24 hours a day. Moreover, teacher attire is not just a personal matter but involves a contractual relationship. According to the court: "Whatever constitutional aspect there may be to one's choice of apparel generally, it is hardly a matter which falls totally beyond the scope of the demands which an employer, public or private, can legitimately make upon its employees."

Summary

STUDENTS

• **Grooming.** Eight out of the 11 U.S. Circuit Courts of Appeals have clearly ruled on the constitutional right of students to choose the length of their hair.* As the map at the end of this chapter indicates, some circuits hold that grooming is a constitutional right and other circuits do not. The arguments used on each side are varied and vigorous and no final decision establishing a uniform law has been reached since the Supreme Court has refused to rule on the issue.

• **Upholding Student Rights.** The following are some of the constitutional arguments used to support a student's right to wear his hair as he wishes: A student's hair style is part of the personal liberty assured to citizens by the Due Process Clause of the Fourteenth Amendment; the "freedom to govern one's personal appearance" is retained by individual citizens under the Ninth Amendment; and it is part of the freedom of expression protected by the First Amendment.

In addition, judges have offered these educational and philosophic arguments: hair regulations bear no reasonable relation to a legitimate educational objective; they teach conformity for its own sake; and they are not necessary for health or safety. Their enforcement projects the prejudices of certain adults in authority and causes more disruption than does the presence of long-haired students. If such students cause others to be disruptive, school officials should teach the disrupters tolerance and

*Although the other three circuits have not ruled directly on this issue, they have indicated how they probably would vote as the footnotes on pp. 367 and 368 indicate.

not suppress diversity. It is dangerous to say the problem is best left to local authorities; such a rationale could support any prohibition of teacher or student rights.

• **Upholding School Rules.** Among the legal reasons courts give for upholding school grooming regulations are: the regulations seek to accomplish "legitimate objectives" and have "a real and reasonable connection" with maintaining school discipline; and the Constitution does not protect grooming, but even if it does, it is one of the "lesser liberties" and not a fundamental right.

In addition, judges upholding school regulations note that their purpose is to eliminate distracting extremes in hair style, to avoid possible conflicts, and to eliminate potential health and safety hazards. Even if some codes restrict student freedom, their effect is temporary and "relatively inconsequential" and still leave students a wide range of choice in grooming. School officials should have discretion and authority to develop dress codes without having to justify their professional judgment in court. Finally, all school regulations restricting student liberty cannot be litigated, for the judicial process is administratively unable to deal with the infringement of every minor right.

CLOTHING
Courts are divided on whether students have a right to wear the clothing of their choice. Most courts, including all those that support the right of schools to regulate hair length, hold that they do not. Each of the arguments used to reject the right of students to wear long hair has been used to reject their right to wear unconventional clothing. Moreover, some courts that protect student hair length reject students' claims to wear the clothing of their choice. Such courts justify the distinction on the grounds that restrictions on hair style are more serious invasions of individual freedom; after all, clothing can be easily changed after school, but the effect of haircuts is more lasting.

A few courts protect clothing as well as grooming. Judges, for example, have ruled that flat prohibitions against boys wearing dungarees or frayed trousers, or girls wearing slacks or long dresses are illegal because they are not reasonably related to the school's responsibility or its curriculum. Even these courts, however, recognize the validity of school regulations prohibiting certain kinds of clothing because of health or safety, or to prevent disturbance or distraction.

Compared to the "great grooming controversy," there are relatively few reported cases concerning clothing. As one federal judge observed, this may indicate that students, parents, and administrators do not view clothes with the same emotion with which they regard hair length, or more probably "that most school boards are no longer concerned with what a student wears to school as long as it is clean and covers adequately those parts of the body that, by tradition, are usually kept from public view."

TEACHERS

• **Grooming.** In the late 1960s and early 1970s, *Finot* was cited as a leading case to indicate that a teacher's grooming is a form of personal expression or symbolic speech entitled to the peripheral protection of the First Amendment. According to *Finot*, only if a school board could prove that a teacher's beard, mustache, or long hair interfered with his effectiveness could officials take action against him.

In recent years, the trend of decision has shifted. Courts seem less inclined to recognize teacher grooming as a constitutional right. Even a federal appeals court that had clearly protected student grooming declined to do so for teachers. Recent decisions seem to indicate that public employees may not have a constitutional right concerning their "style of plumage," or if they do, it deserves less protection than the freedom of school boards to establish reasonable grooming codes for teachers.

• **Dress.** The judicial protection of administrative discretion is even clearer in the area of teacher attire. Most courts have ruled that teachers do not have a constitutional right to dress as they please. In *Blanchet, Brimley,* and other cases, judges have emphasized that schools have the authority to discipline teachers for violating school dress codes—even when this involves necktie requirements or other restrictions the courts think unwise or insignificant. This is because courts assume that all employers can establish some clothing regulations and because such restrictions on teacher freedom are relatively minor.

Courts, however, might be more likely to protect certain nonconforming clothing under special circumstances. Thus they might protect a black teacher of African studies who wears a dashiki as directly relevant to his job or as a matter of academic freedom and racial pride. But it is doubtful that any court would protect a teacher who insisted on going to class in frayed jeans, sandals, and a t-shirt. This would be true even if he could prove that his dress was not distracting and did not interfere with his teaching.

In short, a teacher's grooming may sometimes be protected as a form of personal liberty or symbolic speech. But the trend of decision is to regard the regulation of both dress and grooming as a matter that does not implicate "basic constitutional values" and therefore an area for administrative discretion and not for judicial supervision.

• **Conclusion.** Now, in the 1980s, some readers may find it difficult to understand why so many students and teachers, parents and administrators were so concerned with issues of personal appearance during the last two decades. But the questions raised by these controversies involve far more; they concern such fundamental legal and educational issues as: When can school officials restrict student and teacher freedom? Should nonconformity be guarded or restricted in our schools? Should courts protect individual choices or just "fundamental" freedoms?

In the coming years, dress codes may no longer be the symbol that triggers this larger debate. But the underlying issues will be with us as long as we continue to struggle with the problems of freedom and conformity in the public schools.

NOTES

1. *Blanchet* v. *Vermilion School Board,* 220 So.2d 534 (La. 1969).
2. *Ferrell* v. *Dallas Independent School District,* 393 U.S. 856 (1968).
3. Controversy over hair length has been taking place on this continent at least since 1649 when the magistrates of Portsmouth issued the following regulation: "For as much as the wearing of long hair, after the manner of ruffians and barbarous Indians, has begun to invade New England, we, the magistrates, do declare and manifest our dislike and detestation against the wearing of such long hair, as against a thing uncivil and unmanly, whereby men do deform themselves and do corrupt good manners." Dale Gaddy, *Rights and Freedoms of Public School Students: Directions from the 1960's,* Topeka, Kansas, National Organization on Legal Problems in Education, 1971, p. 25.
4. *Pugsley* v. *Sellmeyer,* 250 S.W. 538 (Ark. 1923).
5. *Karr* v. *Schmidt,* 460 F.2d 609 (5th Cir. 1972).
6. Id. at 610−611.
7. Id. at 617.
8. In conclusion, Judge Morgan wrote:

> The regulations which impinge on our daily affairs are legion. Many of them are more intrusive and tenuous than the one involved here. The federal judiciary has urgent tasks to perform, and to be able to perform them, we must recognize the physical impossibility that less than a thousand of us could ever enjoin a uniform concept of equal protection or due process on every American in every facet of his daily life [Id. at 618].

9. Id. at 620.
10. Id. at 621.
11. Id. at 623−624.
12. *Bishop* v. *Colaw,* 450 F.2d 1069, 1071 (8th Cir. 1971).
13. *King* v. *Saddleback,* 445 F.2d 932 (9th Cir. 1971).
14. In a related case upholding grooming rules, the Tenth Circuit noted the lack of consensus among lawyers for students as to what constitutional provision would protect student grooming. It concluded that "the hodgepodge reference to many provisions of the Bill of Rights and the Fourteenth Amendment shows uncertainty as to the existence of any federally-protected right." *Freeman* v. *Flake,* 448 F.2d 258 (10th Cir. 1971).

15. *Jackson* v. *Dorrier*, 424 F.2d 213 (6th Cir. 1970), cert. denied, 400 U.S. 850 (1970).
16. *Mercer* v. *Board of Trustees, North Forest Independent School District*, 538 S.W.2d 201 (Tex. 1976).
17. Id. at 206.
18. See, for example, *Crews* v. *Cloncs*, 432 F.2d 1259 (7th Cir. 1970). For further discussion of ERAs, see Chapter 11.
19. *Ferrara* v. *Hendry County School Board*, 362 So.2d 371 (Fla. 1978).
20. Id. at 375.
21. *Richards* v. *Thurston*, 424 F.2d 1281 (1st Cir. 1971).
22. Id. at 1286.
23. *Bishop* v. *Colaw*, 450 F.2d 1069 (8th Cir. 1971).
24. *Union Pacific Railway Company* v. *Botsford*, 141 U.S. 250 (1891).
25. *Bishop* at 1077.
26. Id. at 1077–1078. This quotation was from the concurring opinion of Judge Bailey Aldrich of the First Circuit Court of Appeals who lives in Boston and was "sitting by designation" in this Eighth Circuit case.
27. Id. at 1078.
28. Ibid.
29. Ibid.
30. *Massie* v. *Henry*, 455 F.2d 779 (4th Cir. 1972).
31. Id. at 780.
32. *Crews* v. *Cloncs*, 432 F.2d 1259 (7th Cir. 1970).
33. *Arnold* v. *Carpenter*, 459 F.2d 939 (7th Cir. 1972).
34. "After reviewing several decisions which had concluded that the "long hair" problem was not substantial enough to warrant judicial intervention, Judge Kiley observed:

    It is understandable why some judges find students' "long hair" claims constitutionally insubstantial. Measured against today's great constitutional issues (capital punishment, abortion, school segregation), the question of whether a student may or may not have constitutional protection in selection of his hair dress appears *de minimus*. Perhaps even judges who sustain the right are nagged with impatience and doubt when faced with student claims. But we look across a gap of a generation or two, from the Olympian heights of what we consider the great issues. For the high school student claimant, however, the right to wear long hair is an issue vital to him . . . and there appears to be no reason why the values of freedom are less precious in a younger generation than in an older. [Id. at 941–942.]

35. Furthermore, Judge Stevens noted: "It does not take the wisdom of Solomon to recognize that dress codes which have been judicially condemned were doomed to fall in due course in any event. Judicial participation in the process of changing mores can affect the rate of change, but we certainly do not decide whether or not the change will occur," Id. at 945.
36. "I cannot understand," wrote Judge Stevens, "why we should intervene in this case to save a child's parent from walking over to the principal's office" where the only legal relief his son may obtain "is available for the asking.'
37. *Karr* v. *Schmidt*, 401 U.S. 1201 (1971).

38. *Ferrell* v. *Dallas*, 393 U.S. 856 (1968).
39. For example, the Supreme Court declined to review both *Breen* v. *Kahl*, 419 F.2d 1034 (7th Cir. 1969), cert. denied 398 U.S. 937 (1970), which recognized grooming as a constitutional right, and *Jackson* v. *Dorrier*, cert. denied 400 U.S. 850 (1970), which did not recognize such a right. For more information on Supreme Court review, see Appendix B, How the System Works.
40. *Jones* v. *Day*, 89 So. 906 (Miss. 1921).
41. *Bannister* v. *Paradis*, 316 F.Supp. 185 (D. N.H. 1970).
42. *Webster's Third International Dictionary* unsurprisingly defines *dungarees* as "heavy cotton work clothes usually made of blue dungaree." *Bannister* at 186.
43. Section 1983 of the 1964 Civil Rights Act provides that "Every person who, under color of any statute of any state subjects any citizen to the deprivation of any rights . . . secured by the Constitution and laws, shall be liable to the party injured in an action at law." Judge Bownes found that the enforcement of the Pittsfield dress code was clearly an action by the state of New Hampshire, Id. at 187.
44. Ibid.
45. From *Westley* v. *Rossi*, 305 F.Supp. 706, 714 (D. Minn. 1969), as quoted in *Bannister* at 189.
46. *Scott* v. *Board of Education, Hicksville*, 305 N.Y.S.2d 601 (1969).
47. *Dunham* v. *Pulsifer*, 312 F.Supp. 411, 419 (D. Vt. 1970).
48. *Westley* v. *Rossi*, 305 F.Supp. 706 (D. Minn. 1969).
49. *Finot* v. *Pasadena City Board of Education*, 58 Cal. Rptr. 520 (1967).
50. *Braxton* v. *Board of Public Instruction of Duval County, Florida*, 303 F.Supp. 958 (M.D. Fla. 1969).
51. *Miller* v. *School District Number 167, Cook County, Illinois*, 495 F.2d 658 (7th Cir. 1974).
52. See, for example, *Ham* v. *South Carolina*, 409 U.S. 524 (1973), concerning the Supreme Court's ruling that there is no constitutional right to interrogate prospective jurors about their possible prejudice against a defendant because he wore a beard.
53. Judge Stevens observed that "since the acceptance of employment . . . always entails some need to comply with an employer's concept of the manners which are suitable for the position, including matters of speech and behavior as well as appearance and grooming, the deliberate nonconformist inevitably prejudices his own employment prospects." *Miller*, op. cit., 29, pp. 665–666.
54. *Morrison* v. *Hamilton County Board of Education*, 494 S.W.2d 770 (Tenn. 1973).
55. Id. at 773.
56. *Blanchet* v. *Vermilion Parish School Board*, 220 So.2d 534 (La. 1969).
57. Id. at 541.
58. Id. at 540.
59. *East Hartford Education Association* v. *Board of Education of the Town of East Hartford*, 562 F.2d 838 (2nd Cir. 1977).
60. *Tardif* v. *Quinn*, 545 F.2d 761 (1st Cir. 1976).

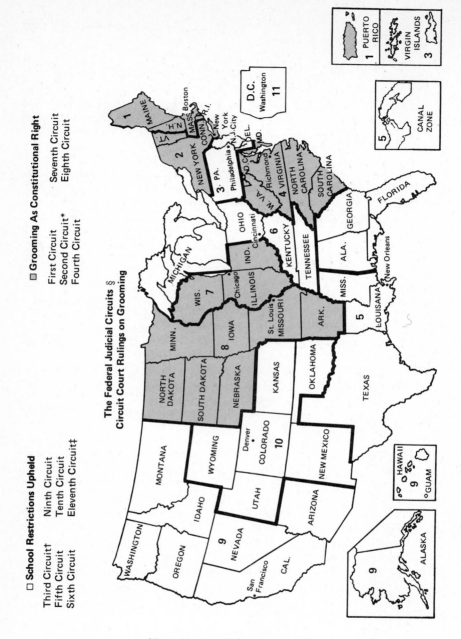

The Federal Judicial Circuits §
Circuit Court Rulings on Grooming

☐ School Restrictions Upheld

Third Circuit†   Ninth Circuit†
Fifth Circuit   Tenth Circuit
Sixth Circuit   Eleventh Circuit‡

■ Grooming As Constitutional Right

First Circuit   Seventh Circuit
Second Circuit*   Eighth Circuit
Fourth Circuit

*Probable. See first note page 367.

†Probable. See first note page 368.

‡Probable. See second note page 185.

§ A new federal circuit court has been added,
   effective October 1, 1981. See map on page 416.

Chapter 15
Other Rights and Frontier Issues

> . . . a school board member is not immune from liability for damages . . . if he knew or should have known that the action he took within his sphere of official responsibility would violate the constitutional rights of the student affected . . .
>
> The Supreme Court in *Wood* v. *Strickland.*

In the preceding chapters we explored the most widely known and litigated rights of students and teachers. Recent years saw the emergence of still other rights—some from new interpretations of the Constitution and others derived from legislation. These are the rights we present in this chapter, together with some frontier issues—issues where there are few if any judicial decisions or clear legislation—issues that will provoke educational and legal debate during the coming years.

Among the rights we explore here are those related to exceptional children, to students of limited English-speaking ability, as well as the complex matter of inequality of school finance. We then highlight some frontier issues.

SPECIAL EDUCATION: RIGHTS OF THE HANDICAPPED

Historically, although most states compelled children to attend school, they also found ways to exclude certain children from the reach of such laws. Children with difficult learning disabilities, and emotional or physical handicaps, had various labels attached to them, but were ultimately branded "uneducable," and excluded from public schools. During any one year hundreds of thousands of children were out of school in our country as a result of such laws. These laws merely reflected the popular belief that most of these children could not be educated or even trained and thus social resources should not be wasted on them.

A very different view is generally accepted today with the support of respectable scientific evidence. The current view holds that *all* human beings can benefit from appropriate education or training. Based on extensive evidence and mounting popular support to extend the benefits of schooling to *all* children, some parents went to court to secure educational rights for their retarded children.

The PARC Case: Retarded Children

Prior to 1972 the laws of Pennsylvania kept children out of school if they were certified by school psychologists as "uneducable and untrainable."[1] In that year, the parents of 17 children, together with the Pennsylvania Association for Retarded Children (PARC), challenged these laws, claiming them to be unconstitutional because (1) they violated due process by not giving parents notice and a proper hearing; (2) they denied equal protection of the laws by assuming certain children to be uneducable without a rational basis in fact; and (3) the state constitution guaranteed education for all children; the laws that excluded retarded children were arbitrary and capricious.

When the federal district court ruled that schools may not exclude retarded children, it gave the contending parties an opportunity to work out an arrangement acceptable to both sides. Once they reached an agreement, the court incorporated it into its decision and thus it came to have the force of law. This decision requires careful and elaborate due process before any child may be placed in special education classes or before any change in such placement may be made.

Since the state constitution guaranteed free public schooling for all children, retarded children could not be excluded. Although some retarded children might be more appropriately educated in special classes, the degree of retardation as well as suitable placement must be individually determined for each child. Furthermore, mistakes in diagnosis have placed some normal children into inappropriate special classes. One important function of due process is to reduce the risk of errors in diagnosis and in educational placement.

The court recognized that labeling a child "retarded" and placing him in a class for the retarded itself creates a handicap; consequently it is very important to guard against inappropriate placement. Although mild cases of retardation can be "mainstreamed" or integrated with normal children, most retarded students benefit from special classes taught by qualified teachers. It was agreed that the least desirable alternative was homebound instruction which should be used as a last resort, according to the court, and then only with qualified teachers. Furthermore, such arrangements must be reevaluated every three months, with proper notice to the parent or the guardian, who may request a hearing on the case.

Are these arrangements applicable only to retarded students or do they also apply to other areas of exceptionality? This issue was faced in the *Mills* case in Washington, D.C.

The Mills Case: Other Disabilities

During the 1972–1973 academic year, close to 18,000 handicapped children were not being educated in Washington, D.C. "Exceptional" or handicapped children included the mentally retarded, emotionally disturbed, physically disabled, hyperactive, and those with serious behavioral problems.[2] Although local law mandated free public education for all children between the ages of 7 and 16, these children were systematically excluded from schools.

When parents challenged these exclusionary school practices, the court ruled in their favor. The children may not be excluded and the constitutional right to due process must be followed before anyone can be labeled "exceptional" and before an educational placement is decided on for such a child.

School officials argued, however, that there were not adequate funds available for the appropriate schooling of all children and that the education of exceptional children is particularly expensive. This argument is often heard, coupled with the notion that society will benefit less from the education of the handicapped than from the schooling of normal children.

Questions to Consider

1. When resources are scarce, should we not use it for the schooling of those children who will benefit society the most?
2. Is the use of equal resources for the education of all children fair and equitable?

The district court ruled that the lack of funds for identifying and educating exceptional children was not a sufficient or acceptable reason for failing to provide them with appropriate schooling. If funds are inadequate, they must nevertheless be used equally for *all* children. And particularly, no child should be completely excluded from publicly supported education. In the words of the court:

> The inadequacies of the District of Columbia Public School System, whether occasioned by insufficient funding or administrative inefficiency, certainly

cannot be permitted to bear more heavily on the "exceptional" or handicapped child than on the normal child.

The court ruled that the exclusion of these children violated both the
Equal Protection and Due Process Clauses of the Constitution. As in the
PARC case, the ruling required that the parents be notified and have
opportunities to be involved every step of the way in the diagnosis and
appropriate placement of their children.

STATUTORY DEVELOPMENTS

Subsequent to the landmark cases in Pennsylvania and the District of
Columbia, similar problems were addressed in other states both through
court cases and legislation. Clearly, many "exceptional" children can
succeed in ordinary classrooms if their teachers are sensitive to their
needs and receive some support services from trained specialists. Thus
large numbers of such children are being "mainstreamed" in many states.

Case law and legislation both support the conviction that children
and their parents have a right to due process and equal protection of the
laws *before* a child is identified as exceptional and *in the process* of
determining an appropriate educational placement. Furthermore, due
process requires periodic reevaluations and altering of placements if
warranted by the reevaluation. Prior to the use of such careful procedures, many children were excluded from schooling altogether and still
others were misdiagnosed and inappropriately placed. Examples could be
given of thousands of children who were misdiagnosed as mentally
retarded simply because their language was different from the one used to
test them. Important steps have been taken to prevent such educational
malpractices in the future. These steps include new state laws as well as a
broadly inclusive federal law—Public Law 94–142, generally known as
the Education for All Handicapped Children Act of 1975.

Public Law 94–142

The purpose of the law is to assure that all handicapped children have
available to them "a free appropriate public education and related
services designed to meet their unique needs." These purposes are stated
in the preamble along with a recognition by Congress that there were
over 8 million handicapped children in the United State at the time the
law was enacted and that most of them were receiving inadequate
education.

What age children come under this law? Initially, the law applied to
children between the ages of 3 and 18 and on September 1, 1980, to all
children between 3 and 21. However, since education is basically a state
responsibility, Public Law 94–142 applies only to the ages covered by the
laws of the individual states. For example, if a state provides schools

between the ages of 4 and 18, the federal law cannot extend it from 3 to 21. The federal law provides for the education of handicapped children only indirectly, by providing funds to states that comply with its provisions. Within each state the funds must go first to handicapped children currently not receiving any education and second to children with the most severe handicaps currently receiving inadequate education.

Where will handicapped children be educated? According to the law, they will be educated in the "least restrictive" environment appropriate to their needs. When possible and for as much time as possible, they should be educated with ordinary children, that is, "mainstreamed." A regular class with appropriate support is preferable to special classes; special classes are preferable to special schools; special schools are preferred to home teaching; and home teaching is better than no teaching at all. If no appropriate public schools are available, private schools may be used with public funds paying the costs. They must, of course, meet the same standards applied to state or local public schools.

Is attention paid to individual children under this law? Yes, the law requires that an individualized educational plan be developed for each handicapped child in cooperation with the parents, and that such plans be reviewed annually. The plan must indicate the child's current level of school performance, the educational services to be provided, and the criteria to measure his progress. Schools must keep records of these individualized educational plans.

What procedures protect students and their parents under this law? The regulations provide for an elaborate set of safeguards that must include at least the following:

a. Access to all relevant school records.
b. Prior notice to parents of any proposed change in their child's educational placement or program and a written explanation of the procedures to be followed in effecting that change.
c. All communications with parents must be in the primary language of the parents; testing of children must not be discriminatory in language, race, or culture.
d. Opportunity for a fair and impartial hearing to be conducted by the State Educational Agency (SEA) or local school district, not by the employee "involved in the education or care of the child." At any hearing, parents have the right to be represented by a lawyer or an individual trained in the problems of handicapped children; the right to present evidence; to subpoena, confront, and cross-examine witnesses; and to obtain a transcript of the hearing and a written decision by the hearing officer. Parents may appeal the decision to the SEA and, if they are still not satisfied, may appeal the SEA ruling in court.
e. The child has a right to remain in his or her current placement until the due process proceedings are completed. If the child is just beginning school, he or she may be enrolled in public school until then.

f.   A "surrogate parent" will be designated for children who are wards of the state or whose parents or guardians are unknown or unavailable.

This landmark statute contains many other provisions, such as those protecting the confidentiality of school records, and the allocation of funds to state and local educational agencies. The law is a great stride toward improving the education of all handicapped children, although some of its provisions will need further clarification through legislative action or through litigation.

One example of such litigation arose in Pennsylvania in 1979, where suit was filed challenging a State Department of Education policy that refused to fund the education for any child, handicapped or not, beyond 180 days per year.[3] The plaintiff claimed that under Public Law 94–142, the law required appropriate education that enabled handicapped children to attain reasonable self-sufficiency, and claimed that children who were severely retarded or emotionally disturbed were seriously hampered by the 180-day rule. They regressed during the long break from schooling and too much time was wasted at the beginning of each year regaining the lost skills.

The district court, after examining the legislative intent behind the federal law, ruled in favor of the plaintiffs. It struck down the 180-day rules as one that deprives these children of an "appropriate education" and therefore violates Public Law 94–142.

The significance of this law is also illustrated in controversies involving the suspension or expulsion of exceptional children. At least one case held that expulsion is forbidden because it is a violation of the child's right to "a free appropriate public education."[4] Not all courts agree with this and one case held that expulsion is a "change in placement" under P.L. 94–142, and therefore, although it may be allowed, it must be preceded by the same evaluation and due process required for other changes in placement.[5] If the disruptive behavior is related to the child's handicap, courts consider that evidence that the child in not appropriately placed. If it is clear that the misbehavior is unrelated to the handicap, some courts will allow the suspension or even expulsion.[6] We may expect many other cases in the future in attempts to clarify and implement this very important and inclusive piece of legislation.

BILINGUAL EDUCATION

Although we are a diverse and pluralistic culture, the English language is the common instructional medium of our public schools. Many, if not most, people also believe that it is a necessary ingredient in the mortar that holds us together as a nation. In the past it was assumed that children who come from non-English-speaking homes will learn the language as they go through our schools. Indeed, many of them did; the others dropped out and took their places in the work force of the nation.

In recent times, as formal schooling and diplomas became increasingly important in the world of work, various issues arose in the schooling of children of limited English ability. Although many of these issues are technical, professional matters for educational theory and research, some legal questions have also surfaced. The most dramatic of these related to the placement of unusually large numbers of Mexican-American and Chinese-American children into classes for the retarded. This phenomenon was identified in California and throughout the Southwest.

When challenged through legal action, trial courts in California ruled that (1) if IQ tests are to be given to children, they are to be administered in their primary language as well as in English; (2) culturally and linguistically different children should be tested only with tests that do not unfairly use unfamiliar vocabulary or verbal questions; (3) minority language children in classes for the retarded must be retested in their primary language and with nonverbal tests; and (4) new standardized tests must be developed, tests that are based on the culture of the children. Since these legal developments in the late 1960s and early 1970s, significant strides have been made in the area of bilingual education. These advances were the results of further lawsuits and of new legislation. The most important case in this area, the *Lau* case, arose in San Francisco.

Lau v. *Nichols*

In 1974 of the thousands of Chinese-American students attending public schools in San Francisco, California, close to 3000 spoke little or no English. The evidence showed that about 1800 of these students received no school services designed to meet their linguistic needs. Yet, when the students and their parents went to court seeking more adequate education, in effect seeking equal educational opportunity, the federal district court ruled against them.

The court held that equal educational opportunity had been provided when "the same education [was] made available on the same terms and conditions to the other tens of thousands of students in the San Francisco Unified School District . . . " as to these students. When the Ninth Circuit affirmed this ruling,[7] the case was appealed to the Supreme Court.[8] The Court, reversing the decision, based its ruling on Title VI of the Civil Rights Act of 1964,[9] even though the plaintiffs claimed their rights under the Equal Protection Clause of the Constitution.*

---

*As a general policy, the Supreme Court will avoid the constitutional issue if a case can be decided on statutory grounds.

To the Court it was clear that students who understand little or no English do not receive equal educational opportunities when English is the sole medium of instruction and when there are no systematic efforts to teach that language to non-English-speaking students. In the words of the Court:

> Under these state-imposed standards there is no equal treatment merely by providing students with the same facilities, textbooks, teachers, and curriculum; for students who do not understand English are effectively foreclosed from any meaningful education.

The Court did not specify what remedy San Francisco should provide. Questions regarding remedies are usually left to the district court judges, as we have seen in desegregation cases. Various educational provisions might satisfy the courts, but disagreements over appropriate remedies have spawned further lawsuits. Often these suits intertwine issues related to bilingual education, questionable ability grouping, and racial or ethnic segregation.[10]

In 1975, the U.S. Office of Education and its Office of Civil Rights (OCR) issued a set of interpretations and recommendations commonly referred to as the "Lau remedies." These indicate acceptable ways to satisfy the law in providing instructional programs for students with limited English. The remedies do not mandate bilingual education; at the secondary level ESL is an acceptable alternative, and it might even be acceptable in lower grades. The important feature of any plan is its demonstrated educational effectiveness.

Since *Lau*, the federal government as well as several states have enacted laws providing for bilingual-bicultural education. Seven months after *Lau*, Congress passed the Equal Educational Opportunity Act of 1974,[11] codifying the Court's holding. The first state to enact such a law was Massachusetts, whose 1971 law became a prototype for other states.[12] The Bilingual Education Act of 1974[13] is a further major step toward the enhancement of bilingual education. Designed to meet the special educational needs of large numbers of children of limited English-speaking ability in the United States, it provides funds for planning and developing bilingual programs and teacher education. It also makes money available for early childhood and adult education, programs for dropouts, vocational programs, and courses in the history and culture of the language minority being served. The law also provides for opportunities for parent involvement in program planning and requires that, at the secondary school level, the students concerned also be involved in program planning and development. Although the law provides for classes in the students' own language and for ESL classes, it stipulates that these children shall attend regular classes in such courses as art, music, and physical education, where language skill is not a major requirement for success.

The Guadalupe Case

After *Lau*, some people came to believe that the Constitution and the federal laws mandate bilingual and bicultural education for language minority children all the way through high school. The *Guadalupe*[14] case in Arizona was based on such a conviction.

Elementary schoolchildren of Mexican-American and Yaqui Indian origin brought suit to compel the schools to provide bilingual-bicultural education. They claimed that the lack of such instruction violated their right to equal protection under the Fourteenth Amendment as well as rights provided for bilingual-bicultural education under federal laws.

The evidence indicated that the schools provided instruction to remedy existing language deficiencies of non-English-speaking students. However, the plaintiffs wanted the schools to provide continuous instruction in English and also in the child's native language, Spanish or Yaqui, from kindergarten to the fourth year of high school. The district court ruled against them and the court of appeals agreed.

The court first recognized that education, although very important, is not a fundamental right guaranteed by the Constitution. "Differences in the treatment of students in the educational process, which in themselves do not violate specific constitutional provisions, do not violate the . . . Equal Protection clause if such differences are nationally related to legitimate state interests."

Thus the Constitution does not require the provision of bilingual or bicultural education. Nor does it prohibit such programs; states may decide to offer such programs if they wish. The *Lau* case and other federal laws guarantee only that children of limited English ability be provided sufficient instruction to remove the language handicap with which they entered school. The *Guadalupe* case also contains some strong judicial opinions about the importance of one unifying language to maintain the social compact upon which our nation-state is based.

In sum, it is clear that significant strides have been made toward achieving equal educational opportunity on behalf of students of limited English-speaking ability. Although some legal issues still remain,[15] the major challenge before us now appear to be educational and financial.

FINANCIAL INEQUALITIES IN SCHOOLING

Even the casual observer realizes that in our country there are both "rich schools and poor schools." This fact results from the way we finance public schools; most of the money to support them comes from local real estate taxes. Enormous differences in school wealth result from the location of schools. Tax-rich schools tend to be those located in districts that have industries, businesses, and/or expensive private homes. Conversely, poor schools are located in districts that rely primarily on taxes levied against poor or working-class homes. Do such discrepancies violate the Equal Protection Clause of the Constitution? This question was raised in the *Rodriguez* case in Texas.

San Antonio Independent School District v. Rodriguez[16]

This was a suit brought on behalf of schoolchildren of "poor families" residing in school districts having low property-tax bases. It challenged the school finance system of Texas, claiming that the scheme violated the Equal Protection Clause of the Constitution. As an example of interdistrict differences in money available for schools, during 1967–1968 the Edgewood District had a total of $356 per pupil to spend from all sources, whereas the Alamo Heights District had $594 per pupil. Such discrepancies occurred in other parts of Texas as well.

Plaintiffs argued that these discrepancies discriminated unfairly against the poor, that education is a fundamental interest, and that the judicial test of strict scrutiny should be applied. This would require Texas to show a compelling state interest to maintain the present scheme of school finance. The state of Texas, however, claimed that its financing scheme was reasonable and that it was reasonably related to the state's purpose of providing a basic education for all its students.

Questions to Consider

1. Do "poor people" live in low-tax school districts?
2. Is education a fundamental value under the Constitution?
3. How should the courts determine the constitutionality of school finance schemes?

When the federal district court ruled against Texas, the state appealed to the U.S. Supreme Court.

Does the Texas system of school finance discriminate against the "poor" or deprive those who live in poor districts? There was no evidence presented that poor people tend to live in the poorest property districts. The Court referred to recent findings of social scientists that challenge the notion that the poor tend to cluster in low tax-base districts. Furthermore, the Court was not convinced that the quality of education may be determined by the amount of money expended for it. This relationship has also been seriously questioned by social scientists in recent years and the Court did not wish to foreclose a question not yet fully settled by educators and other scholars. The state of Texas provided a certain minimum educational program that it considered adequate, one that was available to all children of Texas. Thus the Court concluded "that the Texas system does not operate to the peculiar disadvantage of any suspect class."*

Is education a fundamental right under the Constitution? Plaintiffs argued that even if the Constitution nowhere mentions education explicitly, it is a fundamental right "because it is essential to the effective exercise of First Amendment freedoms and to intelligent utilization of the right to vote." They further urged "that the right to speak is meaningless unless the speaker is capable of articulating his thoughts intelligently and persuasively. The 'marketplace of ideas' is an empty forum for those lacking basic communicative tools. Likewise, . . . the . . . right to receive information becomes little more than a hollow privilege when the recipient has not been taught to read, assimilate and utilize available knowledge."

Although the Court did not dispute the connections between education and other fundamental rights, it was not satisfied that the plaintiff's evidence showed that the schools of Texas had fallen short of preparing people to exercise their right to speak or to vote. Furthermore, it is not the job of the Court "to guarantee to the citizenry the most *effective* speech or the most *informed* electoral choice." The Court saw these as laudable objectives, to be attained by legislative action and not by judicial rule. Thus the Court held that, although very important, education is not a fundamental right under the Constitution. It did indicate that Texas provided "each child with an opportunity to acquire the basic minimal skills necessary for the enjoyment of the rights of speech and of full participation in the political process." Perhaps an absolute denial of educational opportunities to children might lead to different results.

Since the Court found no deprivation of a fundamental right, the strict scrutiny test did not apply. The less demanding rational basis test was used "which requires only that the state's system be shown to bear some reasonable relationship to a legitimate state purpose. Here the Court explained that not only Texas, but also most states have relied on similar means for financing public schools and that states ought to be given room for further experimentation rather than be placed in a straightjacket by a single formula promulgated by the Court. Thus the Equal Protection Clause will be satisfied by various reasonable arrangements in financing our schools, even if significant discrepancies result among school districts.

*The Court has ruled that certain bases of classifying people are suspect, that is, classifying on the basis of race, religion, ethnicity, or wealth. Such classification will be closely examined for legitimacy. This is what is meant by the "strict scrutiny" test.

DEVELOPMENTS UNDER STATE LAW

The Supreme Court even while upholding the constitutionality of the Texas scheme urged states to reconsider historic methods of financing schools. In its own words:

> We hardly need add that this Court's action today is not to be viewed as placing its judicial imprimature on the status quo. The need is apparent for reform in tax systems which may well have relied too long and too heavily on the local property tax.

Even before the above recommendation of the Court, there has been a nationwide effort underway to achieve more equity in school finance. A number of states, recognizing the great disparities in school district wealth, have developed some type of equalization formula. These efforts still continue with most of the action centered in state legislatures. In addition to legislative efforts, suits have been brought under state constitutions to achieve equity in school finance.

The *Serrano* case[17] of California is probably the best known suit that succeeded under a state constitution, but similar suits also succeeded in New Jersey[18] and Connecticut.[19] On the other hand, however, the courts of Arizona,[20] Idaho,[21] and Washington[22] ruled against the equalization efforts. There are two main reasons why different state courts disagree in this area: first, the wording of state constitutions differ, and each court must base its decision on its own state constitution; and second, constitutional provisions tend to be vague and abstract, making it possible for different judges to come up with different interpretations.

After dozens of lawsuits, most experts in the area of school finance believe that appropriate remedies are more likely to result from legislation than from court action. Such legislation will attempt to strike a balance between traditional concerns for local control of schools and the emerging concern for equity in school finance.

FRONTIER ISSUES

The preceding chapters have examined topics about which there has been substantial litigation. In this section we consider questions about which there are few if any judicial decisions. These are the frontier issues— issues that will provoke educational and legal debate during the coming years.

Testing and the Right to Privacy

Schools administer various tests to their students. Among these are psychological tests used to analyze students' emotional health, self-concepts, and even their potential for future drug use. Although society may have a legitimate interest in developing emotionally healthy citizens and in preventing drug abuse, the right to privacy must not be ignored. We believe that one frontier issue in the years ahead will be the conflict between an individual's right to privacy and the social interests pursued through psychological testing. This conflict is heightened by the advent of "humanistic education" in our schools, with its attendant techniques that probe the "private" lives of students. At least one such case has already ruled in favor of the right of privacy. The *Merriken*[23] case involved a program of testing, designed to identify potential drug users among eighth graders in Norristown, Pennsylvania. Students were asked questions about their family life, about themselves, and about their peers. Those identified as potential drug abusers were to be helped by teachers, guidance counselors, their peers, or by outside specialists.

The evidence showed that questionnaires asked the student whether his family is "very close, somewhat close, not too close, or not close at all," whether his parents "hugged and kissed him at night when he was small," whether they told him how "much they loved him or her," and similar questions. Psychiatric testimony indicated that the testing program was dangerous and that the dangers were not pointed out to the students or their parents. For example, one danger was the self-fulfilling prophecy, namely, students labeled potential drug abusers may decide to act out the prediction. The court considered the conflicting interests in the right of privacy on the one hand and the social interest in preventing drug abuse on the other. It recognized that students also have a constitutional right to privacy and in this case neither they nor their parents were given the opportunity to give informed consent. "The letters sent to parents were 'selling devices' aimed at gaining consent without giving negative information" about the testing program and its possible consequences. The study nowhere defined what a potential drug abuser is and, what is still more serious, the students that were so identified would be treated in group therapy sessions by teachers, guidance counselors, and others who have had insufficient training in the requisite skills of therapy. According to the court, "as the program now stands the individual loses more than society can gain in its fight against drugs."

Psychological tests are likely to be carefully scrutinized in the years to come, and it is probable that only those that are clear and specific will be allowed; even then, informed consent by parents and students will be generally required.

TESTING AND DISCRIMINATION

The IQ testing will also come under increasing attack, particularly as applied to racial, ethnic, or language minority students. In San Francisco, for example, parents challenged the heavy reliance on IQ scores in placing students into classes for the retarded.[24] The evidence showed that although black students constituted 28.5 percent of all the students in the district, 66 percent of the students in the classes for the retarded were black. This evidence was sufficient to shift the burden to the school district to justify this imbalance and its reliance on IQ measures. When the district could not come up with satisfactory justification, the IQ testing program had to be suspended. Some other school districts have similarly abandoned the use of IQ tests in favor of achievement tests and teacher judgments.

Serious questions have also been raised concerning the constitutionality of "competency testing" as a means of screening students for graduation and as a way of determining teacher competence for entry into the profession. When the Florida approach to competency testing was challenged, the courts ruled that students were given inadequate notice of the newly formulated standards. The court also found it significant that the 1978–1979 seniors, who failed the tests in disproportionate numbers, had attended segregated schools in their first three years of public education. "In the court's opinion, punishing the victims of past discrimination for deficits created by an inferior education environment neither constitutes a remedy nor creates better educational opportunities,"[25] wrote U.S. District Judge George Carr. Although other law suits are likely to arise in this area, it is probable that such a testing program can meet constitutional standards if the tests are clear, reasonably related to the programs of the school, and students and their parents have adequate notice of the testing requirement and long enough time for preparation.

Teachers have challenged the use of examinations as one means of screening people wanting to enter the profession. Cases have been filed under Title VII of the 1964 Civil Rights Act that forbids discrimination in employment. If a test, such as the National Teacher Examination, is failed by a disproportionate number of black applicants or by some other minority group, does it violate Title VII? So far, courts have upheld the use of such tests since there is a sufficient connection between the test and teacher training programs.[26]

We have also noted earlier that any use of tests in connection with the placement of special needs children or of bilingual students requires careful procedures, including notices to their parents as well as the right on the part of parents to participate in placement decisions.

Grouping and Tracking

Grouping for instruction is a double-edged sword; it can be used to benefit students, but it can also work to their detriment. When students are grouped on the basis of inadequate or discriminatory criteria, or when they are rigidly kept in groups for long periods of time without a reexamination of their placement ("tracking"), these procedures may be held unconstitutional.

Several cases have successfully challenged certain grouping and tracking practices. A Washington, D.C. court ruled unconstitutional a tracking system that had the effect of segregating students along racial and economic lines.[27] And we saw earlier that due process must be followed before students can be placed in classes for the retarded or for the emotionally or physically handicapped. Suits have also successfully challenged the use of tests, written or administered in English, with students of limited English ability.

Although some lawsuits related to grouping have already been adjudicated, it is probable that the procedure will come under increasing legal attack during the next decade. Grouping in schools is a widespread practice, yet the tests used to place students into groups are so inadequate that they are vulnerable to claims that they violate the Due Process and Equal Protection Clauses of the Fourteenth Amendment.*

School Accountability

If students must attend school for approximately 12 years, do they not have the right to expect reasonable returns for their investment of time and energy? If a student "passes" from grade to grade but graduates from high school with academic skills that are substantially below the average of his peers, can the school be held accountable? Is the school district liable in money damages to such a student? Although several lawsuits have raised these questions, so far there are no authoritative answers. To date, no appeals court has found schools liable for such malpractice[28] for no plaintiff has proven negligence on the part of the schools and a causal connection between such negligence and damages suffered by the student. There are so many variables that affect students' learning, with powerful out-of-school factors involved, that the blame cannot simply be placed on the school.

A New York State Court of Appeals, for example, dismissed a $5 million suit by Edward Donahue, a 1976 graduate of Copiague Union High School.[29] Donahue alleged "educational malpractice" on the part of the school that allowed him to graduate, although he was a functional illiterate. Judge Mason dismissed the suit "as a matter of public policy," for "to entertain such a cause of action for 'educational malpractice' would require the courts not merely to make judgments as to the validity of broad educational policies . . . but, more importantly, to sit in review of the day-to-day implementation of these policies." Such complaints,

---

*On the other hand, grouping can be justifiable if carefully done with reasonable and relevant criteria, as long as the groups remain flexible and regrouping occurs often.

according to the court, should be handled through administrative processes. Perhaps the next decade may develop alternative ways of holding schools accountable to students, parents, and taxpayers, but it seems doubtful that courts will require schools to pay damages to students who did not succeed in their programs.

Money Damages

What happens if government officials (such as school administrators) violate the constitutional rights of students or teachers? Does the court merely declare who was correct in a conflict or may it also assess money damages?

In the landmark case of *Wood* v. *Strickland*[30] the Supreme Court ruled that school officials could be held personally liable for money damages if they violate students' constitutional rights. The Court held that . . . "a school board member is not immune from liability for damages . . . if he knew or should have known that the action he took within his sphere of official responsibility would violate the constitutional rights of the student affected. . . ." However, in the subsequent case of *Carey* v. *Piphus*, students were awarded only nominal damages when they were suspended from school without due process.[31] On the other hand, the Court indicated that in cases in which school officials knowingly or maliciously violate constitutional rights, exemplary or punitive damages might be awarded as a way of punishing the violations. Furthermore, the costs of attorney fees might be also assessed against the officials, and these can be considerable.

A federal district court in Delaware also warned school board members to be careful in seeking advice related to the rights of students. It may not suffice, warned the Court, that the board member sought legal advice: "Although a school board member may not be charged with knowing the interplay of complex legal principles and with awareness of subtle changes in case law, a member seeking to establish his official immunity should be required to show at least that he had some reasonable basis for trusting his attorney's advice."[32]

Although the foregoing cases involved students, it is well established that teachers will be also able to recover money damages if school administrators and board members violate their clearly established constitutional rights.* In a suit not related to education the Court ruled that action for money damages may be brought not only against individuals, but also against governmental entities.[33] Thus teachers in such

---

*For example, a teacher who is dismissed because she wrote a letter to the editor criticizing school policy or for union-organizing activities will receive back pay and, at the discretion of the judge, money damages and attorney fees.

situations might sue not only to regain their positions, but also for money damages as well. Furthermore, punitive damages may also be awarded if the violation of rights was malicious. And recently Congress passed a law whereby a "court, in its discretion, may allow the prevailing party . . . a reasonable attorney's fee as part of the costs."[34] Thus it is possible for teachers, whose constitutional rights were violated, to recover compensatory damages for actual loss suffered, punitive damages if the violation was malicious, and, at the judge's discretion, attorney's fees. With the number of unresolved issues related to monetary compensation for violating constitutional rights, the next decade will probably see additional lawsuits that will shed further light on this important matter.

The Use of Drugs to Control Students

The use of drugs to control the behavior of students is fairly widespread. In recent years, newspapers and popular magazines as well as professional journals have carried articles about this controversial practice. If students are compelled to attend school, by what right do schools administer drugs to them to control their behavior? If some children are "hyperactive," cannot schools adjust programs to fit their needs rather than drug them into conforming with existing school programs? Since children cannot consent to drug use, who should properly give such consent? If using drugs might have long-range consequences on students' lives, should parents be able to consent to such use? Since the highest proportion of drug use to control student behavior occurs among minority groups, does this practice constitute racial discrimination? These are some of the difficult questions posed by this issue.

The Right to Choose: Academic Freedom for Students

In recent years, an increasing number of people have argued that high school students should have the right to determine the goals, methods, and content of their education. They believe that students should be able to decide what courses they should take, what books should be used, what kinds of people should teach them, and how they should be evaluated. This, of course, is in sharp conflict with the traditional view that school boards should establish academic policy and resolve all disputes between conflicting educational alternatives. On the other hand, many school boards are currently increasing the range of curricular choice for students, and some are granting student representatives the right to participate in formulating academic policy. In addition, alternative public schools and alternative learning programs within schools are a recent development that could greatly increase student choice.

If teachers are entitled to academic freedom, shouldn't students have a parallel right? Shouldn't they be able to participate in making the academic decisions that will affect their lives? Should schools be required to provide courses that are requested by a significant number of students? Should students have a right to evaluate their teachers? Should students have an equal voice with educators in choosing the books and materials they must use? These are some of the questions we can expect to hear more frequently during the coming years.

The Right Not to Go to School

An increasing number of minority groups see the compulsory education laws as the process by which the dominant majority is training all the children of the community to accept the values, goals, and methods of the American "establishment." Some parents feel that any public school system that reflects the views of a politically selected school board will be in conflict with the beliefs and lifestyle they wish to instill in their children. Therefore, these ethnic, religious, racial, and social minorities believe that their children should have the right not to go to school, and many of their children agree. Such groups range from Christian fundamentalist sects to members of certain counterculture communities. Although these individuals usually recognize the need to "educate" their children, they reject specific state laws concerning teacher qualifications, school building codes, or curricular requirements.*

If the Amish do not have to send their children to schools that endanger their religious community, should not other parents have the right not to send their children to schools that would similarly threaten their values and beliefs? Since Justice Douglas suggested that the views of the Amish children should be considered in determining whether or not they should go to school, should not the views of all children above the age of 12 or 14 be considered in making such decisions? And if there is a dispute between parents and children, should not mature students have a right to have their views considered and respected? Although the Supreme Court limited its ruling in the *Yoder* case to members of established religious communities, this decision, which allowed one minority group to escape the compulsory attendance laws, can be expected to encourage others to seek similar rulings in the coming years.

These appear to be some of the major frontier issues of the decade, but we can expect many others also to emerge out of the diversity and conflict of our rapidly changing society.

---

*In 1981, South Dakota passed a law excusing children from attending school and allowing for greater parental choice in instruction, as long as designated levels of learning are achieved in language arts and mathematics. (Reported in *NOLPE NOTES*, Vol. 16, No. 7, July 1981, p. 7).

A FINAL NOTE

Toward the end of the 1960s we saw a new recognition on the part of the courts that indeed the Constitution applies to the schools and to the daily lives of teachers and students. The best known expression of this recognition came in the *Tinker* case in 1969, whose dictum that the Constitution does not stop "at the school-house gate" was repeated in hundreds of cases in the ensuing years. The 1970s saw a general expansion of the application of the Constitution to the schools and a general realization by teachers, students, administrators, and parents that, indeed, the Constitution is a viable, living document whose provisions must be applied anew to ever-changing times and conditions. The 1980s will continue this trend, and, in all likelihood, will establish clear law in some areas while introducing new complications and uncertainty in others. Thus the law grows, and only by such growing and adaptation do we keep the Constitution relevant to our daily lives and in robust health for its upcoming 200th birthday in 1987.

NOTES

1. *Pennsylvania Association for Retarded Children* v. *Commonwealth of Pennsylvania*, 343 F.Supp. 279 (E.D. Penn. 1972).
2. *Mills* v. *Board of Education of the District of Columbia*, 348 F.Supp. 866 (DDC. 1972).
3. *Armstrong* v. *Kline* (U.S.D.C., E. Penn. 6-21-1979).
4. *Stuart* v. *Nappi*, 443 F.Supp. 1235 (D. Conn. 1978).
5. *Southeast Warren Community School District* v. *Department of Public Instruction*, 285, N.W.2d 173 (1979).
6. *Doe* v. *Kroger*, 480 F.Supp. 225 (1979).
7. *Lau* v. *Nichols* 483 F.2d 791 (9th Cir. 1973).
8. *Lau* v. *Nichols* 414 U.S. 563 (1974).
9. 42 U.S.C. § 2000(d).
10. See, for example, *Morales* v. *Shannon*, 516 F.2d 411 (5th Cir. 1975); *Serna* v. *Portates Municipal Schools*, 499 F.2d. 1147 (10th Cir. 1974); *Aspira* v. *Board of Education of the City of New York*, 423 F.Supp. 647 (S.D. N.Y., 1976); and *Otero* v. *Messa County Valley School District* No. 51, 408 F.Supp. 164 (D. Colo., 1975).
11. 20 U.S.C. 1703 (1975).
12. Mass. Gen. Laws ch. 71A. See also the laws of Texas, Illinois, and California.
13. 20 U.S.C.A.880b.
14. *Guadalupe Organization, Incorporated* v. *Temple Elementary School District No. 3*, 587 F.2d 1022 (9th Cir. 1978).
15. For a thorough analysis of the legal issues involved, see Herbert Teitelbaum and Richard J. Hiller, "Bilingual Education: The Legal Mandate," *Harvard Educational Review*, 47, No. 2, 1977, 138–170.

16. 411, U.S. 1 (1973).
17. *Serrano* v. *Priest*, 557 P.2d 929 (Cal. 1976).
18. *Robinson* v. *Cahill*, 303 A.2d 273 (N.J. 1973).
19. *Hopton* v. *Meskill*, 332 A.2d 113 (Conn. 1974).
20. *Shofstall* v. *Hollins*, 515 P.2d 590 (Ariz. 1973).
21. *Thompson* v. *Engelking*, 537 P.2d 635 (Idaho 1975).
22. *Northshore School District No. 417* v. *Kinnear*, 530 P.2d 178 (Wash. 1974).
23. *Merriken* v. *Cressman*, 364 F.Supp. 913 (E.D. Penn. 1973).
24. *Larry P.* v. *Riles*, 343 F.Supp. 1306 (N.D. Cal. 1972).
25. *Debra P.* v. *Turlington*, 474 F.Supp. 244 (M.D. Fla. 1979).
26. *United States* v. *State of South Carolina*, 445 F.Supp. 1094, aff'd. 434 U.S. 1026 (1978).
27. *Hobson* v. *Hansen*, 269 F.Supp. 401 (D. D.C. 1967).
28. The best known case is *Peter W.* v. *San Francisco Unified School District*, 31 Cal. Rptr. 854 (1976).
29. This decision was affirmed in *Donahue* v. *Copiague Union Free School District*, 418 N.Y.S.2d 375 (1979). The case of *Hoffman* v. *Board of Education of City of New York*, 410 N.Y.S.2d 99 (1978) should be distinguished from the foregoing "malpractice" cases. Hoffman initially won an award of $500,000 for damages suffered as a result of the school's negligence. Hoffman was placed in classes for the retarded at the age of five and he remained in such classes throughout his school life despite the school psychologist's recommendation that he be retested after two years. His initial test score showed him one point below normal and later tests placed him within the normal range. The court held the school negligent and found that the negligence imposed additional crippling burdens by his long-term placement in classes for the retarded. However, the New York State Court of Appeals dismissed the judgment, holding that "the court system is not the proper forum to test the validity" of educational decisions or to "second-guess" such decisions. Thus, once again an appeals court reiterated the oft-used principle that "the courts ought not interfere with the professional judgment" of educators.
30. 420 U.S. 308 (1975).
31. *Carey* v. *Piphus*, 435 U.S. 247 (1978).
32. *Eckerd* v. *Indian River School District*, 475 F.Supp. 1350 (D. Del. 1979).
33. *Morrell* v. *New York Department of Social Services*, 436 U.S. 658 (1978).
34. 42 U.S.C., 1988.

Appendix A
Selected Constitutional Amendments

AMENDMENT I [1791]

Congress shall make no law respecting an establishment of religion, or prohibiting the free exercise thereof; or abridging the freedom of speech, or of the press; or the right of the people peaceably to assemble, and to petition the Government for a redress of grievances.

AMENDMENT IV [1791]

The right of the people to be secure in their persons, houses, papers, and effects, against unreasonable searches and seizures, shall not be violated, and no Warrants shall issue, but upon probable cause, supported by Oath or affirmation, and particularly describing the place to be searched, and the persons or things to be seized.

AMENDMENT V [1791]

No person shall be . . . compelled in any criminal case to be a witness against himself, nor be deprived of life, liberty, or property, without due process of law; nor shall private property be taken for public use, without just compensation.

AMENDMENT VIII [1791]

Excessive bail shall not be required, nor excessive fines imposed, nor cruel and unusual punishments inflicted.

AMENDMENT IX [1791]

The enumeration in the Constitution, of certain rights, shall not be construed to deny or disparage others retained by the people.

AMENDMENT X [1791]

The powers not delegated to the United States by the Constitution, nor prohibited by it to the States, are reserved to the States respectively, or to the people.

AMENDMENT XIII [1865]

Section 1. Neither slavery nor involuntary servitude, except as a punishment for crime whereof the party shall have been duly convicted, shall exist within the United States, or any place subject to their jurisdiction.

Section 2. Congress shall have power to enforce this article by appropriate legislation.

AMENDMENT XIV [1868]

Section 1. All persons born or naturalized in the United States, and subject to the jurisdiction thereof, are citizens of the United States and of the State wherein they reside. No State shall make or enforce any law which shall abridge the privileges or immunities of citizens of the United States; nor shall any State deprive any person of life, liberty, or property, without due process of law; nor deny to any person within its jurisdiction the equal protection of the laws.

AMENDMENT XXVII [*Proposed*]

Section 1. Equality of rights under the law shall not be denied or abridged by the United States or by any State on account of sex.

Section 2. The Congress shall have the power to enforce, by appropriate legislation, the provisions of this article.

Section 3. This amendment shall take effect two years after the date of ratification.

Appendix B
How the System Works[1]

In this section we examine questions laymen often ask about our legal system. Among others, we consider why local school officials are governed by the federal Constitution; how the federal and state judicial systems are organized; and how to find the law. There are other matters that lawyers must know in order to understand how the system works. These, however, are too technical for inclusion in this book.[2]

EDUCATION AS A STATE FUNCTION

One must understand the relationship between the schools and their respective states to realize that when a school official acts it is a state action within the meaning of constitutional law. When the school board of a town in Massachusetts prescribes that each school day begin with a prayer, it is a state action that violates the "separation of church and state" doctrine. When a school psychologist in California, using a standarized test written in English, determines that Chicano children are mentally retarded and therefore must be placed in separate classes, he is acting as a state official and is violating the Equal Protection and Due Process Clauses of the Fourteenth Amendment. And when teachers or principals systematically treat some children differently from others because of the color of their skin or their national origin, such actions are state actions for civil rights purposes. Similarly, when teachers frisk students' briefcases and lockers, or when a counselor systematically "guides" black and brown students into vocational classes, these are also state actions.

Another important principle of constitutional law is that the basic liberties of our Bill of Rights apply to state actions through the Fourteenth Amendment. This was a controversial development at one point in American history. However, today it is widely accepted by scholars and certainly by the courts that the adoption of the Fourteenth Amendment made "national citizenship primary and state citizenship derivative therefrom."[3] Consistent with this principle, for example, is the pronouncement of the Supreme Court that "the fundamental concept of liberty embodied in the Fourteenth Amendment embraces the liberties guaranteed by the First Amendment."[4] Thus, although the words of the first ten amendments restrained only the federal government, after the Fourteenth Amendment was adopted in 1868, it became possible to apply some of these restraints to the states as well. This was accomplished by the Court's interpretation that the Fourteenth Amendment incorporated the basic protections of the First Amendment and specifically applied them to all state actions. In practice this means that all the civil rights protections of the First Amendment apply to the actions of all public school officials just as much as those of the Fourteenth Amendment.

THE CONSTITUTION AND SCHOOLING

Our federal Constitution is strangely silent on schooling. Scholars have speculated through the years about the reasons for this omission and tend to agree that were the Constitution to be reframed today, education would occupy a prominent place in it.[5]

By implication the federal government could move into the field of public education under several provisions of the Constitution. Prominent among these is Article I, Section 8: "The Congress shall have power to lay and collect taxes, duties, imports and excises, to pay the debts and provide for the common defense and general welfare of the United States." The welfare clause has been used without difficulty or distortion to imply congressional power to legislate in school matters.[6]

Although it is arguable that under the implied powers embodied in the Constitution our federal government could have developed a system of schools, as a matter of fact it did not do so. Instead, another provision of the Constitution has been relied on to establish the principle that education is primarily a state function. The Tenth Amendment, ratified in

1791, stipulates that "the powers not delegated to the United States by the Constitution, nor prohibited by it to the States, are reserved to the States respectively, or to the people." Consistent with this principle, every state constitution makes provision for a system of state-supported schools. These provisions vary from state to state; some are quite general, whereas others are more specific and include such matters as the minimum length of the school year and the age range between which schooling must be freely provided.[7]

The courts have accepted the general principle that power over the schools is among those reserved to the states. In the words of Supreme Court Justice Jackson:

> A Federal Court may interfere with local school authorities only when they invade either a personal liberty or a property right protected by the Federal Constitution. . . .
> We must have some flexibility to meet local conditions, some chance to progress by trial and error.

Justice Jackson further warned that adoption by the Court of "an unchanging standard for countless school boards . . . is to allow zeal for our own ideas of what is good in public instruction to induce us to accept the role of a superior board of education for every school district in the Nation."[8]

It is clear, then, that education is primarily a state function to be carried out pursuant to the constitutions, legislative enactments, and administrative agencies of the several states. All of these, of course, are subject to the principles of the federal Constitution as interpreted by the Supreme Court of the United States. That Court itself has addressed this matter as follows:

> The Fourteenth Amendment, as now applied to the states, protects the citizen against the State itself and all of its creatures—Boards of Education are not excepted. These have, of course, important delicate and highly discretionary functions, but none that they may not perform within the limits of the Bill of Rights. That they are educating the young for citizenship is reason for scrupulous protection of Constitutional freedoms of the individual, if we are not to strangle the free mind at its source and teach youth to discount important principles of our Government as mere platitudes.[9]

State responsibility has often been forgotten in our historical emphasis on local control of schools. It is true that states may delegate certain powers over schooling to regions within the states such as counties, cities, towns, or other political subdivisions. However, the basic authority remains with the states. Thus local school boards, superintendents, principals, and teachers perform state functions when they act in their professional capacities.

THE STRUCTURE OF THE SYSTEM

Perhaps a more accurate heading for this section would be "The Structure of the Systems," for in the United States we have a system of federal courts and 50 systems of state courts. For our purposes, general descriptions of the federal system and the state systems will suffice.

The Federal Courts

The Supreme Court was specifically created by the Constitution (Article III, Section 2), but the other federal courts were established by Congress. Congress also has the power to alter the federal court system, creating new courts and abolishing existing ones to meet the needs of our changing culture. Currently, except for some special courts, like the Court of Claims, Court of Customs, and Patent Appeals, and Tax Court, we have a hierarchic system of three levels. The first level, the trial court, is the U.S. District Court. Each state has at least one district court, and some more populous states have as many as four. Cases from these courts, as a general rule, are reviewable by the U.S. Court of Appeals, of which there are 12, including one in the District of Columbia. (See map, p. 416.) The top level, of course, is the Supreme Court of the United States. This three-level hierarchy is depicted in the chart on p. 415.

Except for the Supreme Court, whose jurisdiction is specified in the Constitution (Article III, Section 2, Clause 1), Congress determines which cases shall be tried where,* the route each type of case will follow, and the relationship between the courts and the many administrative agencies of the government.

The State Courts

Since state courts are created by state constitutions and legislative bodies, they vary considerably in titles, authority, and procedures. Nevertheless there are commonalities among them that make a general description and schematic presentation possible.

The court systems of the states are organized on four levels. At the lowest level are the small claims, traffic, and police courts, justices of the peace, and magistrates' courts. Cases heard at this level usually cannot be appealed to higher courts. At the next higher level we find probate, municipal, and superior courts, as well as special trial courts such as juvenile courts. From this level appeal is possible to the next, the intermediate appellate courts, variously named in the different states. At

---

*This is where disagreements arose between Congress and President Nixon during the spring of 1972, when the President proposed to limit the jurisdiction of the courts (eliminate court power) over desegregation cases.

A Typical State Court System

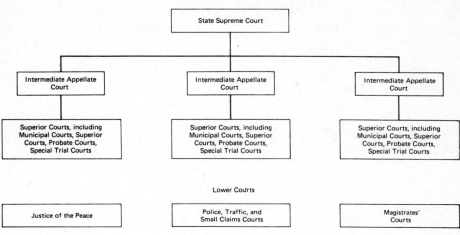

```
                          ┌──────────────────────┐
                          │  State Supreme Court  │
                          └──────────────────────┘
```

Intermediate Appellate Court	Intermediate Appellate Court	Intermediate Appellate Court
Superior Courts, including Municipal Courts, Superior Courts, Probate Courts, Special Trial Courts	Superior Courts, including Municipal Courts, Superior Courts, Probate Courts, Special Trial Courts	Superior Courts, including Municipal Courts, Superior Courts, Probate Courts, Special Trial Courts

Lower Courts

Justice of the Peace	Police, Traffic, and Small Claims Courts	Magistrates' Courts

The Federal Court System

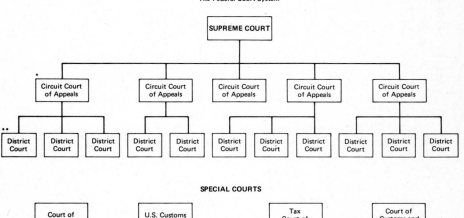

```
                     ┌─────────────────┐
                     │  SUPREME COURT  │
                     └─────────────────┘
```

Circuit Court of Appeals	Circuit Court of Appeals	Circuit Court of Appeals	Circuit Court of Appeals	Circuit Court of Appeals

District Court	District Court	District Court	District Court	District Court	District Court	District Court	District Court	District Court	District Court	District Court

SPECIAL COURTS

Court of Claims	U.S. Customs Court	Tax Court of the U.S.	Court of Customs and Patent Appeals

*There are currently 11 Circuit Courts of Appeals including one in the District of Columbia. Several judges may serve on any of these courts, on District Courts as well as other courts.
**There are currently 89 District Courts, including one in the District of Columbia.

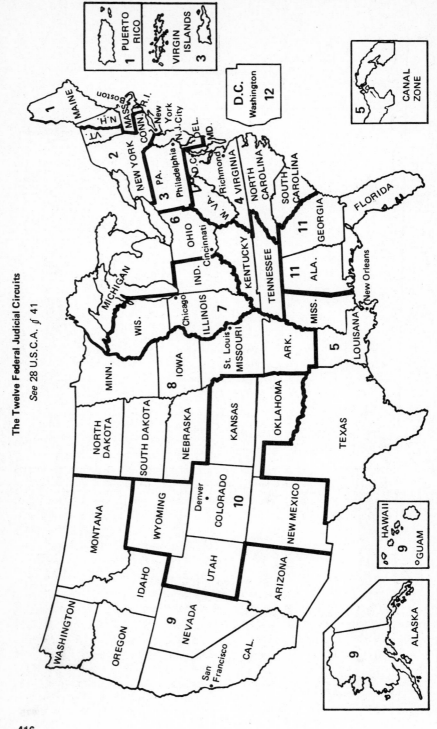

The Twelve Federal Judicial Circuits

See 28 U.S.C.A. § 41

the zenith of the state court hierarchy is the state supreme court; in Massachusetts, the Supreme Judicial Court; in Kentucky, the Court of Appeals; in Connecticut, the Supreme Court of Errors. The chart on p. 415 depicts the general pattern of state court hierarchies.

The appellate courts within a state also have power to review the decisions of state administrative agencies. Since states vary in their provisions for appeal from both courts and administrative agencies, it is necessary to know the laws of the particular state involved. One final but significant point must be noted in this brief sketch of our legal structures. Although it may appear that the state and federal systems are completely parallel, it must be remembered that the Supreme Court of the United States has final authority on all questions of federal law. Consequently, cases litigated in the state courts that involve questions related to the U.S. Constitution or to federal laws may be appealed from the state supreme courts to the highest court of the land.

A NOTE ON APPEALS

Trial courts, both state and federal, determine (1) what the facts are in a particular controversy and (2) what legal principles should be applied. Appeals courts do not retry the case; they usually accept the facts as determined by the trial court unless it is clear that the evidence for such facts was inadequate. Thus appeals courts hear arguments by counsel for each side and resolve conflicts about the proper legal principles to be applied to the particular case.

A school, for example, might want to suspend or expel John Doe, a student, for disrupting the educational process by allegedly entering classrooms and offices to hand out an "underground" paper and recruit students to demonstrate against the school's grading system. The trial court must decide what the facts were, whether or not John Doe performed the acts alleged against him. When, where, and under what circumstances did these occur? To whom and under what circumstances did he hand out the papers, and were his acts actually disruptive. After the facts are established, the appropriate legal principles are applied to them. Where is the law found? In legislation, other cases, and the state and national constitutions that govern these particular facts.

The state courts handle all matters arising under state law, but they must also handle claims arising out of federal law.* The latter is required by Article IV of the Constitution which provides that the Constitution and the "Laws of the United States" and "Treaties . . . shall be the supreme Law of the Land" and that "Judges in any State shall be bound thereby."

---

*For example, if a suspended student editor claims that her suspension violated the state education laws and her rights under the First Amendment, the state court where she filed suit must consider the applicable state laws as well as the relevant constitutional principles.

The state appeals court hierarchy will be the final authority on laws created by that state or by the state constitution unless federal questions are also involved. In other words, the federal courts and the U.S. Supreme Court are not superior to state courts in all matters, only in those that involve federal laws, treaties, the Constitution, or conflicts among state laws. This is one reason why we cannot talk about the court system of the United States, but must recognize that there are 51 systems—50 state and 1 federal.

As our chart of the federal judicial circuits indicates each circuit except that of the District of Columbia includes several states and a large number of federal district courts. The circuit courts of appeals, however, have no power over states courts and do not hear appeals from them; their decisions are not binding precedents for state courts. Their rulings are authoritative only for the federal district courts within their circuits. This is exemplified by the different holdings in various circuits on school regulation of students' hair length. Thus a case tried initially in a state court is appealed to higher state courts and not to federal courts, whereas a case tried in a federal district court is appealed to higher federal courts and never to higher state courts.

At the pinnacle of the court systems stands the Supreme Court of the United States. As indicated before, in all cases that involve federal law, this court is the final authority. The Court, however, has great discretion over which cases it will review. It cannot possibly handle all the appeals addressed to it plus the cases it must take as specified in the Constitution (Article III, Section 2, Clause 1) and in federal law. It hears relatively few cases and each year renders about 120 full opinions. Approximately two-thirds of these are in civil cases, the rest criminal.[10]

Review by the Supreme Court is usually sought under a "petition for *certiorari*." The petitioner, through this document, tries to convince the Court that the issues involved are of national significance and therefore warrant attention by the Court. Of the approximately 3000 petitions for *certiorari* submitted annually to the Court, only a small percentage are granted.[11]

CONGESTION AND DELAY

"Justice delayed is justice denied" is a popular saying that reflects an old concern. "Delay, of course, is no newcomer to the law. It was condemned in the Magna Carta, criticized by Shakespeare, and immortalized by Dickens in 'Bleak House.' About a century ago, a legislative committee in Massachusetts was pondering again the famous statement in the Magna Carta: to no one will we sell, to no one will we deny or delay right or justice."[12]

The congestion and delay in the administration of justice in U.S.

courts, however, are unprecedented in its seriousness.* Thoughtful scholars, lawyers, and judges are raising alarming questions about the very survival of the "rule of law" under present conditions. In fact, Chief Justice Burger of the Supreme Court considers the streamlining of judicial administration among his highest priorities. Such an effort must involve the courts and the various legislatures; it may require constitutional amendments; and it will certainly necessitate attitudinal changes on the part of lawyers and the public.[13]

WHERE TO FIND THE LAW

With many different governmental units creating law and with various courts adjudicating cases, the task of "finding the law" can be very complicated. A little knowledge in this instance may indeed be dangerous, for when one is faced with a real problem a thorough search of the law library is necessary. Short of a good course in legal research or its equivalent in experience, one cannot master the tools of legal research. Consequently, it is wise to seek counsel from legal aid, legal services, or a private lawyer. The following explanations are merely introductory and should enable the reader to understand references we have used and to look up cases we have cited.

Decisions of appellate courts, state and federal, are published both as official reports and by private publishing houses. The decisions of the Supreme Court of the United States, for example, are published officially as the *United States Reports* (cited "U.S.") by the U.S. Government Printing Office and in the *Supreme Court Reporter* (cited "S.Ct.") by the West Publishing Company, the best known private publishing firm in this field. These decisions are also published by Lawyers Cooperative Publishing Company as the *United States Supreme Court Reports or Lawyers Edition* (cited "L.Ed."). Thus the same case may be followed by three separate citations—for example, *Brown* v. *Board of Education of Topeka*, 349 U.S. 294, 75 S.Ct. 753, 99 L.Ed. 1083 (1955). This means that the *Brown* case can be found in volume 349 of the *United States Reports* at page 294, in volume 75 of the *Supreme Court Reporter* at page 753, or in volume 99 of the *Lawyers Edition* at page 1083, and that the decision was handed down in 1955.

The most recent Supreme Court decisions appear weekly in a looseleaf publication called the *United States Law Week*. Similar to other legal references, a citation in this publication looks like the following: *Bessie B. Givhan* v. *Western Line Consolidated School District et al.* 47 U.S.L.W. 4102, January 9, 1979. This means that the *Givhan* case is

---

*In some cities it takes a year or more for a criminal case to reach trial and a civil suit might take four to five years before the trial stage.

reported in volume 47 of *United States Law Week* at page 4102 and that the decision was announced on January 9, 1979.

Cases brought in federal courts are generally tried in a U.S. District Court and reported in a series of publications entitled the *Federal Supplement* (F.Supp.). From here cases are appealed to the U.S. Court of Appeals whose decisions appear in the *Federal Reporter*, currently in its *Second Series* (F.2d), and ultimately to the Supreme Court. Thus, in the *Tinker* case, for example, action was first brought in the U.S. District Court for the Southern District of Iowa, reported in 258 F.Supp. 971, appealed to the Court of Appeals of the Eight Circuit, reported in 383 F.2d 988, and finally to the Supreme Court, whose decision may be found in 393 U.S. 503 (1969).

The National Reporter System of the West Publishing Company includes both federal and state courts in a comprehensive regional reporting system. It is advisable that anyone interested in doing legal research become acquainted with these reporters and practice using them. Librarians specifically trained in the search for legal materials can be found in most libraries that have such holdings, and they can be quite helpful.

The cases adjudicated by the appellate courts of the various states are reported by the National Reporter System in nine regional units as follows:

Title	*States Included*	*Cited*
The Pacific Reporter	Montana, Wyoming, Idaho, Kansas, Colorado, Oklahoma, New Mexico, Utah, Arizona, Nevada, Washington, Oregon, California, Alaska, and Hawaii	"P." or "P.2d"
The South Western Reporter	Kentucky, Tennessee, Missouri, Arkansas, and Texas	"S.W." or "S.W.2d"
The North Western Reporter	Michigan, Wisconsin, Iowa, Minnesota, North Dakota, South Dakota, and Nebraska	"N.W." or "N.W.2d"
The Southern Reporter	Florida, Alabama, Mississippi, and Louisiana	"So." or "So.2d"
The South Eastern Reporter	Virginia, West Virginia, North Carolina, South Carolina, and Georgia	"S.E." or "S.E.2d"
The Atlantic Reporter	Maine, New Hampshire, Vermont, Connecticut, New Jersey, Pennsylvania, Maryland, and Delaware	"A." or "A.2d"

The North Eastern Reporter	Massachusetts, Rhode Island, New York, Ohio, Indiana, and Illinois	"N.E." or "N.E.2d"
The New York Supplement	New York	"N.Y.Supp."
The California Reporter	California	"Cal. Rptr."

The reader will notice that all of the states are included in regional reporters and that various states such as New York and California have separate series in addition. Where there are state reports, a case is reported by its official state citation, followed by the regional reporter citation together with the year of the decision—for example, *Morse* v. *San Diego High*, 34 Cal. App. 134, 166 P. 839 (1917).

Notice that as the regional reporters climb to high numbers owing to the many volumes of cases reported, the publisher begins a second series. For example, in the *Pacific Reporter* series, "P.2d" is a continuation of "P.," as in *School District* v. *Bruck*, 255 Ore. 496, 358P.2d 283 (1960).

A further important tool in legal research is the American Digest System, an index of cases to the National Reporter System. A publication of the West Publishing Company, it consists of the Century Digest, spanning cases from 1658 to 1896, the Decennials for cases in each ten-year period from 1897 to 1956, and the General Digest, third series, covering cases since 1957.

For the beginner or for anyone interested in an overview of a particular topic, a variety of legal encyclopedias are available. Among these perhaps the best known are *Corpus Juris Secundum* (cited as "C.J.S.") and *American Jurisprudence* (cited as "Am. Jr."). Note, however, that although the materials cited should suffice to introduce educators to the highly organized mysteries of legal research, the sources of law as well as the research tools necessary to find them are more extensive than indicated here.[14]

Warning

The brief descriptions and explanations we have provided should lead no one to believe that he can now act as his own legal counselor. In fact, even among trained lawyers there is a widely accepted saying: "He who is his own lawyer has a fool for a client." It might be of interest to the reader to know that when Clarence Darrow, one of the country's great criminal lawyers, was accused of tampering with a jury, he hired a lawyer to defend him.

Our goal is to sensitize students and educators to the range of civil rights problems that permeate the public schools. We want to inform them of overall principles as well as some problem areas and unanswered questions. However, anyone who suspects that he is involved in a civil rights violation should discuss his situation with a lawyer. In addition, advice and help are often available from the American Civil Liberties Union (ACLU), a nonpartisan organization long active on behalf of the civil rights of all Americans. Since the enforcement of one's constitutional rights is often an expensive, prolonged, and technical process, it is highly recommended that an aggrieved individual seek help and support of interested organizations.

NOTES

1. This appendix draws heavily on Appendix 1 in Louis Fischer and David Schimmel, *The Civil Rights of Teachers*, New York, Harper & Row, 1973.
2. For a brief but excellent analysis comparing the American and British legal systems, see Delmar Karlen, *Judicial Administration, The American Experience*, Dobbs Ferry, N.Y., Oceana Publications, 1970.
3. Edward S. Corwin, *The Constitution and What It Means Today*, New York, Atheneum, 1963, p. 248.
4. *Cantwell* v. *Connecticut*, 310 U.S. 296 (1940).
5. See, for example, Ellwood P. Cubberley, *Public Education in the United States*, Boston, Houghton Mifflin, 1934, pp. 84–85; see also Corwin, op. cit.
6. In fact, as many as 14 different parts of the Constitution have influenced educational development in the United States. *Federal Relations to Education*, Part II: Basic Facts, Report of the National Advisory Committee on Education, Washington, D.C., National Advisory Committee on Education, 1931, pp. 4–9.
7. See Cubberley, op. cit., and Edward C. Bolmeier, *The School in the Legal Structure*, Cincinnati, Anderson, 1968, pp. 65–77.
8. *McCollum* v. *Board of Education*, 33 U.S. 203 (1948).
9. *West Virginia State Board of Education* v. *Barnette*, 319, U.S. 624 (1943).
10. The annual November issue of the *Harvard Law Review* is one of the sources of analysis of the work of the Court and a statistical summary of the disposition of its cases.
11. See *Harvard Law Review*, annual November issue.
12. Karlen, op. cit., p. 60.
13. For a hard-hitting analysis, see Karlen, ibid., chap. 3.
14. A useful little volume we recommend is Arthur A. Rezny and Madeline Kinter Remlein, *A Schoolman in the Law Library*, Danville, Ill., Interstate Printers, 1962.

Appendix C
Glossary

Action: A judicial proceeding.

Adjudicate: To render judgment.

Administrative law: The branch of law dealing with the operation of the various governmental agencies that administer specific branches of the law.

Admissible: Allowable in evidence.

Adversary system: System of law in America, where justice is thought to be best achieved through a clash in the courtroom between opposite sides to a dispute.

Affidavit: A written statement sworn to before a person officially permitted by law to administer an oath.

Amicus curiae: "Friend of the court"; a person or organization allowed to appear in a lawsuit to file arguments in the form of a written brief supporting one side or the other, even though not party to the dispute.

Answer: The first pleading by the defendant in a lawsuit. This statement sets forth the defendant's responses to the charges contained in the plaintiff's "complaint."

Appeal: Asking a higher court to review the actions of a lower court in order to correct mistakes or injustice. "An appeal" is the process whereby such a request is made.

Appellant: One who appeals a judgment.

Beyond a reasonable doubt: The level of proof required to convict a person of a crime. This is the highest level of proof required in any type of trial. Compare with *by a preponderance of the evidence*, the level of proof in civil cases.

Brief: A written summary or condensed statement of a case. Also a written statement prepared by one side in a lawsuit to explain its case to the judge.

Burden of proof: The duty of proving to the court that one's assertions are in fact the truth by showing that the evidence favors them.

By a preponderance of the evidence: The level of proof required in a civil case. This level is lower than that required in criminal cases. See also *Beyond a reasonable doubt*.

Cause of action: Facts sufficient to allow a lawsuit.

Certiorari: A request addressed to a higher court to review a lower court decision. This request may be refused by the higher court.

Civil case: Every lawsuit other than a criminal proceeding. Most civil cases involve a lawsuit brought by one person against another and usually concern money damages.

Civil rights: The legal rights of individuals as guaranteed by the Constitution.

Class action: A lawsuit brought by one person on behalf of himself or herself and all other persons in the same situation; persons bringing such suits must meet certain statutory criteria and must follow certain notice procedures.

Code: A compilation of laws; most states have an education code containing all state laws related to education.

Common law: "Judge-made" rather than "legislature-made" law. The body of law which has developed from judicial decisions based on customs and precedents, as distinct from laws enacted by legislatures and written in statutes and codes.

Compensatory damages: Damages which relate to the actual loss suffered by a plaintiff, such as loss of income.

Complaint: The first main paper filed in a civil lawsuit. It includes, among other things, a statement of the wrong or harm done to the plaintiff by the defendant and a request for specific help from the court. The defendant responds to the complaint by filing an "answer."

Confidentiality: Requirement that the privacy of certain relationships (lawyer-client, doctor-patient, etc.) receives legal protection. For example, a lawyer may not repeat information obtained in confidence from a client.

Conspiracy: A criminal offense consisting of the joining of two or more persons for the purpose of doing an unlawful act.

Criminal case: Cases involving crimes against the laws of the state; unlike civil cases, the state is the prosecuting party.

Cross-examination: The questioning of a witness for the opposition in order to test the truth of his statements.

Damages: Money awarded by a court as compensation for an injury or wrong caused by another. They are classed as (1) actual or compensatory—as compensation for the actual injury or (2) punitive (exemplary)—in excess of the actual damage, but intended as punishment.

De facto: In fact; actual; a situation that exists in fact whether or not it is lawful. *De facto* segregation is that which exists regardless of the law or the actions of civil authorities. See also *De jure*.

Defamation: Injuring a person's character or reputation by false or malicious statements. This includes both *libel* and *slander*.

Defendant (appellee):   The person against whom a legal action is brought. This legal action may be civil or criminal. At the appeal stage, the party against whom an appeal is taken is known as the appellee. Usually, the appellee is the winner in the lower court.

De jure: Of right; legitimate; lawful, whether or not in actual fact. *De jure* segregation is that which is sanctioned by law. See also *De facto*.

De minimus: Small; unimportant; not worthy of concern.

Demurrer: The formal means by which one party to a lawsuit argues against the legal sufficiency of the other party's claim. A demurrer basically contends that even if all the facts which the other part alleges are true, they do not constitute a legal cause of action.

De novo (Latin):   New; over again.

Deposition: A written statement, given under oath, usually outside of court for use in court.

Dictum (Latin; plural, dicta):   A digression in the court's opinion, not necessary to explain the holding in the case at hand.

Disclaimer: The refusal to accept certain types of responsibility. For example, a college catalogue may disclaim any responsibility for guaranteeing that the courses contained therein will actually be offered since courses, programs, and instructors are likely to change without notice.

Double jeopardy: The trying of a person twice for the same offense. This is prohibited by the Fifth Amendment to the Constitution.

En banc: The full panel of judges assigned to a court sit to hear a case. A federal appeals court may sit *en banc*, for example, to reconsider a case of special significance.

Equity: Fairness; the name of a type of court originating in England to handle legal problems when the existing laws did not cover some situations in which a person's rights were violated by another person. In the United States, civil courts have both the powers of law and equity. If only money is represented in a case, the court is acting as a law court and will give only monetary relief. The court provides a jury if the parties want one, and it enters a judgment in favor of either the plaintiff or the defendant. If something other than money is requested—injunction, declaratory judgment, specific performance of a contractual agreement, and so on—then the court takes jurisdiction in equity and will grant a decree ordering acts to be done or not done. There is no jury in an equity case. Actions at law and suits in equity involve civil cases, not criminal.

Estoppel: Being stopped from proving something (even if true) in court because of something said or done before that shows the opposite.

Et al.:   And others. When the words "et al." are used in an opinion, the court is thereby indicating that there are unnamed parties, either plaintiffs or defendants, who are also before the court in the case.

Ex parte: With only one side present; an *ex parte* judicial proceeding involves only one party without notice to, or contestation by, any person adversely affected.

Ex post facto law: A law that retrospectively changes the legal consequences of an act which has already been performed. Article 1, Section 10, of the U.S.

Constitution forbids the passage of *ex post facto* laws.

Ex rel: On behalf of; when a case is titled *State ex rel. Doe* v. *Roe*, it means that the state is bringing a lawsuit against Roe on behalf of Doe.

Exclusionary rule: The rule that prevents illegally obtained evidence from being admitted in a criminal case.

Expert witness: A person who is so knowledgeable on a subject that he is allowed to testify as to his conclusions. An ordinary witness is allowed to testify only to facts.

Expunge: Blot out. For example, a court order requesting that a student's record be expunged of any references to disciplinary action during such and such a period means that the references are to be "wiped off the books."

Federal question: A case or lawsuit that involves the U.S. Constitution or federal laws.

Fiduciary: A relationship between persons in which one person acts for another in a position of trust.

Hearing: An oral proceeding before a court or quasi-judicial tribunal. Hearings which describe a process to ascertain facts and provide evidence are labeled "trial-like hearings" or simply, "trials." Hearings that relate to a presentation of ideas as distinguished from facts and evidence are known as "arguments." The former occur in trial courts and the latter occur in appellate courts. The terms *trial, trial-type hearing, quasi-judicial hearing, evidentiary hearing,* and *adjudicatory hearing* are all used by courts and have overlapping meanings.

Hearsay: Second-hand evidence; facts not in the personal knowledge of the witness, but a repetition of what others said that is used to prove the truth of what those others said. Hearsay is generally not allowed as evidence in trial-type hearings, although there are many exceptions.

Holding: The rule of law in a case; that part of the judge's written opinion that applies the law to the facts of the case and about which can be said "the case means no more and no less than this." A holding is the opposite of *dictum*.

In camera: In chambers; in a judge's private office; a hearing in court with all spectators excluded.

Incriminate: To involve in a crime; to cause to appear guilty.

Informed consent: A person's agreement to allow something to happen (such as surgery) that is based on a full disclosure of facts needed to make the decision intelligently.

Injunction: A court order requiring someone to do something or refrain from taking some action.

In loco parentis: In place of the parent; acting as a parent with respect to the care, supervision, and discipline of a child.

In re: In the matter of; this is a prefix to the name of a case often used when a child is involved. For example, "*In re Mary Smith*" might be the title of a child neglect proceeding even though it is really against the parents.

Inter alia: Among other things; usually used when what is being mentioned is only part of what there is; for example, "We found in the box, *inter alia*, a book."

Ipso facto: By the fact itself; by the mere fact that.

Judgment: The final determination by a court in a proceeding before it.

Judgment-proof: A person against whom a judgment for money is useless because the person is unable to pay or is somehow protected from paying.

Judicial notice: The recognition by a judge that certain commonly known and indisputable facts are true even though they have not been presented as evidence.

Judicial review: The power of a court to declare a statute unconstitutional; also the power to interpret the meaning of laws.

Judiciary: The branch of government that interprets the law and administers justice through a system of courts.

Jurisdiction: A court's authority to hear a case; also the geographical area within which a court has the right and power to operate. *Original jurisdiction* means that the court will be the first to hear the case; *appellate jurisdiction* means that the court reviews cases on appeal from lower court rulings.

Jurisprudence: The study of the law.

Laches: Neglect to do something at the proper time; an undue delay to do a thing that should be done or failure to enforce a right at the time required.

Law: Basic rules of order as pronounced by a government. Common law refers to laws originating in custom or practice. Statute law refers to laws passed by legislatures and recorded in public documents. Case law are the pronouncements of courts.

Libel: Written defamation; published false and malicious written statements that injure a person's reputation.

Litigant: A person engaged in a lawsuit.

Litigate: To carry on a lawsuit.

Malpractice: Incompetence or misconduct by a professional, usually a doctor or a lawyer.

Mandamus: A writ issued by a court commanding that some official duty be performed.

Material: Important; going to the heart of the matter; for example, a material fact is one necessary to reach a just decision.

Misrepresentation: A false statement; if knowingly done, misrepresentation may be illegal and result in punishment.

Mitigation: The reduction in a fine, penalty, sentence, or damages initially assessed or decreed against a defendant.

Moot: Abstract; not a real case involving a real dispute.

Motion: A request made by a lawyer that a judge take certain action, such as dismissing a case.

Obiter dictum (Latin):   Unnecessary words in an opinion. See also *Dictum.*

Opinion: A judge's statement of the decision reached in a case.

  Majority opinion: The opinion agreed in by more than half the judges or justices hearing a case; sometimes called the opinion of the court.

  Concurring opinion: Agrees with the majority opinion, but gives different or added reasons for arriving at that opinion.

  Dissenting opinion: Disagrees with the majority opinion.

Ordinance: The term applied to a municipal corporation's legislative enactments. An ordinance should be distinguished from a statute.

Parens patriae: The historical right of all governments to take care of persons under their jurisdiction, particularly minors and incapacitated persons.

Per curiam (Latin):   By the court. It denotes an opinion of the whole court as opposed to an opinion of a single judge.

Petitioner: One who initiates a proceeding and requests some relief be granted on his behalf; a plaintiff. When the terminology "petitioner" is used, the one against whom the petitioner is complaining is referred to as the respondent.

Plaintiff: One who initiates a lawsuit; the party bringing suit.

Plaintiff in error: The party who initiates a review of a court judgment or other proceeding. The plaintiff in error could have been either the plaintiff or the defendant in the earlier proceeding.

Pleading: The process of making formal, written statements of each side of a case. First the plaintiff submits a paper with facts and claims; then the defendant submits a paper with facts and counterclaims; then the plaintiff responds; and so on until all issues and questions are clearly posed for a trial.

Police power: Generally, the power of the government to regulate the activities of the populace.

Political question: A question that the courts will not decide because it concerns a decision more properly made by another branch of government such as the legislature.

Precedent: A court decision on a question of law that gives authority or direction on how to decide a similar question of law in a later case with similar facts. Ruling by precedent is usually conveyed through the term *stare decisis*.

Prima facie: Clear on the face of it; presumably, a fact that will be considered to be true unless disproved by contrary evidence. For example, a *prima facie* case is a case that will win unless the other side comes forward with evidence to dispute it.

Probable cause: Reasonable cause under the circumstances.

Proximate cause: The cause that actually leads to an injury; the one event without which the injury could not have taken place.

Publish: To make known to the public.

Punitive damages: Money awarded to a person by a court that is over and above the damages actually sustained. Punitive damages are designed to serve as a deterrent to similar acts in the future.

Quasi-judicial: The case-deciding function of an administrative agency.

Quo warranto: A proceeding whereby the right of a person or office to exercise a certain power is challenged. This proceeding is designed to prevent the illegal exercise of government or governmentally conferred powers.

Redress: To set right, remedy, make up for, remove the cause of a complaint or grievance.

Remand: Send back. A higher court may remand a case to a lower court with instructions to take some action in the case.

Res judicata: A thing decided. Thus, if a court decides a case, the matter is settled and no new lawsuit on the same subject may be brought by the persons involved.

Respondent: One who makes an answer in a legal appellate proceeding. This term is frequently used in appellate and divorce cases, rather than the more customary term, defendant.

Restitution: The paying back or restoration to a person who has been deprived of what was rightfully his.

Restraining order: An injunction.

Reverse: To set aside; for example, an appellate court can reverse the decision of a lower court.

Search and seizure: The discovery and confiscation by law enforcement officials of property belonging to a suspected criminal.

Search warrant: A written authorization from a judge or magistrate allowing the police, upon a showing of probable cause, to search a designated area for specific evidence of a crime.

Sectarian: Characteristic of a sect.

Secular: Not specifically religious, ecclesiastical, or clerical; relating to the worldly or temporal.

Sic (Latin): Literally; so; in this manner. Used in citing a quotation containing an error to indicate that the error was in the original material.

Sine qua non: A thing or condition that is indispensable.

Slander: Oral defamation; the speaking of false and malicious words that injure another person's reputation, business, or property rights.

Sovereign immunity: The government's freedom from being sued for money damages without its consent.

Standing: A person's right to bring a lawsuit because he or she is directly affected by the issues raised.

Stare decisis: "Let the decision stand"; a legal rule that when a court has decided a case by applying a legal principle to a set of facts, that court should stick by that principle and apply it to all later cases with clearly similar facts unless there is a good reason not to. This rule helps promote fairness and reliability in judicial decision-making and is inherent in the American legal system.

Statute of limitations: A statute that sets forth the time period within which litigation may be commenced in a particular cause of action.

Sui generis: Unique; one of a kind.

Tort: A civil wrong done by one person to another. For an act to be a tort, there must be (1) a legal duty owed by one person to another; (2) a breach of that duty; and (3) harm done as a direct result of the action. Examples of torts are automobile accidents, students hurt due to lack of supervision, and libel.

Trial: A process occurring in a court whereby opposing parties present evidence, subject to cross-examination and rebuttal, pertaining to the matter in dispute.

Trial court: The court in which a case is originally tried, as distinct from higher courts to which the case might be appealed.

Ultra vires: Going beyond the specifically delegated authority to act; for example, a school board which is by law restricted from punishing students for behavior observed at a private weekend party.

Unfair labor practice: An act by an employer that in any way coerces or intimidates employees who wish to organize for collective bargaining or in any other way violates a labor relations statute.

Unilateral: One-sided.

Venue: The locale where a case is to be tried. Where several courts may have jurisdiction, venue may be set at the court most convenient for the parties. If venue is not properly set originally, it may be changed later.

Verdict: The decision of a jury.

Void: Not valid; having no effect; null.

Waiver: The intentional relinquishment of a right or privilege.

Index

Procedural due process, 299n,
302–303, 324–325
Professional Problems of Teachers
(Stinnet), 214
Protest and demonstrate, right to, 32n,
183–186, 195. *See also*
Association, freedom of (students)
Public Law 94-142, 392–394
Pugsley v. *Sellmeyer* (1923), 351–352
Pyle v. *Washington County School
Board* (1970), 136

Quarterman v. *Byrd* (1971), 59–60,
72
Quong Wing v. *Kirkendall* (1912), 295

Racial and ethnic discrimination, 5, 13,
27, 236–264
Brown v. *Board of Education*,
239–243, 245, 247, 252, 261, 264n
busing, 237, 246–252, 262
de facto-de jure distinction, current
status of, 253–256, 263
freedom-of-choice, 244–246, 262
historical trends, 236–238
Plessy v. *Ferguson*, 238–242, 259,
261
testing and, 401–402
Rackley v. *School District* (1966), 223
Randle v. *Indianola Municipal
Separate School District* (1974),
212–213
Rankins v. *Commission On Professional
Competence* (1977), 169
*Ratchford, President, University of
Missouri* v. *Gay Lib* (1978), 182n
Rational basis test, 278, 285, 399
Reasonableness test, 15, 144
Reckless accusations, 88
Reduction in force, 309–310
Reed v. *Nebraska School Activities
Association* (1972), 271–272
Reed v. *Reed* (1971), 296
Rehnquist, William, 83, 84, 182n
Reineke v. *Cobb County School
District* (1980), 70n
Relevance, 105–107

Religion, freedom of (students),
138–148, 152–161. *See also*
Conscience, freedom of
antireligious texts, 159–160
armbands, 160–161
Bible reading and prayers, 144–147,
166
compulsory flag salute, 138–144,
166
compulsory high school attendance,
152–158, 166–167
school-required dancing, 158–159
sex education, 159
skullcaps, 160
Religion, freedom of (teachers),
161–165
compulsory flag salute, 162–163,
166
refusal to participate in certain
activities, 165, 167
religious holidays, personal leave for,
163–164, 167
Religious groups, 182–183
Religious holidays, personal leave for,
163–164, 167
Religious indoctrination, 108
Resegregation, 256–257
Reverse sex discrimination, 285
Rhode Island rulings
due process, 304
speech, freedom of, 32–33
Richards v. *Thurston* (1971), 360, 370
"RIF"-ing, 309–310
*Right to Read Defense Committee of
Chelsea* v. *School Committee of
the City of Chelsea* (1978), 36–37,
39
Right versus privilege doctrine, 286,
300–301
Robinson v. *Cahill* (1973), 407
Robinson v. *Sacramento City Unified
School District* (1966), 172–173
Rolando v. *School Directors of District
No. 125, La Salle County* (1976),
349
ROTC training, 148–150, 166
Rourke v. *Walker* (1925), 349

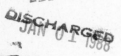